# SKILLS *for* EXAM SUCCESS GEOGRAPHY

Stacy Kenny
&
Andrew Horan

Gill Education
Hume Avenue
Park West
Dublin 12
www.gilleducation.ie

Gill Education is an imprint of M.H. Gill & Co.

© Stacy Kenny and Andrew Horan 2022

ISBN: 978-0-7171-93950

All rights reserved. No part of this publication may be copied, reproduced or transmitted in any form or by any means without written permission of the publishers or else under the terms of any licence permitting limited copying issued by the Irish Copyright Licensing Agency.

Design: Síofra Murphy
Print origination: Mike Connor
Illustrations: Andriy Yankovskyy

At the time of going to press, all web addresses were active and contained information relevant to the topics in this book. Gill Education does not, however, accept responsibility for the content or views contained on these websites. Content, views and addresses may change beyond the publisher or author's control. Students should always be supervised when reviewing websites.

Ordnance Survey Ireland Permit No.9260 © Ordnance Survey Ireland/Government of Ireland

For permission to reproduce photographs, the authors and publisher gratefully acknowledge the following:

© Adobe Stock: 105T, 115CL, 303; © Alamy: 30L, 30R, 46T, 51, 52R, 65, 73T, 75,83TR, 82TR, 82BR, 85, 115BL, 118, 132BR, 135, 155, 228CL, 264; © All-Island Research Observatory (AIRO) at Maynooth University: 217L; © AP Photo/Olivier Matthys: 256; © Central Statistics Office: 225; © Condor Publishers Ltd., 2021. Whilst every care has been taken to ensure that all the information contained in this map is correct, Condor Publishers Ltd. cannot accept responsibility for any errors or omissions which may have occurred: 121C; © Cork County/City Council: 222, 234; © Curtis Abert: 89; © Daft.ie: 228TL; © Department of Agriculture, Food and the Marine, *Forest Statistics Ireland 2021*: 268B; © Department of Foreign Affairs: 279C; © Dublin Chamber of Commerce, *A Vision for Dublin 2050*: 226B; © Environmental Protection Agency: 180; © Food and Agriculture Organization of the United Nations: 271; © Galeria del Ministerio de Defensa del Perú, flickr.com/photos/ministeriodedefensaperu/39935939755: 82BL; © 'Gathering the Data', *ResearchGate*, researchgate.net/figure/Map-of-Africa-showing-colonies-after-the-Berlin-conference-of-1884_fig4_343277531: 257BR; © Getty Images: 90; © Google Earth: 230C; Google Earth © CNES/Airbus, Data SIO, NOAA, U.S. Navy, NGA, GEBCO: 238R; Google Earth © Data SIO, NOAA, U.S. Navy, NGA, GEBCO, Landsat/Copernicus: 238L; Google Maps, Imagery © 2021 CNES/Airbus, Landsat/Copernicus, Maxar Technologies, Map data © 2021: 220, 248; Google Maps, Imagery © 2021 TerraMetrics, Map data © 2021 Mapa GISrael: 208B; Copyright © 2021, Government of Ireland, *Our Rural Future 2021 – 2025*: 226C; © International Energy Agency: 47; © International Volcanic Health Hazard Network, ivhhn.org: 12; © Ireland Aerial Photography: 241; © iStock/Getty Premium: 7T, 29, 52L, 53, 55, 56TL, 56BL, 61, 69, 73B, 79, 83TL, 83BR, 83BL, 115TL, 115CR, 115BR, 132CL, 132CR, 132BL, 134, 142, 149, 163, 164, 171, 182, 192T, 193, 200BC, 200BR, 207, 210L, 210R, 228R, 237, 254CL, 254CR, 255TL, 255CR 263, 287; © Luis Paquito, flickr.com/photos/gabirulo/238461606: 72; © Met Éireann: 58; © NASA Earth Observatory: 249; © National Council for Curriculum and Assessment: 8; © NOAA, National Centers for Environmental Information: 9T; World Energy Balances © OECD/IEA 2018 Sustainable Energy Authority of Ireland (SEAI): 64; © Ordnance Survey Ireland: 92, 100; © Seth Wynes and Kimberly Nicholas, 2017, *Environmental Research Letters*, permission granted by IOP Publishing: 184; © Shutterstock: 4, 9B, 48, 52C, 56TR, 56BR, 82TL, 115TR, 128, 133, 144, 154, 158, 183, 192B, 200BL, 216, 254BL, 255TR, 304, 305; © South Dublin County Council/Clonburris SDZ Planning Scheme: 230B; © Statista, statista.com/chart/13417/atlantic-overfishing_-europes-worst-offenders: 266; © Trócaire: 279T; © UN Women: 291; © UNHCR/Gordon Welters: 208T; © UNHCR/Will Swanson: 203; © UNICEF/UN057220/Makundi: 284; © United Nations Sustainable Development Goals, un.org/sustainabledevelopment. The content of this publication has not been approved by the United Nations and does not reflect the views of the United Nations or its officials or Member States: 205, 253, 289; © University of the West Indies Seismic Research Centre, Volcanic Hazard Map for St. Vincent and the Grenadines. Produced by The UWI Seismic Research Centre under the Volcano Ready Communities Project and adapted from the Volcanic Hazard Atlas of the Lesser Antilles (J.M. Lindsay et al. 2005): 11; © World Bank: 251, 252, 279B; © Worldometer: 288.

The authors and publisher have made every effort to trace all copyright holders. If, however, any have been inadvertently overlooked, we would be pleased to make the necessary arrangement at the first opportunity.

The paper used in this book comes from the wood pulp of sustainably managed forests.

# CONTENTS

# Introduction

## For Students

In writing *Skills for Exam Success Geography*, we wanted to create a resource that would become an important means of exam revision, without generating additional material to cover. This resource offers organised and detailed advice to accompany each question within. Following this advice will bring out your knowledge and understanding of each topic/learning outcome. It is written in language you will find quick and easy to follow, helping you to write your best possible answers. You will also find a Learning Checklist at the beginning of each topic that breaks down the material covered into manageable sections, making it easier for you to revise.

## For Teachers

We wanted to create a resource that allows you to take a step back, confident that the students can guide themselves through each question and apply the knowledge and exam skills they learned in the classroom. It is the aim of this book to help students build a bank of revision material by completing exam-style questions that fulfil the Learning Outcomes from the specification.

# Exam Advice for Students

## Preparing for the Exam

- This book will support you in compiling your own notes as you work through each topic. You will be given lots of opportunities to apply your knowledge by answering various types of exam question. This will build your confidence for the Junior Cycle exam.
- As you complete the topic mind maps, you will build notes on each topic. You should add colour to highlight key points/terms.
- You will be given lots of opportunities to recall your case studies throughout this book. This will help you to create a list of several examples to use across various topics.
- As you approach the exam date, you will have completed all of your revision and you can look over your notes the night before. The work will all have been done!
- Don't stay up late the night before your exam cramming. Go to bed early and have a good night's sleep – this is vital to be in top form for the next day.
- On the morning of your exam, get up early. Eat a healthy breakfast and set off in good time. You don't want to rush or be under pressure on the day.
- Check that you have all necessary equipment for your exam – two blue/black pens, a red pen, some colouring pencils, a pencil, a sharpener, an eraser, a ruler and a calculator.

## The Exam

- Get to the exam centre in plenty of time. This will help you to stay calm and feel prepared.
- You will have two hours to complete the exam paper. As soon as the exam begins, take some time to read through the paper and highlight key words in the questions. As you read the paper, you will notice that certain questions stand out and information to answer them will begin to flow back.
- If you come across a question that you don't initially recognise, do not panic. You need to focus on what you feel confident with initially and relax into answering the paper. Take time to read over the

questions that you feel less sure of, looking at the key words in the questions and trying to identify the topic that is being examined. Consider the question that comes before or after a tricky question; is there any connection between them?

- The exam has ten questions. You must answer ALL questions.
- Some questions may require longer answers than others, so be careful to monitor your time.
- Do not spend too much time on tricky questions that you feel less sure of. Attempt them and move on. You can always go back to them at the end if you have time.
- Do not leave any blank spaces. Always attempt every question.
- You will write all answers directly onto the exam paper. Space has been provided under each question for this, so be careful to stick to the space given. Keep in mind that it is quality not quantity that is important!
- Make sure your answers are clear and easy for the examiner to read. If you make a mistake, simply draw a line through it and move on.
- Be mindful of two-part questions. Make sure that you are answering everything that is asked. Always read back over the question to be sure that you have answered every part of it.
- Make sure to place clear labels on diagrams.
- If you are asked to calculate an answer in the exam, make sure to show your workings.
- If there are numerical answers required, make sure that you include the units in your answer (e.g. km, cm, mil).
- If a question asks you to tick the correct box and you accidentally tick the wrong one, make sure to cancel the wrong answer. Then, carefully highlight for the examiner which box you meant to tick.
- At the end of the exam, make sure to leave five to ten minutes to read back over your answers. This is your opportunity to alter or add any additional information.

## Diagrams, Graphs and Maps

- When asked to draw or complete a diagram, always use a pencil. Make sure to label your diagram clearly. Try to be as neat as possible, and use colour if time allows.
- When drawing any graph use a ruler/compass. Label each axis or section depending on the type of graph. Give your graph a heading. Draw it neatly and add shading if time allows.
- When answering aerial photograph questions, use the correct directions based on the angle of the photograph. Label your sketch map.
- When giving directions from an Ordnance Survey (OS) map, look for a north arrow on the map.
- Be aware of the grid referencing system for differently scaled maps:
  - When locating features on 1:50 000 and 1:25 000 OS maps, remember it's LEN – Letter, Easting and then Northing.
  - When locating features on maps with a 1:10 000 scale grid, it is the x-axis first, followed by the y-axis.
- Use the legend provided. It's there to help.
- If asked to draw or complete a sketch of an aerial photograph/OS map, always use a pencil. Draw a complete border on four sides and only draw what the question asks. Label each feature on your sketch. Be as neat as possible and use shading if time allows. Include a title on your sketch and provide a legend.

## Learning Outcomes

### Strand 1: Exploring the physical world

1.1 Describe the formation and global distribution of volcanoes, earthquakes, and fold mountains in the context of plate tectonics and structure of the Earth

1.2 Distinguish between different categories of rock type, referring to composition and formation

1.3 Analyse the processes and effects of weathering and mass movement on our landscape

1.4 Assess a soil type in a local area in relation to composition and vegetation

1.5 Explain how the processes of erosion, deposition and transportation shape our fluvial, marine, and glacial landscapes

1.6 Classify global climates, and analyse the factors that influence the climate in Ireland

1.7 Investigate the formation and behaviour of a significant weather event

1.8 Gather, record and interpret weather data

1.9 Differentiate between the types of energy resources produced by the physical world

1.10 Investigate a range of physical processes active in a chosen location and the connections between them

### Strand 2: Exploring how we interact with the physical world

2.1 Describe the economic and social impacts of how we interact with the occurrence of volcanoes, earthquakes, and fold mountains

2.2 Evaluate the environmental, economic, and social consequences of rock exploitation and energy resources

2.3 Identify how the physical landscape influences the development of primary activities

2.4 Assess the exploitation of water, fish stocks, forestry, and soil as natural resources

2.5 Describe a local secondary activity in relation to its function and the factors that influence its location

2.6 Examine the causes and implications of climate change

2.7 Investigate examples of how people interact with and manage surface processes

2.8 Investigate how people respond to a natural disaster

2.9 Assess the interrelationships between the physical world, tourism and transport

### Strand 3: Exploring people, place and change

3.1 Use the demographic transition model to explain populations' characteristics and how populations change

3.2 Investigate the causes and consequences of migration

3.3 Examine population change in Ireland and in a developing country

3.4 Consider the factors affecting the location and origin of rural and urban settlement in Ireland

3.5 Examine the causes and effects of urban change in an Irish town or city

3.6 Identify global patterns of economic development

3.7 Compare life chances for a young person in relation to gender equality, health care, employment and education opportunities in a developed and a developing country

3.8 Evaluate the role of development assistance in human development

3.9 Synthesise their learning of population, settlement and human development within the process of globalisation.

## Exam Dictionary: Key Terms

**Analyse** Use data to arrive at a conclusion

**Apply** Use information in a new way

**Calculate** Work out the value of something

**Comment** Make a judgement based on information/data

**Compare** Identify similarities and differences

**Conclusion** A judgement or decision reached

**Define** To explain something clearly

**Describe** Give a detailed account of

**Discuss** State the key points

**Distinguish** List the differences between different things

**Draw** Produce a diagram

**Estimate** Give a rough answer

**Evaluate** Judge something from the information/data given

**Explain** Make something clear by giving detail about it

**Give** Write the main facts

**How** In what way or manner

**Identify** Point out and describe the main ideas

**Illustrate** Explain with diagrams to support

**Indicate** Show clearly

**Insert** Put into the correct place

**Interpret** Look at information and draw conclusions

**Justify** Give valid information to support your answer

**List** List a number of points (no detail needed)

**Name** Name what is being asked (no detail required)

**Outline** Set out the main points or ideas

**Show** Provide structured evidence to show something

**Suggest** Give reasons

**Synthesise** Make connections and draw conclusions between two or more aspects

**With the aid of a diagram** Draw a diagram and write an explanation of what is being asked

# 1 The Earth

In this section, the Learning Outcome we will look at is: **1.1**

## Learning Checklist:

- ☐ I can explain the structure of each layer of the Earth.
- ☐ I can explain how convection currents cause plates to move.
- ☐ I can describe what happens at constructive, destructive and conservative plate boundaries.
- ☐ I can name examples of boundaries where plates are separating, colliding or sliding past each other.
- ☐ I can review maps and diagrams to extract information.
- ☐ I can sketch and label relevant physical geography diagrams.

## The Structure of the Earth

1. Complete the drawing below showing the different layers of the Earth. Place the labels provided onto your sketch.

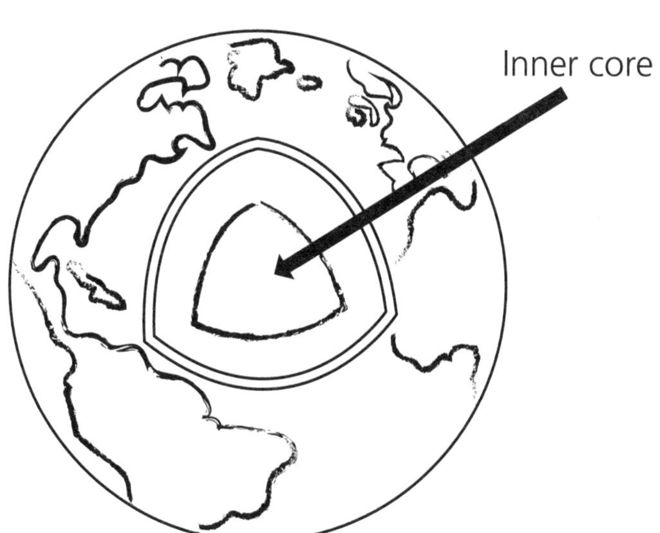


| **Labels** |
| --- |
| Inner core |
| Outer core |
| Mantle |
| Crust |
| Plate boundary |
| Plate |

### Remember!

- Draw diagrams in pencil.
- Make sure the lines are neat.
- Do not cross lines when labelling.
- Only label what you have been asked to.
- Only shade in diagrams once all questions have been answered.

2. Match each term in Column A with its definition in Column B. In Column C, insert an additional piece of information relating to the term that hasn't already been given.

| Column A |
|---|
| Outer core |
| Mantle |
| Crust |
| Inner core |

| Column B | | Column C |
|---|---|---|
| Made of solid rock, mostly granite and basalt | → | |
| Solid centre of the Earth | → | It is very hot, with temperatures of over 4,000°C |
| Consists of liquid nickel and iron | → | |
| The layer found beneath the crust | → | |

**Remember!**

Clear connecting lines between columns make it easy for the examiner to read your work.

3. Fill in the blanks using the following terms:

| Crust | Plates | Layers |
|---|---|---|
| Continental crust | Oceanic crust | Plate boundary |

The Earth is made up of a number of different ________________. The outer layer is known as the ________________ and it is made up of solid rock. The crust is broken up into a number of sections known as ________________, which are 5 to 70 km in depth. The plates that have land on top of them are known as ________________ ________________; the ones with oceans on top are known as ________________ ________________. Plates meet at a place known as a ________________ ________________.

**Remember!**

Always attempt the question in full. Even if unsure, you should never leave a blank space in the exam.

4. Tick (✓) the correct box for each of the questions below.

| | | True | False |
|---|---|---|---|
| **(i)** | Ireland is moving towards North America at a rate of 5 cm per year. | ☐ | ☐ |
| **(ii)** | Oceanic crust is thicker than continental crust. | ☐ | ☐ |
| **(iii)** | The crust is divided into sections known as plates. | ☐ | ☐ |
| **(iv)** | Plates float on the liquid nickel and iron found in the outer core. | ☐ | ☐ |
| **(v)** | Millions of years ago, the continents were joined together in a huge landmass known as Pangaea. | ☐ | ☐ |
| **(vi)** | Plates are colliding in the middle of the Atlantic to form the Mid-Atlantic Ridge. | ☐ | ☐ |

| | | True | False |
|---|---|---|---|
| **(vii)** | The San Andreas fault line is found in California. | ☐ | ☐ |
| **(viii)** | Ireland is located on the Eurasian Plate. | ☐ | ☐ |
| **(ix)** | Plates can only separate or collide. | ☐ | ☐ |
| **(x)** | Ireland has been in its current location for 250 million years. | ☐ | ☐ |

## Convection Currents

**5.** The movement of magma in the mantle causes the movement of the Earth's crust above. Using the numbered diagram below, **describe** how this movement takes place. Number 1 has been completed for you.

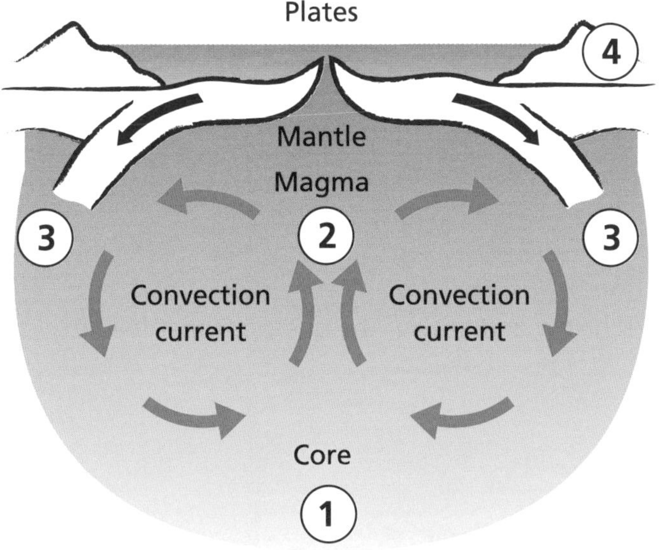


(1) The core heats the magma found above. As the magma heats, it rises slowly upwards towards the crust.

(2) As the magma reaches the crust, it then …

___

___

___

(3) Convection currents move in …

___

___

___

(4) The plates above very slowly begin to …

___

___

### Remember!

The verb in the question is asking you to 'describe' – this means to write about what it is like. You should give plenty of detail. You can use words and sketches to do this.

### GeoSkill

You may be presented with a diagram in the exam that you are unfamiliar with. The information can be presented in many ways. Look carefully at labels and titles: these will help you to understand what is shown.

### Exam Hint

Some key terms to help you in this answer:

- Cools
- Sinks
- Cycle
- Circular movement
- Dragged apart (separate)
- Pushed together (collide)
- Sliding

## Continental Drift

**6.** What effect has continental drift had on the shape of the Earth's surface?

In your description, make sure to include the following:

| | |
|---|---|
| Alfred Wegener | Pangaea |
| Continents fit together | Laurasia |
| Gondwanaland | Convection currents |

The idea of continental drift was first studied back in 1912 by a German scientist named ___________

_______________________________________________

_______________________________________________

_______________________________________________

_______________________________________________

_______________________________________________

### Exam Hint

How does the Earth look now compared to 250 million years ago?

In your answer, write about the theory of continental drift and any evidence that confirms it is occurring.

## Plate Tectonics

**7.** Review the diagram of the Earth's plates below and answer the questions that follow.

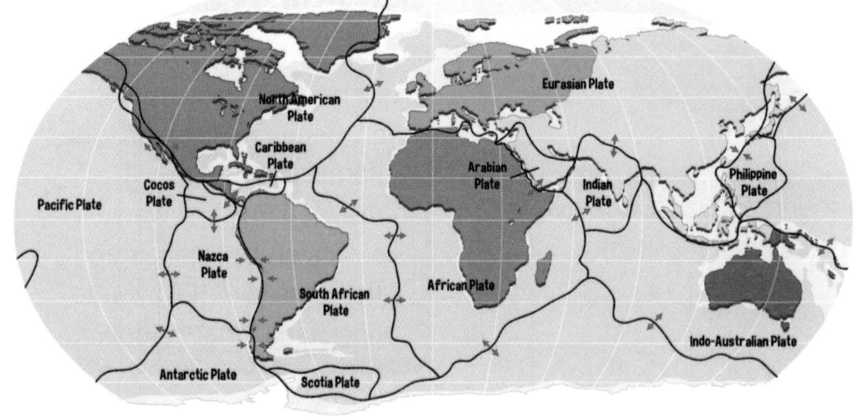


### GeoSkill

When presented with a map/graphic, it is important to spend time looking at it carefully. Try to identify what is familiar to you. Can you locate Ireland here to use as your reference point? What boundary is closest to Ireland?

**(i)** Name two colliding plate boundaries:

**1.** _______________________________________________

**2.** _______________________________________________

Name two separating plate boundaries:

**1.** _______________________________________________

**2.** _______________________________________________

**(ii)** In the space below, draw diagrams to show what is happening at a destructive and a constructive boundary.

**Remember!**

Destructive = Crust is being destroyed.
Constructive = Crust is being created.

| **Destructive (Colliding) Boundary** | **Constructive (Separating) Boundary** |
|---|---|
| | |

**GeoSkill**

Make sure your diagrams are clear, drawn using pencil. Be careful with your timing and don't spend too long on diagrams. Always show your labels clearly.

**(iii)** Describe what happens at each of the boundaries mentioned in part **(ii)**.

**Exam Hint**

Things to consider in your answer:

- How are plates moving at this type of boundary?
- What happens as the plates collide/separate?
- What features do we find at these boundaries?
- Give examples of where these features can be seen.

| **Destructive (Colliding) Boundary** | **Constructive (Separating) Boundary** |
|---|---|
| | |

**Answer the questions to complete the mind map. This will support your revision.**

## Prompt Questions for Mind Map

**(a)** Describe the layers of the Earth.

**(b)** Explain the theory of continental drift. What is Pangaea?

**(c)** How do convection currents work? In what way do plates move because of convection currents?

**(d)** Describe how plates move at constructive plate boundaries. What features do we find here? Give examples. Where can I see this type of boundary?

**(e)** Describe how plates move at destructive plate boundaries. What features do we find here? Give examples. Where can I see this type of boundary?

**(f)** Describe how plates move at conservative plate boundaries. What features do we find here? Give examples. Where can I see this type of boundary?

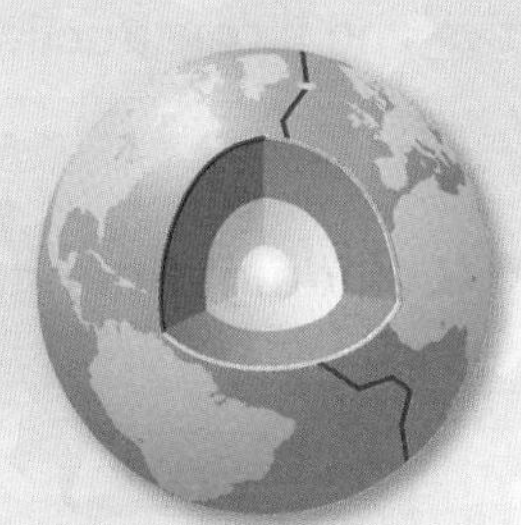

(a) The Earth

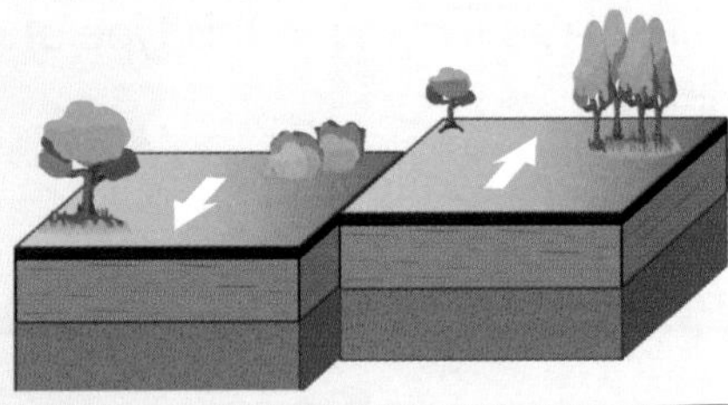

(f) Conservative Boundary

(b) Continental Drift

(c) Convection Currents

The Earth

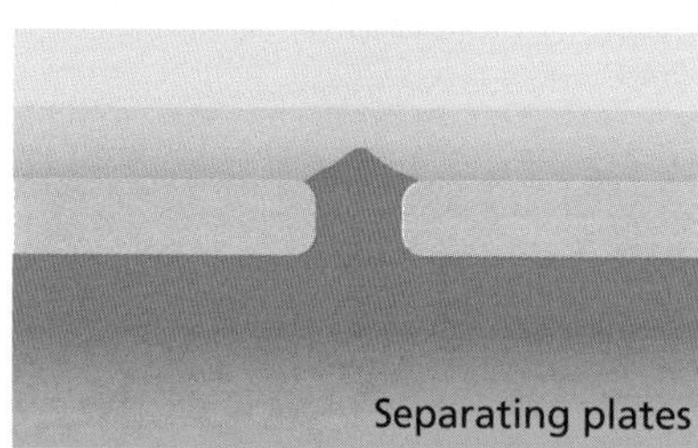
Separating plates

(d) Constructive Boundary

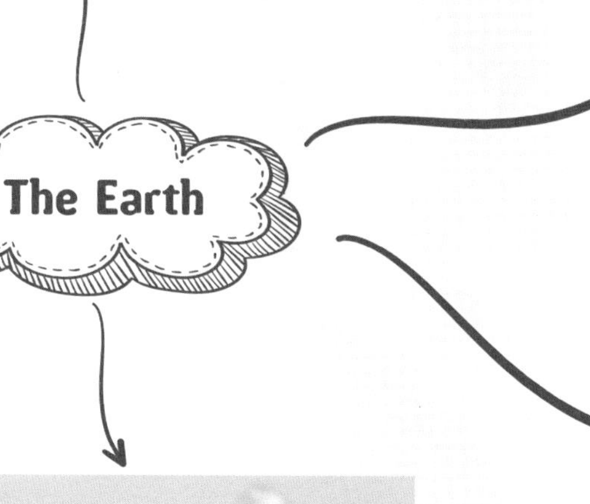
Colliding plates

) Destructive Boundary

## NCCA Sample Questions

### Question 1

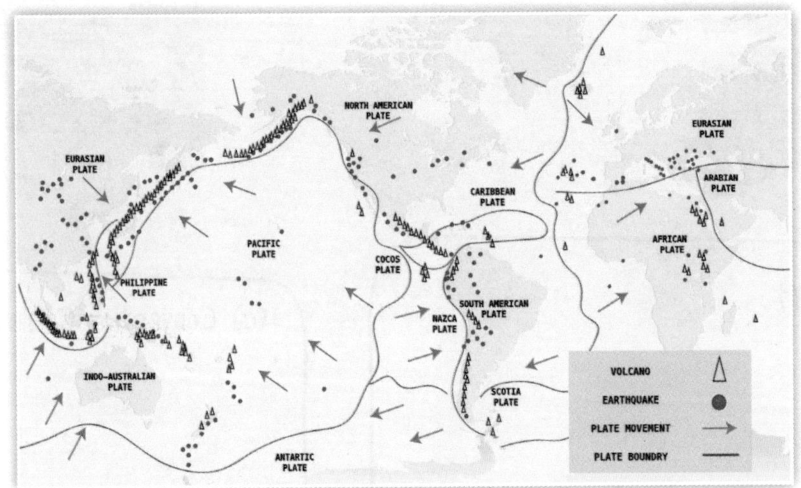


**(i)** Using your pen or pencil, **mark in** 'The Pacific Ring of Fire' on the map above.

**(ii)** **Describe** the pattern of tectonic activity along the 'The Pacific Ring of Fire'.

_______________________________________________

_______________________________________________

_______________________________________________

_______________________________________________

_______________________________________________

_______________________________________________

_______________________________________________

Look at the map provided, and review the arrows and the key. Does this area have more or fewer volcanoes/earthquakes than other boundaries? Describe what you see.

### Question 2

**Fill in the blanks** in the paragraph below. Use the words provided.

| An earthquake | Core | A fold mountain | Passive | Tectonic plates |
|---|---|---|---|---|
| Mantle | A volcano | Subduction | Magma | |

The Earth is made up of three layers consisting of the crust, ______________ and ______________. The Earth's crust is made up of many plates that fit together like a jigsaw. These plates are called ______________. The place where these plates meet is called a plate boundary. Plates that are moving apart are called divergent or constructive plate boundaries; a landform associated with this boundary is ______________. Plates that are colliding are known as convergent or destructive plate boundaries. Where one plate is pushed under another ______________ occurs. ______________ plate boundaries are plates that are sliding past each other; this may cause a build-up of pressure, resulting in ______________.

**Exam Hint**

If you are unsure of the meaning of any of the words provided above, now is the time to look them up and write out the definitions.

## Question 3

**Examine** the map below and **circle the correct answer** in each of the following statements.

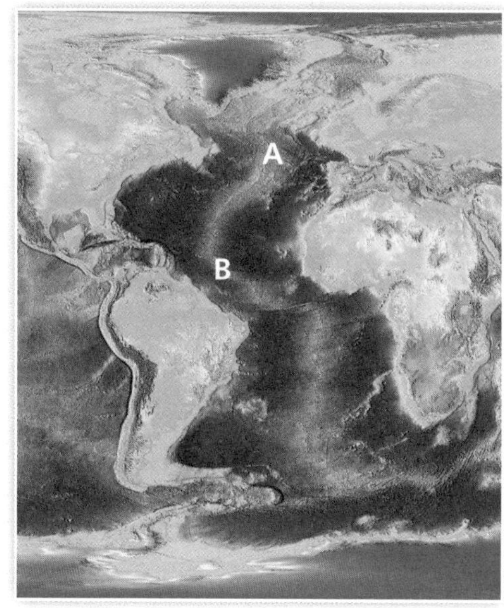


**Remember!**

Always choose an answer when given an option of answers, even if you are unsure. Attempt every question.

**(i)** The area indicated along the raised line AB on the map is called the Pacific Ring of Fire / Mid-Atlantic Ridge.

**(ii)** Plates are colliding / separating in the area along the line AB.

**(iii)** Plates move because of convection currents / ocean currents.

**(iv)** The plates found along this boundary are the American-Eurasian / Eurasian-Pacific Plates.

**(v)** The country located close to point A and containing many active volcanoes is Greenland / Iceland.

## Sample Question and Answer

## Question 4

**(i)** What type of plate boundary is shown on the map opposite? [3 marks]

**(ii)** **Name** the two plates at this boundary. [4 marks]

**(iii)** **Explain** why this region is prone to earthquakes. Use at least one diagram to help you. [8 marks]

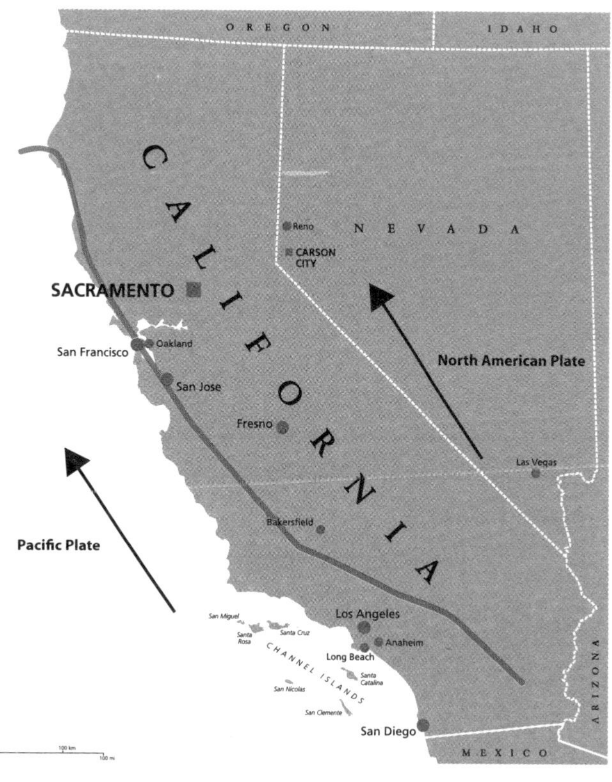


**Exam Dictionary**

**Explain:** Make something clear by giving detail about it.

We can see on the map that the arrows are both pointing upwards, this means the plates are sliding alongside each other. In the answer, be direct and state exactly what was asked. Use the terms that you know. Here we have said conservative and stated that the two plates are sliding.

(i) The type of plate boundary shown here is a conservative one. Two plates are sliding past each other.

(ii) 1. The North American Plate

2. The Pacific Plate

We are asked to name the plates, so no further information is needed. The plates are named on the map, so it is important to look carefully at any image or map given.

(iii) This region is prone to earthquakes because it is located on a boundary where two plates are sliding beside each other. The North American Plate is moving very slowly and sliding in the same direction as the faster-moving Pacific Plate. The plates are always moving, but where they touch off each other they can lock together. This means a lot of pressure builds up.

Over time, one plate will jump forward suddenly or slip, and this causes the energy to be released as an earthquake.

The red line on the map is called the San Andreas Fault. This is a large crack (fault line) in the crust along this plate boundary.

This question uses the action verb 'explain', so it requires a detailed account. It is important to use the information on the map but to also draw on your knowledge of how an earthquake occurs. Is there anything that you would remove or add to this answer? Space is typically limited in the exam, so it is important to be direct in your answers. Check back on the question and only answer what is asked.

**Diagram**

**Marks Awarded**

**(i)** Type of plate boundary named – 3 marks

**(ii)** Two plate boundaries named – 4 marks (2 + 2)

**(iii)** A detailed account given that provided the causes/reasons for earthquakes at this location – 6 marks

A fully labelled diagram was provided – 2 marks (6 + 2 = 8 marks)

# 2 Volcanic Activity

In this section, the Learning Outcomes we will look at are: **1.2**, **2.1**, **2.8**, **2.9**

## Learning Checklist:

- ☐ I can draw and label a diagram of a volcano.
- ☐ I can describe the life cycle of a volcano (active, dormant, extinct).
- ☐ I can describe, using a case study, some of the social and economic impacts of a volcanic eruption.
- ☐ I can draw sketches of physical features.
- ☐ I can describe how plate movement led to the formation of a volcano.
- ☐ I can explain what happens at a mid-ocean ridge.
- ☐ I can interpret information from infographics, maps and satellite images.

## Impact of Volcanic Activity

**1.** To the right is a volcanic hazard map for La Soufrière volcano on the Caribbean island of St Vincent, and on the next page is advice for locals on how to protect themselves from volcanic ash. Review the two images and answer the questions that follow.

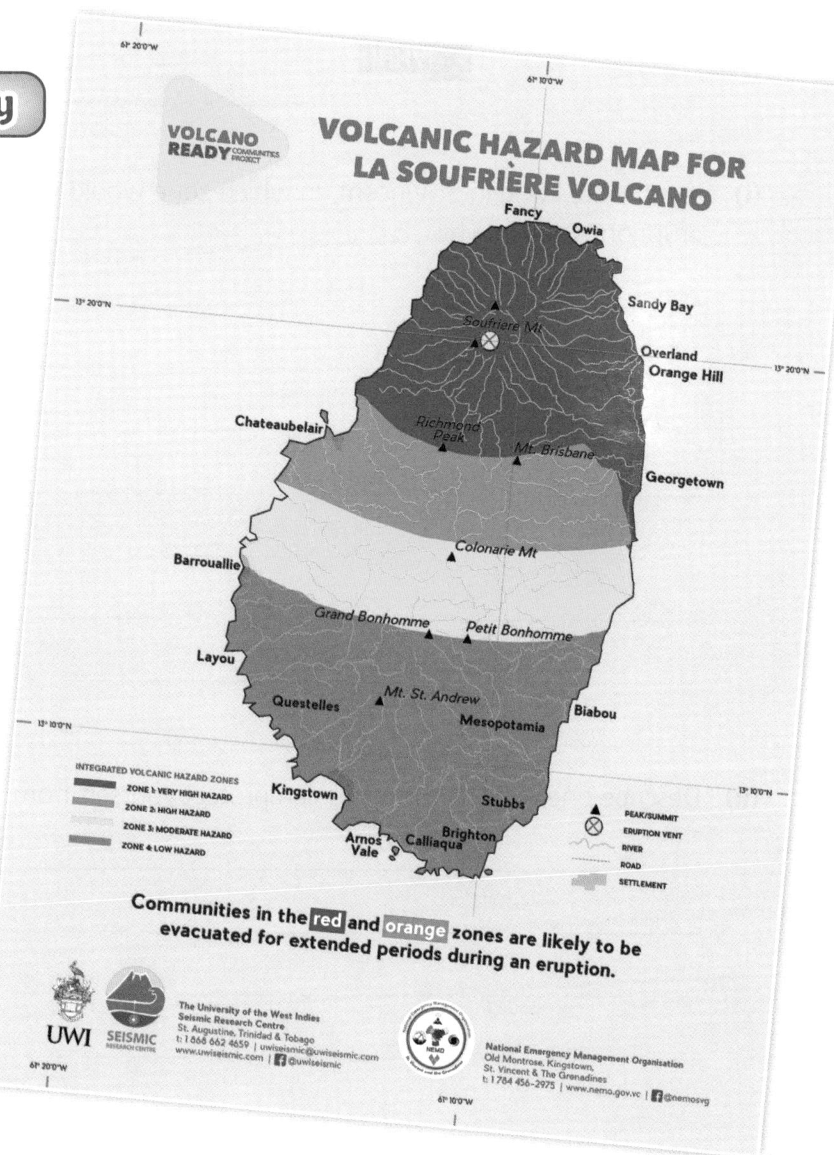


### GeoSkill

When provided with infographics in an exam, make sure to read the key information. Look at the headings and the key facts and figures. If there is a key or legend, remember to look at it and identify what it is showing on the map.

HOW CAN I PROTECT MYSELF FROM BREATHING VOLCANIC ASH?
RESPIRATORY PROTECTION
A facemask should fit well to your face but should not make breathing difficult.
Industry-certified masks (e.g., N95-style) provide the best protection.
Cloth materials (e.g., handkerchief) will not be as effective as a well-fitting facemask.
STAY INDOORS
The best way to reduce your exposure to ash is to shelter indoors, especially for children, older people and people with respiratory or cardiovascular disease.
Close windows and doors and seal up large gaps and spaces to the outdoors.
Keep indoor air as clean and cool as possible.
CLEANING UP
Once volcanic ash has settled, carefully dampen the ash with water and remove it. Wear a well-fitting facemask whilst doing this.
CONTACT A HEALTH PROFESSIONAL IF YOU ARE CONCERNED ABOUT YOUR HEALTH
IVHHN
Pan American Health Organization
World Health Organization Americas
IAVCEI
For more information see: www.ivhhn.org/ash-protection


Image reproduced, with permission, from the International Volcanic Health Hazard Network (www.ivhhn.org).

**(i)** If you were living in St Vincent, in which zone would you be safest during this volcanic eruption? Explain why.

Zone: ______________________________

______________________________

______________________________

______________________________

______________________________

______________________________

______________________________

______________________________

**(ii)** Describe one way in which you can protect yourself from breathing volcanic ash.

______________________________

______________________________

______________________________

______________________________

______________________________

**(iii)** Imagine that you are on the island of St Vincent during the eruption. Write a letter to a friend in Ireland that describes the impact of the eruption. Your letter must include each of the following: Tick (✓) each part as you complete it.

- **(a)** One social impact of the eruption on the local community. ☐
- **(b)** One economic impact for the island. ☐
- **(c)** An impact that the eruption has had on the local environment. ☐

## Exam Hint

For the impacts, it is important to consider how the eruption impacted the areas mentioned **socially**, **economically** or **environmentally**. You might like to consider connections to primary activities (farming), secondary (local businesses) or tertiary (tourism) in your answer.

## Volcanic Mountains

2. (i) Describe, with the aid of diagrams, how the process of plate movement can lead to the formation of a volcano such as La Soufrière. The diagrams have been started for you below.

**Exam Hint**

Below are some useful terms to include in your answer and diagrams:

| | |
|---|---|
| Convection currents | Constructive/Destructive boundary |
| Crater | Lava |
| Magma chamber | Ash cloud |
| Repeated eruptions | Old layers of ash and lava |
| Cone | Vent |

**Remember!**

- Highlight what you are being asked.
- Use the key words in your description and fully label your diagrams.

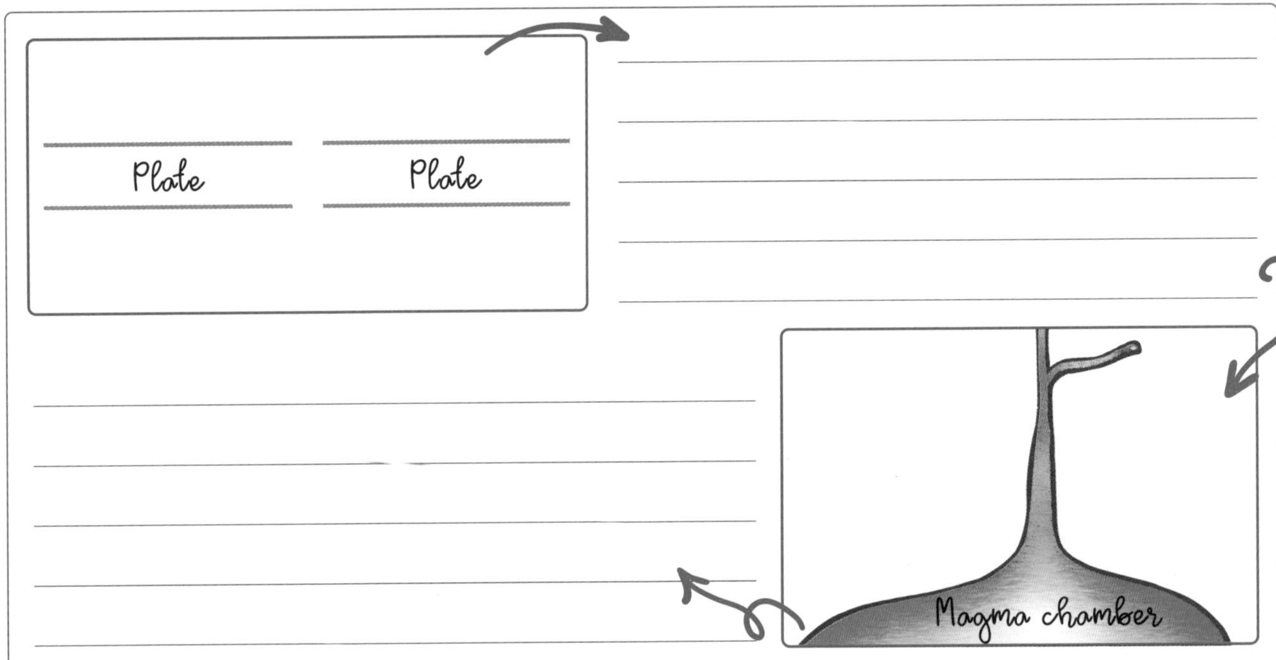


(ii) Complete the table below by writing a definition for each of the key terms provided.

| Key Term | Definition |
|---|---|
| Crater | |
| Magma chamber | |
| Magma | |
| Lava | |
| Vent | |
| Cone | |

**Exam Hint**

Revising the key terms from each topic will make you much more confident with the information. Test yourself on these regularly.

**(iii)** Answer the following short questions.

**Remember!**

These are short-answer questions so they require a brief answer. Pay attention to the action verb. Only answer what is asked of you.

**(a)** What happens to magma when it reaches the Earth's surface?

______________________________

**(b)** Why might I expect to find a volcano at a constructive plate boundary?

______________________________

______________________________

**(c)** Name two active volcanoes, other than the one mentioned in **(i)**, and state where they can be found.

**1.** ______________________________

**2.** ______________________________

**(d)** What name is given to a scientist who studies volcanic activity?

______________________________

**(e)** Name the scale used to measure volcanic eruptions.

______________________________

**(f)** Why might the pieces of equipment listed below be useful to a scientist who is at the scene of a volcanic eruption?

Video camera: ______________________________

Gas mask: ______________________________

Thermal suit: ______________________________

**(g)** Name the rock formed when lava cools quickly at the Earth's surface.

______________________________

**(h)** Circle the correct answer in each of the following statements:

- Iceland is found on the Pacific Ring of Fire / Mid-Atlantic Ridge.
- A volcano that has not erupted in a long time but is expected to erupt again in the future is active / dormant.
- The type of energy used to generate heat from volcanic eruption is geothermal / hydroelectric.

**(iv)** Volcanic eruptions are a natural disaster event that can have local, national and international impacts. Using an example of an eruption that you have studied, fill in the case study below.

## Case Study

Name and location of volcano: ______________________________

When the eruption occured: ______________________________

**Impacts:**

Local

______________________________

______________________________

______________________________

______________________________

National

______________________________

______________________________

______________________________

______________________________

International

______________________________

______________________________

______________________________

______________________________

## Mid-ocean Ridges

3. Look at the satellite image below showing the Mid-Atlantic Ridge and answer the questions that follow

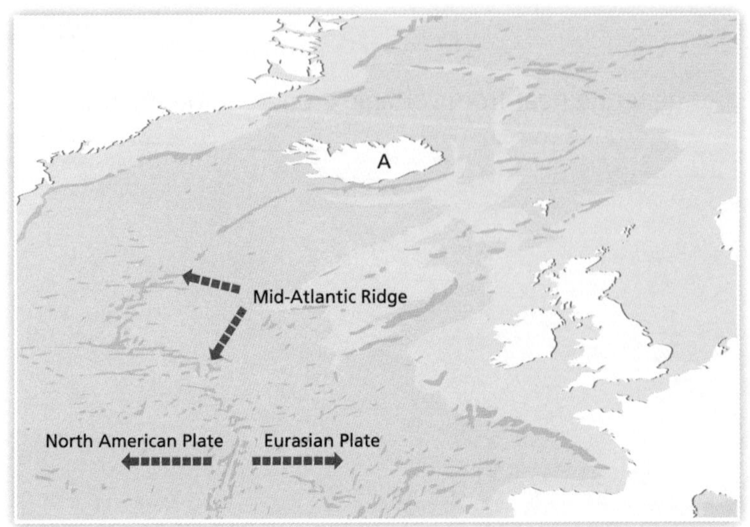


### GeoSkill

Interpreting information from satellite images is an important geo skill. Try to identify familiar features by reviewing the labels on the image. Look at the landmasses shown. Ocean/ water will be blue; land masses are typically green. Upland areas may be shaded brown.

**(i)** Name the country labelled A on the map. ______________________________

**(ii)** Describe the tectonic processes occurring at this plate boundary. You may support your answer with diagrams.

## Exam Hint

Some key points to include in your answer:

- What plates are involved here? Name them.
- In what direction are they moving? Are they pushing together or pulling apart?
- What makes plates move? Describe the process.
- What is the result of the movement? Is new land being created/destroyed?
- What features might we find on this boundary? Can you name any?
- If you have included a diagram, is it a basic sketch that has clear labels?

## Remember!

Some key words that will be helpful in this answer.

- North American Plate
- Eurasian Plate
- Magma/Lava
- Volcanic islands
- Pulling apart
- Atlantic ocean
- Constructive
- Mid-ocean ridge
- Iceland

**Diagrams**

**Answer the questions to complete the mind map. This will support your revision.**

## Prompt Questions for Mind Map

**(a)** How are volcanic mountains formed? At what type of plate boundaries do we find them? Give examples.

**(b)** What are the three stages in the life cycle of a volcano? How is each stage in the life cycle different? Can you give an example of a volcano in each stage?

**(c)** How is a mid-ocean ridge formed? What type of boundary is it on? Give an example. What does it look like?

**(d)** Describe some economic impacts of a volcanic eruption that you have studied. What was the financial cost of the eruption? Did it impact on local businesses?

**(e)** Describe some social impacts of a volcanic eruption that you have studied. Did anyone lose their life? Were homes impacted? Did people require emergency food or shelter?

**(f)** Describe some environmental impacts of a volcanic eruption that you have studied. Was the local landscape badly damaged? Local ecosystems? Loss of wildlife?

(a) Volcanic Mountains

(f) Environmental Impacts of Volcanic Eruption

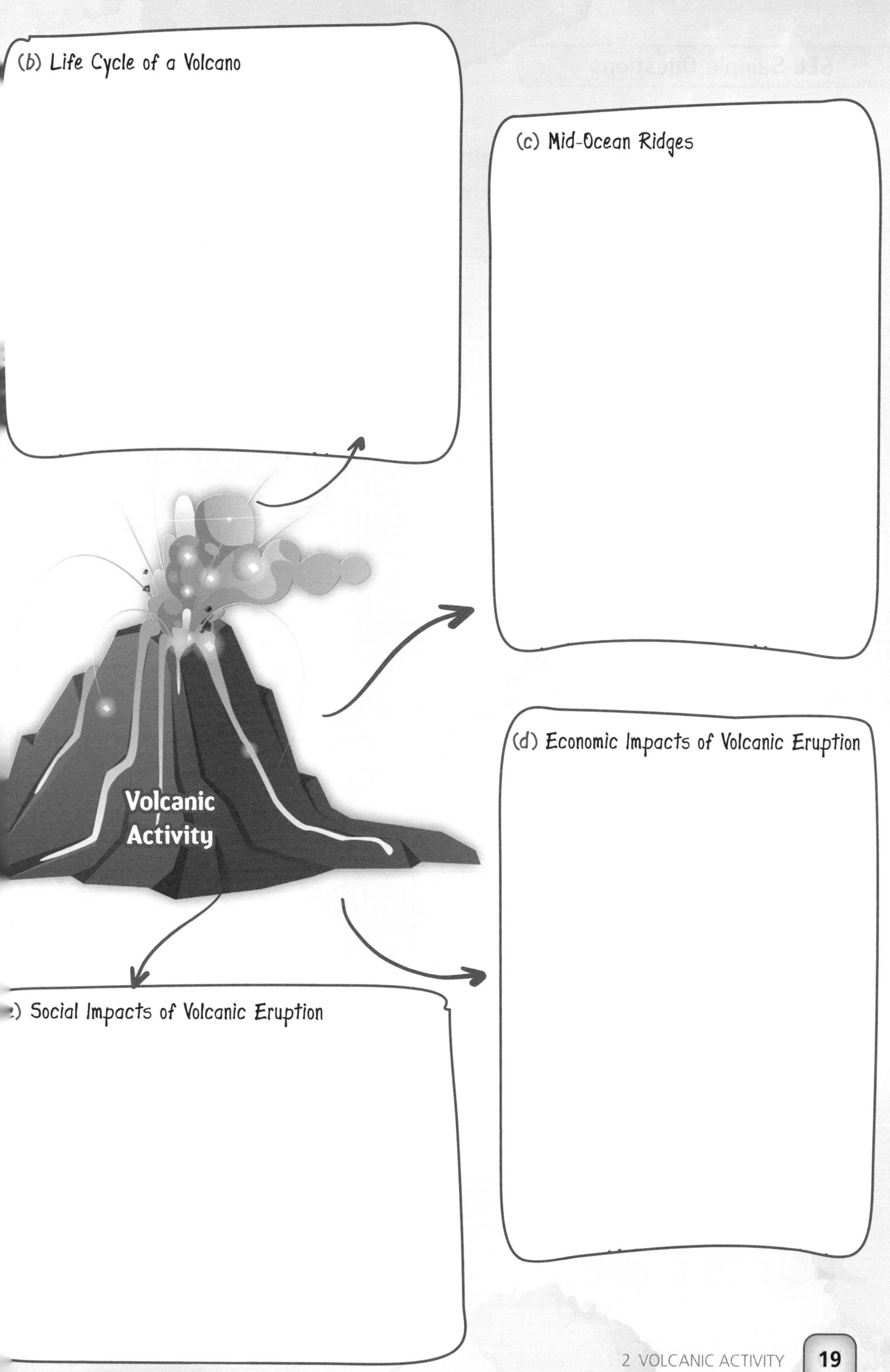
(b) Life Cycle of a Volcano
(c) Mid-Ocean Ridges
Volcanic Activity
(d) Economic Impacts of Volcanic Eruption
) Social Impacts of Volcanic Eruption

## SEC Sample Questions

### Question 1

**(i)** Use the space below to **draw a diagram** of an active volcano. Show and label each of the following on your diagram:

Magma chamber Cone Vent Crater ash cloud

**(ii)** **Name** one example of a rock that forms when molten rock cools.

### Question 2

Imagine you are a journalist sent to the site of a recent volcanic eruption. Write a report describing some of the negative impacts of the volcanic eruption.

**Exam Hint**

This question asks you to describe 'some' negatives. In this instance, aim for **at least three** and keep in mind that a limited amount of space will be provided in the exam for you to write your answer. You are describing them, so you should give a detailed account.

## NCCA Sample Question and Answer

### Question 3

(i) Look at the map on page 8 showing the Pacific Ring of Fire. What **conclusions** can you draw about the direction plates are moving at the location of a volcano? You may support your answer with diagrams. [12 marks]

The question asks you what conclusions you make after reviewing the map. 'Conclusion' means a judgement or a decision reached by reasoning. You make your judgement by looking closely at the location of volcanoes on the map and at the type of boundary they are found on.

*Using the map and key, I can conclude that a large number of volcanoes are located along the Pacific Ring of Fire where the Pacific Plate and Eurasian/North American Plates are colliding. From my knowledge of plate tectonics, I can conclude that as the plates are forced together at this boundary, one plate is pushed downwards into the mantle and melts to form magma. The magma can then rise up due to great pressure and escapes to form a volcano. This is a subduction zone.*

*I can also conclude that the Pacific Ring of Fire is a very active zone and the plates must be pushing together continuously at this boundary. I conclude this because of the very large number of volcanoes that are visible along the boundary: there are more volcanoes there than at any other boundary shown on the map.*

**Marks Awarded**

(i) Conclusions stated – 4 marks (2 + 2)

Conclusions outlined using evidence from map – 8 marks (4 + 4)

*Evidence can also be in the form of a diagram.

**Diagrams**

Space has been left here for you to draw a basic diagram of the boundary. Make sure to use clear labels and insert a title.

**(ii)** Volcanic activity in an area can bring destruction and risk but also provides many social, environmental and economic benefits to the area and country. Choose **one** from the list below (circle the one selected) and **explain** the benefits of volcanic activity. [10 marks]

**SOCIAL** **ENVIRONMENTAL** **ECONOMIC**

For this question, you must choose to write about the benefits of volcanic activity either **socially**, **environmentally** or **economically**. Select one of them and circle it.

You should then:

- state two benefits for the heading selected
- explain how each benefit impacts the local area
- explain how each benefit impacts the country.

You can use information from your case study to support your answer by giving examples.

# 3 Earthquakes

In this section, the Learning Outcomes we will look at are: **1.1**, **2.1**, **2.8**

## Learning Checklist:

- ☐ I can draw a basic diagram of an earthquake and fully label it to show what is happening.
- ☐ I can name the equipment used to measure earthquakes.
- ☐ I can describe how a tsunami occurs using words and diagrams.
- ☐ I can discuss some of the economic and social impacts of an earthquake in a specific region that I have studied.
- ☐ I can describe ways to lessen the impact of an earthquake in an area.

## Earthquakes

**1.** Read the article below and answer the questions that follow.

**Croatia Earthquake**

An earthquake of magnitude 6.4 struck in Petrinja, Croatia, on Tuesday.

A series of aftershocks followed on Wednesday, just as rescuers had arrived to look for people trapped beneath the rubble. 'This morning we were hit by the third, if not the fourth earthquake,' the mayor of Petrinja, stated. 'Everything that has not yet fallen is falling,' he added.

At least seven people are known to have died in the quake. Almost half of the town was destroyed, with nearly 200 people having to sleep in the local army barracks. Large parts of the town had no electricity.

The government have promised that funds will be made available to rebuild homes and businesses.

**Adapted from a BBC article.**

### Exam Hint

When reading articles in the exam, underline or highlight the key points. If visual material is given alongside the text, make sure to also look at it.

(i) **(a)** What was the magnitude of the earthquake and where did it strike?

Magnitude: ______________________________

______________________________

Location: ______________________________

______________________________

## Exam Hint

Underline the action verbs in the question – this will help you to be clear on what you are being asked.

**(b)** Look at the map on the previous page. Where would you expect to find the greatest damage caused by the earthquake? Circle your answer. Explain your choice in the space below.

Glina Petrinja Sisak Zagreb

______________________________

______________________________

______________________________

**(c)** Describe one type of short-term aid and one type of long-term aid that may be needed in the areas impacted by this earthquake.

Short-term aid: ______________________________

______________________________

______________________________

Long-term aid: ______________________________

______________________________

______________________________

**(ii) (a)** Use the terms to correctly label the diagram of an earthquake below.

Shock waves Focus Epicentre Plate movement

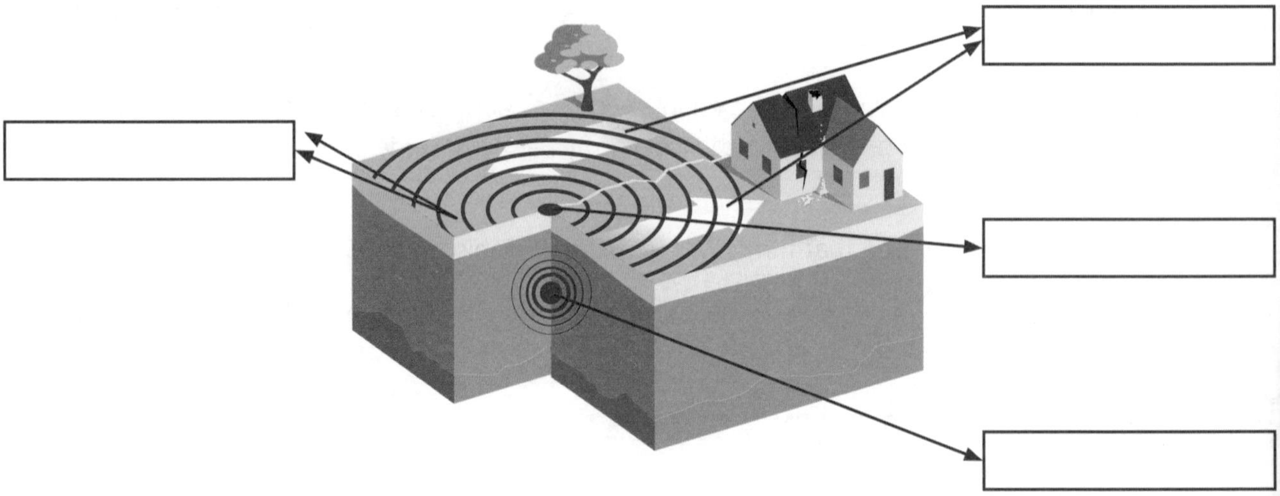

**(b)** The local council have started to rebuild the areas impacted by the earthquake. **Write a report** for the local Croatian Council suggesting some ideas they could consider that will help to limit the damage caused from future earthquakes.

Complete the report in the space provided below.

**Remember!**

It is important to consider sustainability in your answer.

Dear Petrinja Council,

I have some ideas that I would like to share with you that I think will help to limit the impact of future earthquakes in your region …

________________________________________

________________________________________

________________________________________

________________________________________

________________________________________

________________________________________

________________________________________

________________________________________

________________________________________

## Tsunami Waves

2.

**Japanese Earthquake and Tsunami, 2011**

On 11 March 2011, Japan experienced the strongest earthquake in its recorded history. A magnitude 9.0 earthquake occurred off the Japanese coastline with the epicentre east of the Tohoku region.

The earthquake lasted 6 minutes and caused a tsunami wave that reached heights of over 40 metres. Japan is located in one of the most active earthquake zones on Earth, with the earthquake occurring on a destructive plate boundary.

**(i)** **(a)** Where was the epicentre of the earthquake located?

________________________________________

**(b)** Define the following terms mentioned in the above article:

| | |
|---|---|
| **Epicentre** | |
| **Magnitude** | |
| **Destructive plate boundary** | |

**(c)** Match each term with the correct definition in the table below. The first one has been completed for you.

| | |
|---|---|
| **A** | Seismograph |
| **B** | Richter scale |
| **C** | Moment magnitude scale |
| **D** | Seismic waves |

| | |
|---|---|
| **1** | Shock waves that spread out from the focus of an earthquake. |
| **2** | Replaced the Richter scale because it is more reliable for larger earthquakes. |
| **3** | Instrument used to measure and record an earthquake and how long it lasted. |
| **4** | Original scale used to measure earthquake magnitude. |

| | |
|---|---|
| **A** | 3 |
| **B** | |
| **C** | |
| **D** | |

**(d)** Complete the diagram below showing the formation of a tsunami and, in the space provided, explain how a tsunami wave is formed.

Include the following terms in your diagram and explanation:

Focus     Tsunami wave     Fault

Epicentre     Shock waves

**Remember!**

Clearly draw and label your diagram. Use a pencil.

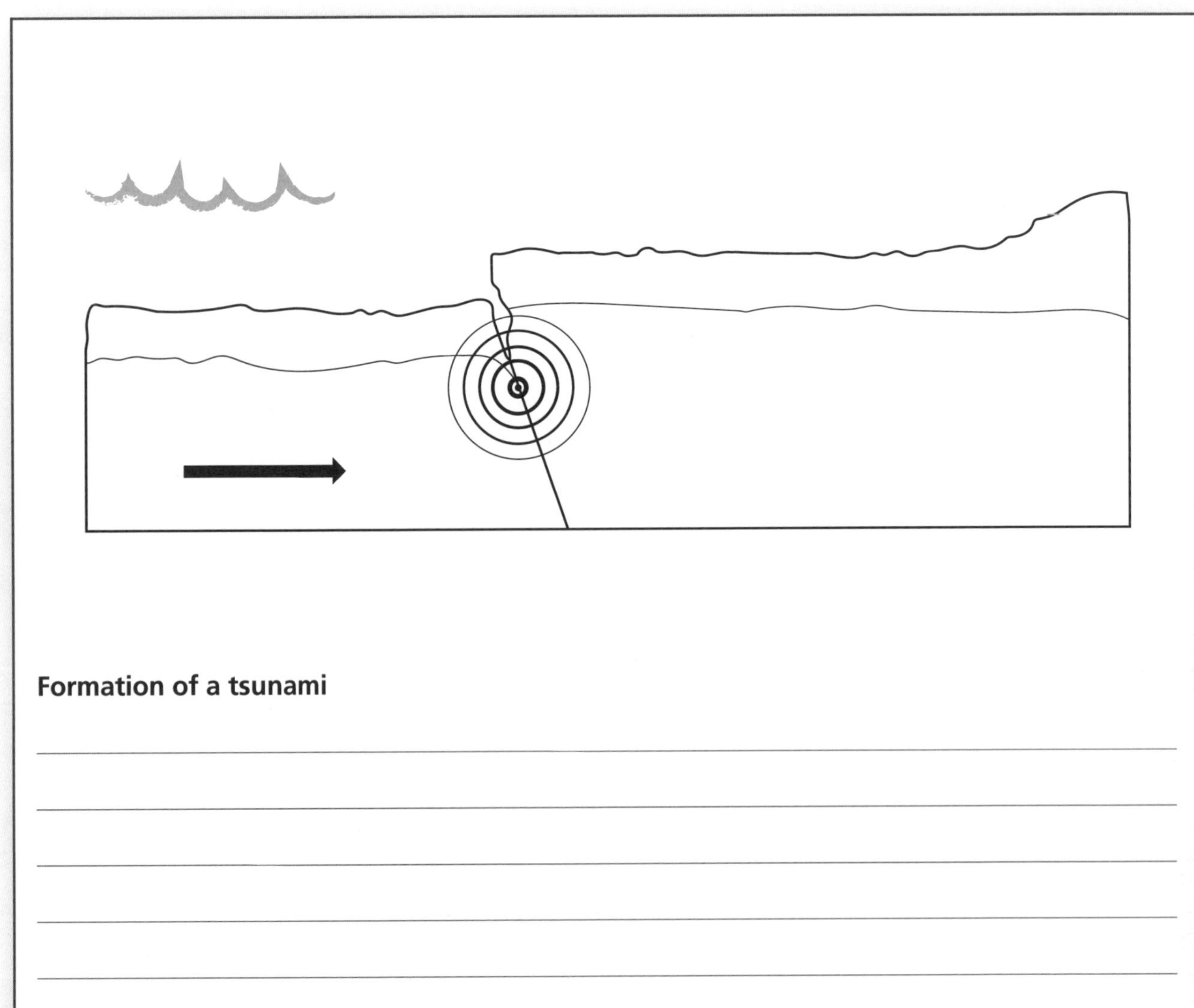

**Formation of a tsunami**

## Case Study

Other than the tsunami event named on page 25, name an example of a natural disaster that you have studied and state where and when it happened.

Natural disaster: ______________________________

Where: ______________________________

When: ______________________________

**Exam Hint**

You have been asked to 'Name and explain' in this question. This means that once you have named the consequences (impacts), you must also write an explanation for each one.

Name and explain one economic, one social and one environmental consequence of this event.

Economic: ______________________________

______________________________

______________________________

Social: ______________________________

______________________________

______________________________

______________________________

Environmental: ______________________________

______________________________

______________________________

______________________________

**Answer the questions to complete the mind map. This will support your revision.**

**Prompt Questions for Mind Map**

**(a)** How do plate movements trigger earthquakes? Can you name the types of plate boundary that earthquakes occur at? Can you name some very active earthquake zones?

**(b)** List and explain the key terms associated with an earthquake. Can you draw a basic sketch of an earthquake?

**(c)** What is a tsunami wave and how does it occur? Can you identify and name each key term associated with a tsunami?

**(d)** Name and explain the equipment used in measuring earthquakes.

**(e)** What can be done to reduce the impact and potential destruction of an earthquake?

**(f)** Describe an earthquake event that you have studied. Where, when and how did it occur? What was the magnitude? Can you name the social and economic impacts?

(f) Case Study

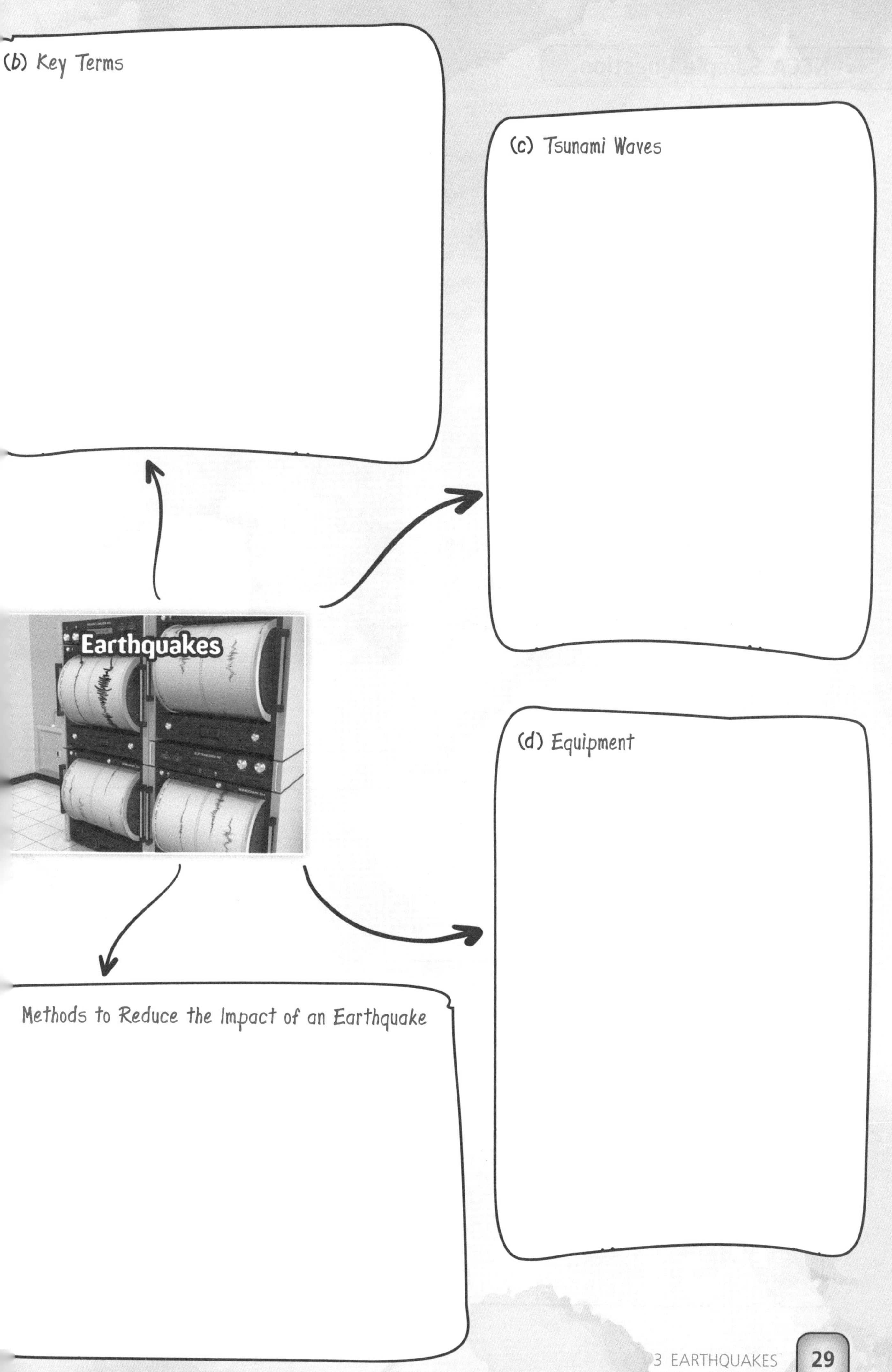
(b) Key Terms
(c) Tsunami Waves
Earthquakes
(d) Equipment
Methods to Reduce the Impact of an Earthquake

## NCCA Sample Question

### Question 1

In 2010, two earthquakes occurred of similar magnitude and depth, close to built-up areas. One of these earthquakes occurred in Christchurch, New Zealand; the other in Port-au-Prince, Haiti. Haiti experienced devastating results compared to New Zealand, which experienced mild damage. Haiti is located on an island in the Caribbean. It is classified as a low-income country. It is densely populated, with many of its population living in extreme poverty. New Zealand is an island located in the Pacific Ocean. It is classified as a high-income country, with a very high standard of living.

**Exam Hint**

In this question, you are comparing the damage caused by an earthquake in a high-income country (New Zealand) with a low-income country (Haiti).

Explain **three** factors that may have caused the effects to be felt worse in Haiti.

| Factor | Explanation |
|---|---|
| 1. | |
| 2. | |
| 3. | |

## Sample Question and Answer

### Question 2

Examine the map opposite and answer each of the following questions.

**(i)** Explain what is meant by the term 'epicentre'. [3 marks]

**(ii)** Explain why the effects of the earthquake were greater in Christchurch than in Wellington. [4 marks]

**(iii)** Describe **two** ways to reduce the impact of earthquakes. [8 marks]

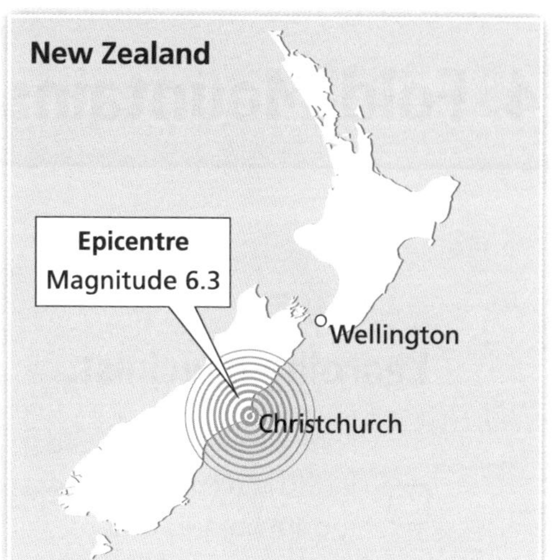


**Sample Answers**

*(i) The term 'epicentre' is used to describe the point on the Earth's surface directly above the focus of an earthquake. The shock waves released by the earthquake are felt most strongly at the epicentre and they reduce in strength as they move further away. The most severe damage caused by an earthquake will usually occur close to the epicentre.*

*(ii) From looking at the map, the epicentre (6.3) of the earthquake is shown to be located in Christchurch. The shock waves are moving outwards from this epicentre. The effects would be much greater in Christchurch than in Wellington because the epicentre is located in Christchurch. As the shock waves move outwards, they would have a much smaller impact in Wellington.*

*(iii) Two ways to reduce the impact of an earthquake are:*

1. ***Construct buildings that are designed and built to withstand the impact of an earthquake**. To do this, architects and engineers need to design buildings with foundations that allow a certain degree of movement so they can withstand the shaking that takes place during an earthquake. Roller foundations have been used in other locations to help with this.*
2. ***Practise by having earthquake drills**. In areas where earthquakes occur, local people should take part in training drills to practise the steps to take if an earthquake occurs similar to how we take part in fire drills. This will help them to take the necessary steps to protect themselves and their families.*

(i) This question uses the action verb 'explain'. We need to give a detailed account of what an epicentre is. We state where it can be found, what its role is in an earthquake and how it relates to damage caused.

(ii) This part also uses 'explain', so we provide a detailed account of why being close to the epicentre will cause greater damage in Christchurch. We use our key terms, such as 'shock waves'.

(iii) This question uses the action verb 'describe'. So, we must build a detailed picture of two ways to reduce the impact of an earthquake. We receive 1 mark for stating each method, but to achieve full marks, we must build the full picture by developing our answer.

**Marks Awarded**

**(i)** Correct explanation of term given – 3 marks

**(ii)** Proximity to epicentre explained, shock waves – 4 marks

**(iii)** Two ways to reduce impact stated – 1 mark each (1 + 1 = 2 marks)
Descriptions then provided – 3 marks each (3 + 3 = 6 marks)

Total = 15 marks

# 4 Fold Mountains

In this section, the Learning Outcomes we will look at are: **1.1**, **2.1**, **2.9**

**Learning Checklist:**

- ☐ I can explain how plate movements led to the formation of a fold mountain and I can draw/label a diagram of the formation.
- ☐ I can describe the economic and social impact of fold mountains, giving real-life examples.
- ☐ I can discuss the three main periods of folding.

## Fold Mountains – OS Maps

**1.** The map extract on the opposite page shows part of the MacGillycuddy's Reeks mountain range in Co. Kerry. They are a fold mountain range, formed during the Armorican folding period 250 million years ago. Review the map extract and answer the questions that follow.

**GeoSkill**

When reading grid references from 1:50 000 OS maps, remember **LEN**:

Letter Easting → Northing ↑

**(i)** Suggest two ways that this fold mountain range has been used by people. Use evidence from the map to support your answer.

**Exam Hint**

When you are asked to use evidence from the map, make sure to point out specific map features and use grid references to give their location.

1. ______________________________

______________________________

______________________________

______________________________

2. ______________________________

______________________________

______________________________

______________________________

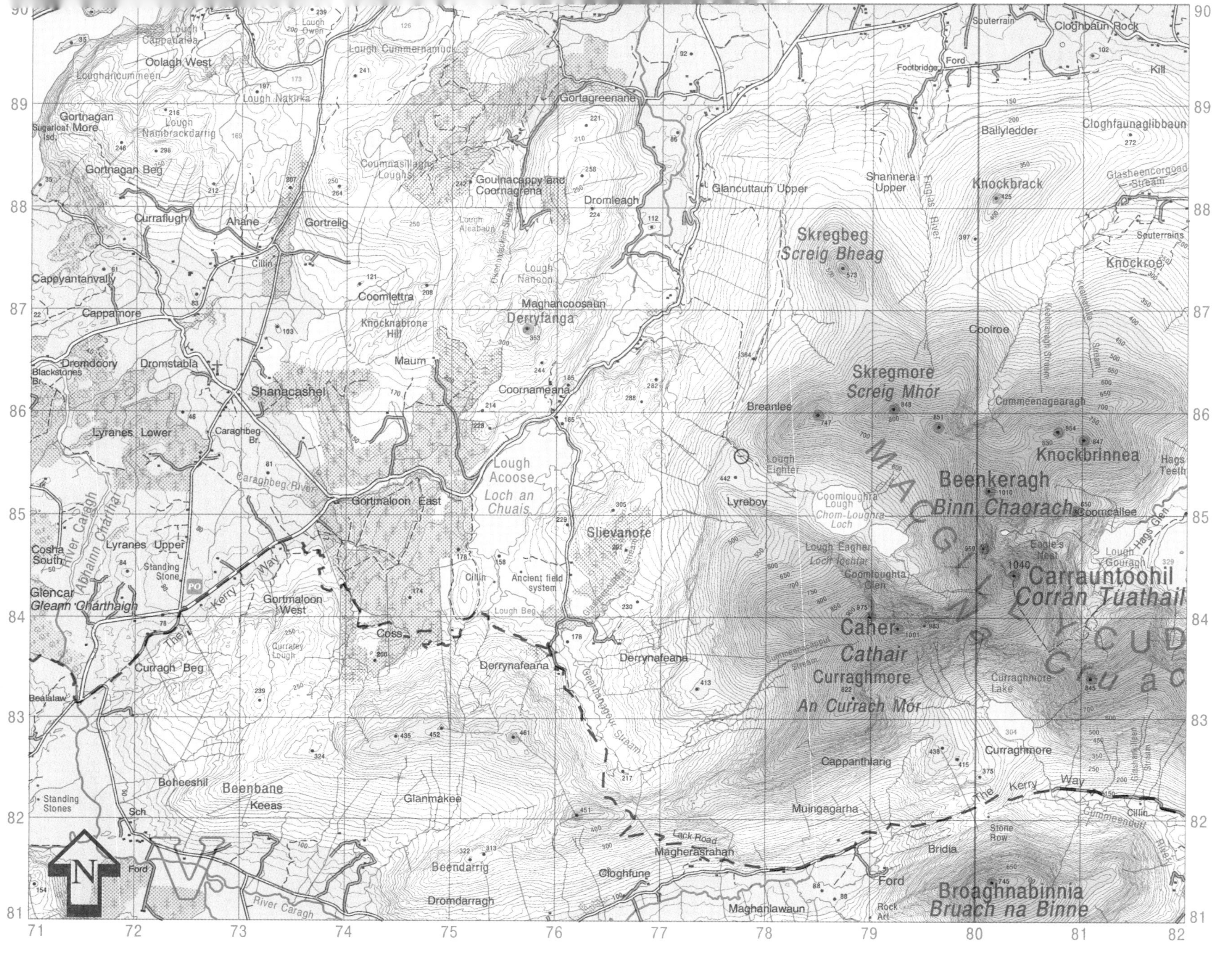
Carrauntoohil
Corrán Tuathail
Beenkeragh
Binn Chaorach
Caher
Cathair
Curraghmore
An Currach Mór
Skregmore
Screig Mhór
Skregbeg
Screig Bheag
Knockbrinnea
Broaghnabinnia
Bruach na Binne
Lough Acoose
Loch an Chuais
Knockbrack
Derryfanga
Slievanore
Breanlee
Lyreboy
Gortmaloon East
Shanacashel
Lyranes Lower
Lyranes Upper
Glencar
Gleann Chárthaigh
Beenbane
Cappanthlarig
Muingagarha
The Kerry Way

**(ii)** Measure the curved line distance in km along the Kerry Way from the post office at V72 84 to the northern edge of Lough Acoose at the top of grid square V75 85.

---

**GeoSkill**

When measuring curved line distance, use a piece of paper and pencil. Hold the paper carefully as you twist and mark along the page to mark the distance. Then, hold the first and last mark on the scale bar to find out your measurement in km.

**(iii)** Place these periods of folding onto their correct position on the timeline below.

35 million years ago 400 million years ago 250 million years ago

**(a)** Armorican **(b)** Alpine **(c)** Caledonian

**(iv)** You have decided to set up a sustainable tertiary economic activity located within this fold mountain region. Complete the business plan on the opposite page, ensuring that you include the following information:

**(a)** State the type of activity that you will establish. ☐

**(b)** Explain what makes your business sustainable. ☐

**(c)** Give the grid reference of the location you feel is most suitable for your selected activity. ☐

**(d)** Explain two reasons why you selected the above location. ☐

**(e)** Describe one way that your business will benefit the local community. ☐

**Exam Hint**

If there are a few parts to answer within a question, make sure to tick (✓) each part as you complete it. This way, you can be sure that you have not left anything out.

## My Business Plan

**Type of economic activity**

**Sustainability considerations**

**Location**

**Explanation for choice of location**

**Remember!**

Always include grid references when explaining the reasons for your chosen location.

**Benefit of my business to the local community**

## Formation of Fold Mountains

2. The map below shows the distribution of fold mountains across the globe. Review the map and answer the questions that follow.

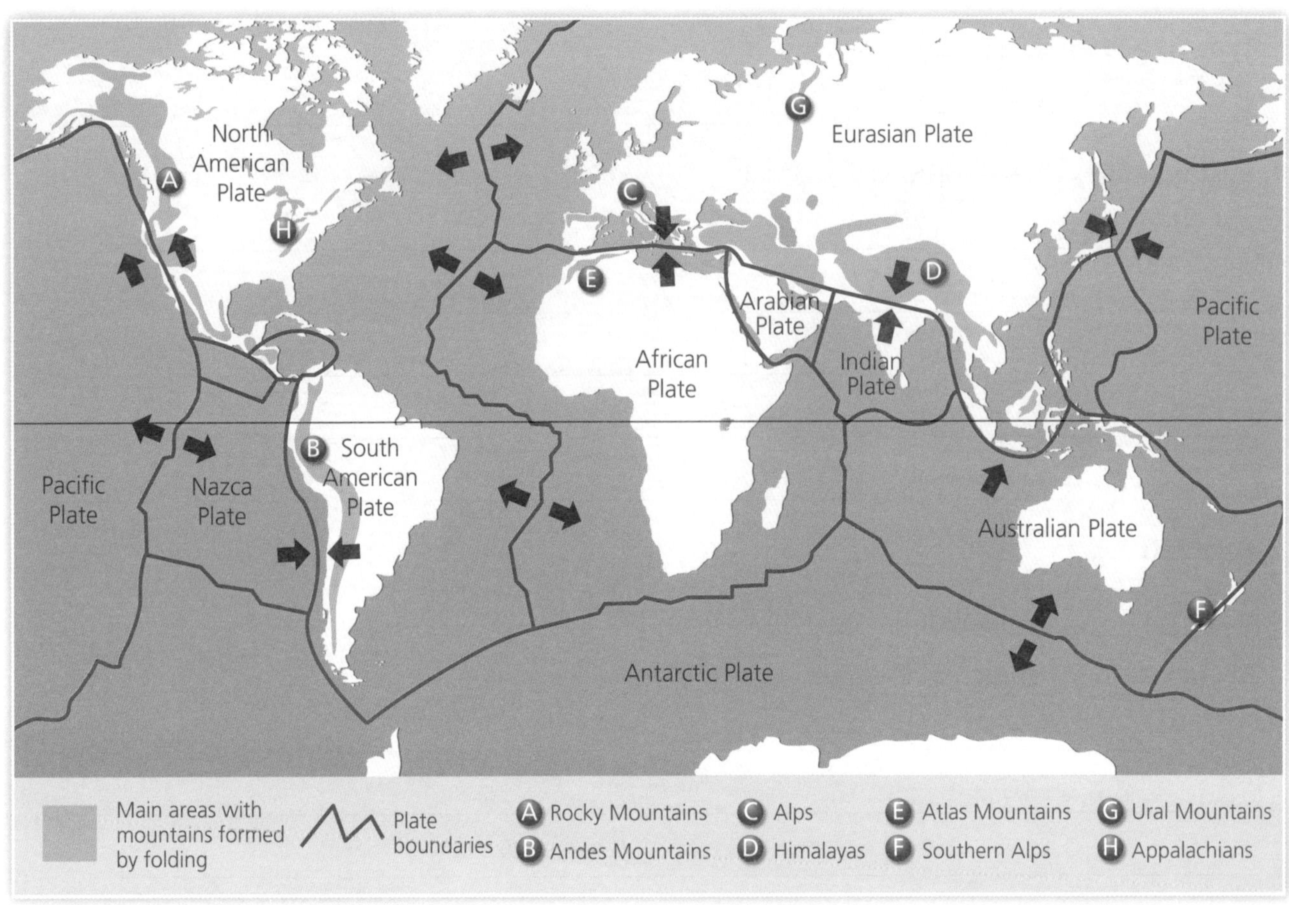


(i) Using the map, describe the distribution of fold mountains across the globe in relation to plate boundaries and movement.

**Exam Dictionary**

**Distribution** means how they are spread out.

(ii) On a hike with a friend on a walking trail in the Alps, you stop to talk about how this magnificent fold mountain range was formed. In the space below, write the description that you would give to your friend, detailing how fold mountain ranges such as this are formed. Include a diagram to support your answer.

**Remember!**

Some key terms that might be useful to include here are:

Plate boundaries, colliding, plates pushing together, forces, compression, buckled, upwards, anticline, syncline.

**Description of formation**

**Diagram**

## Exam Hint

You were asked to include a diagram to support your answer. Make sure that it is clear and well labelled, and that it includes additional information to enhance your written answer.

## The Alps

**3. (i)** Read the information below and answer the questions that follow.

The Alps are a fold mountain range located in central Europe. The Alps were formed when the Eurasian Plate collided with the African Plate 35 million years ago.

Tourism plays a key role in the economic life of the Alps. In wintertime, local businesses such as hotels, ski schools, restaurants and entertainment centres help to support over 100 million visitors each year. In summertime, tourism continues, with hiking, climbing, mountain biking and outdoor activities bringing people to the region. This provides a steady income all year for locals.

The Alps are also a great resource for generating power. Energy companies have built dams to generate hydroelectric power. The high rainfall and regular supply of water from melting snow provides plenty of water to power the hydroelectric power plants.

**(a)** Name the two plates that collided to form the Alps.

**1.** ____________________

**2.** ____________________

**(b)** The Alps were formed 35 million years ago. What was the name given to this period of folding?

____________________

**(c)** Describe one economic and one social impact of fold mountains for people living in this region.

**Remember!**

You have been given a lot of information about the Alps in this question. Make sure to go back over the information and use it in your answer here.

**Economic:**

____________________

**Social:**

**(ii)** Read the information below and answer the questions that follow.

The climate of the Alps is mainly temperate. However, climate predictions show that due to climate change, the air temperature in the Alps may rise in the future. This could result in less snowfall, which would have an impact on industries across the region.

Describe two ways in which the Alps would be impacted by the climate change prediction mentioned above.

**1.**

**2.**

**Answer the questions to complete the mind map. This will support your revision.**

**Prompt Questions for Mind Map**

**(a)** Why are fold mountains found on plate boundaries? Can you describe how plate movement creates fold mountains? Where in the world can we see examples of fold mountains?

**(b)** What are the three main periods of folding known as? When did they each occur?

**(c)** Can you draw a small diagram showing how a fold mountain is formed? Can you label all parts?

**(d)** Describe some economic impacts of fold mountains for people living near them. Do you have a case study of a fold mountain region that you have studied?

**(e)** Describe some social impacts of fold mountains for people living in a fold mountain region. Again, can you refer to your case study here?

(a) Plate Boundaries

(e) Social Impacts of Fold Mountains

(b) Periods of Folding

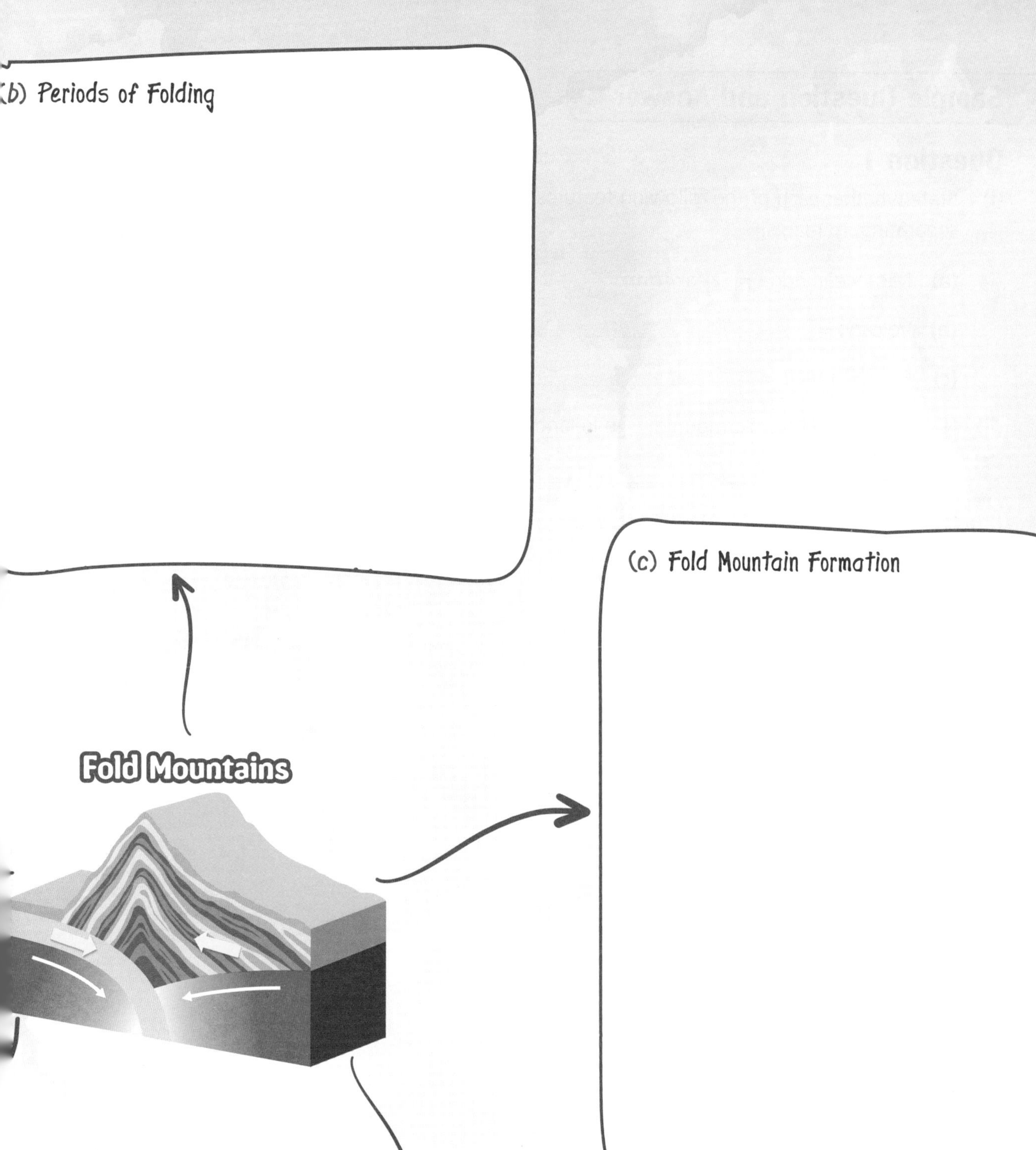


(c) Fold Mountain Formation

Economic Impacts of Fold Mountains

## Sample Question and Answer

### Question 1

**(i)** State whether each of the following features is formed as a result of plates colliding or plates separating. [6 marks]

**(a)** Mid-ocean ridge = *Separating*

**(b)** Volcano = ______________________________

**(c)** Fold mountain = ______________________________

**(ii)** Name one range of fold mountains in Ireland. [3 marks]

______________________________________________________________

**(iii)** Using a labelled diagram, show how fold mountains are formed. [8 marks]

*Here you will need to draw a diagram showing how a fold mountain is formed when two plates collide. You receive marks for the accuracy of your diagram, so make sure to use pencil and keep it neat and clear. You should place clear labels and arrows onto the diagram to make sure that it is easy to understand.*

**(iv)** Explain two advantages of hydroelectric power generation in fold mountain regions. [8 marks]

1. *One advantage of hydroelectric power generation in fold mountain regions is the positive impact that it has on climate change. It is a renewable source of energy and this makes it cleaner than burning fossil fuels. There is a lot of power in moving water in these regions, and it is very good environmentally to tap into this.*

*You need to state two advantages of hydroelectric power. One has been stated and described for you. You must now follow this with a second positive. Marks are awarded for stating the positive and then developing the description.*

**2.** ______________________________

______________________________

______________________________

______________________________

**(v)** Outline two objections that might be made to the development of a hydroelectric power station. [8 marks]

1. *In some places, hydroelectric power can disrupt wildlife habitats in the area. They may disrupt or destroy certain habitats and this is not good for the local environment. Locals may object, as the loss of one wildlife habitat can have knock-on impacts for others in the area.*

*You are asked to outline two objections. The first has been written for you. You must state what the objection is and then develop the point further to outline why people would object.*

**2.** ______________________________

______________________________

______________________________

______________________________

**Marks Awarded**

**(i)** Correct answers stated – 2 marks for each (2 + 2 + 2 = 6 marks)

**(ii)** Fold mountain range named – 3 marks

**(iii)** Accurate diagram drawn – 4 marks

Diagram includes full labels showing plate collision and folding – 4 marks

(4 + 4 = 8 marks)

**(iv)** Advantages stated – 2 marks for each (2 + 2 = 4 marks)

Advantages developed – 2 marks for each (2 + 2 = 4 marks)

(4 + 4 = 8 marks)

**(v)** Objections stated – 2 marks for each (2 + 2 = 4 marks)

Objections developed – 2 marks for each (2 + 2 = 4 marks)

(4 + 4 = 8 marks)

# 5 Rocks

In this section, the Learning Outcomes we will look at are: **1.2**, **2.2**

## Learning Checklist:

- ☐ I can describe how rocks move through the rock cycle.
- ☐ I can read grid references from OS maps.
- ☐ I can explain the formation of igneous, sedimentary and metamorphic rocks.
- ☐ I can describe the economic, social and environmental impacts of rock exploitation, giving examples.
- ☐ I can discuss examples of rocks from each rock group.
- ☐ I can extract relevant information from news articles.
- ☐ I can measure straight line distance on a map.
- ☐ I can read information from graphs.

## Rock Formation

**1.** **(i)** Fill in the blanks in the paragraph below using the key words provided.

Inorganic Resources Texture Metamorphic Compressed Sedimentary

The surface of our Earth is covered in rocks. Rocks can have different colour, ________________, mineral content and hardness. Rocks can be made up of a single mineral or of many minerals ________________ together. Minerals are ________________ materials, which means that they do not come from an animal or plant. The rocks that make up our landscape provide us with many valuable ________________. Rocks are divided up into three groups: igneous, ________________ and ________________.

**(ii)** Correctly label the diagram of the rock cycle.

Metamorphic rock

Heat and pressure

Sediments

Igneous rock

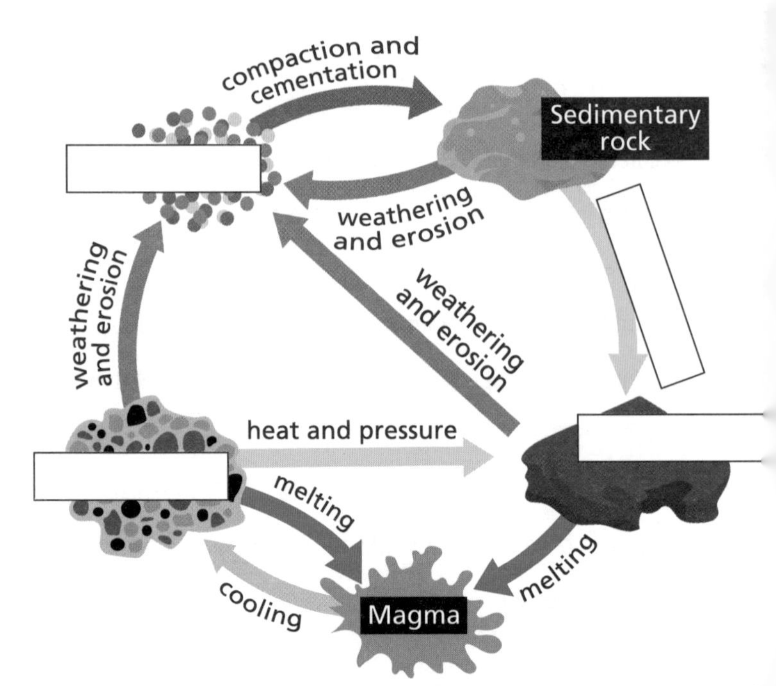

**(iii)** You have just completed a really exciting lesson where you learned all about the rock cycle. Write an email to a friend to explain how rocks are constantly changing as they move through this cycle.

**Exam Hint**

The first one has been completed for you. Some key information to consider including in this answer:

**Igneous:** Intrusive and extrusive igneous rock.

**Sedimentary:** Layers, compression, sea floor.

**Metamorphic:** Great heat, pressure, changing of other rocks.

New Message

To:

Subject: **The Rock Cycle!**

**1.** As magma rises from the mantle it cools to form igneous rocks. If it cools slowly below the surface we call it intrusive igneous rock, and if it cools quickly on the Earth's surface we call it extrusive igneous rock. Examples are granite and basalt.

**2.** ________________________________________

________________________________________

________________________________________

________________________________________

________________________________________

**3.** ________________________________________

________________________________________

________________________________________

________________________________________

________________________________________

Send

**(iv)** Match each term in Column X with the correct location in Column Y. In Column Z, insert one characteristic for each rock type. One has been completed for you.

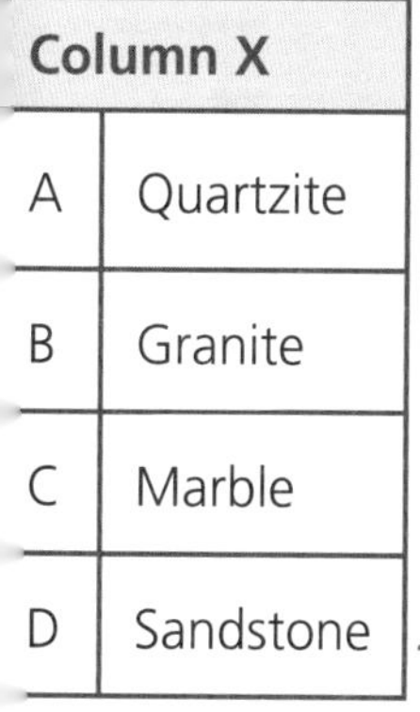

| Column X | |
|---|---|
| A | Quartzite |
| B | Granite |
| C | Marble |
| D | Sandstone |

| Column Y | |
|---|---|
| 1 | MacGillycuddy's Reeks, Co. Kerry |
| 2 | Connemara, Co. Galway |
| 3 | Croagh Patrick, Co. Mayo |
| 4 | Wicklow Mountains, Co. Wicklow |

| Column Z |
|---|
| Sandstone is typically brown to red in colour |
| |
| |
| |

## Rock Groups

2. (i) Examine the photograph of this limestone area in Co. Clare and answer the questions that follow.

(a) Circle the rock group below that limestone belongs to.

Igneous Sedimentary Metamorphic

(b) Read the statements below and circle the correct answer as **True or False**.

- Limestone is a permeable and soluble rock. True / False
- Limestone is used to create agricultural lime used in farming. True / False
- Limestone is formed when lava cools quickly on the Earth's surface. True / False

(c) What metamorphic rock is formed when limestone is placed under great heat and pressure?

______________________________

(d) Describe one impact of **human activity** on a limestone region that you have studied.

______________________________
______________________________
______________________________
______________________________
______________________________
______________________________
______________________________
______________________________

**Remember!**

Consider: What are humans doing to the landscape that could impact on a soft limestone landscape? Think of the link with weathering.

(ii) Take a look at the geological map of Ireland opposite. Answer the questions that follow.

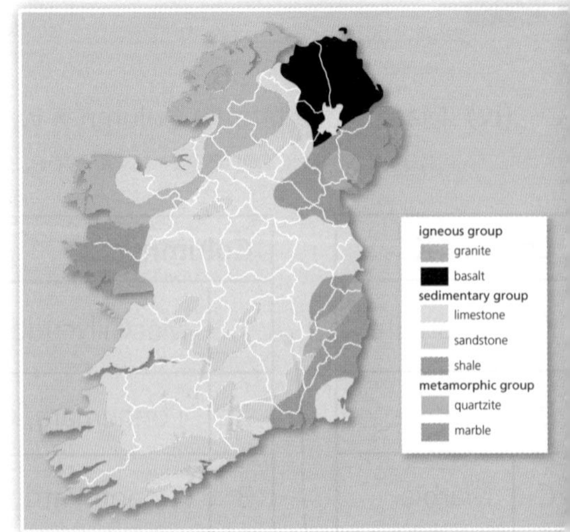


(a) What is the most common rock found in Ireland?

______________________________

(b) Select one igneous **or** metamorphic rock from the geological map above and describe how it was formed. Include a diagram to support your answer.

## Exam Hint

To answer this question, pick the rock you feel most comfortable with.

- ▢ Start by naming the rock and stating which rock group it belongs to.
- ▢ Next, describe the steps involved in its formation.
- ▢ Then, describe its colour and texture.
- ▢ State one thing that the rock is used for in everyday life.
- ▢ Finally, give an example of where it can be located in Ireland.

The rock that I have chosen to describe the formation of is …

**Diagram**

## Human Interaction

3. (i) The table opposite shows the total energy supply by source in Ireland from 1990 to 2019. Review the table and answer the questions on the next page.

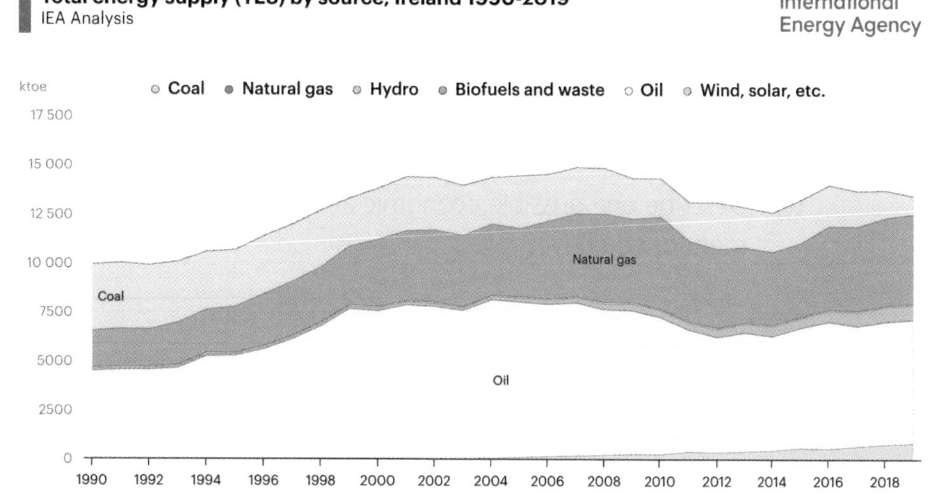

**(a)** Which natural energy source is used in the largest quantity in Ireland over the time period shown? Tick the correct answer.

| Source | Tick |
|---|---|
| Coal | |
| Oil | |
| Wind, solar | |

**(b)** Name the two sources of renewable energy that increase in supply from 2006 to 2019.

________________ ________________

**(c)** State one environmental and one economic impact that drilling for gas or oil can have on a local area.

Environmental impact: ________________

Economic impact: ________________

**(ii)** Read the news article below and answer the questions that follow.

**Mining in Ireland Has Key Role in Ensuring Sustainable Future, Geoscientists Warn**

On Monday a campaign was launched to raise awareness of the role of mineral exploration and mining in meeting Ireland's future social, economic and environmental needs.

The switch from using fossil fuels to moving towards renewable energy options such as wind energy, solar energy, geothermal energy and battery storage will create a huge demand for important metals. Mining for these items is essential to ensure the supply of these metals.

Europe is 75 per cent dependent on imports for almost all metals. The Republic of Ireland has only two working mines. The zinc that is mined at the Tara Mines in Co. Meath is sent all over Europe.

'Ireland can offer more. Strong potential exists to explore for zinc and other known metals that are really important to the green economy which are also found in Ireland, such as silver, gold, copper, lead, cobalt and rare earth elements,' the Irish geoscientists warn. The green economy aims to reduce environmental risks and ecological scarcities, and that aims for sustainable development without degrading the environment.

*Source: The Irish Times*

**(a)** Name two sources of renewable energy mentioned in the article.

________________

________________

**(b)** The article mentions the 'green economy'. Explain what is meant by this term.

________________

________________

**(c)** Describe one possible economic advantage for Ireland in mining for the essential metals mentioned above.

________________

________________

________________

**(iii)** A mining company has proposed to build a new quarry very close to Macroom, Co. Cork, at grid reference W315 735. Review the map on the next page and answer the questions that follow.

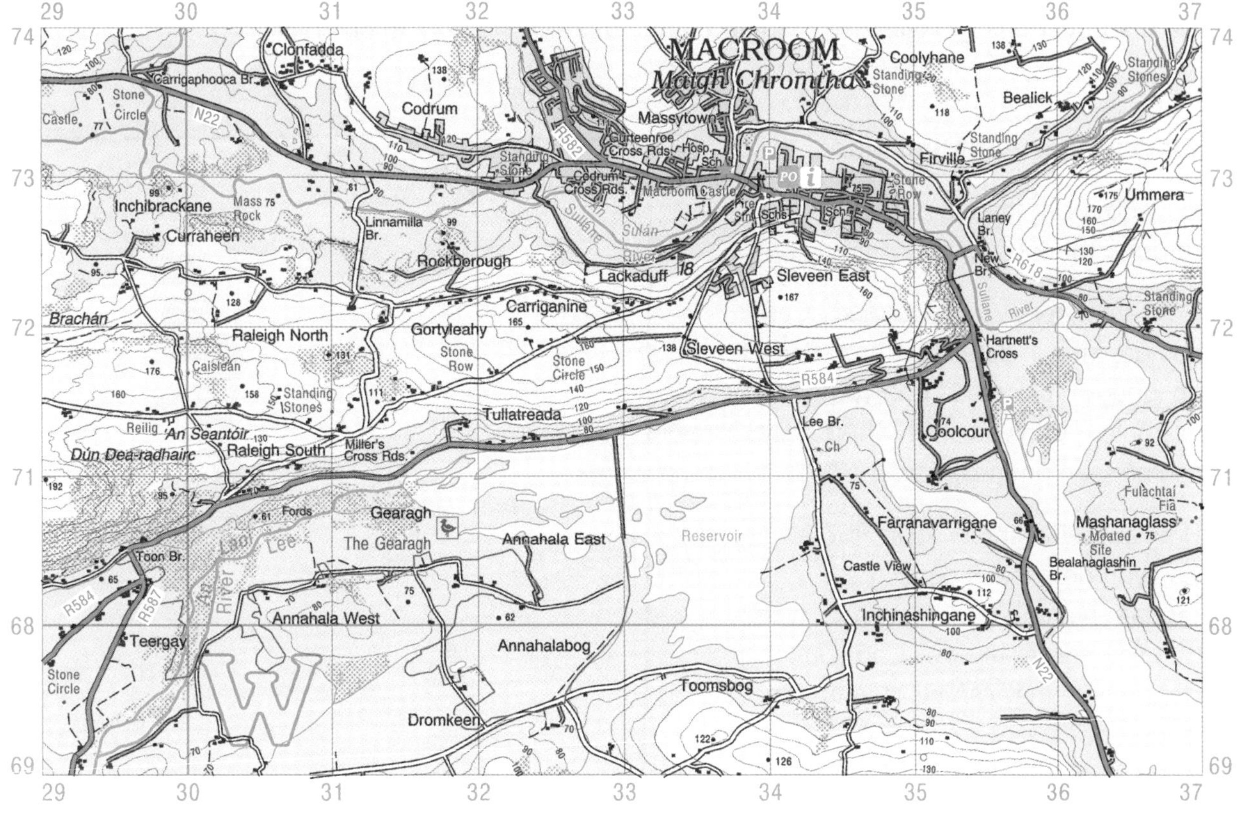


**(a)** Measure the straight line distance in km from the proposed quarry site at W315 735 to the post office in the centre of Macroom town.

________________________________________

**Remember!**

Always include the correct unit in your answer.

**(b)** Local residents are unhappy that the new quarry will be located so close to their homes and schools. Provide a six-figure grid reference for an alternative site for the location of this new quarry. Give one reason for your choice.

Six-figure grid reference for new site: ________________________

Reason for selection:

________________________________________

________________________________________

________________________________________

________________________________________

**(c)** Describe one environmental impact and one economic impact that the new quarry could have on the town of Macroom.

**Environmental impact:**

________________________________________

________________________________________

________________________________________

**Economic impact:**

________________________________________

________________________________________

________________________________________

**Answer the questions to complete the mind map. This will support your revision.**

**Prompt Questions for Mind Map**

**(a)** How do rocks change as they move through the rock cycle?

**(b)** How are igneous rocks formed? Can you describe in detail the formation of an igneous rock type? Can you give examples? Can you state where they can be seen on the landscape?

**(c)** How are sedimentary rocks formed? Can you describe in detail the formation of a sedimentary rock type? Can you give examples? Can you state where they can be seen on the landscape?

**(d)** How are metamorphic rocks formed? Can you describe in detail the formation of a metamorphic rock type? Can you give examples? Can you state where they can be seen on the landscape?

**(e)** How do humans interact with rocks? Describe some of the environmental and economic impacts of this interaction.

(a) Rock Cycle

(e) Human Interaction with Rocks

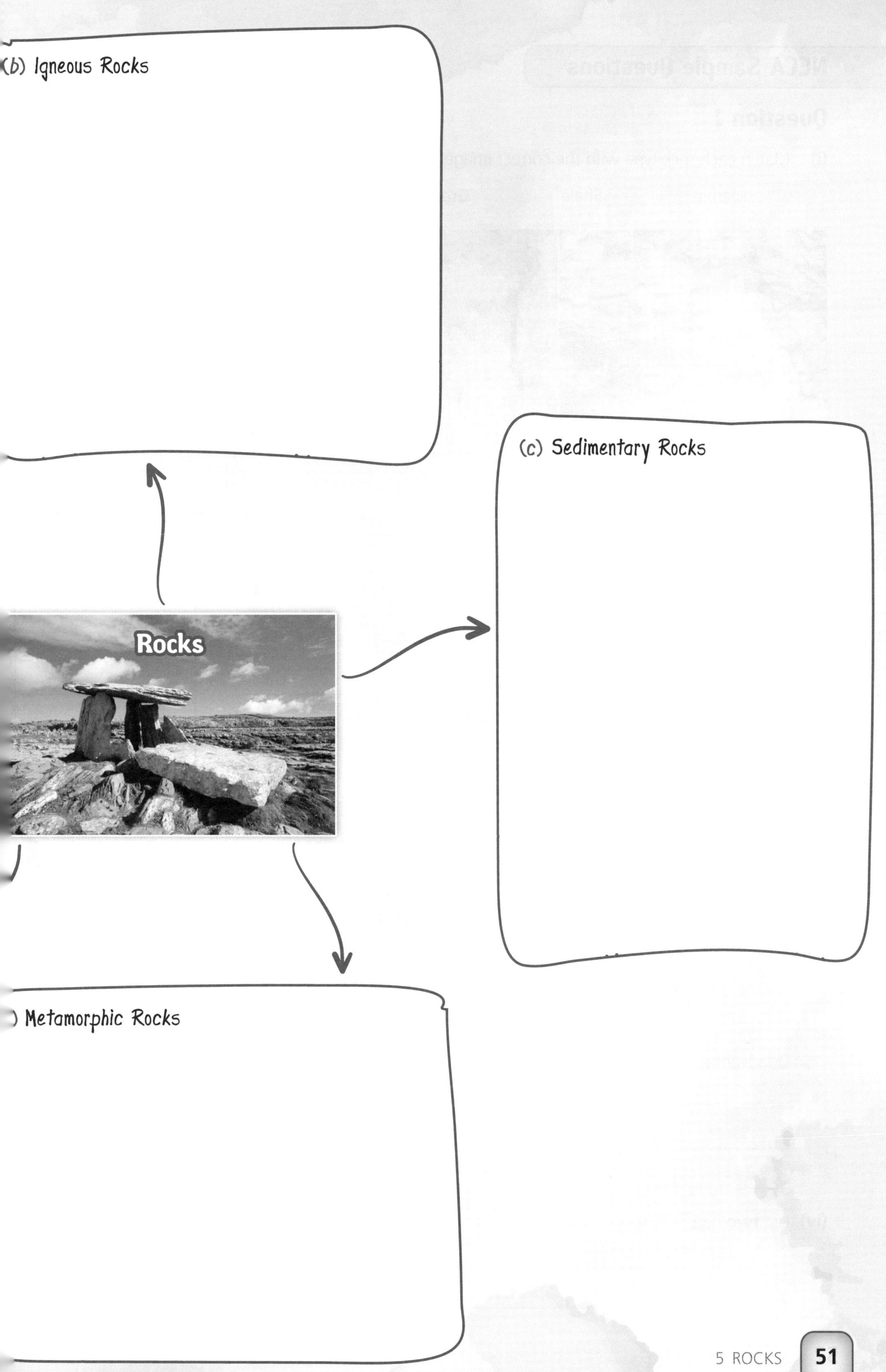
(b) Igneous Rocks
(c) Sedimentary Rocks
Rocks
) Metamorphic Rocks

## NCCA Sample Questions

### Question 1

**(i)** Match each rock type with the correct image below.

Marble Shale Granite

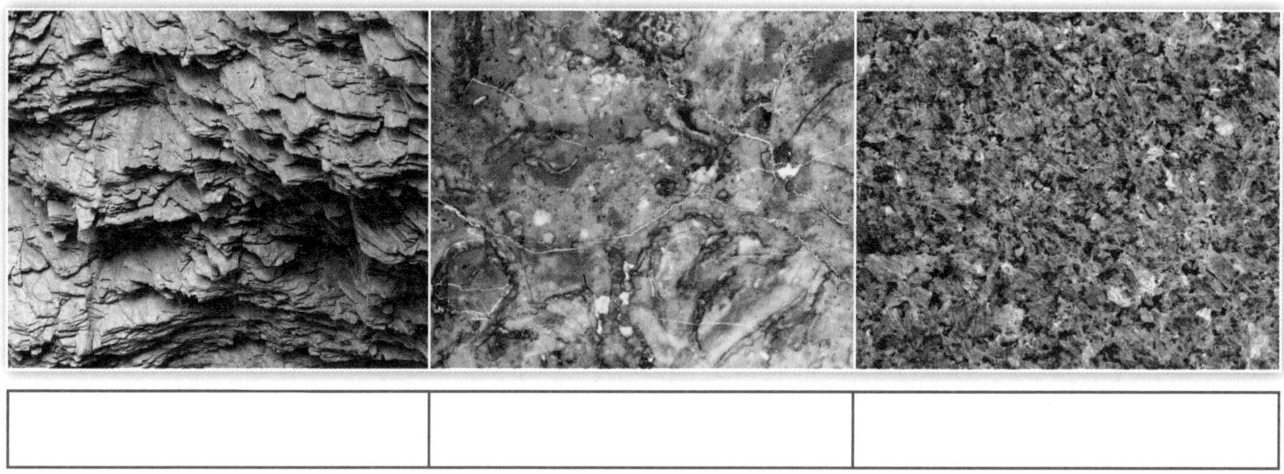

| | | |
|---|---|---|
| | | |

**(ii)** Fill in the following table.

| Category | Formation | Characteristics | Human uses/ Economic uses |
|---|---|---|---|
| Igneous | Magma from the Earth's core cooled to form rock | | |
| Sedimentary | Many sediments compacted together to form rock | | |
| Metamorphic | Rocks that have changed due to extreme heat and/or pressure | | |

**(iii)** Rock exploitation in Ireland provides many advantages and disadvantages. Explain **one** advantage and **one** disadvantage.

Advantage: ______________________________

______________________________

______________________________

______________________________

Disadvantage: ______________________________

______________________________

______________________________

______________________________

**(iv)** List **two** natural resources **other than rocks** found in your local area.

**1.** ______________________________

**2.** ______________________________

## Sample Question and Answer

### Question 2

Examine the photograph below and answer each of the following questions.

**(i)** State whether the photograph shows an igneous, a sedimentary or a metamorphic rock. [3 marks]

**(ii)** Name an example of a sedimentary rock. [3 marks]

**(iii)** Describe and explain how the sedimentary rock named by you in part **(ii)** above was formed. [8 marks]

**Sample Answer**

*(i) The rock shown in the photograph is an igneous rock.*

*(ii) An example of a sedimentary rock that I have studied is limestone.*

*(iii) Limestone is formed when the remains of dead sea creatures, shells, sediments and bones become piled up on the seabed. Over many millions of years, and under great pressure, all of these remains become compressed and cemented in layers. The layers are known as strata. Sometimes, old fossils can be found preserved in the rock.*

*Limestone is a permeable rock, which means that water can pass through it. It is also soluble; this means that it can dissolve in water.*

*Limestone is the most common rock type in Ireland. I have seen limestone being used in old buildings and monuments.*

(i) Brief answer is required here as the action verb is 'state'. State the rock type for 3 marks.

(ii) A brief answer is also required here, as the action verb is 'name'.

(iii) In this question we are asked to describe and explain, so we must build a picture in our answer. We start by explaining the formation of the rock, which will get us 4 marks. Next, we move on to describe the rock, its characteristics and its uses.

**Marks Awarded**

**(i)** Rock correctly named – 3 marks

**(ii)** Correct example named of any sedimentary rock – 3 marks

**(iii)** Explanation of how the rock is formed – 4 marks. Description of the rock, characteristics, uses, etc. – 4 marks (4 + 4 = 8 marks)

Total = 14 marks

# 6 Soil

In this section, the Learning Outcomes we will look at are: **1.4**, **2.4**

**Learning Checklist:**

- ☐ I can explain what soil is.
- ☐ I can explain how leaching and plant litter can impact soil.
- ☐ I can understand what soil is made of and how it is formed.
- ☐ I can interpret information from maps, infographics and weather charts.

## What Is Soil?

**1.** **(i)** Soil has five main ingredients. Match these five ingredients with their correct definitions in the table below.

Mineral particles Water Organic matter Humus Air

| Ingredient | Definition |
|---|---|
| | Makes up 4% of soil. A mixture of anything living found in the soil (earthworms, beetles, etc.). |
| | Makes up 1% of soil. Formed from dead organic matter, such as plant litter (dead leaves and twigs). A dark gel-like substance that increases soil fertility. |
| | Makes up 25% of soil. Found between soil particles, it provides oxygen for the soil. |
| | Largest ingredient found in soil at 45%. It is made up of sand, silt and clay. It is created by denudation and weathering. |
| | Makes up 25% of the soil. It binds or sticks the soil together. Plants soak this up through their roots to get nutrients. |

**(ii)** Correctly label each section of the pie chart to show the five main ingredients of soil and the percentage of the soil they make up.

**Composition of soil**

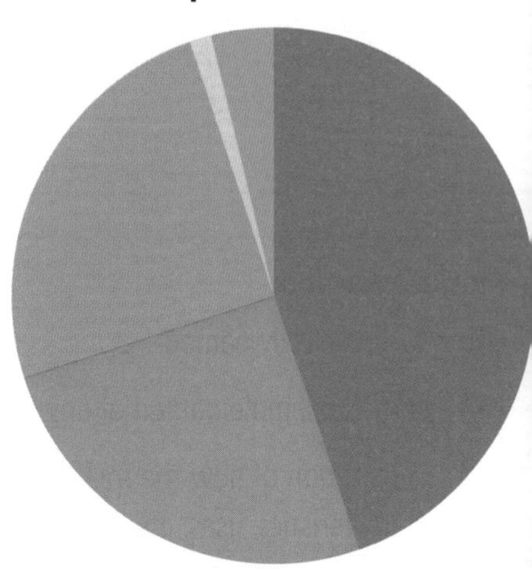

**Exam Hint**

When answering part (b) on the following page, make sure to define what a natural resource is.

**(iii)** **(a)** Is soil a natural resource? Tick the correct box to answer.

Yes ☐ No ☐

(b) Give a reason for your answer:

(c) List four uses for soil (one has been filled in for you already).

1. ______
2. ______
3. *Building materials*
4. ______

## How Is Soil Formed?

2. Complete the poster below and on the following page to explain how soil is formed.

### How Soil Is Formed

#### Parent Material

The type of rock from which soil is formed. Different types of rock will make different soils when broken down. For example, when limestone is broken down it makes soil more fertile.

#### Vegetation

What happens when vegetation dies? What does it become? What does it do for soil fertility?

#### Living Organisms

## How Soil Is Formed (contd.)

### Landscape

**Upland areas:**

**Lowland areas:**

### Climate

How can a hot, cold or temperate climate affect soil? Think of precipitation, temperature, etc.

### Time

### Human Activity

Farming, building, searching for natural resources. How do human activities like these and more affect soil formation?

**Exam Hint**

This question is asking you to explain the impact each factor has on soil formation. Read the completed 'Parent Material' section on the previous page. Keep your points short and use the hints provided. You can use bullet points or complete sentences.

## Soil Profiles and Impacts on Soil

3. **(i)** This is a diagram of a typical soil profile. Describe each horizon (A–C). The O horizon has been described for you in detail. You should use the words provided here to help.

| Horizon | Topsoil | Most fertile | Dark in colour |
|---|---|---|---|
| Lighter in colour | Bedrock | Solid rock | Parent material |

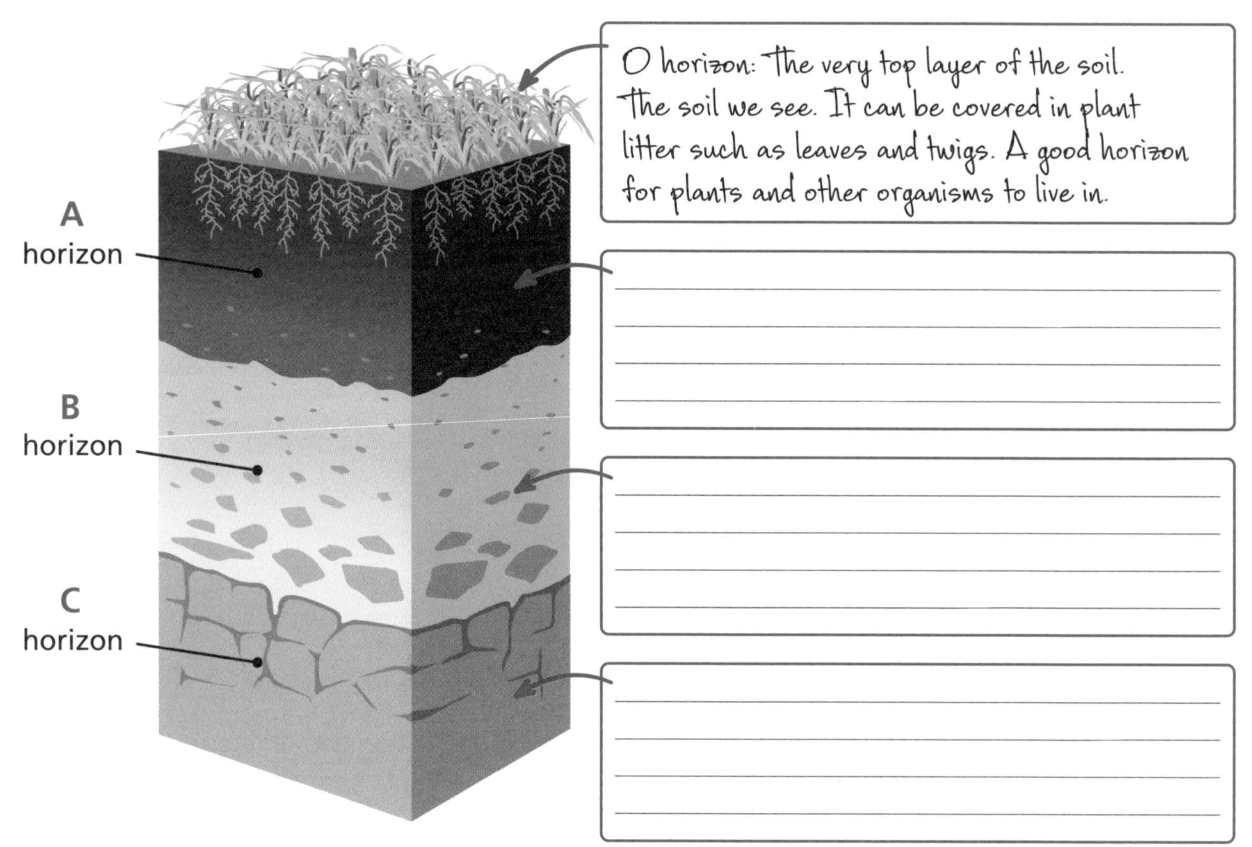

O horizon: The very top layer of the soil. The soil we see. It can be covered in plant litter such as leaves and twigs. A good horizon for plants and other organisms to live in.
A horizon
B horizon
C horizon

**Exam Hint**

Clearly define the difference between each horizon. What colour is it? What is it made of? How does it affect fertility? Use bullet points or sentences to answer.

**(ii) (a)** Leaching affects soil fertility. Give a brief description of what leaching is.

**(b)** Examine the cartoon image. On the following page, explain **two** reasons why severe leaching is bad for soil.

Leaching

**Exam Hint**

Interpreting information from a cartoon is a popular exam question. Describe what you see in an image.

1: ______________________________

______________________________

2: Hardpan: ______________________________

______________________________

______________________________

______________________________

**Exam Hint**

A hint has been given; what is a hardpan?
If hints like this are given in exam questions, make your best effort to refer to them in your answer.

**(iii)** Examine the two weather maps (A and B) below.

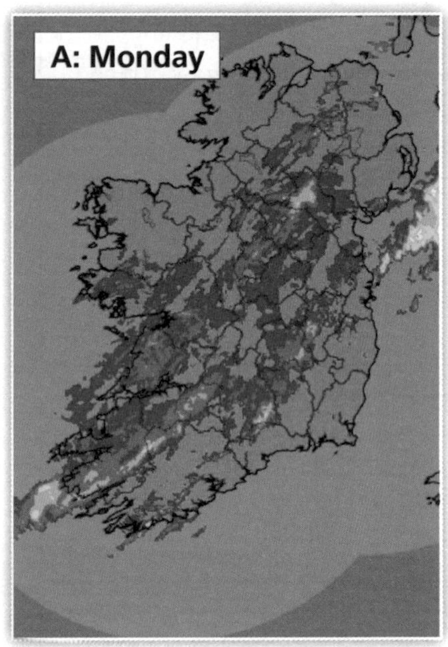


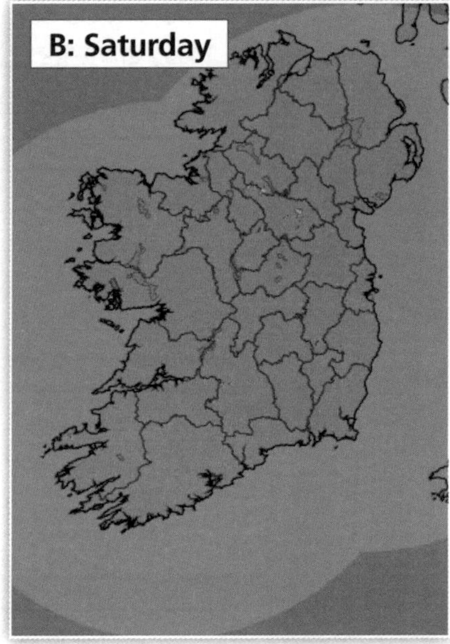


**Remember!**

Two Learning Outcomes linked to soil are being questioned here: Weather and Natural Resources.

The maps show Ireland experiencing different levels of rainfall on two different days in the week: Monday and Saturday. A farmer in Co. Clare is looking to spread pesticides on his crops. Which day would be a better day for the farmer to do this?

______________________________

Explain the reason for your choice.

______________________________

______________________________

______________________________

**Exam Hint**

When asked to explain your choice, use the information from the maps and include examples to back up your answer.

**(iv)** Using the words provided, fill in the blanks in the paragraph below to explain the breakdown of plant litter.

Humification   Dead leaves and twigs   Humus   A horizon   Oxygen

Plant litter, which is made up of ________ ________ ________ ________ that have fallen on top of the ________ ________________, is broken down by insects and microorganisms into a black jelly-like substance called ________________. This makes soil fertile. ________________ is also needec to help the breakdown of plant litter, as it helps keep organisms alive. This entire process is called ________________.

## Ireland's Soil Types

4. **(i)** Look at the map of Ireland's soil types to the right and answer the questions that follow.

 **(a)** What is Ireland's most common soil type?

 ______________________________

 **(b)** Which soil is most common in Donegal?

 ______________________________

 **(c)** Which province has the most fertile soil?

 ______________________________

 **(d)** What is the least common soil type found in Ireland?

 ______________________________

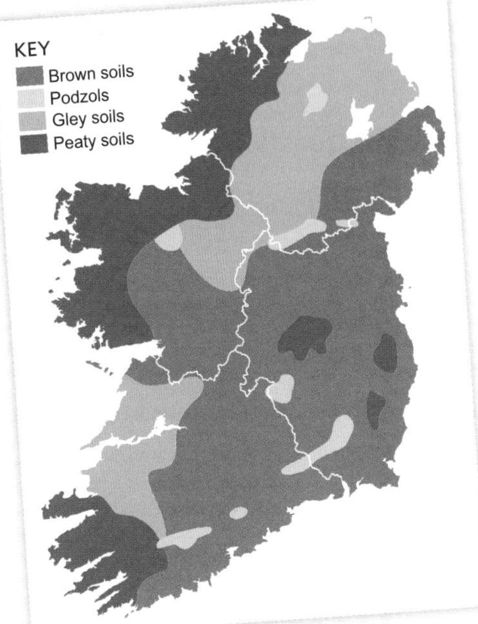


### Exam Hint

Short questions like these are asking for direct answers. Make sure to attempt them all.

**(ii)** Choose **three** soil types that you have studied and describe the soils in the report below. You can use **three** of the soils shown on the map above. Use the headings provided for guidance.

| **Soil type** | | | |
|---|---|---|---|
| **Profile: Sketch your profile here. Note the height of each horizon and the difference in colour.** | | | |
| **Colour** | | | |
| **Formation and location** | | | |
| **Is there leaching or humification?** | | | |
| **Uses** | | | |

### Exam Hint

List the colour(s) of each soil clearly. Know one county where each soil is dominant, and whether there is leaching. For uses, think of primary economic activities.

**Answer the questions to complete the mind map. This will support your revision.**

## Prompt Questions for Mind Map

**(a)** Can you define what soil is and name some of its uses?

**(b)** Do you know the make-up (composition) of soil in percentages?

**(c)** Can you explain the importance of each ingredient of soil?

**(d)** How is soil formed?

**(e)** Can you explain how leaching and humification affect soil?

**(f)** Can you explain in detail a fertile and infertile soil?

(a) Soil

(f) Fertile and Infertile Soil

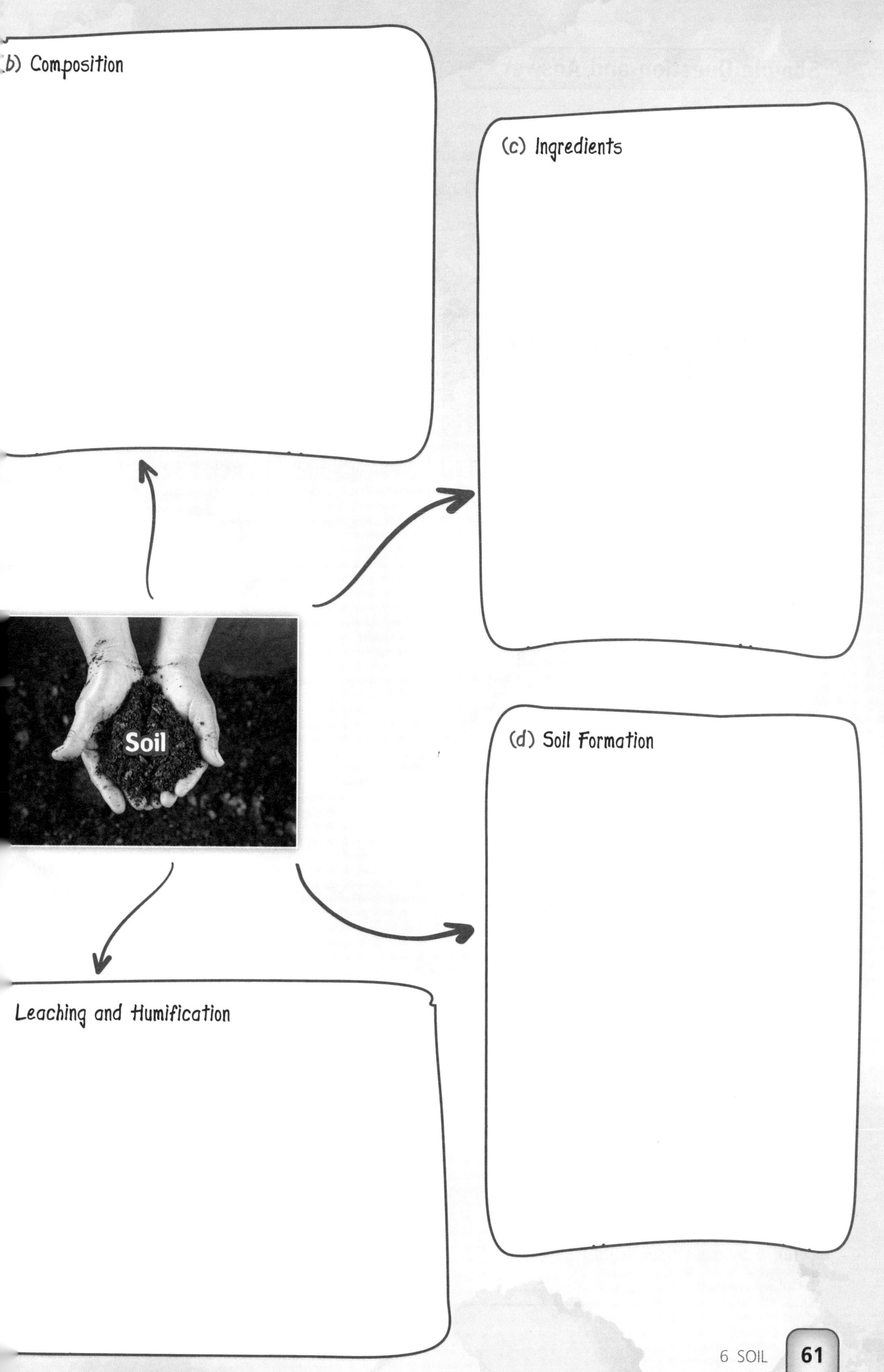
b) Composition
(c) Ingredients
Soil
(d) Soil Formation
Leaching and Humification

## Sample Question and Answer

### Question 1

**(i)** Describe and explain the formation of the soil profile shown in the image below. [9 marks]

**(ii)** Name Ireland's most common soil type. [1 mark]

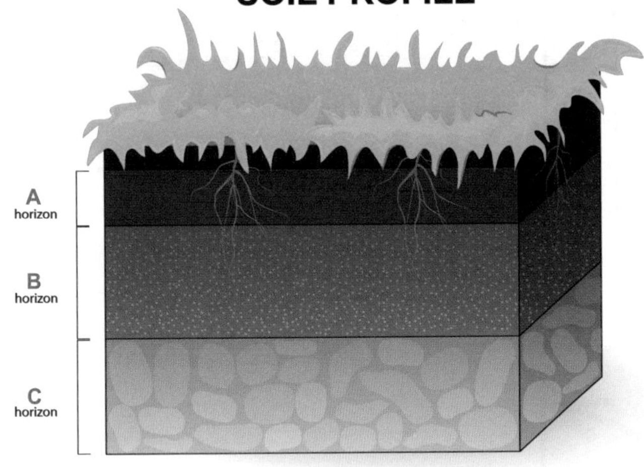


*Breaking your answer down into three separate paragraphs will make it easier for you to show your knowledge. You can see how each factor is developed and includes an example to ensure full marks are achieved.*

**Sample Answer**

*(i) There are a number of factors that contribute to the formation of soil. These are Parent Material, Vegetation, Time, Climate, Landscape and Human Activity.*

*I will describe how three of these – Parent Material, Climate and Time – affect the formation of soil.*

*Parent Material: Some rocks break down slowly, e.g. granite, compared to other rocks that break down quickly, e.g. sandstone. This will affect the length of time it can take the soil to form. The type of rock can affect the fertility of a soil also. Limestone when broken down can make soil very fertile, whereas igneous rocks can make soil very acidic.*

*Climate: Climate has a significant impact on the type of soil in an area. Precipitation and temperature will affect how quickly soil breaks down. In warm climates, like tropical climates, humification will happen faster. In a cold climate, freeze-thaw action will break rocks down, adding to soil fertility.*

*Time: Soil takes hundreds of years to form (1 cm of soil takes 400 years to form). Any factor which slows down or speeds up this process will directly affect the length of time for soil to form in an area.*

*(ii)* ______________________

**Marks Awarded**

**(i)** Three factors contributing to formation of soil listed – 1 mark each (1 + 1 +1 = 3 marks)

Each factor explained – 2 marks each (2 + 2 + 2 = 6 marks)

(3 + 6 = 9 marks)

**(ii)** Most common soil named – 1 mark

Total = 10 marks

# 7 Natural Energy Resources

In this section, the Learning Outcomes we will look at are: **1.9**, **2.2**

**Learning Checklist:**

- ☐ I can explain what natural energy resources are.
- ☐ I can tell the difference between renewable and non-renewable energy.
- ☐ I can explain how natural resources affect the national economy.
- ☐ I can identify ways that the environment is affected by using natural energy resources.
- ☐ I can interpret information from diagrams, images and graphs.

## What Are Natural Energy Resources?

**1.** In the space below define natural energy resources. Then give an example of the different types.

Definition of natural energy resources: ______________________________

______________________________

______________________________

______________________________

______________________________

**Exam Hint**

When writing the definition think:

- What are natural energy resources?
- Where are they found?
- Who uses natural resources?

**Remember!**

Some questions might not ask to give examples directly. You should try give examples in answers where possible.

Give examples of Earth's natural energy resources:

Metal ores, e.g. zinc. Name another: ______________________________

Precious metals/stones, e.g. diamonds. Name another: ______________________________

Building materials, e.g. stone. Name another: ______________________________

Energy sources, e.g. oil. Name another: ______________________________

2. The pie chart opposite displays information on Ireland's usage of **non-renewable energy sources** and **renewable energy sources** in 2018. Attempt the questions below.

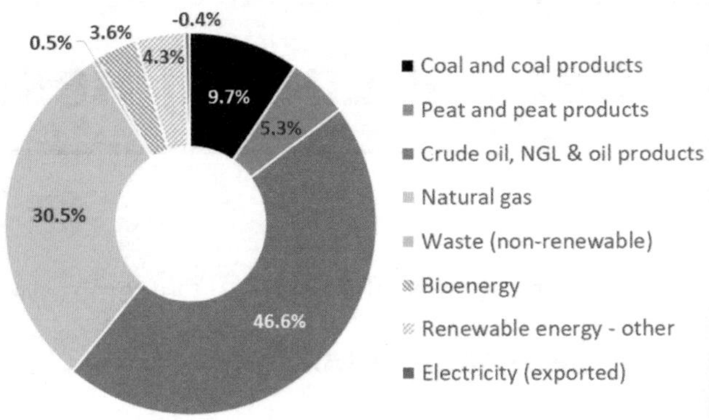

0.5% 3.6% 4.3% -0.4% 9.7% 5.3% 46.6% 30.5%

- Coal and coal products
- Peat and peat products
- Crude oil, NGL & oil products
- Natural gas
- Waste (non-renewable)
- Bioenergy
- Renewable energy - other
- Electricity (exported)

**GeoSkill**

When examining a pie chart, make sure to pay attention to the legend with it. Take the information exactly from the pie chart.

**(i)** Give an explanation of the two terms highlighted in the statement above.

Non-renewable energy sources: ____________________

____________________

Renewable energy sources: ____________________

____________________

**(ii)** Place each resource listed on the pie chart under the correct heading in the table below.

| **Non-renewable** | **Renewable** |
|---|---|
| | |
| | |
| | |
| | |
| | |

**(iii)** To the nearest whole number, what percentage of Ireland's energy comes from non-renewable energy, according to the pie chart? ____________________

**(iv)** What is the largest renewable energy source used, according to the pie chart?

____________________

**(v)** What is the largest non-renewable energy source used to create energy, according to the pie chart? ____________________

**(vi)** Explain one negative impact the use of non-renewable energy sources can have on the environment.

____________________

____________________

____________________

**(v)** The government has placed an extra tax on households that still burn non-renewable solid fuel such as coal or peat.

How might this tax discourage people from using non-renewable solid fuels?

____________________

____________________

____________________

**(vi)** How could the money gained from this tax be used to help reduce damage caused by non-renewable energy source usage?

______________________________

______________________________

______________________________

**3.** On this blank map of Ireland, mark with an 'X' the location of a natural energy resource that you studied. It can be renewable or non-renewable (think offshore also). Then write about the following:

- **Environmental impact:** What impact does the exploitation of your chosen resource have?
- **Economic impact:** What is this resource worth to the economy of the local area and to Ireland (employment and money made from the sale of the resource)?
- **Social benefit:** How has the resource improved the local area? Has money been put back into the area from which it was taken?

## Case Study

**Natural Resource**

Name of the resource:

______________________________

Environmental impact:

______________________________

______________________________

______________________________

______________________________

______________________________

______________________________

______________________________

______________________________

______________________________

Economic impact:

______________________________

______________________________

______________________________

______________________________

______________________________

Social benefits:

______________________________

______________________________

______________________________

______________________________

______________________________

### Exam Hint

Read the question carefully. Preparing some key information from case studies is very helpful before your exam. In each of the spaces provided, try to write two or three facts on each heading and your chosen resource. Keep the facts to the point.

4. **(i)** Complete either part **(a)** or part **(b)** below.

**(a)** Correctly label parts 1 to 4 in the diagram below of how acid rain forms.

**or**

**(b)** Write a short paragraph on 'How Acid Rain Forms'.

Key words can be used for both.

**Remember!**

Oil, gas and peat are examples of energy sources used to generate electricity.

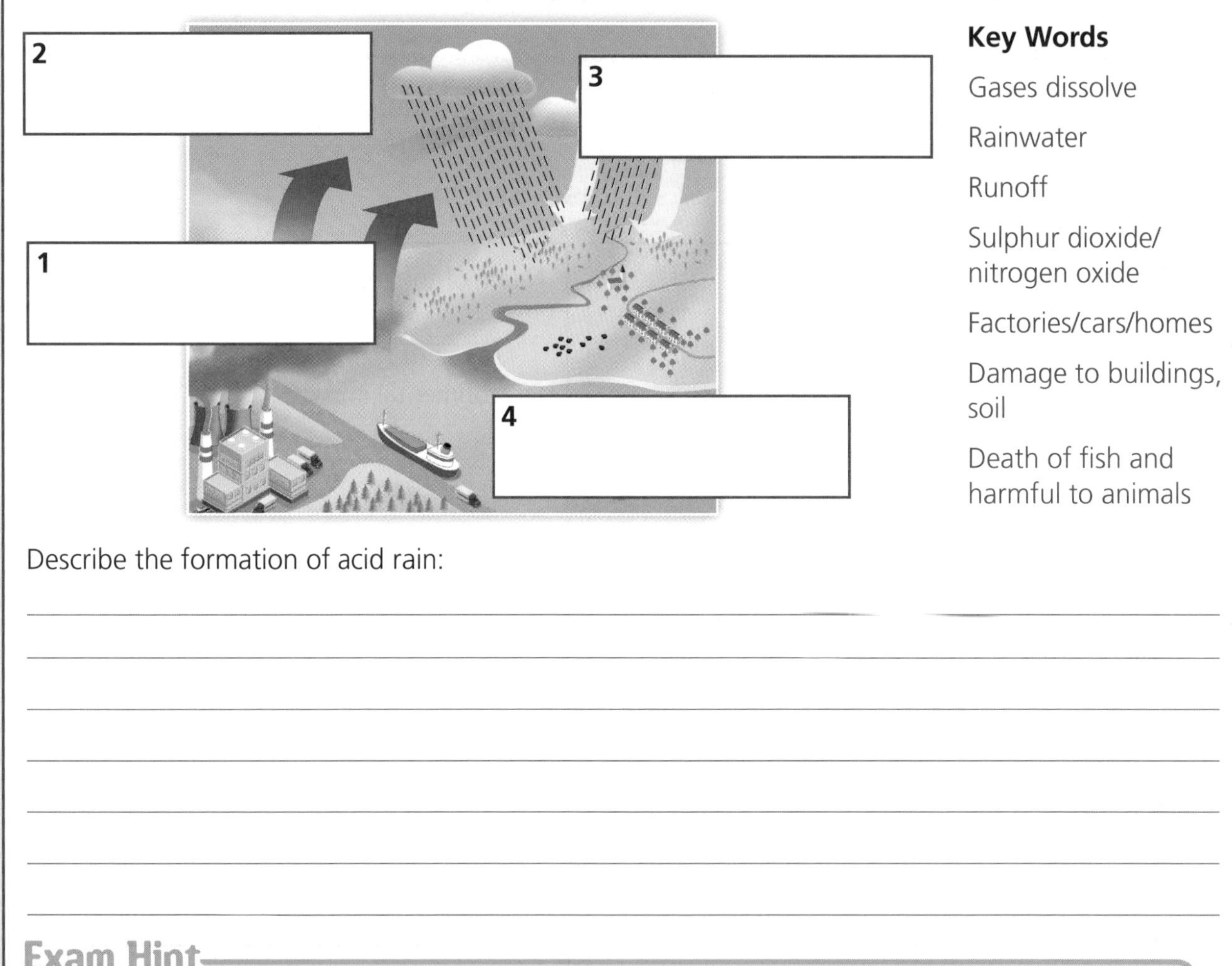


**Key Words**

Gases dissolve

Rainwater

Runoff

Sulphur dioxide/ nitrogen oxide

Factories/cars/homes

Damage to buildings, soil

Death of fish and harmful to animals

Describe the formation of acid rain:

**Exam Hint**

When presented with a question that gives you key words, make sure to use them all and explain as many as you can. If you choose to label a diagram, use the image to help your explanation. If you choose to write a paragraph, make sure to write only what is needed.

**(ii)** Read the following newspaper article from March 2021.

> EirGrid, Ireland's main supplier of electricity, has been set a task by the government – to transform the electricity system in anticipation of a future without coal, oil, peat and, ultimately, gas-based generation. Specifically, it has been asked to prepare for 70 per cent of Ireland's electricity coming from renewable sources by 2030, up from the current 40 per cent.

Imagine you are employed by EirGrid Ireland. You are to help make the decision on what is the best choice of **renewable energy resource** for Ireland to use to meet the challenges mentioned in the article above.

In the space below:

- Choose your renewable energy resource
- Explain your reason(s) for choosing this resource
- Explain how it works and how it can be best exploited
- Evaluate the environmental, economic and social benefits of your chosen renewable energy source.

Your chosen renewable energy resource: ______________________________

Your reason(s) for choosing this resource:

______________________________
______________________________
______________________________
______________________________
______________________________
______________________________

How does this resource work and how is it exploited:

______________________________
______________________________
______________________________
______________________________
______________________________
______________________________
______________________________

Environmental impact:

______________________________
______________________________
______________________________
______________________________
______________________________
______________________________
______________________________

Economic impact:

______________________________
______________________________
______________________________
______________________________

Social impact:

______________________________
______________________________
______________________________
______________________________

**Exam Hint**

Think about these questions as you write your answer:

- What is the resource?
- Why did you choose this resource? Why is it exploited?
- Who exploits this resource: the government or private companies?
- Where is it exploited?
- How is it exploited?

**Answer the questions to complete the mind map. This will support your revision.**

## Prompt Questions for Mind Map

**(a)** Can you explain what natural energy resources are and give some possible uses?

**(b)** List some of the natural energy resources Ireland has at its disposal and briefly explain how one is exploited.

**(c)** In your own words, explain the differences between renewable and non-renewable energy.

**(d)** List one of the social, economic and environmental impacts of the exploitation of a renewable energy resource.

**(e)** List one of the social, economic and environmental impacts of the exploitation of a non-renewable energy resource.

(a) Natural Energy Resources and Uses

(e) Non-renewable Energy Resource:

Social Impact:

Economic Impact:

Environmental Impact:

b) Irish Natural Energy Resources

(c) Renewable Vs Non-renewable

Renewable Energy Resource:

Social Impact:

Economic Impact:

Environmental Impact:

## NCCA Sample Question and Sample Answer

### Question 1

(i) List **two** natural resources **other than rocks** found in your local area. [4 marks]

1. ______________________

______________________

2. ______________________

______________________

**Exam Hint**

Read the question carefully. You are asked about natural resources; you cannot mention rocks.

'Local area' can mean your village, town, city or anywhere in Ireland.

When asked to explain think of the 5 Ws: Who? What? Where? When? and Why?

(ii) Explain **two** ways in which the natural resources are used in your locality. [10 marks]

1. ______________________

______________________

______________________

______________________

______________________

2. ______________________

______________________

______________________

______________________

______________________

**Marks Awarded**

**(i)** Two natural resources listed – 2 marks each
(2 + 2 = 4 marks)

**(ii)** Natural resource explained – 2 marks
Explained two ways in which the natural resources affect your locality – 4 marks each
(4 + 4 = 8 marks)
(2 + 8 = 10 marks)

Total = 14 marks

### Question 2

Describe **two** environmental impacts of using renewable energy sources. [10 marks]

1. Switching from a non-renewable energy source like oil to a renewable energy resource like solar power will have a positive impact on the environment. The burning of fossil fuels releases huge amounts of $CO_2$ into our atmosphere every year. This increases global warming (the increasing of the Earth's temperature) and affects everything from crop growth to climates around the world. Switching to solar power, which makes clean energy, will reduce $CO_2$ emissions and reduce global warming, helping our environment.

2. Using renewable energy sources such as wind energy will reduce acid rain. Acid rain is made when harmful gases, such as nitrogen, dissolve in rainwater, making it more acidic. The resulting rain can damage forests by affecting soil nutrients and kill wildlife, such as fish. Wind energy creates no acid rain and does no damage to our environment.

Breaking your answer down into separate paragraphs will make it easier for you to show your knowledge. Note how each factor is developed and includes an example to ensure full marks are achieved.

**Marks Awarded**

5 marks for each impact:
Impact named – 2 marks
Impact explained in detail – 2 marks
Examples of energy sources given – 1 mark
Total = 10 marks

# 8 Weathering and Erosion

In this section, the Learning Outcomes we will look at are: **1.2, 2.9**

**Learning Checklist:**

- ☐ I can describe the processes involved in mechanical weathering – freeze-thaw action.
- ☐ I can explain how chemical weathering occurs, using carbonation as an example.
- ☐ I can describe how chemical weathering can lead to the formation of underground features such as limestone caves, and surface features such as limestone pavements.
- ☐ I can explain how biological weathering occurs.
- ☐ I can discuss the human impact on the landscape, using examples from real life.
- ☐ I can describe the connection and relationship between tourism and the physical world, using an example studied.
- ☐ I can interpret information from photographs of the landscape. I can read contour lines on OS maps to discover upland and lowland areas.
- ☐ I can label diagrams of physical features of weathering and erosion.

## Weathering vs Erosion

1. **(i)** Complete the paragraph below using the key words provided.

| Moves | Chemical | Sediments | Wind |
|---|---|---|---|
| Biological | Gravity | Transported | Physically |

Weathering is the process that ________________ changes solid rock into small pieces or ________________. The three main types of weathering are mechanical, ________________ and ________________.

Erosion is the process that breaks down and ________________ the sediments away from their original location. Erosion is caused by water, ________________, moving ice and ________________. The broken material will be ________________ to a new location and deposited.

**(ii)** Describe the main difference between weathering and erosion.

______________________________________________

______________________________________________

______________________________________________

______________________________________________

**Remember!**

Think about what happens to the broken sediments …

**(iii)** Match each type of weathering with the correct example in the table below.

| | |
|---|---|
| 1 | Mechanical weathering |
| 2 | Chemical weathering |
| 3 | Biological weathering |

| | |
|---|---|
| A | Rocks worn away by plants and animals |
| B | Freeze-thaw action |
| C | Carbonation |

| | |
|---|---|
| 1 | |
| 2 | |
| 3 | |

## Mechanical Weathering

**GeoSkill**

Identifying key features and processes on the landscape from photographs.

**2.** Freeze-thaw action is the most common type of mechanical weathering. It is common in upland areas such as the area shown in the image opposite. Describe how the process of freeze-thaw action weathers rocks and changes the landscape.

What do we call the material found at the bottom of the slope?

**Exam Hint**

Some prompts have been completed below to help you get started. Remember to include your key words and terms, such as freezing, expanding, melting, pressure, rock shattering, scree.

The most common type of mechanical weathering is freeze-thaw action. It occurs as follows:

1. As it rains or snows, this precipitation falls and lands in the cracks in rocks. This can happen, for example, on the side of a mountain.
2. At night … ______________________________
3. The next day, the ice will thaw and melt again.
4. Over time, this repeated freezing and thawing … ______________________________
5. Pieces of rock break off and … ______________________________

**Diagram**

**By night**

**By day**

**Over time**

Describe here what happens when you have repeated freezing and thawing.

## Chemical Weathering

3. (i) The image opposite shows a limestone sculpture that has been impacted by weathering. What type of weathering is most likely to have caused the damage to this sculpture? Tick the correct answer.

| Type of weathering | Tick |
|---|---|
| Freeze-thaw action | |
| Carbonation | |

(ii) Chemical weathering is caused by chemical changes when rock is dissolved or decayed. The below diagram shows the steps involved in carbonation. Answer the questions.

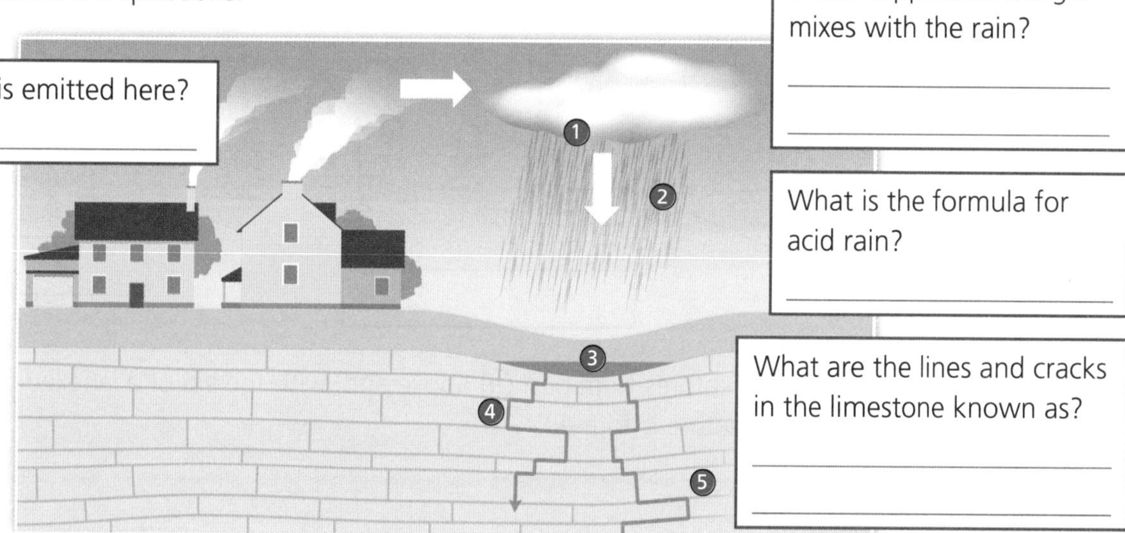
What gas is emitted here?
What happens as the gas mixes with the rain?
1
2
What is the formula for acid rain?
3
4
5
What are the lines and cracks in the limestone known as?

Statements A to E below represent Steps 1 to 5 in the carbonation process as shown on the diagram above. Read each of the statements and then place them in the correct order in the table below.

A. Carbon dioxide mixes with the rainwater to form a weak carbon acid (acid rain).
B. The calcium carbonate in the limestone starts to dissolve (carbonation) and it seeps downwards through the rock.
C. As the limestone is permeable and soluble, the water continues to seep down and easily passes through the joints and cracks in the limestone.
D. As rainwater falls and passes through the air, it dissolves carbon dioxide from the atmosphere.
E. Limestone on the Earth's surface contains calcium carbonate. When the weak carbonic acid falls onto the limestone surface, a chemical reaction takes place.

| Step 1 | Step 2 | Step 3 | Step 4 | Step 5 |
|---|---|---|---|---|
| | | | | |

(iii) Label the image of a limestone pavement below.

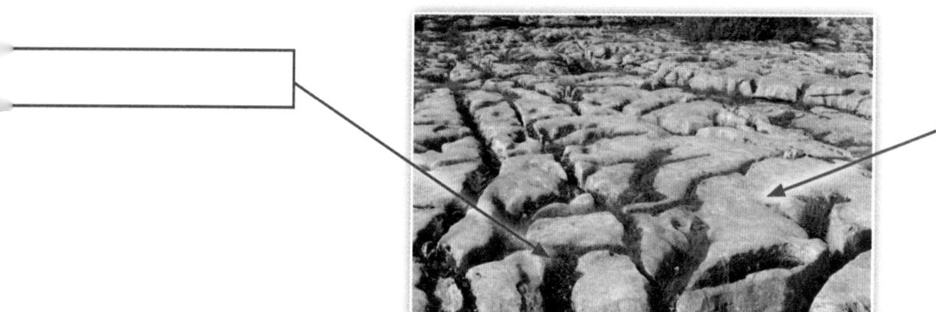

**(iv) (a)** Carbonation can create many interesting underground features in karst areas. Look at the diagram below and correctly label the features shown. One has been completed for you.

| Cave | Pillar | Stalactite | Stalagmite | Joints |
|---|---|---|---|---|

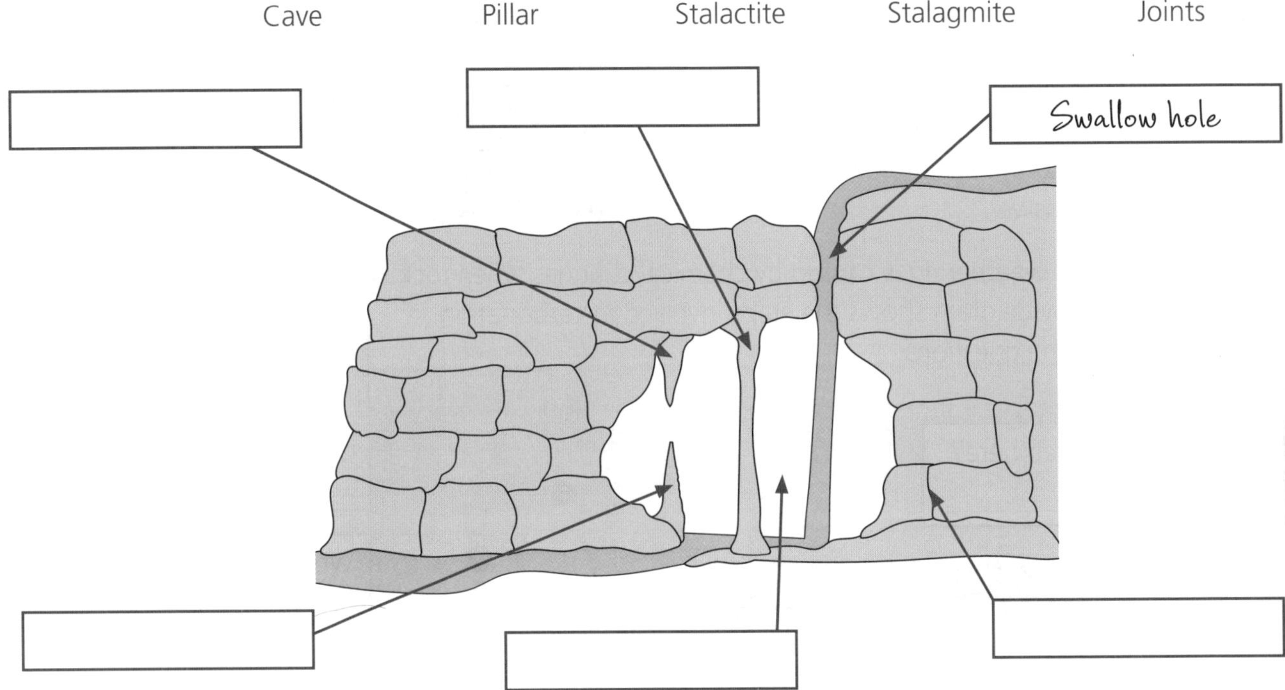


**(b)** Select one of the features from part **(a)** above and, with the aid of a labelled diagram, explain how the feature is formed.

## Exam Hint

When asked to explain how a feature on the landscape is formed, use the FEED method.

| | | |
|---|---|---|
| F | = Feature | Name the feature you are writing about. |
| E | = Explanation | Explain how it is formed. |
| E | = Example | Give an example of where the feature can be seen. |
| D | = Diagram | Draw and label a brief diagram. |

**Diagram**

## Biological Weathering

**4.** Using the photo below, describe how biological weathering takes place.

**Exam Hint**

Describe what you can see in the photo. What is happening to the rock?

Why is it happening? What is causing it?

In the image above, I can see… ______________________________

______________________________

______________________________

______________________________

______________________________

______________________________

## Physical World and Tourism

**5.** **(i)** Draw a sketch map of the area shown on the OS map on the next page. Place the following features onto your sketch:

- An area of forestry
- The full route of the N67
- A historical site
- A named walking trail
- Moneen Mountain

**Remember!**

You only draw the items asked in the questions onto your sketch map. Tick them off as you draw them and place them into the key.

**Exam Hint**

Checklist for sketch:

- Use pencil
- Title
- North arrow
- All items drawn on
- All items placed in key

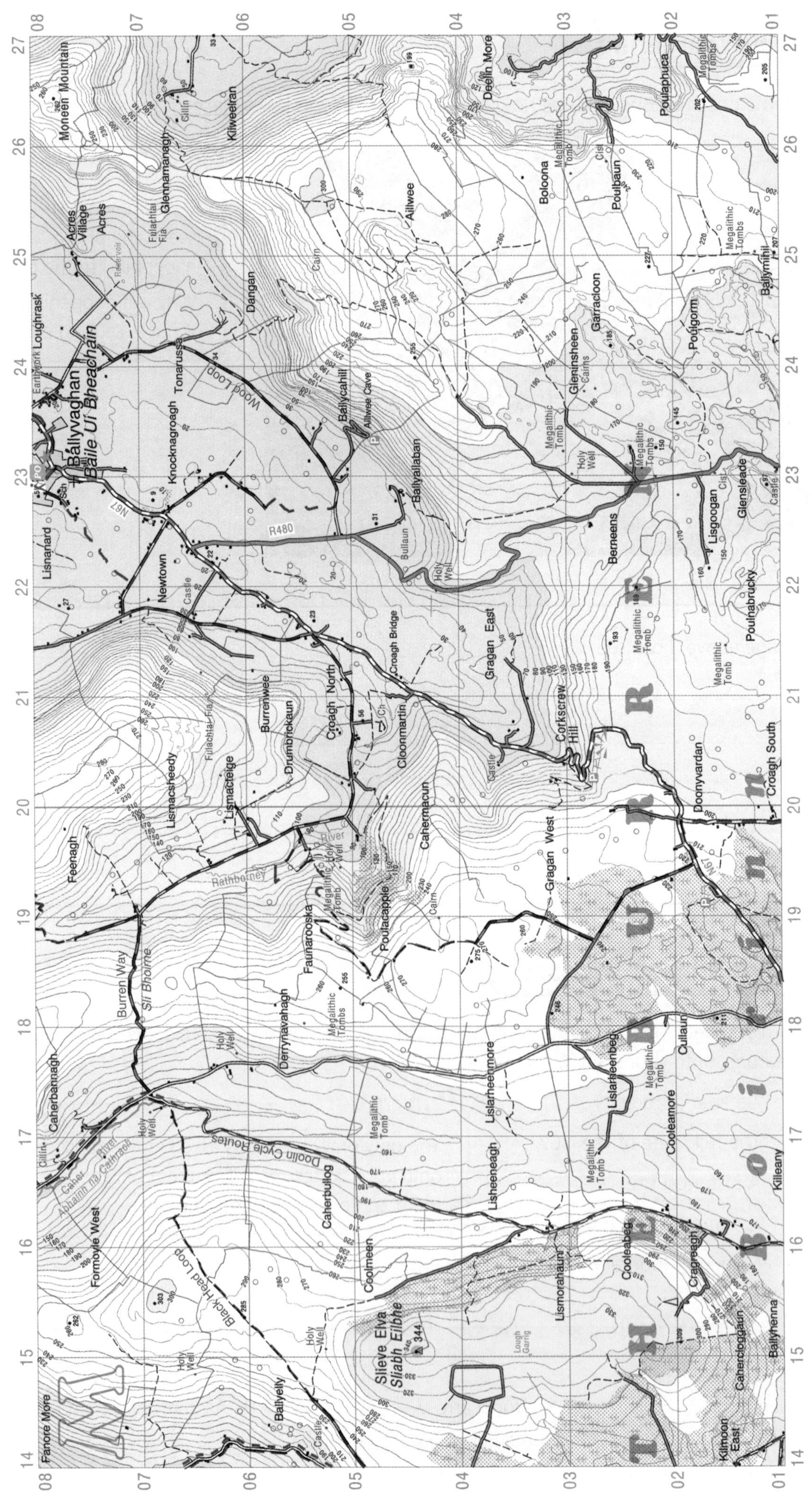
Ballyvaghan
Baile Uí Bheacháin
Loughrask
Lisnanard
Newtown
Knocknagroagh
Tonarussa
Acres Village
Acres
Glennamanagh
Moneen Mountain
Kilweelran
Dangan
Ailwee
Aillwee Cave
Ballycahill
Ballyallaban
Wood Loop
R480
N67
Boloona
Deelin More
Poulbaun
Poulaphuca
Garracloon
Gleninsheen
Berneens
Poulgorm
Ballymihil
Gleansleade
Lisgoogan
Poulnabrucky
Croagh South
Doonyvardan
Corkscrew Hill
Gragan East
Gragan West
Croagh Bridge
Croagh North
Gloonmartin
Burrenwee
Drumbrickaun
Lismacteige
Lismacsheedy
Cahermacun
Rathborney
Poulacapple
Faunarooska
Feenagh
Burren Way
Slí Bhoirne
Derrynavahagh
Caherbannagh
Lislarheenmore
Lislarheenbeg
Cullaun
Cooleamore
Killeany
Lisheeneagh
Caherbullog
Coolmeen
Doolin Cycle Routes
Black Head Loop
Formoyle West
Caher River
Abhainn na Cathrach
Slieve Elva
Sliabh Eilbhe
Lismorahaun
Cooleabeg
Cragreagh
Caherclogaun
Ballyhenna
Kilmoon East
Ballyelly
Fanore More
Megalithic Tomb
Holy Well
THE BURREN
Boireann

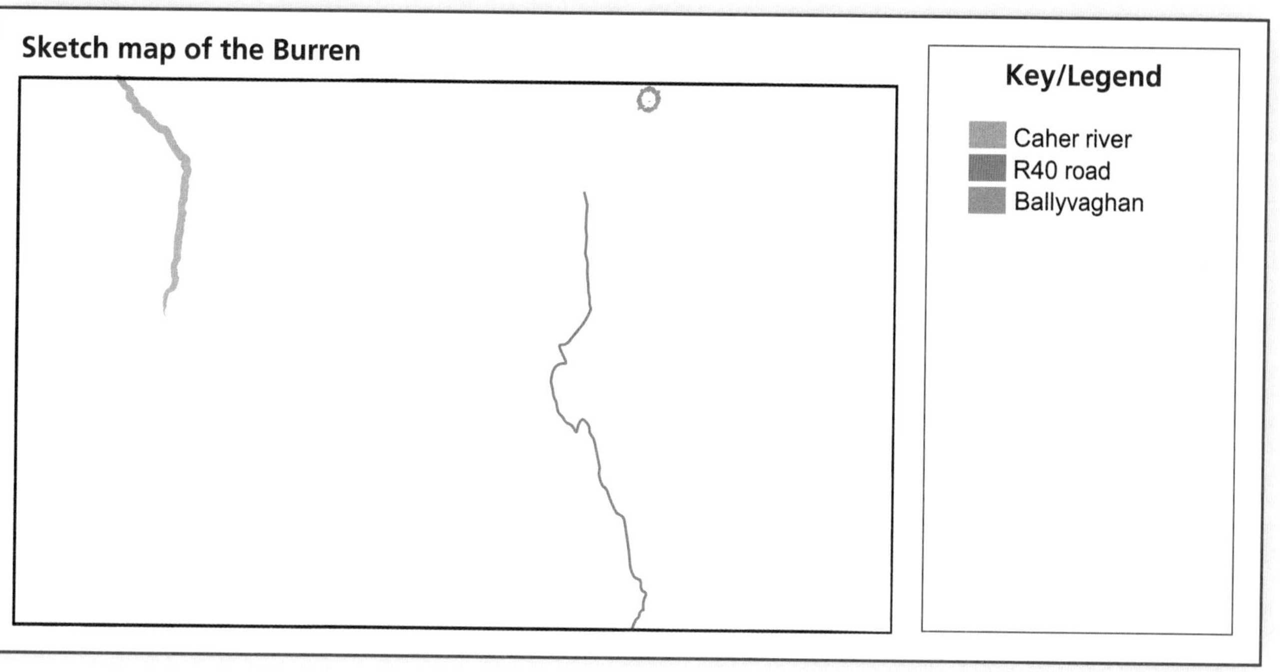


**(ii)** Your family has settled in this area and wants to open a bike rental business to cater for locals and tourists. Give a six-figure grid refence for a suitable location for this new business.

______________________________

State **two reasons** for your choice of location:

**1.** ______________________________

**2.** ______________________________

**(iii)** A waste company has proposed to build a new landfill site at M23 06. The local residents' group are very unhappy about this new development, as they are worried about the impact on the local natural environment. Write a letter to your local TD to explain some of your concerns and suggest an alternative location for the landfill.

**Date** ______________________________

**Dear** ______________________________

______________________________

______________________________

______________________________

______________________________

______________________________

______________________________

______________________________

______________________________

______________________________

**Answer the questions to complete the mind map. This will support your revision.**

## Prompt Questions for Mind Map

**(a)** Explain what is meant by the terms 'weathering' and 'erosion'. Can you outline the main difference between the two?

**(b)** Describe the process of freeze-thaw action and how it impacts on the landscape. Can you draw a sketch to show how it occurs? Can you give an example of where it occurs on the landscape?

**(c)** Describe the process of carbonation. What features do we find both above and below ground in karst regions? Can you name them? What processes occur in their formation?

**(d)** Explain what happens during biological weathering. Can you give examples?

**(e)** Using an example that you have studied, e.g. the Burren, describe how the physical world and tourism are interconnected and linked.

(a) Weathering and Erosion

(e) Relationship Between Physical World and Tourism

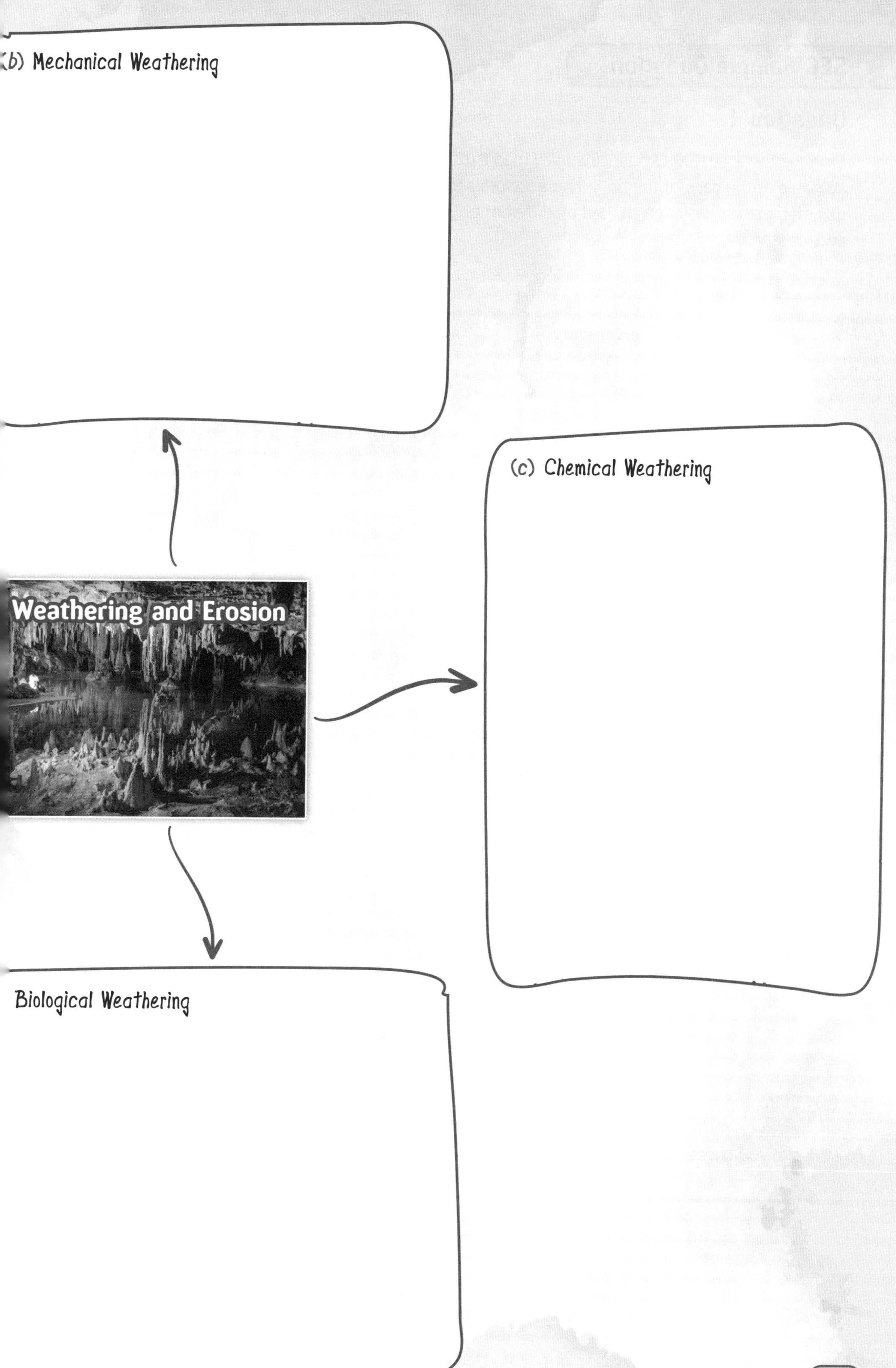
(b) Mechanical Weathering
Weathering and Erosion
(c) Chemical Weathering
Biological Weathering

## SEC Sample Question

### Question 1

Examine the 1:50 000 Ordnance Survey map extract below and the accompanying legend which is available at the back of the book and answer each of the following questions. The landscape shown on this map extract has been shaped by different physical processes, including river erosion, glacial erosion and weathering.

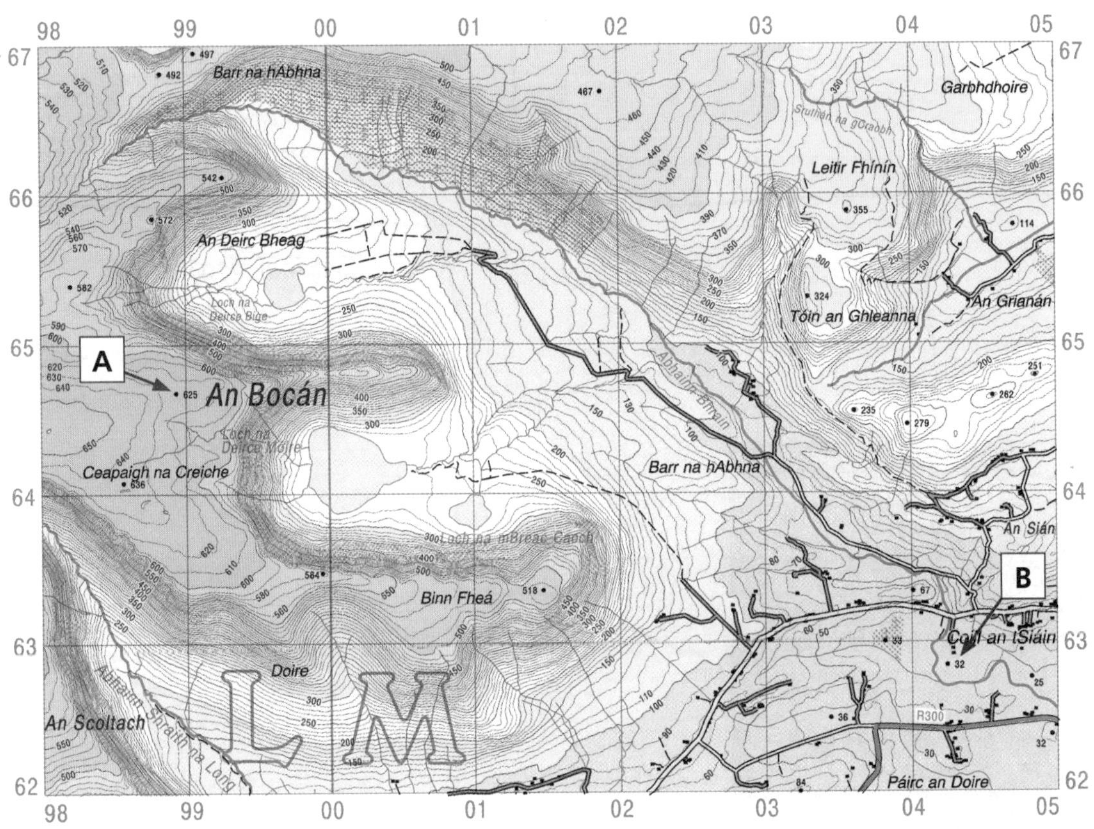


**(i)** At which site on the map extract, A or B, is freeze-thaw action most likely to occur? Tick (✓) the correct box. [3 marks]

A ☐ B ☐

*Carefully look at the map. A is showing an upland area, the colouring is brown and the contour lines are closely spaced and increasing by number. At B, we see a lowland area with green colouring and well-spaced contour lines. Which area is more likely to experience freeze-thaw action?*

**(ii)** State one reason why freeze-thaw action is most likely to occur at the site you chose. [4 marks]

*Here the action verb is 'state'. This requires you to simply state the reason why freeze-thaw action is likely to occur at the site you selected in part (i) above.*

________________________________________

________________________________________

**(iii)** Circle the correct answer in each statement below. [8 marks]

*Here you need to circle the term that makes the most sense to you when describing what occurs during the process of freeze-thaw action. For each correct answer, you are awarded 2 marks.*

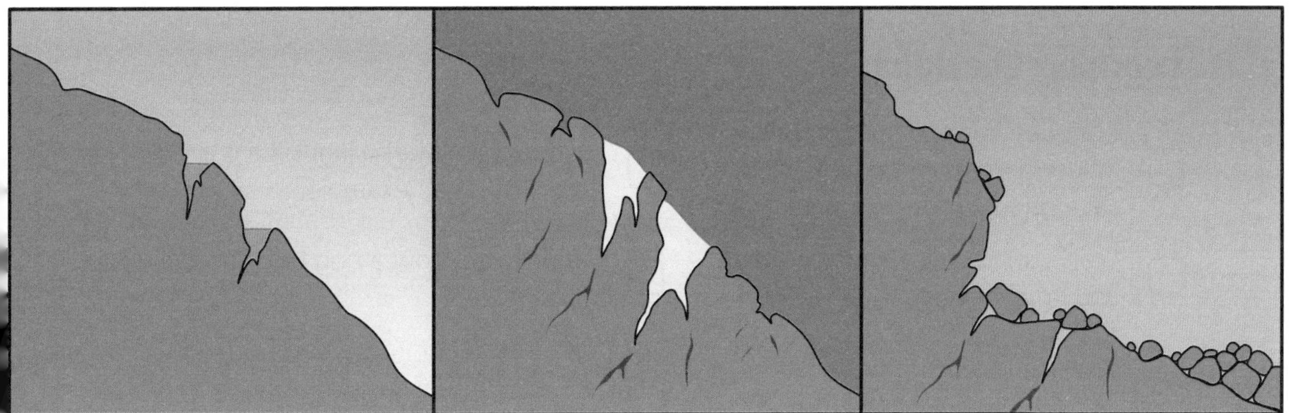


**(a)** The diagram above is showing freeze-thaw action / carbonation.

**(b)** This is a type of mechanical / biological weathering.

**(c)** We expect to see this type of weathering occuring in lowland / upland areas.

**(d)** The loose rock that breaks off and gathers at the base of the hill is known as scree / grikes.

**Marks Awarded**

**(i)** Correct box ticked – 3 marks

**(ii)** Correct reason stated – 4 marks

**(iii)** Four correct answers given – 2 marks each (4 × 2 = 8 marks)

Total = 15 marks

# 9 Mass Movement

In this section, the Learning Outcomes we will look at are: **1.3**, **2.8**

## Learning Checklist:

- ☐ I can describe the factors that influence mass movement (slope, vegetation, water, human activity).
- ☐ I can explain what a landslide is and how it occurs using an example.
- ☐ I can explain what soil creep is and how it occurs.
- ☐ I can explain how a bog burst occurs using an example.
- ☐ I can explain how mudflows occur, using an example that I have studied.
- ☐ I can interpret information from aerial images and photographs showing physical features on the landscape. I can draw sketches to highlight important physical features on the landscape.

## Factors Influencing Mass Movement

1. (i) Take a look at the images below showing the four main types of mass movement. Place the correct name for each type of mass movement below the relevant picture. One has been completed for you.

| | |
|---|---|
| Bog burst | Landslide |
| Soil creep | Mudflow |

### GeoSkill

When presented with aerial images or photos, look at each image and try to identify any features or processes that are familiar to you. If you are provided with a list of possible answers, select the one that makes most sense based on the evidence that you can see.

*Bog burst*

**(ii)** Complete the mind map below to describe how each of the four factors influence mass movement (use the question prompts to help you complete the mind map).

**Prompts for Mind Map**

**Water**

- How does the quantity of precipitation that falls impact the soil?
- If soil is saturated, where does the water go?
- Does water impact on the weight of soil?

**Human Activity**

- What types of activities can humans be involved in that can impact the ground in an area?
- What impact can these activities have on soil? On hillsides? On how stable the ground is?

**Vegetation**

- What impact does vegetation have on the ground in which it is located?
- How does a plant hold the soil in place?
- What impact might deforestation have on the soil in an area?

**Slope/Gradient**

- How does a steep gradient impact the soil and loose material on that slope?
- If the slope is gentle, how is this different to a slope that is very steep?

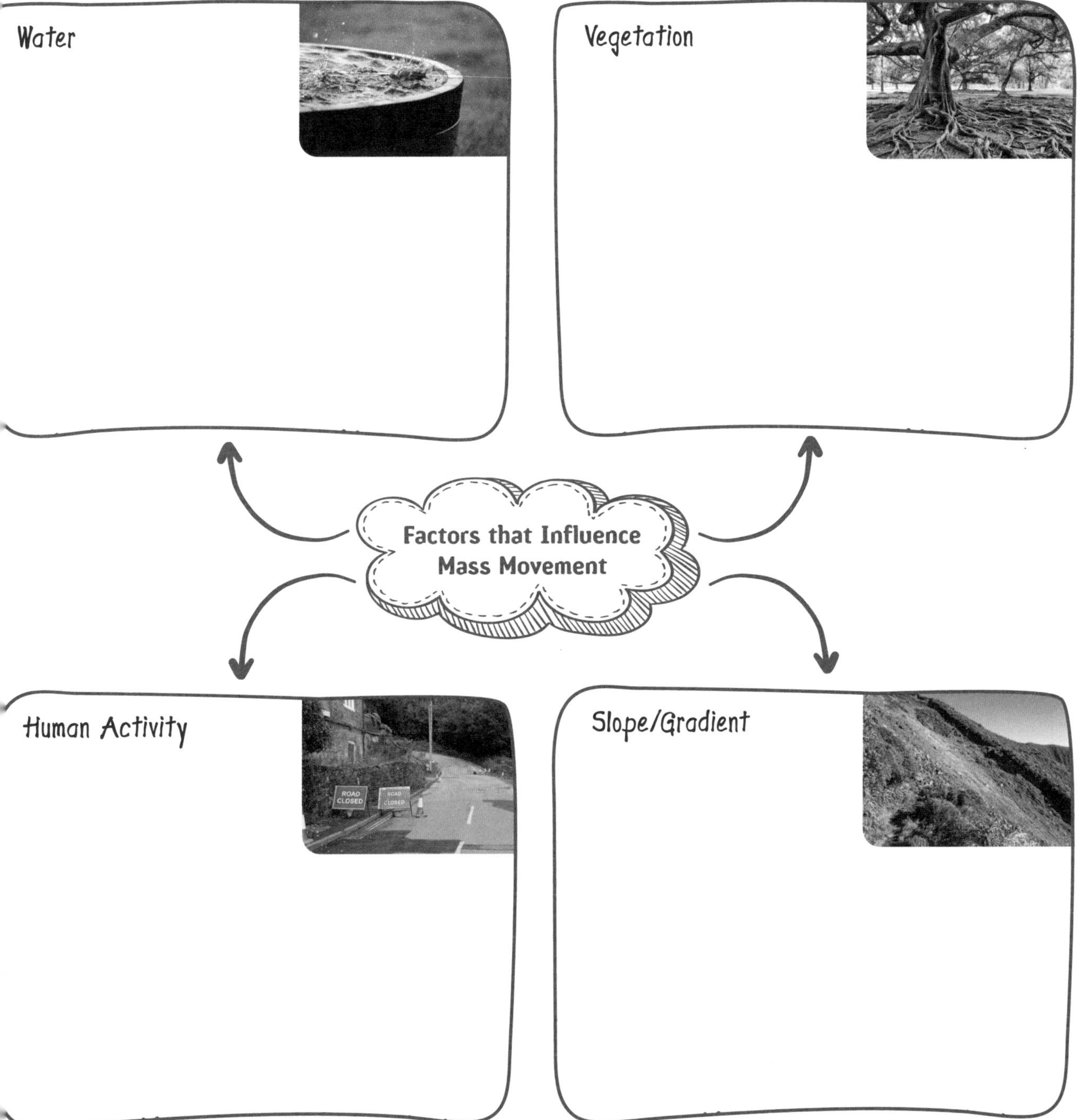

## Soil Creep

Remember!

You can use FEED here for your report!

**F**eature
**E**xplanation
**E**xample
**D**iagram

2. (i) Your grandparents' house is located on a rural hillside in Co. Cork. You have noticed that soil creep is occurring on their land and you must write a brief report about this for a class project. In the space provided below, describe the soil creep that you can see occurring and complete the sketch to highlight its impact on your grandparents' land.

### My Report

My grandparents' house is located on a hillside in Co. Cork. I have noticed evidence of soil creep on their land. I will describe the evidence that I have seen for this below:

**Sketch**

GeoSkill

This sketch has been started for you. When sketching physical features, always use pencil and fully label them.

For a sketch of soil creep, it would be important to include the following features:

- Curved tree trunks
- Cracks in walls of house
- Tilted poles
- Garden walls falling
- Soil build-up behind walls
- Terracettes
- Slope/gradient of the land

**(ii)** Indicate whether the statement below is true or false by placing a tick (✓) in the correct box.

'Soil creep is the slowest form of mass movement.'

**True** ☐ **False** ☐

## Landslides, Mudflows and Bog Bursts

**3. (i)** Read the article below and answer the questions that follow.

### Indonesia Landslide: Rescuers Buried as They Help Victims

**Rescuers searching for victims of a landslide in Indonesia were buried by a second landslide just hours later, officials say.**

The first landslide was triggered by high rainfall and unstable soil conditions. The second occurred while rescuers were still trying to evacuate people who were trapped in the local area. At least 11 people were killed and 18 people were injured. It was reported that 34 houses were impacted by the landslide.

The government responded to the disaster by sending out a number of staff and support workers to help the local people. Emergency field kitchens were set up to feed locals who could not return to their homes.

Landslides are common in Indonesia during rainy season. They are blamed on deforestation that is occurring in the local area and on gold-mining activities that are making hillsides unstable.

*Source: bbc.com*

**(a)** Where did the landslide occur?

________________________________________

**(b)** State one social and one economic impact of this landslide event.

Social: ________________________________________

________________________________________

________________________________________

Economic: ________________________________________

________________________________________

________________________________________

**(c)** Who responded to this natural disaster event and what was their response?

**Exam Hint**

In this question you are asked two things:

Who responded?

**AND**

What was their response?

Remember to answer both parts.

**(d)** This landslide event was blamed on heavy rainfall in an area that has suffered deforestation and gold mining. Describe how heavy rainfall and gold-mining activities could result in a landslide such as this.

**Exam Hint**

Use your knowledge of the factors that influence mass movement here.

- What impact will heavy rainfall have on the soil?
- How does a human activity such as mining impact the land?

**(ii)** Natural disasters require an immediate response in the short term, but they can also require ongoing support in the long term.

Other than the natural disaster named in part **(i)**, name an example of either a landslide, mudflow or bog burst event you have studied and state where and when it happened. Explain one short-term and one long-term response to the event that you have studied.

## Case Study

I have chosen a: Landslide ☐ Mudflow ☐ Bog burst ☐

Named event: ____________________

Where and when it occurred: ____________________

**Remember!**

It is important that you have a case study to use here.

You can use this case study in your exam if asked about a mass movement event.

Short-term response: ____________________

Long-term response: ____________________

**Answer the questions to complete the mind map. This will support your revision.**

### Prompt Questions for Mind Map

**(a)** How do water, slope, human activity and vegetation impact on mass movement? Are they connected? Show how.

**(b)** Explain the process of soil creep. How does it occur? Is it fast or slow? What does it look like on the land?

**(c)** Describe how a mudflow occurs. Where is it likely to occur? Is it fast or slow? How do people respond to such natural disasters? What type of short-term and long-term support should be offered?

**(d)** Describe what happens to cause a landslide. Where is it likely to happen? Is a landslide fast or slow? What are some economic or social impacts?

**(e)** Explain how a bog burst occurs. Where does it happen? Are there any social or economic impacts for local communities?

(a) Factors Influencing Mass Movement

(e) Bog Burst

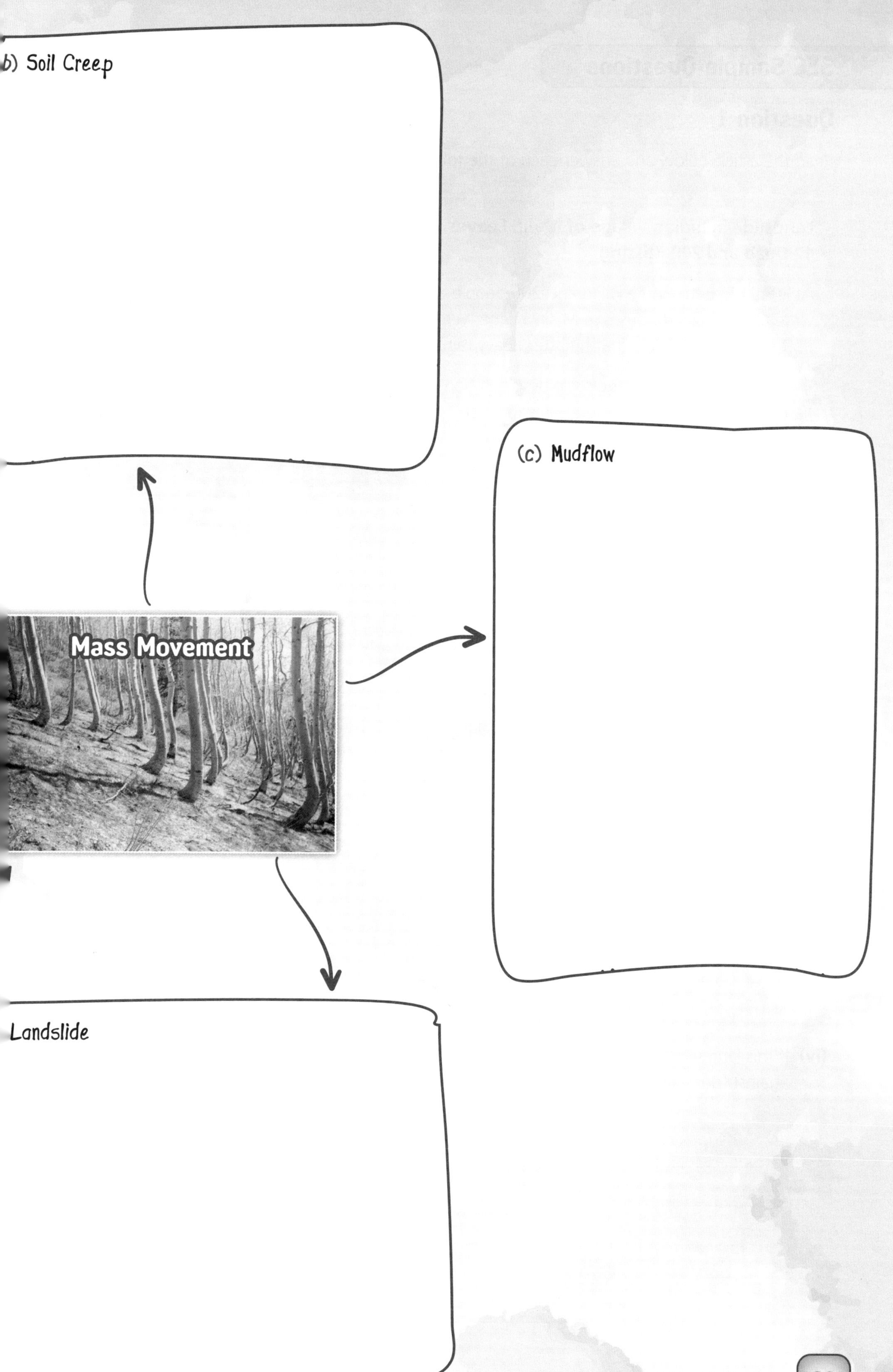
b) Soil Creep
Mass Movement
(c) Mudflow
Landslide

## SEC Sample Questions

### Question 1

Read the article below and answer each of the following questions.

**Landslide in Indian village of Malin Leaves 17 Dead and 200 Missing**

At least 17 people were killed and 200 people were trapped as 44 houses in Malin village were flattened by a landslide that hit after heavy rain.

Environmentalists said large-scale deforestation had made the place vulnerable. An expert on landslides said 'the cause of the landslide appears to be the clearing of land on the hill for farming and the removal of trees'.

**(i)** In what country did this landslide take place?

______________________________

**(ii)** Name one effect of the landslide mentioned in the article.

______________________________

**(iii)** The article states that one cause of this landslide was the 'removal of trees'. Briefly explain how the removal of trees can lead to a landslide.

______________________________

______________________________

______________________________

______________________________

______________________________

______________________________

**Remember!**

Deforestation is the removal of vegetation. How does that impact on the land?

**(iv)** If this land was reforested (replanted with trees), it would help protect against future landslides. Describe another benefit of planting trees.

______________________________

______________________________

______________________________

______________________________

______________________________

______________________________

**Exam Hint**

Think of sustainability and climate change in this answer.

## Sample Question and Answer

### Question 2

**(i)** Name one slow type of mass movement and describe two effects of this slow mass movement. [8 marks]

**(ii)** Explain the impact of precipitation and gradient on mass movement. [6 marks]

(i) *One type of slow mass movement is soil creep.*

*Soil creep is very slow so the effects can take a long time to be visible.*

*Two effects of this slow form of mass movement are:*

1. *As the soil moves slowly down a gentle hill, it can begin to build up behind walls. This build-up of soil can put added pressure on the wall and cause it to break, crack or fall.*
2. *If there are telephone poles in the area that is experiencing soil creep, the polls can begin to tilt and lean in the direction that the soil is moving. This means that some poles will be tilted to one side and, over time, this could become dangerous.*

(ii) *Both precipitation and gradient have an impact on mass movement.*

1. *Precipitation: As water falls onto the surface, it is absorbed into the soil. If too much precipitation falls, the soil can become oversaturated.*

______________________________

______________________________

______________________________

______________________________

2. *Gradient: The steeper the gradient, the faster the loose material can move down a slope.*

______________________________

______________________________

______________________________

______________________________

This question is asking us two different things. It first uses the action verb 'name', so we must name a type of slow mass movement. This requires only a brief answer; one sentence is enough. It then asks us to 'describe' two effects, requiring us to give a detailed account. You could also use a diagram here to help you in your answer if you wish.

This question is using the action verb 'explain', so it requires you to give a detailed account of how precipitation and gradient impact on mass movement. The answer has been started, but only a statement about each has been made. In order to achieve full marks, you must elaborate and add more detail. Space has been provided for you to do this.

You should now complete part (ii) using the advice to guide you.

**Marks Awarded**

**(i)** One type of slow mass movement named – 2 marks
Two effects named – 1 mark each (1 + 1 = 2 marks)
Two named effects described – 2 marks each (2 + 2 = 4 marks)
(2 + 2 + 4 = 8 marks)

**(ii)** Two correct explanations given – 3 marks each (3 + 3 = 6 marks)

Total = 14 marks

# 10 OS Maps and Aerial Photographs

**Element: Geographical Skills**

- Students will develop their ability to understand and use a map or photograph.
- Students will be able to analyse and interpret data.

## Learning Checklist:

- ☐ I can measure curved and straight-line distances on an OS map.
- ☐ I can read grid references on 1:50 000, 1:25 000 and 1:10 000 scale maps.
- ☐ I can identify upland areas, drainage areas and other features on OS maps.
- ☐ I can measure area on an OS map.
- ☐ I can identify direction on aerial photographs.
- ☐ I can sketch OS maps and aerial photographs.
- ☐ I can identify items on an aerial photograph and locate them on the corresponding OS map.

## 1:50 000 Scale Maps

1. **(i)** **(a)** Scale is the relationship between a distance on a map and its corresponding distance on the ground.

Convert the distances in the box below into centimetres (cm) and kilometres (km) using the scale 1:50 000.

**Exam Hint**

For maps with a scale of 1:50 000, the scale is 2 cm:1 km.

| cm | km |
|---|---|
| 6 cm | |
| 5 cm | |
| | 10 km |
| | 22 km |

**(b)** This is the scale you will see on the legend of any OS map you study.

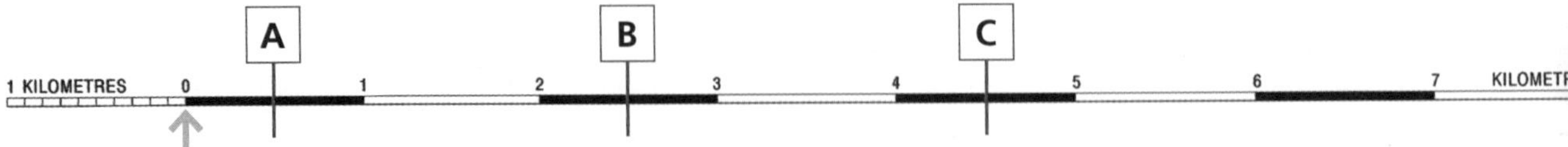


Write the distance in km for A to C, which are marked on this scale approximately. Then convert into cm.

**Exam Hint**

When using the scale, remember distances start at zero kilometres.

| Letter | Distance in km | Distance in cm |
|---|---|---|
| A | | |
| B | | |
| C | | |

**(ii)** Examine the 1:50 000 OS map extract of Waterford below and answer the questions on the following page.

## Exam Hint

When measuring distance, answers are given in km.
When measuring area, answers are given in km².

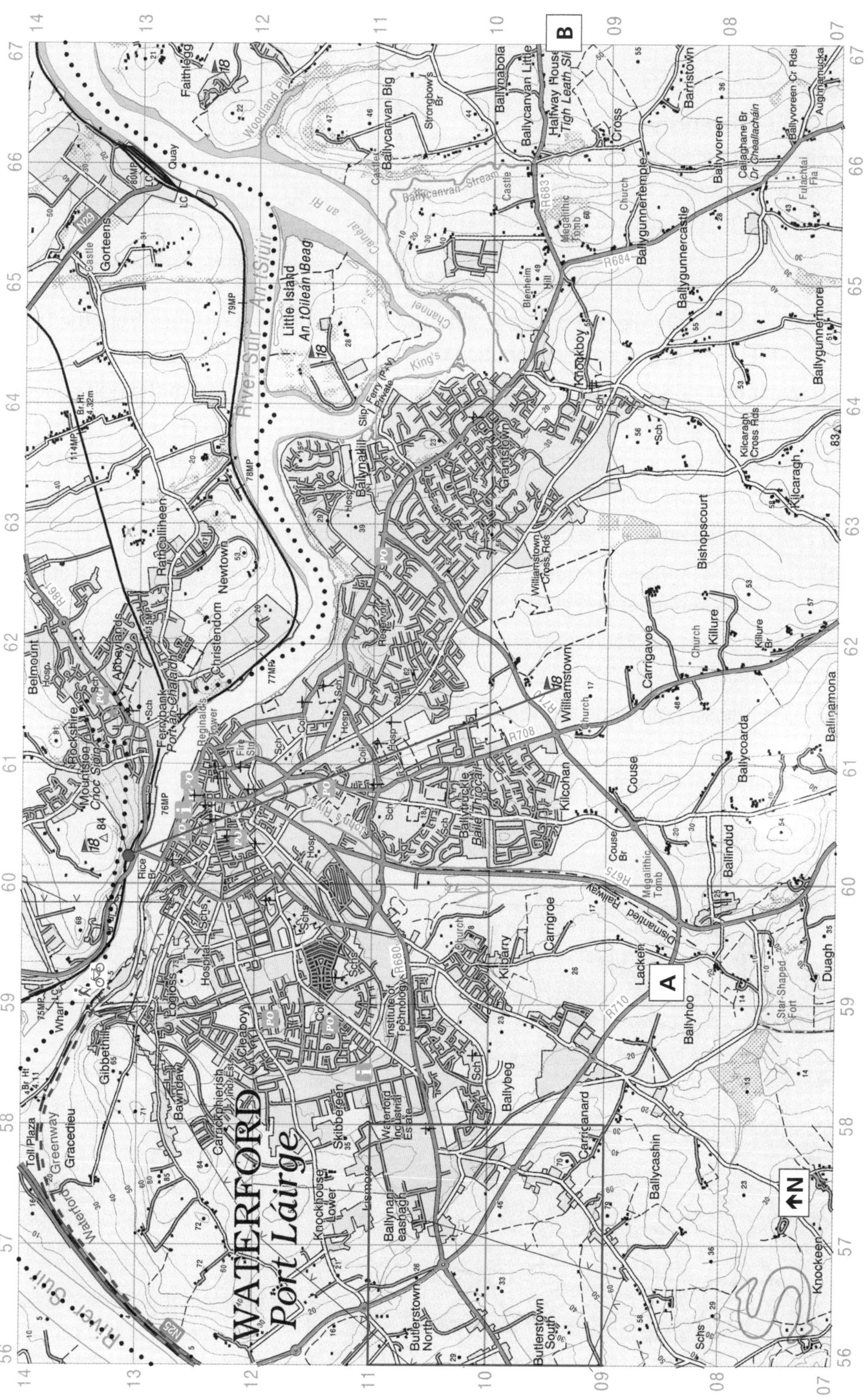

## GeoSkill

**Four-figure grid referencing**

LEN for the grid ref: **L**etter **E**asting **N**orthing

Start along the x-axis at the top or bottom of your map.

Then go up the y-axis located on the left and right side of the map.

Do not forget to add in the zonal letter.

**Six-figure grid referencing**

Break down each square into 10×10 individual squares. This will allow you to add a digit to the easting and northing references to give a six-figure reference.

## GeoSkill

When measuring straight-line distances without a ruler, simply mark both spots on a straight piece of paper and use the scale given with the OS map.

When measuring a curved line, divide the curved line into a number of straight segments. Using a straight piece of paper, mark the distances between each straight-line segment. You now have a number of straight-line distances, which can be added together to give the curved-line distance.

**(a)** Using the scale/ruler on page 92, measure the straight-line distance from the train station to the 18-hole golf course identified on the map extract. ________________

**(b)** What direction would a person be travelling if they travelled from the golf course back to the train station in a straight line? ________________

**(c)** Measure the curved-line distance of the R710 and R683 roads on this map extract from point A on the map to where it leaves the map at point B. ________________

**(d)** What is the area of the grid square highlighted in red on this map? ________________

**(e)** Count the number of squares filled and more than half-filled by the River Suir to calculate the approximate area it covers in the extract. ________________

**(f)** What is the four-figure grid reference for the forested area located in the south-west of the map? ________________

**(g)** Give the six-figure grid reference for the train station located on this map extract.

________________

**(h)** What historical feature is located at S 65 4, 09 5? ________________

## Altitude and Slope

**2.**

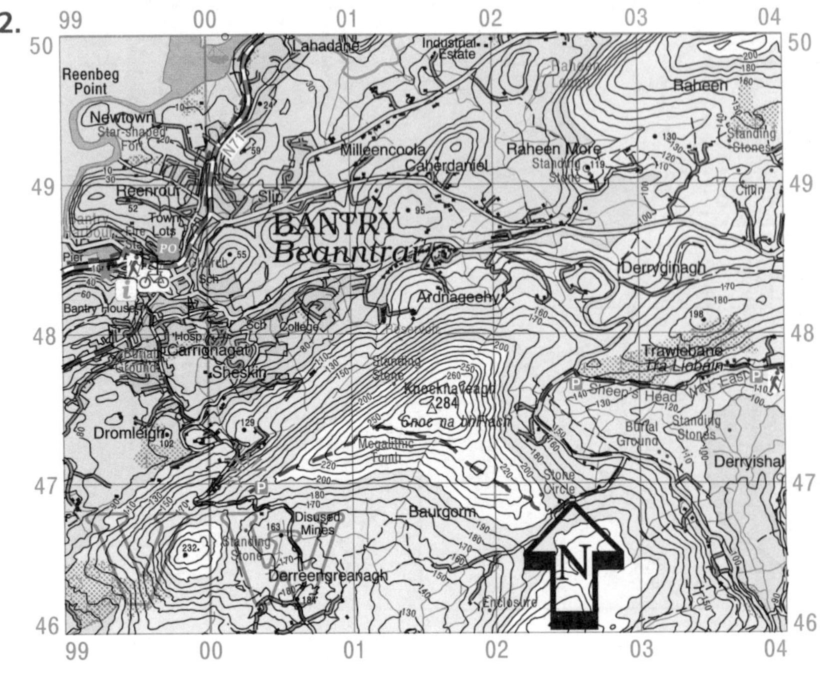


## Exam Hint

When measuring height, answers are given in metres (m).

**(i)** What is the height in metres of the highest point on this map extract? ________________

**(ii)** What is the six-figure grid reference for this point?

________________

**(iii)** What is the spot height in metres at V 03 5, 48 2?

________________

**(iv)** By what height is the land (contour lines) increasing in square V 01, 46? ______________

**(v)** Give a four-figure grid reference for the following:

**(a)** A square covered mostly in flat land: ______________

**(b)** A square covered in gentle or steep sloping land: ______________

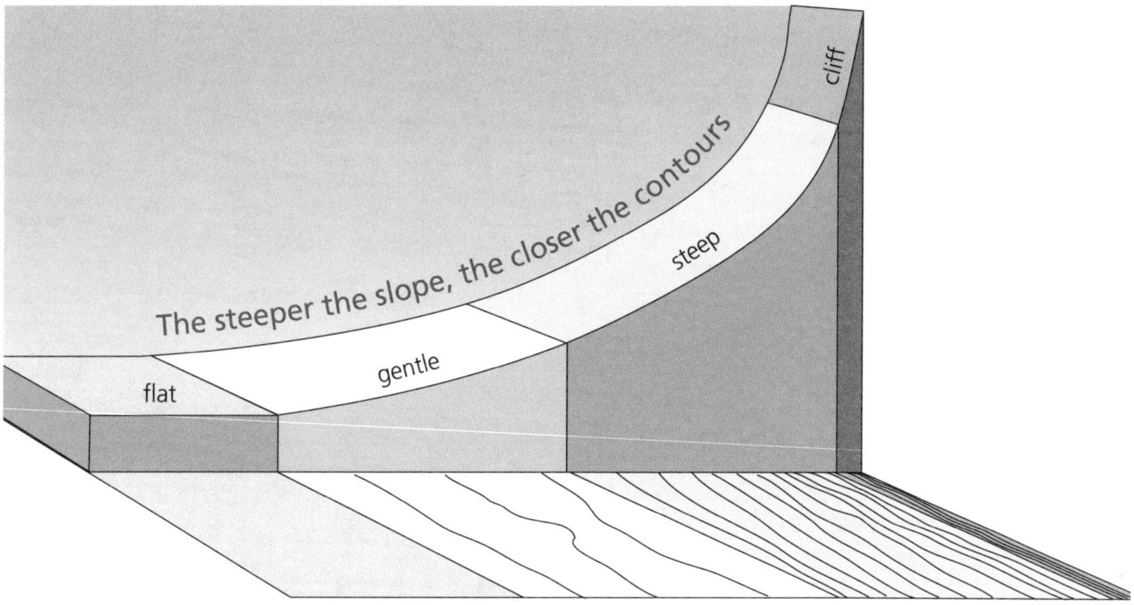

The steeper the slope, the closer the contours

flat

gentle

steep

cliff

**(vi)** Choose a suitable location for a farmer to set up an arable farm near Bantry, e.g. growing barley. Give the four-figure grid reference, and explain one reason for your choice.

**Location grid reference:** ______________________________

______________________________

______________________________

______________________________

______________________________

______________________________

______________________________

**Remember!**

Altitude and slope play a significant part in farming. How would farming crops be difficult on a steep slope?

**(vii)** Choose a suitable location for a farmer to set up a pastoral farm near Bantry, e.g. sheep rearing. Give the four-figure grid reference, and explain one reason for your choice.

**Location grid reference:** ______________________________

______________________________

______________________________

______________________________

______________________________

______________________________

______________________________

**Exam Hint**

Arable farming means the growing of crops. For farmers to access the land and the crops growing on it, what type of land is most suitable?

For pastoral farming, is the height/slope of the land an issue?

## Drainage and Transport

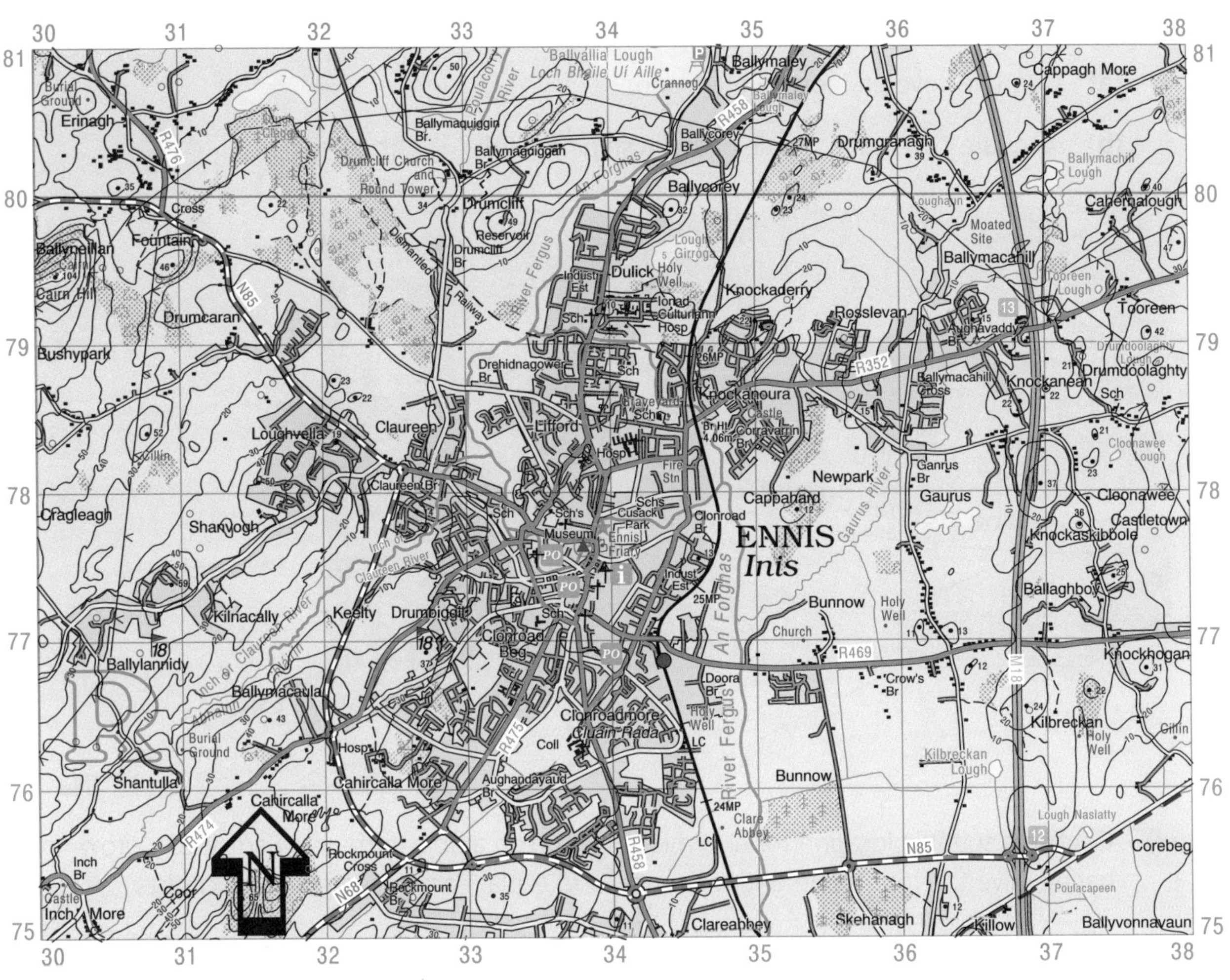


**3.** **(i)** 'The built-up area of Ennis and the surrounding lands have good drainage.'

Examine the OS map of Ennis. Use evidence from this map to support this statement.

**Remember!**

Think back to your chapter on rivers. How do they act as drainage for the basin they are in?

**Exam Hint**

To answer this question, name and give a four-figure grid reference for a number of rivers in the land around Ennis. Then explain how rivers help control flooding in a drainage basin.

(ii) Identify one area on the map you believe has poor drainage and give at least one reason for your answer.

**Exam Hint**

To attempt this question, locate an area (using four-figure referencing) on the map with a lack of settlement with a river nearby.

______________________________________________

______________________________________________

______________________________________________

______________________________________________

______________________________________________

______________________________________________

(iii) The town of Ennis is served by many different types of transport. Using the legend, identify the following:

(a) The six-figure grid reference for the train station: ____________________

(b) The six-figure entry point of the motorway on the north of the map and its six-figure entry point on the south of the map.

North entry point: ____________________ South entry point: ____________________

## Settlement: Rural and Urban

4. (i) Using the Bantry and Ennis map extracts (on pages 94 and 96), identify an example of the following types of settlement, using four- or six-figure grid referencing.

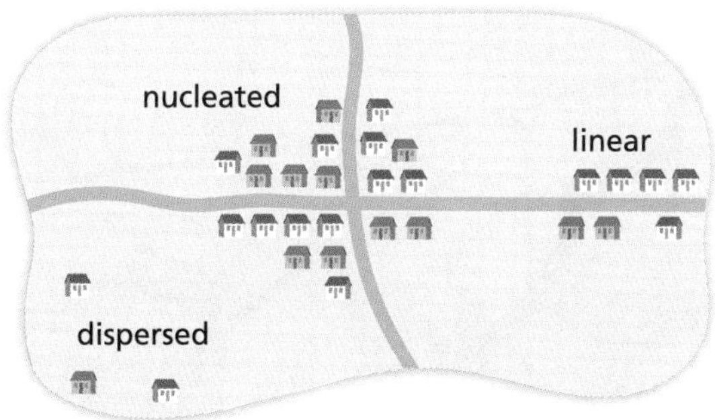


| | Bantry | Ennis |
|---|---|---|
| Linear | | |
| Nucleated | | |
| Dispersed | | |

(ii) Choose either the Bantry or Ennis map extract and draw a sketch map of the area in the space on page 98. Sketch and label the following:

- The built-up area of Bantry/Ennis
- A river
- A railway line
- A national, primary or secondary road
- A historical antiquity
- A tourist attraction

**GeoSkill**

When sketching a 1:50 000 OS map, keep the same layout (landscape or portrait).
Always include a title: Sketch Map of ______ (insert town name).
Include the scale. If your sketch is the same size as the map, keep the same scale.
Include a border (frame), a north sign (arrow) and a legend (key).
Include all required features in the question.
Use graph paper if provided.

## GeoSkill

**Grid referencing 1:25 000**

This is the same as for 1:50 000.

Remember LEN: **L**etter **E**asting **N**orthing

## 1:25 000 Scale Maps

5.

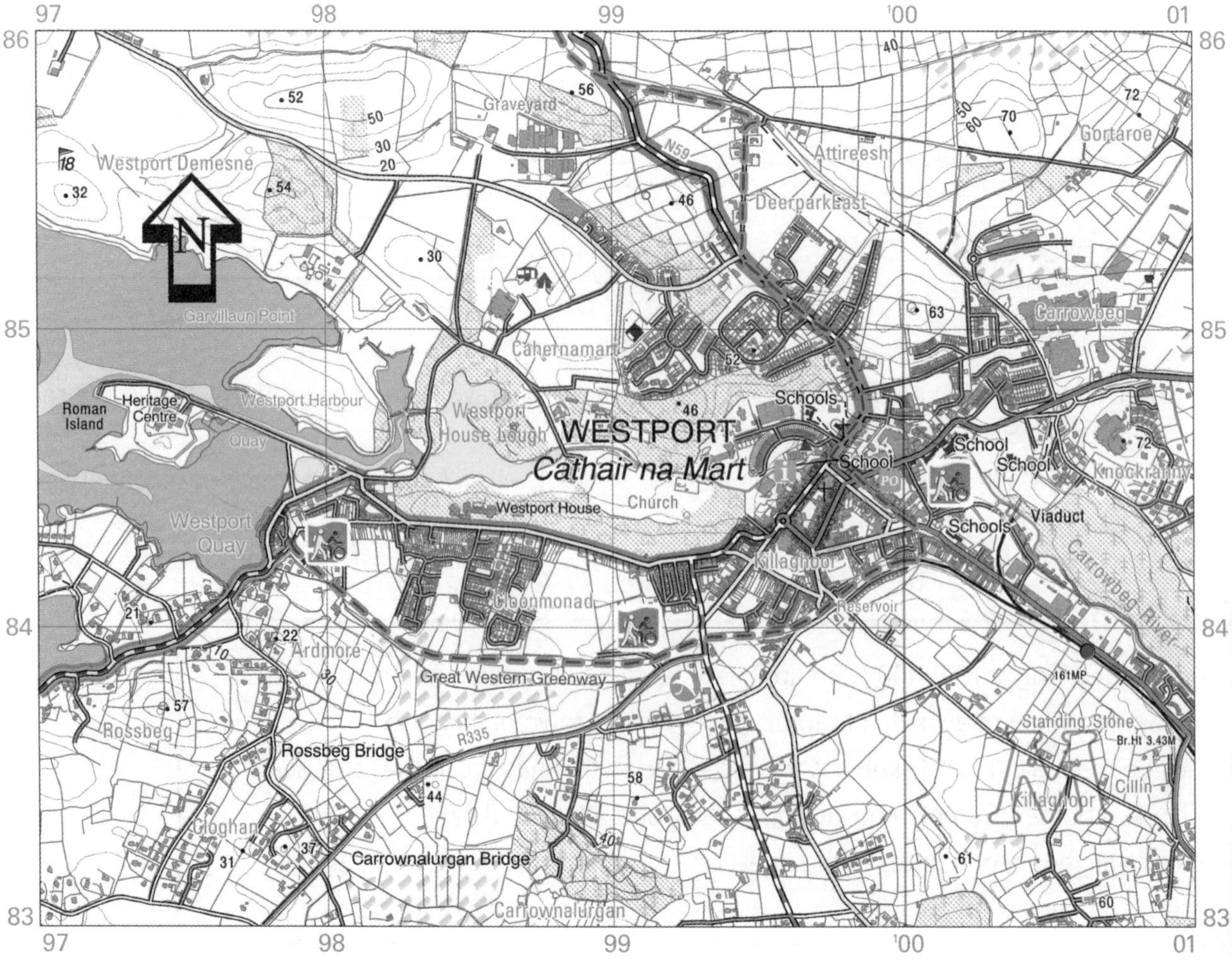

Examine the map extract of Westport on the previous page and choose a location for a **secondary economic activity** of your choice. Then fill in the report below.

## Exam Hint

Name two different types of transport on this map. Why is transport needed for secondary economic activities? Think about raw materials and finished products.

| **Secondary Economic Activity:** |
|---|
| **Six-Figure Grid Reference:** |
| **How would the types of transport on this map help your secondary economic activity?**<br>(Road and rail) |
| **Give the grid reference of two other services that already exist in the town which may help your economic activity and state why.**<br>**1.**<br>**2.** |

6. **Exam Hint**

For maps with a scale of 1:10 000, the scale is 1 cm = 0.1 km/100 m, e.g. 2 cm = 0.2 km = 200 m

**SCÁLA 1:10,000 / SCALE 1:10,000**

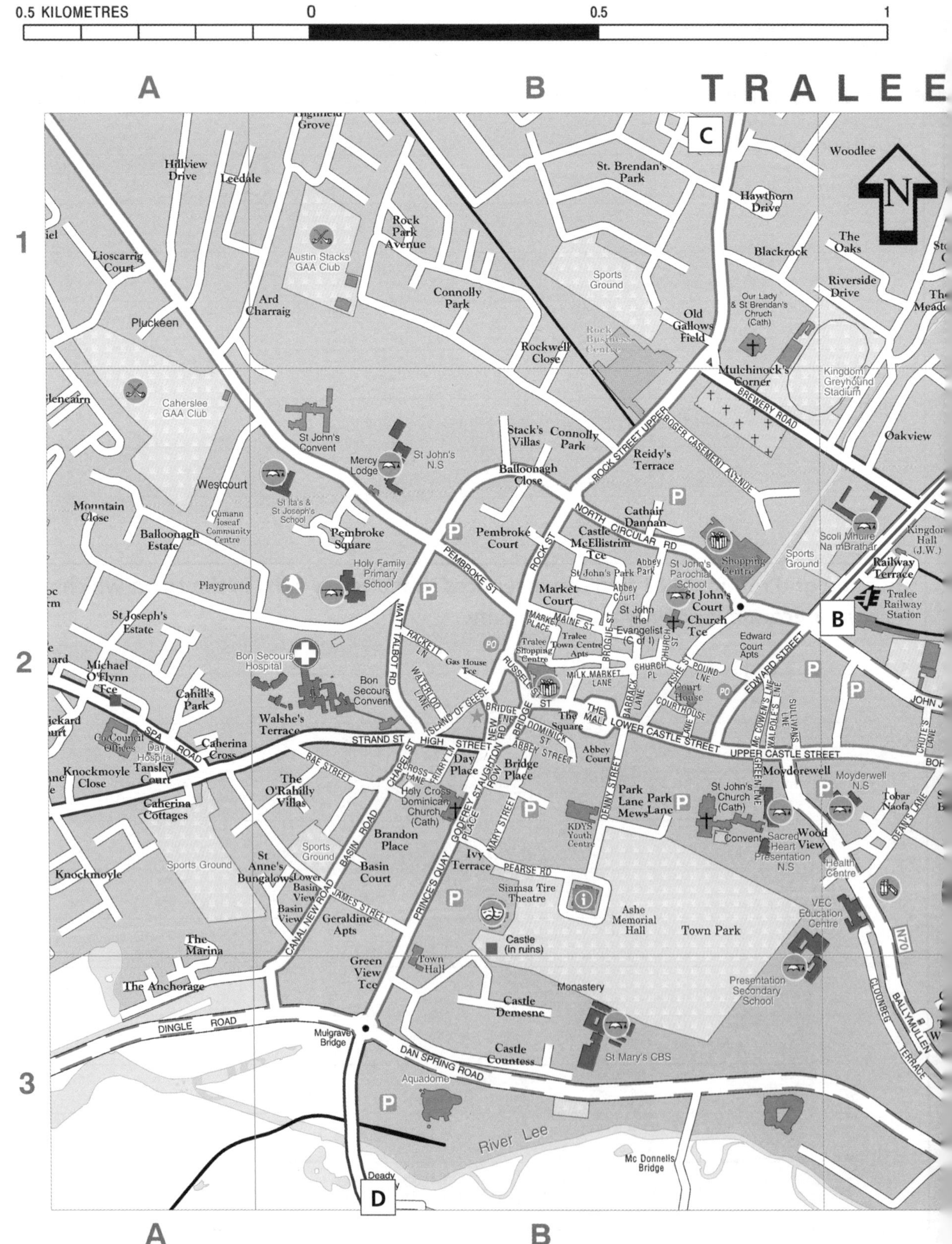

## GeoSkill

**Grid referencing on a 1:10 000 map**

X-axis first, followed by y-axis, e.g. A2.

**(i)** **(a)** What is the approximate length of the straight stretch of road (A–B) highlighted in red on the map? ________________km

**(b)** What is the approximate length of the curved stretch of road (C–D) on the map? ________________km

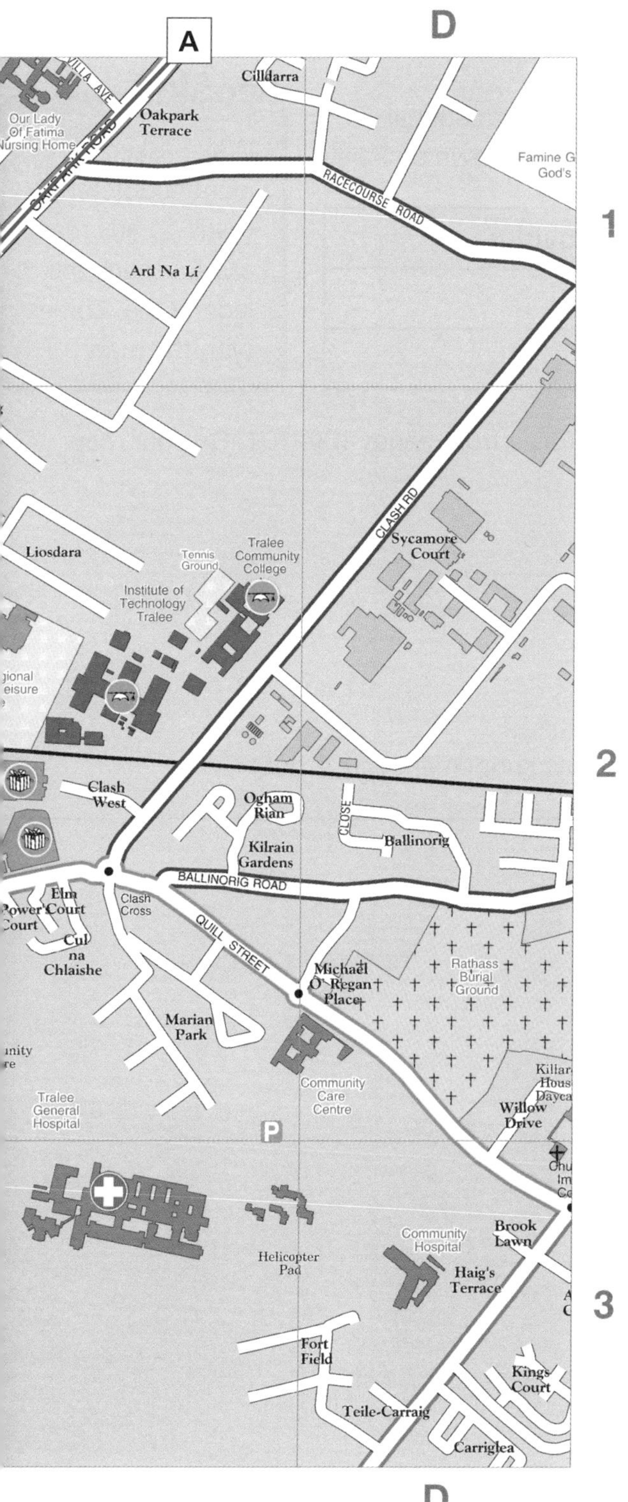

**(ii)** Give the grid square and evidence for the following types of functions found in Tralee. One has been completed for you already.

**Remember!**

If you are unsure of the meaning of any of these terms, now is the time to check them and write their definitions down.

| Function | Grid Square on Map | Evidence/Name |
|---|---|---|
| **Residential** | | |
| **Recreational** | | |
| **Educational** | | |
| **Bridging Point** | B3 | Mulgrave Bridge |

**(iii)** Traffic jams or a build-up of traffic can often occur where roads of different importance meet, or when large crowds gather for recreational events.

Give the grid square and type of roads or name the recreational activity of two locations where this might occur in the town of Tralee.

**GeoSkill**

When asked to identify different roads on any map, always check the legend that comes with the map.

| Grid Square | Type of Roads/Recreational Activities |
|---|---|
| | |
| | |

**(iv)** Draw a sketch map of the 1:10 000 OS map of Tralee from pages 100–101. On your map sketch the following:

- A national primary road
- A regional road
- A roundabout
- A recreational area
- A church
- A location you believe is best suited for a sports shop (mark with a dot)

**(v)** You wish to open a sports shop in the town of Tralee. A town councillor would like to read your report on the following: the reasons for your choice of location, the existing services that will benefit your shop, and the benefit your shop will bring to the area.

**Exam Hint**

Give two reasons behind your choice and explain both briefly.

Name and give grid references for the existing services your shop will rely on.

Think of the social and economic benefits of the shop.

Location of choice: __________

The reason(s) for your choice of location: __________

The existing services that will benefit your sports shop (give the grid square): __________

The benefit(s) your sports shop will bring to the area: __________

. Choose one of the following map extracts:

- Waterford/Ennis 1:50 000 (page 93/96)
- Westport 1:25 000 (page 98)
- Tralee 1:10 000 (page 100/101)

Explain how the town you chose developed by filling in the profile on the following page.

**Exam Hint**

Bullet points can be used here for the majority of the factors asked.

You must give grid references to back up your points.

Choice of town: ______________________________

| Factor | Description |
| --- | --- |
| Altitude (height above sea level) | |
| Drainage (rivers) | |
| Bridging point | |
| Transport (types/importance) | |
| Function (list two and explain) | |
| Influence of primary economic activities | |
| Influence of secondary economic activities | |
| An example of a physical feature, e.g. sea, mountain, glacier, that influenced location | |

## Aerial Photographs

3. (i) Examine the two aerial photographs below: Dingle (A) and Kilrush (B). Label each photograph as either vertical or oblique in the spaces provided.

| A: | B: |
| --- | --- |

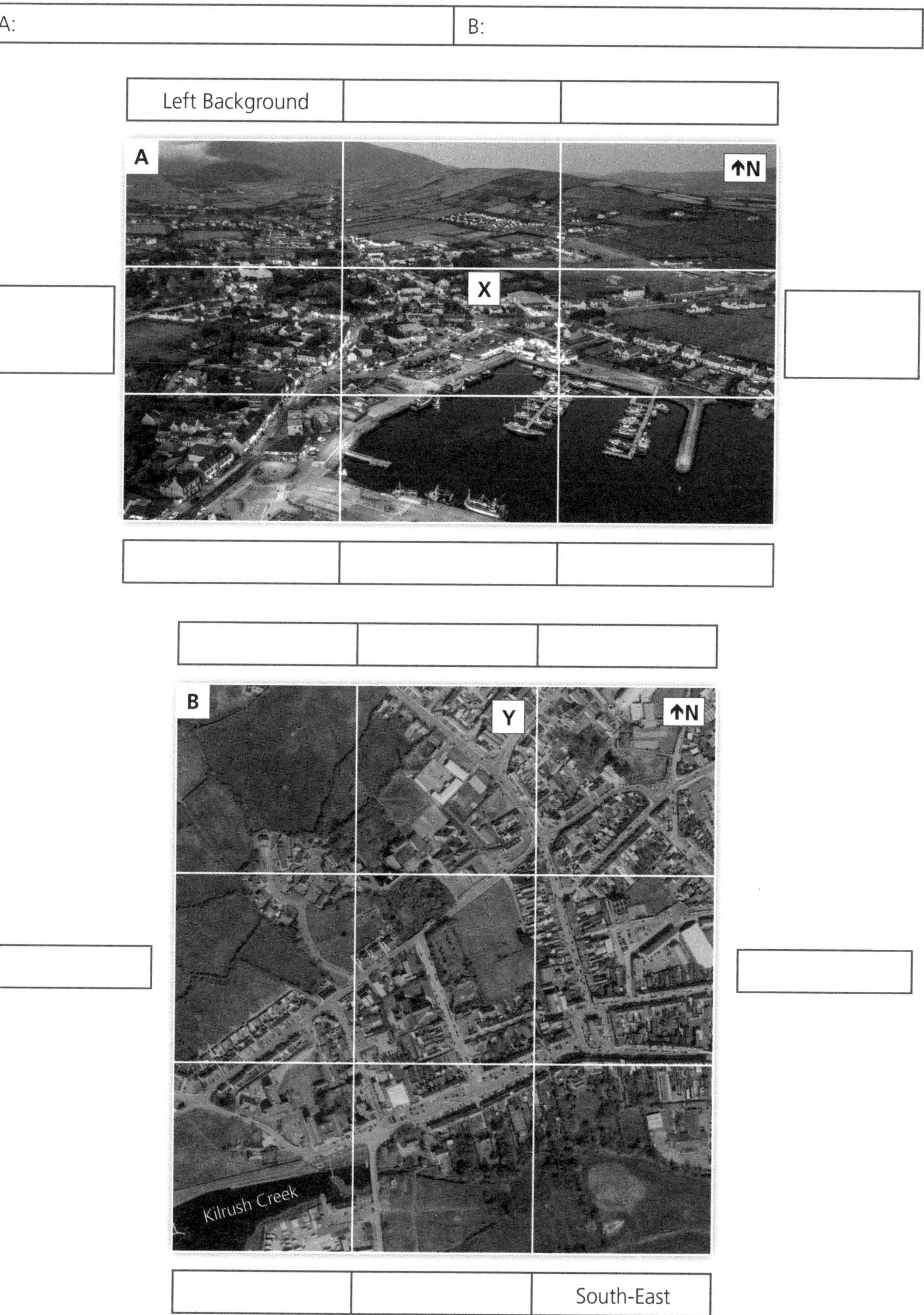

**(ii)** Photographs A and B have been divided up into nine equal segments. Using a pencil, label each segment on each photograph correctly. One segment on each has been filled in for you.

**(iii)** Now that you have labelled each segment on both photographs, in what areas can the following features be found?

| Feature | Area |
|---|---|
| The harbour in Dingle | |
| Kilrush Creek | |
| Factory marked X on Photograph A | |
| Residential estate marked Y on Photograph B | |

**(iv)** Draw a sketch map of Dingle. Include the following:

- The harbour
- A residential area
- A recreational area
- A roundabout and two roads coming from it
- A factory

## Identifiying Physical Features on OS Maps and Aerial Photograghs

**9.** On the following page are an OS map and an aerial photogragh of the same area, Glenbeigh in Co. Kerry. Using four-figure grid referencing and the correct directions on the vertical photograph, locate the features mentioned in the table below.

| Feature | OS Map | Photograph |
|---|---|---|
| Coastal erosion | | |
| Meander | | |
| Coastal deposition | | |
| An area of higher elevation | | |
| A lake | | |
| An estuary | | |

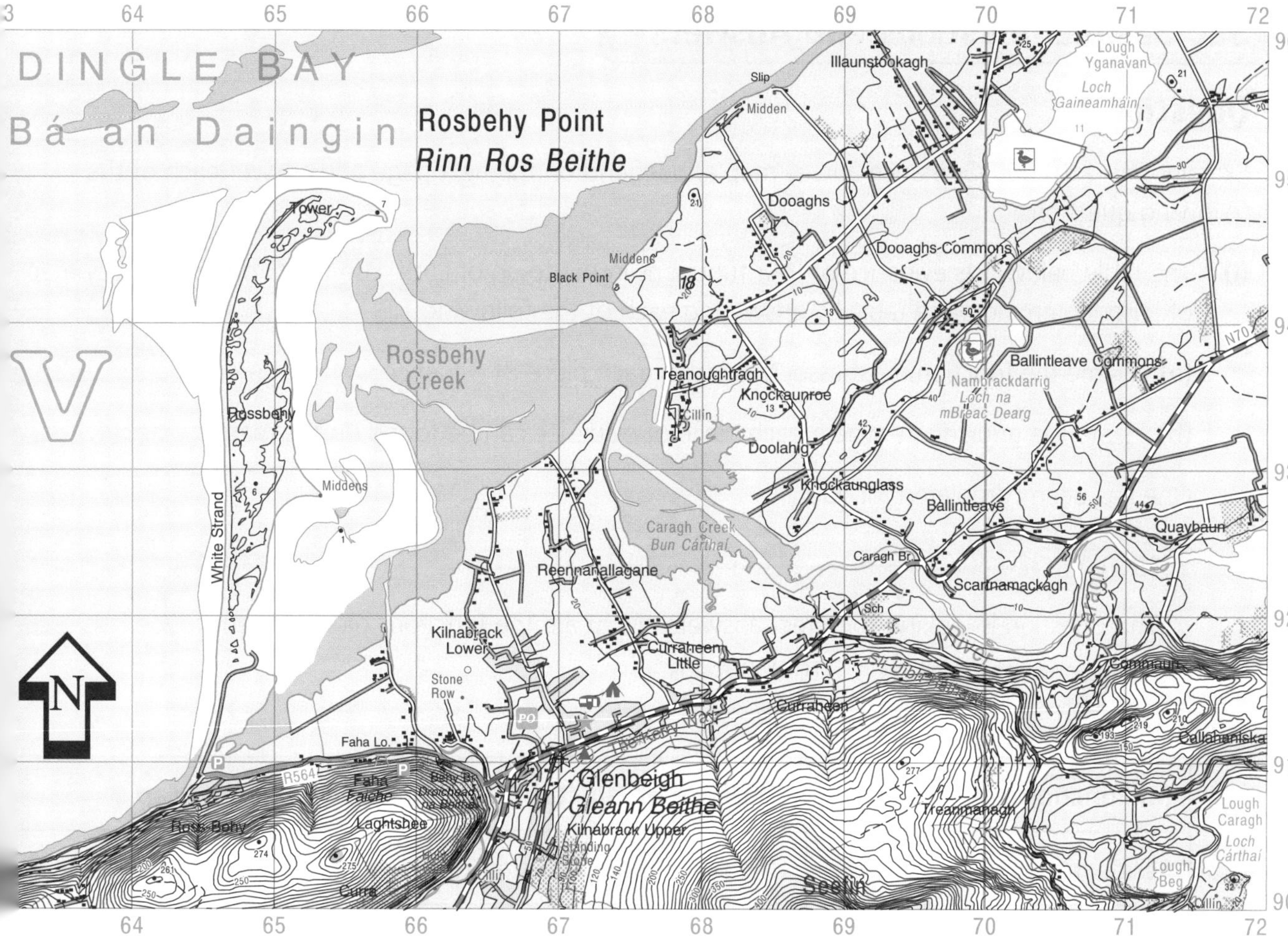

## SEC Sample Questions and Answers

### Question 1

Examine the 1:10 000 Ordnance Survey map and legend on the next page and answer each of the following questions.

**(i)** The table below lists evidence of four functions in the town of Lusk. Use the Ordnance Survey map of Lusk to complete the table by answering each of the following:

**(a)** Name the function most associated with each piece of evidence.

**(b)** State the grid square where each piece of evidence can be found on the map.

One has been completed for you.

**Exam Hint**

This question is looking for direct answers. What are the functions of settlement? Revise grid referencing on 1:10 000 maps.

| (a) Function | Evidence of Function | (b) Grid Square on Map |
|---|---|---|
| Residential | 'The Forge' housing estate | B 3 |
| | Lusk Community College | |
| | St Maccullin's Church | |
| | Lusk Town Centre | |

**(ii)** Measure the length of Rathmore Road, in kilometres, from the Raheny roundabout to the Dublin Road roundabout.

______________________________

**Marks Awarded**
(i) (a) 1 mark for each function ($1 \times 3 = 3$ marks)
(b) 1 mark for each correct grid reference ($1 \times 3 = 3$ marks)
6 marks in total
(ii) 4 marks for correct distance given to the nearest 0.5 km

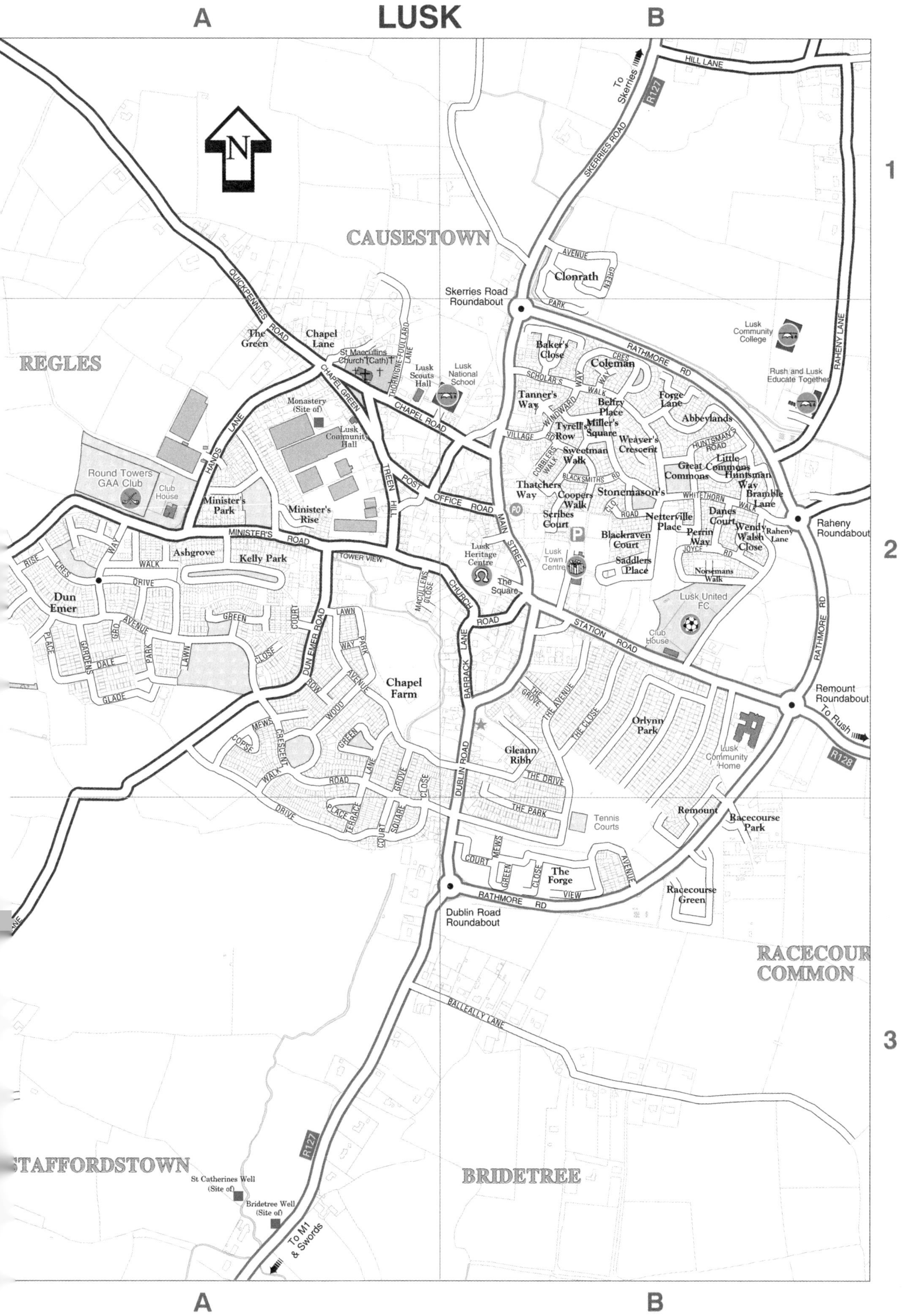
A
LUSK
B
1
2
3
N
CAUSESTOWN
REGLES
RACECOUR
COMMON
TAFFORDSTOWN
BRIDETREE
To Skerries
R127
SKERRIES ROAD
HILL LANE
RAHENY LANE
Skerries Road Roundabout
Clonrath
AVENUE
GREEN
PARK
Lusk Community College
Rush and Lusk Educate Together
RATHMORE RD
QUICKPENNIES ROAD
The Green
Chapel Lane
St Maccullins Church (Cath)
THORNIGNE-POULLARD LANE
Lusk Scouts Hall
Lusk National School
CHAPEL GREEN
CHAPEL ROAD
Monastery (Site of)
Lusk Community Hall
Baker's Close
Coleman
CRES
WAY
SCHOLAR'S
WALK
Tanner's Way
WINDWARD
Belfry Place
Forge Lane
Abbeylands
Tyrell's Row
Miller's Square
VILLAGE
Weaver's Crescent
HUNTSMAN'S ROAD
Sweetman Walk
COBBLERS WALK
Little Commons
Great Commons
Huntsman Way
BLACKSMITHS RD
Thatchers Way
Coopers Walk
Stonemason's
WHITETHORN
Bramble Lane
WALK
Scribes Court
Netterville Place
Danes Court
Wendy Walsh Close
Raheny Lane
Raheny Roundabout
Perrin Way
JOYCE RD
Blackraven Court
Saddlers Place
Norsemans Walk
Lusk Town Centre
HANDS LANE
Round Towers GAA Club
Club House
Minister's Park
Minister's Rise
TREEN HILL
POST OFFICE ROAD
MAIN STREET
MINISTER'S ROAD
Ashgrove
Kelly Park
TOWER VIEW
Lusk Heritage Centre
The Square
MACULLENS CLOSE
CHURCH ROAD
STATION ROAD
Lusk United FC
Club House
RISE
CRES
WALK
WAY
DRIVE
Dun Emer
AVENUE
GREEN
GRO
COURT
DUN EMER ROAD
LAWN
PARK
WAY
PLACE
GARDENS
DALE
PARK
LAWN
CLOSE
GLADE
ROW
AVENUE
Chapel Farm
BARRACK LANE
THE GROVE
THE AVENUE
THE CLOSE
Orlynn Park
Remount Roundabout
To Rush
R128
Lusk Community Home
MEWS
COPSE
CRESCENT
WOOD
GREEN
WALK
ROAD
LANE
GROVE
CLOSE
Gleann Ribh
DUBLIN ROAD
THE DRIVE
THE PARK
Tennis Courts
Remount
Racecourse Park
DRIVE
PLACE
TERRACE
COURT
SQUARE
COURT
MEWS
GREEN
CLOSE
The Forge
AVENUE
VIEW
RATHMORE RD
Racecourse Green
Dublin Road Roundabout
BALLEALLY LANE
R127
St Catherines Well (Site of)
Bridetree Well (Site of)
To M1 & Swords
A
B

**(iii)** Complete the sketch map of Lusk below by showing and naming each of the following:

- The full route of Rathmore Road
- A post office
- Lusk Heritage Centre
- **One** named recreational area

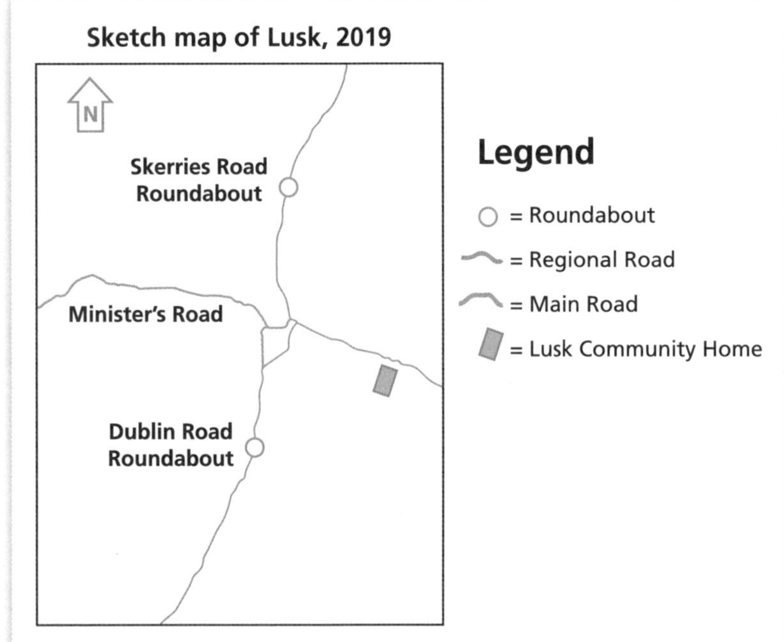


**Exam Hint**

Where possible, use different colours and shading to identify each feature asked for in this question.

**Marks Awarded**

**(iii)** 2 marks for each item shown on the sketch
1 mark for each item correctly placed into the key
2 marks for overall presentation, orientation, neatness

Total = 14 marks

## Question 2

Lusk is one town in Ireland where the population increased between 1996 and 2016. Study each of the following:

- The aerial photograph below showing Lusk in 2000
- The 1:10 000 Ordnance Survey map showing Lusk in 2019 (page 109).

**(i)** What was the area labelled **A** on the photograph being used for in 2000?

Tick (✓) the correct box.

Industry ☐

Agriculture ☐

Quarrying ☐

**Marks Awarded**

(i) 2 marks for correct answer

**(ii)** The area labelled A on the photograph is now being used for housing estates, as can be seen on the Ordnance Survey map of Lusk from 2019 (page 109).

Explain why this area was a good location to build housing estates. Use evidence from the aerial photograph **or** the Ordnance Survey map to support your answer.

Choose three pieces of evidence to support your answer.

**Transport:** *From the aerial photograph we can see existing housing estates in the west, southeast and south of the town. These are well serviced by a number of regional roads in and around the town. On the 1:10 000 map we can see that the R128 acts as a ring road around the town, which means additional traffic brought by the housing estate to the area should not cause traffic problems. These roads link with more important roads, which means the residents can travel to nearby cities/ towns for work.*

Here transport, drainage and existing services have been selected for you.

Name the roads that service the area. These will connect Lusk to other parts of Ireland, which is important for work and recreation. The site chosen is also near a road, meaning residents will be able to access it.

**Drainage:** ________________________________________________________

**Existing Services:** ________________________________________________________

**(iii)** Examine the aerial photograph from 2000 on page 110 and the Ordnance Survey map from 2019 on page 109. Other than housing, describe **one** change in land use between 2000 and 2019.

# 11 Rivers

In this section, the Learning Outcomes we will look at are: **1.5**, **1.10**, **2.7**, **3.4**

## Learning Checklist:

- ☐ I can explain the key terms associated with the journey of a river from source to sea.
- ☐ I can describe each of the three stages of a river (upper course, middle course, lower course).
- ☐ I can describe with the help of diagrams how the processes of erosion can lead to the creation of particular river features (waterfall, V-shaped valley, etc.).
- ☐ I can describe with the help of diagrams how the processes of deposition can lead to the creation of particular river features (levee, delta, ox-bow lake, etc.).
- ☐ I can explain the processes of erosion that are at work on a river (hydraulic action, attrition, abrasion, solution).
- ☐ I can explain the processes of river transportation (traction, saltation, suspension, solution).
- ☐ I can discuss the economic, social and environmental impacts of river flooding.
- ☐ I can explain the impact that rivers have on settlement.
- ☐ I can explain how a river deposits its load.
- ☐ I can interpret information from aerial images and photographs. I can read information from different types of maps.

## Source to Mouth

1. (i) Correctly place the labels onto the diagram of a river's journey from source to mouth.

**Labels**

A. Source
B. Tributary
C. Flood plain
D. Mouth
E. Estuary
F. Ox-bow lake
G. Meander

*Draw a delta onto the sketch in its correct location and clearly label it.*

**(ii)** Match each process of river erosion with its correct definition in the table below. One has been completed for you.

| Process | Definition |
|---|---|
| Hydraulic action | The water can dissolve some of the minerals on the riverbed and banks. |
| Abrasion | Broken material is thrown against the bed and banks of the river and wears them down. |
| Attrition | The fast-moving water breaks and wears away material from the bed and banks of the river. |
| Solution | The load itself can be broken down further as rocks bang against each other and become smooth and rounded. |

**(iii)** Look at the aerial photographs below of different features found along the course of a river. Place the correct name for each feature in the box below it.

Meander    Tributary    Ox-bow lake    Floodplain    Waterfall    V-shaped valley

## GeoSkill

It is very helpful to look at aerial images of river features on the landscape. This will help you to quickly identify features if presented with them in the exam. You should also be able to state and explain the processes that formed the features.

**(iv)** The course of a river is broken up into three different stages. Complete the fact files below for each of the three stages of a river.

**Exam Hint**

Having this information in one place will help with your revision before the exam. Knowing the features in each stage and the processes that helped in their formation will help you to feel confident.

It is also important to always include real-life examples.

**UPPER COURSE**

APPEARANCE AND CHARACTERISTICS OF RIVER

PROCESSES AT WORK

FEATURES FOUND HERE/EXAMPLES

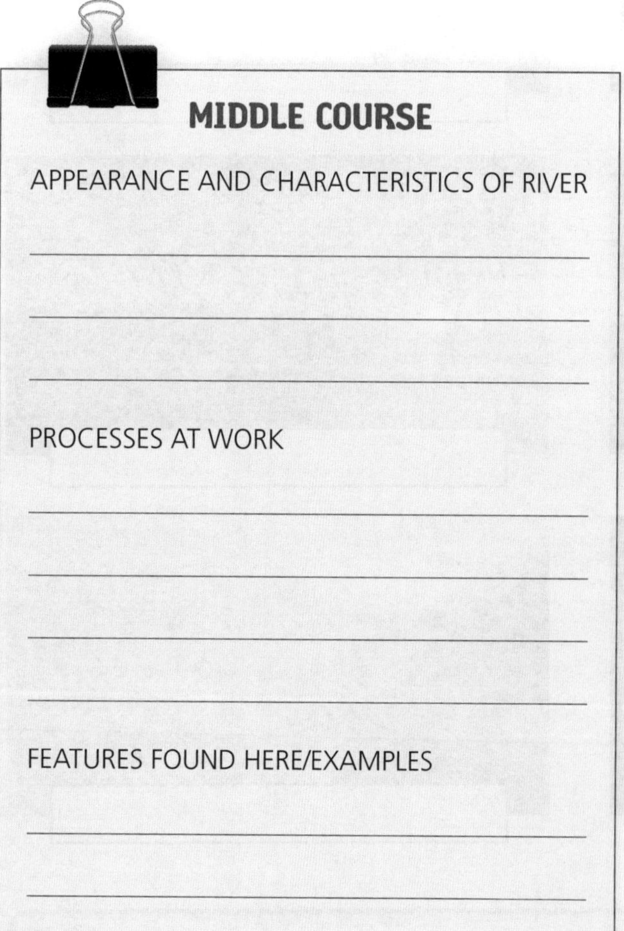
**MIDDLE COURSE**

APPEARANCE AND CHARACTERISTICS OF RIVER

PROCESSES AT WORK

FEATURES FOUND HERE/EXAMPLES

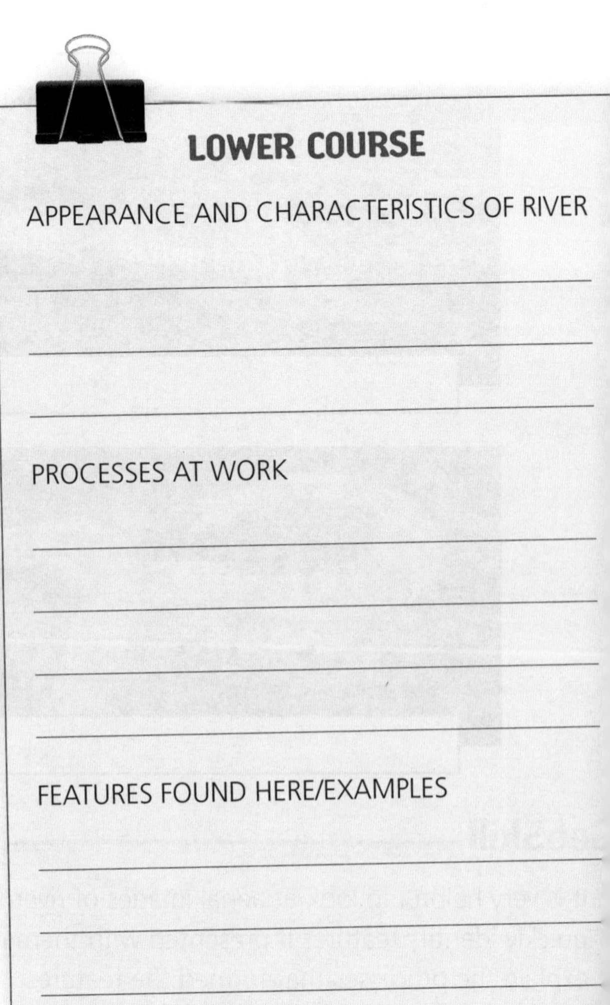
**LOWER COURSE**

APPEARANCE AND CHARACTERISTICS OF RIVER

PROCESSES AT WORK

FEATURES FOUND HERE/EXAMPLES

**(v)** Complete the paragraph below using the words provided:

suspension dropping calcite dragged traction
saltation solution energy sea

As a river moves from source to mouth, it transports its load in a number of ways. Large pebbles and stones are rolled and ______________ along the riverbed by the force of moving water. This is known as ______________. Smaller pebbles and stones are bounced along the riverbed, which is known as ______________. Tiny particles are held in the water by ______________. The water is moving quickly so this prevents the small particles from ______________ to the riverbed. The river water can also dissolve minerals such as ______________ and carry these in ______________. They cannot be seen in the water.

Rivers drop their load when they begin to slow down and lose ______________. This usually happens when a river reaches flat ground or enters a lake or the ______________.

**(vi)** Answer all of the short questions below.

**(a)** What are interlocking spurs?

______________________________________

______________________________________

______________________________________

______________________________________

**Exam Hint**

If you are unsure of the answers to any of the short questions, this will highlight topics that may require some further revision.

**(b)** Why does a river have a V-shaped valley in its youthful stage?

______________________________________

______________________________________

**(c)** What processes are at work in the formation of a waterfall?

______________________________________

______________________________________

**(d)** In what stage of a river's journey would you expect to find a floodplain? Why?

______________________________________

______________________________________

**(e)** What is the name of the fertile material deposited on a floodplain that is very good for farming?

______________________________________

**(f)** What are levees and how are they formed?

______________________________________

______________________________________

______________________________________

**(g)** What processes are involved in the formation of an ox-bow lake?

______________________________________________

______________________________________________

**(h)** What are the small channels that break through a delta known as?

______________________________________________

## Feature of Erosion/Deposition

**2.**

Y

X

### GeoSkill

You have been provided with an aerial image. Look closely at it to identify the features of river erosion or deposition that you can see here.

**(i)** Above is an image of the River Swale in the UK. Name the process taking place at point X on the image.

______________________________________________

**(ii)** Name the river feature found in the box labelled Y.

______________________________________________

**(iii)** Describe the processes that led to the formation of feature Y. You may use diagrams to support your answer if you wish.

### Remember!

Look closely at the river's course in the image. Use your fluvial knowledge to identify the feature. You should describe the processes that have helped to create this feature.

### Remember!

**F.** Feature
**E.** Explain
**E.** Example
**D.** Diagram

Feature: ______________________________________________

Explanation:

______________________________________________

______________________________________________

______________________________________________

______________________________________________

______________________________________________

______________________________________________

______________________________________________

Example:

**Diagrams:**

## Flooding

3. Read the article below that reports on a recent flooding event in Co. Cork and answer the questions that follow.

**Shock Flooding for Cork City**

Around 100 buildings and dozens of parked cars were damaged by flooding in Cork city centre following Tuesday morning's high tide, with damage estimated to run to millions of euro.

Many streets in Cork city were under up to a metre of water. Cork County Council said that a storm surge and high winds that are likely associated with Storm Barbara moved over from Portugal and are making their way across western Europe.

Flood warnings were issued in advance but the speed at which the waters rose appeared to have taken many people by surprise. Many business owners had to bail out water after the River Lee burst its banks.

Cork City Council advised motorists to avoid the city centre for a number of hours up to mid-morning. Gardaí were forced to close off a number of low-lying streets as floodwaters began to make them impassable.

Cork City Council
@corkcitycouncil
Cork City Council asks road users to please avoid low lying areas of Cork City Centre until 11am this morning, due to serious flooding
Cork City Council Operations crews, @CorkCityFire & @cc_civildefence are on site to assist as serious flooding has occurred #CorkFloods
Cork City Civil Defence
@cc_civildefence
Swift Water Responder teams with @corkcitycouncil operations crews and @CorkCityFire are currently providing support to some business premises in #Cork city following flood damage this am.
CIVIL DEFENCE
10:49 AM · Oct 20, 2020


In a statement, Taoiseach Micheál Martin said the government would ensure supports are given to businesses affected by the flooding.

*Source: irishcentral.com*

**(i)** What was the cause of the flooding event in Cork city?

**(ii)** Explain one potential economic impact and one environmental impact of this flooding event in Cork.

Economic: ______________________________

______________________________

______________________________

Environmental: ______________________________

______________________________

______________________________

**(iii)** Describe the response to this natural disaster event.

______________________________

______________________________

______________________________

**(iv)** Look at the two tweets that were issued by Cork City Council and Cork City Civil Defence during the flooding event. What are the benefits of social media use during natural disaster events such as this?

______________________________

______________________________

______________________________

______________________________

______________________________

**Exam Hint**

Think about the social media applications that you use. How might they help during an emergency situation?

**(v)** Other than the flood event mentioned in the article on the previous page, name a natural disaster flooding event that you have studied. State where and when it occurred.

Describe what led to your selected flooding event and explain one social and one economic impact that it had on the local area.

## Case Study

Event: ______________________________

Where and when it occurred: ______________________________

______________________________

______________________________

______________________________

______________________________

______________________________

**Remember!**

Writing case studies for natural disaster events is very useful preparation for your exam.

Social impact:

______________________________

______________________________

______________________________

Economic impact:

______________________________

______________________________

______________________________

## Settlement and Rivers

4. **(i)** Examine the map opposite, which shows Norman towns in Ireland. These towns are situated mainly along rivers in which of the following parts of the country? Tick (✓) the correct answer.

The North and West ☐  The South and East ☐

The North and East ☐  The South and West ☐

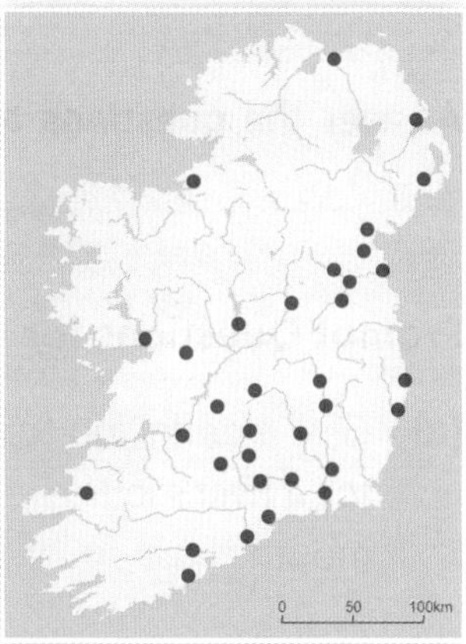

**(ii)** Kilkenny is a medieval city found on the River Nore, and was once a Norman settlement. Review the street map of Kilkenny city opposite and answer the questions that follow.

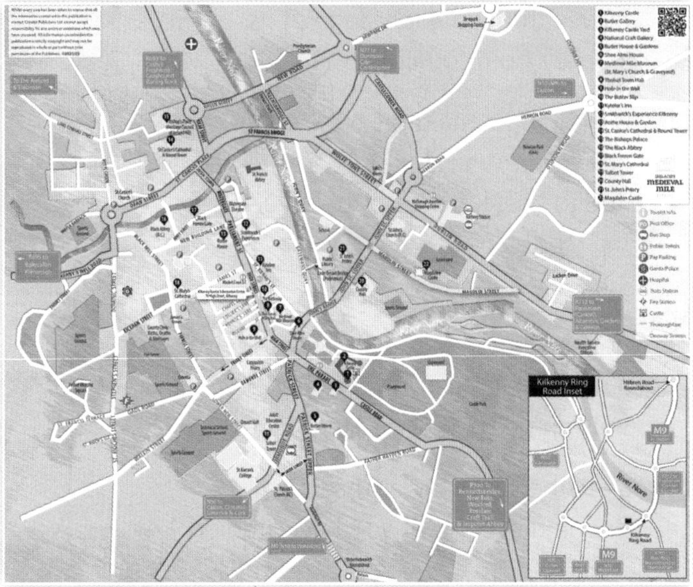

### GeoSkill

You could be presented with many different types of maps in the exam. Getting familiar with maps of different types and scales is great practice. Always read the map key/legend and scan across the full map to take it all in.

**(a)** Outline one piece of evidence on the map that suggests that the area shown was part of a medieval Norman settlement.

______________________________________________

______________________________________________

______________________________________________

______________________________________________

**(b)** Briefly explain how each of the factors below may have influenced the Normans in settling close to a river such as the Nore in Kilkenny.

How did they use rivers for transport? Why didn't they use roads?

**Influence of Rivers on Settlement**

What might early settlers need water for? What do you use water for?

When castles were built, what was built around them? Were they built in upland or lowlands?

| Transport | Water | Defence |
|---|---|---|
| | | |

**Answer the questions to complete the mind map. This will support your revision.**

**Prompt Questions for Mind Map**

**(a)** Give a definition for all key terms/words for a river's journey from source to mouth.

**(b)** Describe how a river changes as it moves through each stage of its journey from source to sea.

**(c)** Describe the main processes of erosion on a river. What features are created due to these processes being active on the landscape?

**(d)** Describe the processes of transportation and deposition along a river. What features are shaped by these processes?

**(e)** Describe some social impacts of a flooding event that you have studied.

**(f)** What impact do rivers have on settlement?

(a) Journey of a River

(f) Settlement

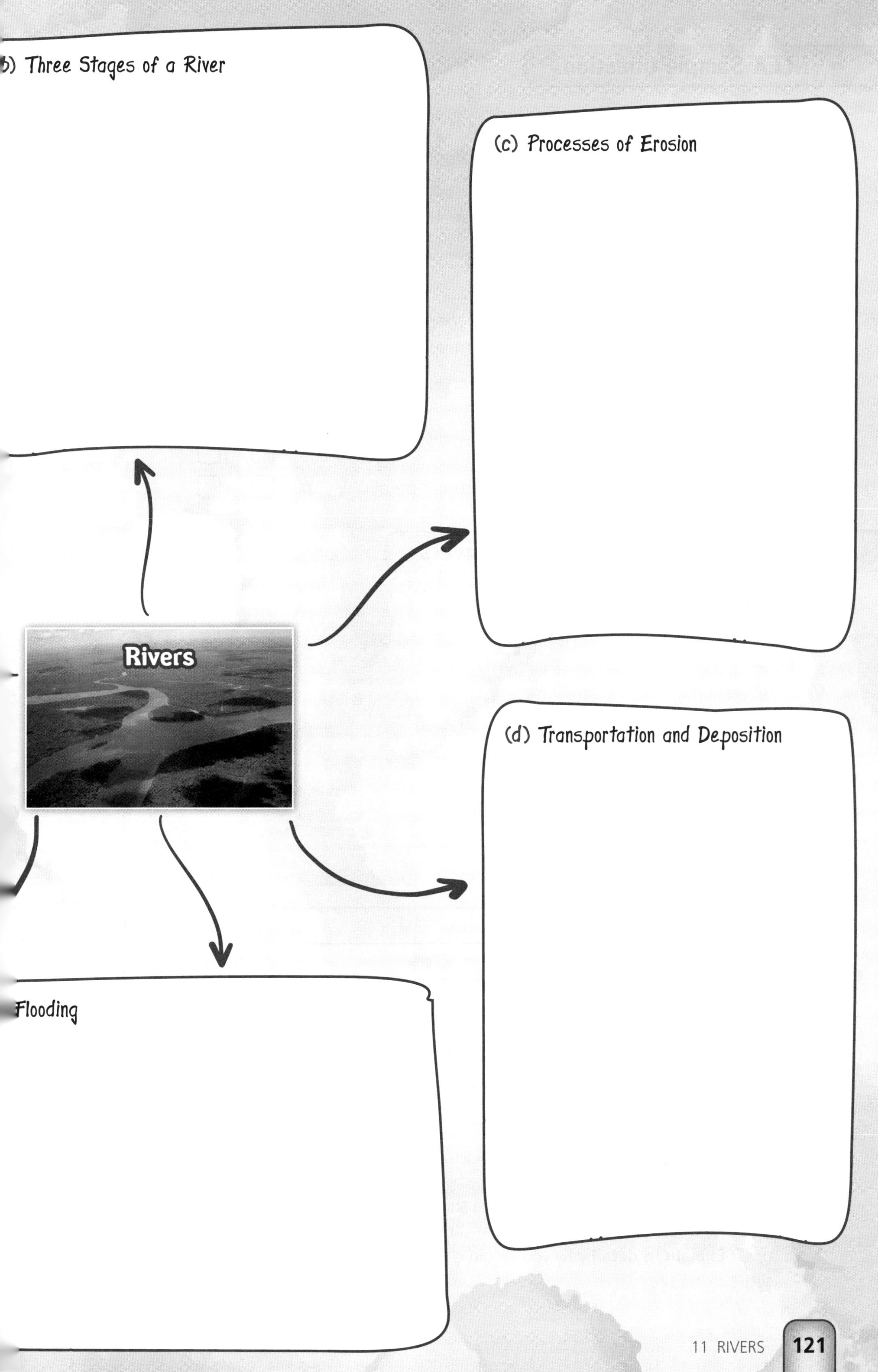
b) Three Stages of a River
(c) Processes of Erosion
Rivers
(d) Transportation and Deposition
Flooding

## NCCA Sample Question

### Question 1

Identify the following statements as true or false.

| | | True | False |
|---|---|---|---|
| **1.** | A river source is generally found in high mountainous areas. | ☐ | ☐ |
| **2.** | A narrow, fast-flowing river would generally mean it is in a youthful stage. | ☐ | ☐ |
| **3.** | It is uncommon to find a settlement along a river. | ☐ | ☐ |
| **4.** | Soils found close to rivers are rich and fertile. | ☐ | ☐ |
| **5.** | Freeze-thaw action is a type of weathering. | ☐ | ☐ |
| **6.** | Abrasion is a type of deposition. | ☐ | ☐ |
| **7.** | Beaches are examples of deposition. | ☐ | ☐ |
| **8.** | 20,000 years ago, ice covered most of the continent of Europe. | ☐ | ☐ |

**Exam Hint**

When presented with a question like this, always attempt each part. Do not leave any blank.

## SEC Sample Questions and Answers

### Question 2

**(a)** Examine this diagram which shows a landscape that has been shaped by different physical processes including erosion, transportation and deposition by rivers and the sea.

In the table below, **match** each of the features labelled 1 to 5 on Figure 1 with the correct term from the box. One has been completed for you.

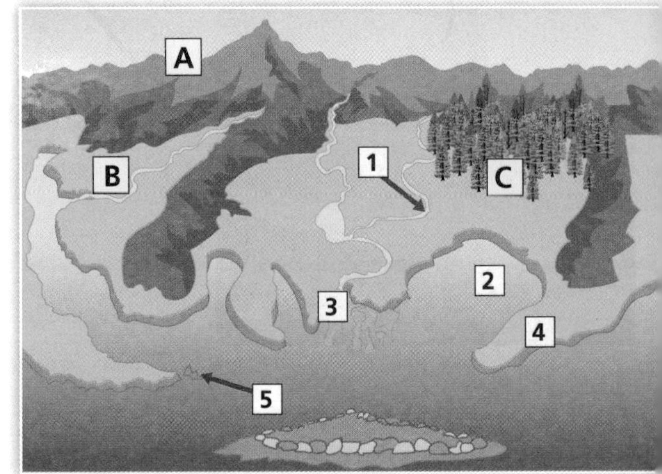


| Terms |
|---|
| Bay |
| Meander |
| Source |
| Headland |
| Delta |
| Sea stack |

| Number | Feature |
|---|---|
| **1** | |
| **2** | |
| **3** | |
| **4** | Headland |
| **5** | |

**(b)** Figure 1 shows an area along the coast similar to the area that Ireland's first settlers arrived. If you were one of the first settlers in the area shown in Figure 1, would you choose to settle at site A or B or C? **Explain in detail** why you would choose to settle at this site.

**Exam Hint**

Take your time reviewing the diagram above. Consider things such as: location in relation to coast/river, topography of the site, protection, access.

Site: A ▢ or B ▢ or C ▢

## Question 3

Name one feature formed by river erosion, and, with the aid of a labelled diagram, explain how the processes of erosion helped in its formation. [10 marks]

**Remember!**

**F.** Feature
**E.** Explain
**E.** Example
**D.** Diagram

**Feature:** *Waterfall*

**Explanation:**

*Waterfalls are formed in the upper/youthful course of a river because of the impact of vertical erosion by the processes of hydraulic action, abrasion and solution. Most waterfalls develop where a river meets a band of softer, less resistant rock like sandstone, after flowing over a harder, more resistant rock like granite.*

**Example:**

**Diagram:**

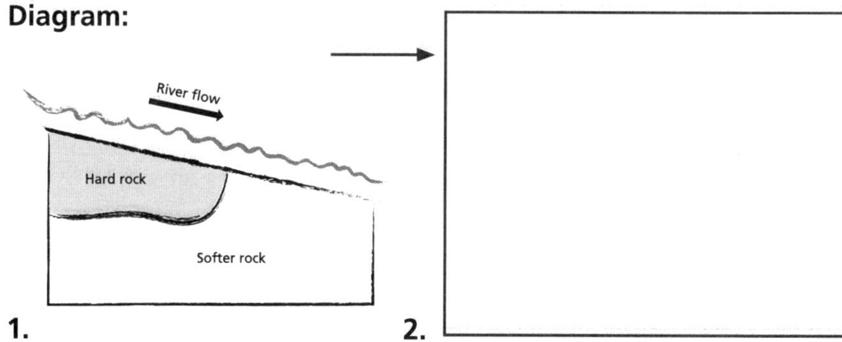


In answering this question, you should ensure you:
- State the name of the feature that you will explain.
- State how the feature is formed. In your explanation, you must mention at least two processes of erosion that have helped to form a waterfall, and you should explain how the processes do this.

Some processes that can be used here are:
- Hydraulic action
- Abrasion
- Solution
- Attrition

The final 2 marks are for a fully labelled diagram/s. This has been started for you and you should complete it.

**Marks Awarded**

Feature named = 1 mark
Explanation of formation: Statement 2 marks + Development (1 + 1 + 1 + 1 + 1)
Two development marks must be for processes
Labelled diagram = 2 marks
Total = 10 marks

# 12 The Sea

In this section, the Learning Outcomes we will look at are: **1.5**, **1.10**, **2.7**, **2.9**, **3.4**

## Learning Checklist:

- ☐ I can explain the processes of sea erosion (hydraulic action, abrasion, compressed air, attrition, solution).
- ☐ I can describe the processes of transportation by the sea (longshore drift).
- ☐ I can describe how the processes of erosion help in the formation of coastal features such as bays and headlands, sea caves/arches/stacks, etc.
- ☐ I can describe how the process of coastal deposition helps in the formation of features such as beaches, sand spits, bars, tombolos, etc.
- ☐ I can explain how people manage surface processes at the coast by installing coastal protection barriers such as groynes, sea walls, gabions, etc.
- ☐ I can discuss why coastal areas attract tourists and are popular destinations.
- ☐ I can identify features of coastal erosion, deposition and protection from OS maps and photographs.

## Erosion at the Coast

**1.** **(i)** As the sea moves, it is constantly shaping our coastlines. Waves approach the coast and have great powers of erosion. Complete the definitions below for each of the key terms of erosion by waves. One has been completed for you.

| Key Term | Definition |
|---|---|
| Hydraulic action | |
| Abrasion | Waves pick up stones as they move and throw them against the coast. The force of the stones hitting against the coast causes erosion. |
| Compressed air | |
| Attrition | |
| Solution | |

**(ii)** Review the OS map below showing Moore Bay near Kilkee, Co. Clare, and answer the questions that follow.

## GeoSkill

This is a 1:50 000 OS map, so you should try to provide a six-figure grid reference to identify the feature that you are discussing in your answer.

It is also important to be able to identify marine, fluvial or glacial features on OS maps.

**L.** Letter

**E.** Easting →

**N.** Northing ↑

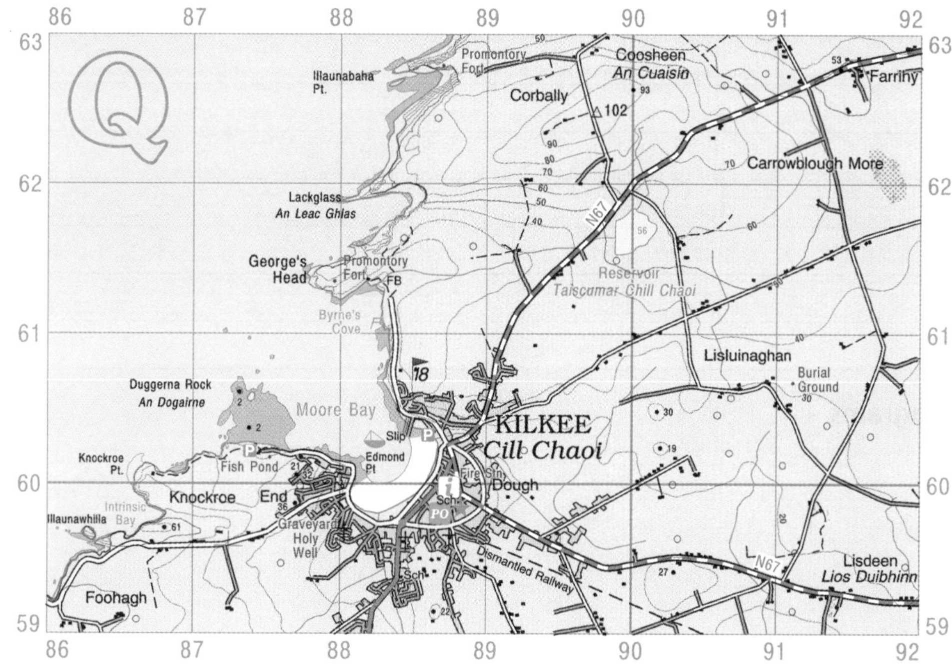


**(a)** Name two different pieces of evidence from the map extract above that show how this area has developed to support tourism, and state how each can be used by tourists.

Evidence 1: ____________________

How it can be used by tourists:

____________________

____________________

____________________

____________________

Evidence 2: ____________________

How it can be used by tourists:

____________________

____________________

____________________

____________________

**(b)** Give the six-figure grid reference for the location of the main named headland shown on the map.

____________________

____________________

(c) What are bays and headlands are a feature of?
Tick (✓) the correct answer.

Erosion ☐ Deposition ☐

(d) Describe how bays and headlands, such as the one shown on the OS map on the previous page, are formed at the coastline by the processes of coastal erosion. Use diagrams to support your answer.

**Remember!**

**F.** Feature
**E.** Explain
**E.** Example
**D.** Diagram

______________________________________________
______________________________________________
______________________________________________
______________________________________________
______________________________________________
______________________________________________
______________________________________________
______________________________________________
______________________________________________

**Diagrams**

(iii) You are on holiday in a coastal region and take a photograph of the beautiful coastal landscape.

(a) Label the features of coastal erosion that are shown in your photograph below.

Sea stump    Sea arch    Sea cliff    Sea stack    Sea cave

**GeoSkill**

Identifying landforms of coastal erosion from photographs.

**(b)** Write a postcard to a friend back home naming **one** of the features that you photographed on the previous page and explain to your friend how this feature was formed by the processes of coastal erosion.

**Remember!**

**F.** Feature
**E.** Explain
**E.** Example
**D.** Diagram

## Transport by Sea

**(i)** Match each term in column A with its definition in column B.

| Column A | Column B |
|---|---|
| Destructive waves | Powerful waves that can cause erosion along the coastline. |
| Swash | Water that can move material back down the beach. |
| Constructive waves | These break on the shores and deposit beach material, building up the beach. |
| Backwash | This can move material up the beach. |

**(ii)** Complete the sketch below to show how the sea transports its load by the process of longshore drift. You must provide full labels and brief written descriptions on the next page. The first step has been completed for you.

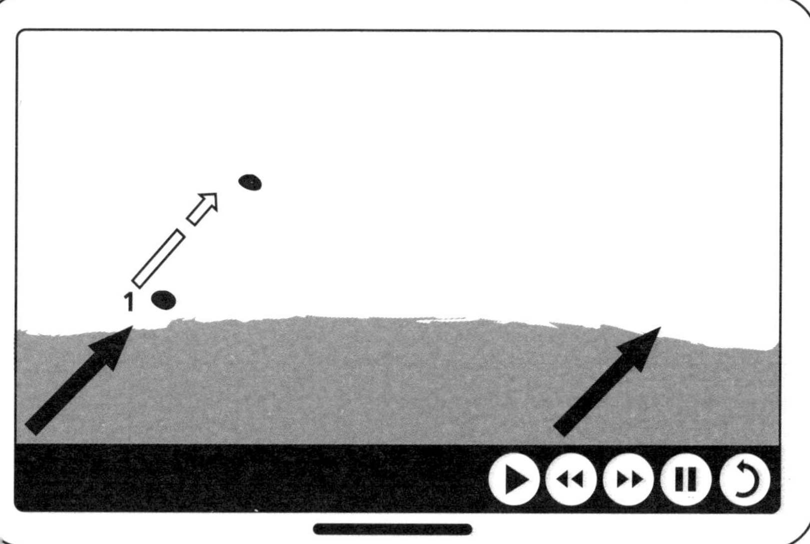


**Remember!**

Use a pencil to complete the sketch. As this has been started for you by numbering the first step as 1, this might be helpful to continue – label your next step as 2 and so on.

**Exam Hint**

You should try to use the following key words to help you in your answer: swash, backwash, zig-zag, angle, drags, longshore drift, destructive and constructive waves.

**Step 1.** The waves approach the beach at an angle. The prevailing wind will affect this. The swash carries the material at an angle up the beach.

## Sea Deposition

**3.** **(i)** Answer all short questions below.

**(a)** Why is marram grass sometimes planted in sand dunes?

**(b)** Explain what a 'storm beach' is.

**(c)** Name the processes at work in the formation of a beach.

**(d)** Where in Ireland can we see an example of a sand spit?

**(ii)** Below is a diagram showing a sand spit. Label the diagram, and, in the space provided, describe how this feature was formed by the processes of coastal deposition.

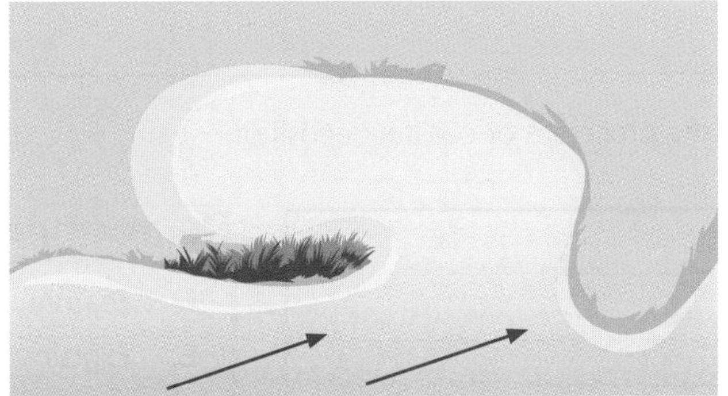

## Exam Hint

Remember to write about **the processes** of coastal deposition that helped in the formation of this feature.

**Labels**

Bay
Spit
Silt
Marram grass
Longshore drift

## Remember!

**F.** Feature
**E.** Explain
**E.** Example
**D.** Diagram

**Formation of feature**

________________________________________

________________________________________

________________________________________

________________________________________

________________________________________

________________________________________

________________________________________

________________________________________

**(iii)** If the sand spit above continued to grow in size, it could reach across to the other side of the bay and seal it off. What do we call this new feature?

________________________________________

________________________________________

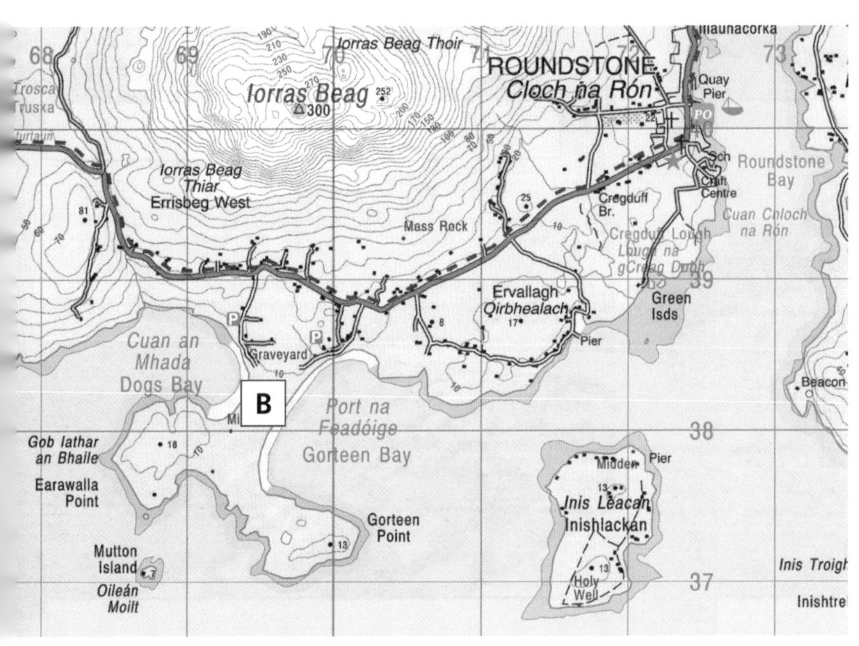


**(iv)** Opposite is an OS map showing a coastal area near Roundstone, Co. Galway. Name the feature highlighted at point B on the map.

## GeoSkill

Identifying features of coastal deposition from an OS map.

**Remember!**

Do not be thrown by an image/diagram that seems unfamiliar. You have studied this topic and know the information to attempt the question. Look at the area on the map and read the names of features as this may help you.

B = ______________________________

**(v)** Explain how this feature was formed by the processes of coastal deposition.

**Remember!**

**F.** Feature
**E.** Explain
**E.** Example
**D.** Diagram

## Managing Coastal Processes

**GeoSkill**

Identifying coastal defence measures from images.

**4. (i)** Name each of the coastal protection measures shown below.

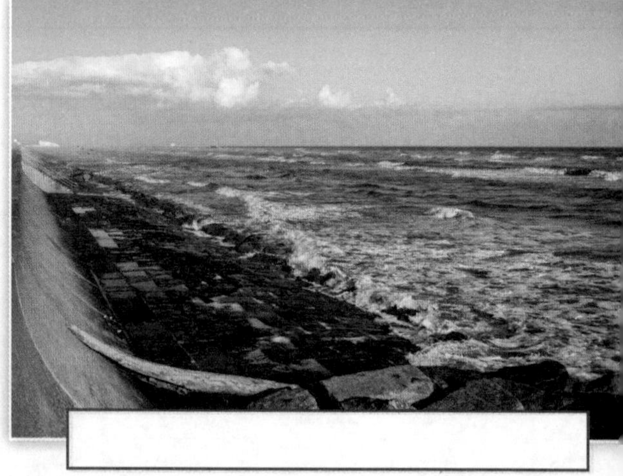

**(ii)** Your home is located along a coastal stretch that is being heavily impacted by coastal erosion. Write a letter to the local county council to describe the coastal management measures that you feel are necessary to help protect your property. Space has also been provided to draw a sketch of your proposed solution(s).

## Exam Hint

If a template for a letter is provided, follow the directions given.

1. In this answer, you must suggest some coastal defence measures to protect your home, such as:
   - Groynes
   - Gabions
   - Rock armour
   - Sea wall

   Look at the image to decide what is most suitable.
2. Describe the methods that you have selected and explain how they will protect your home from coastal processes.
3. Draw a sketch to show what the measures look like and make sure to label them.

**Dear Councillor,**

**Answer the questions to complete the mind map. This will support your revision.**

## Prompt Questions for Mind Map

**(a)** Describe how waves erode at the coastline.
What processes are at work? Name them.
What do they do?

**(b)** Describe how the processes of erosion create different coastal features.
Give examples: where can they be found?

**(c)** How does the process of longshore drift help to transport material by sea?

**(d)** Describe how the sea deposits its load.
Name the features formed by coastal deposition.
Can you give examples?

**(e)** How can humans protect the coastline from the processes of coastal erosion?
What measures can be put in place?

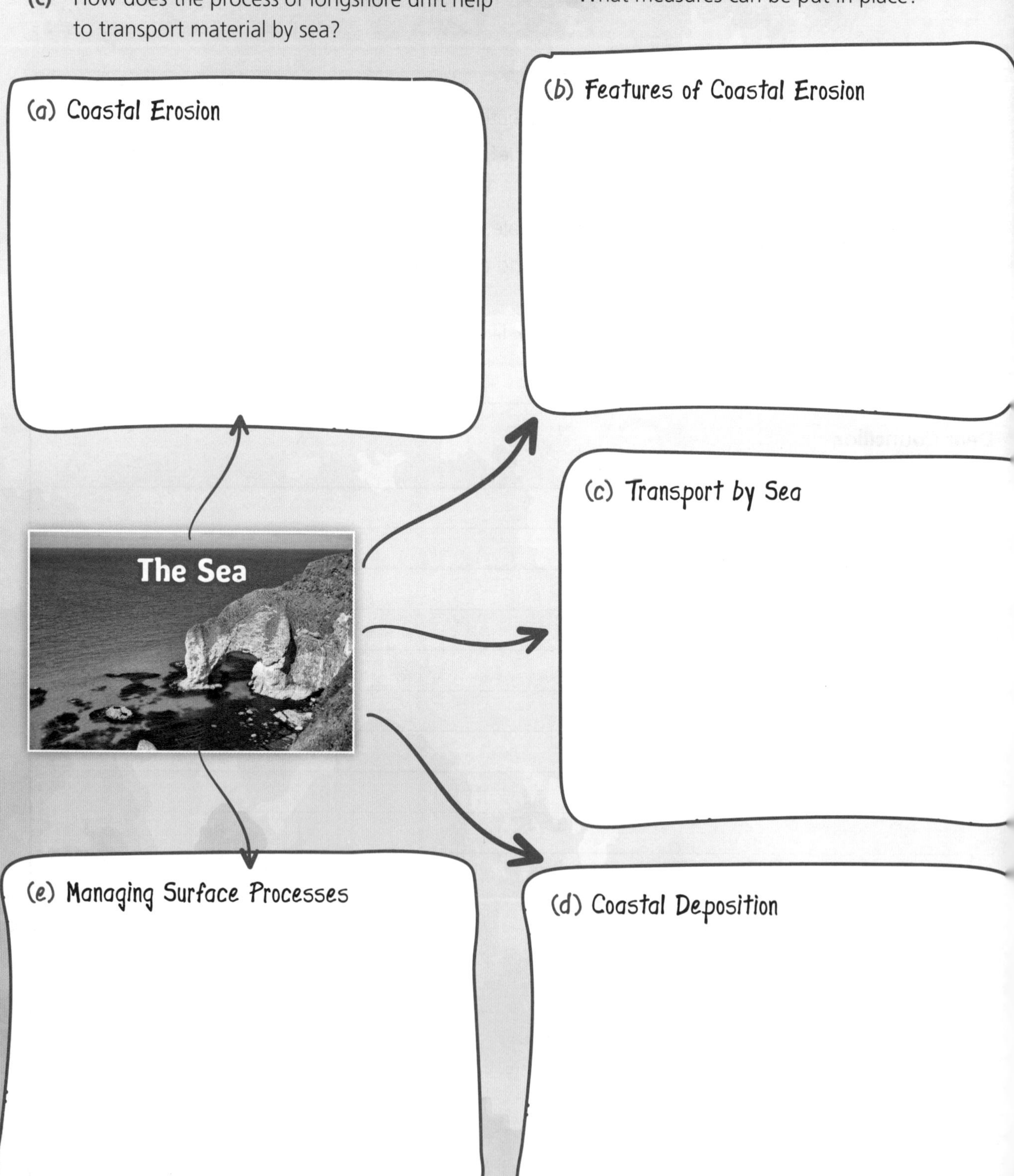

## NCCA Sample Question and Sample Answers

### Question 1

Below are a photograph taken from the top of Croagh Patrick, a mountain in Westport, Co. Mayo; and a map of the area seen in the photograph.

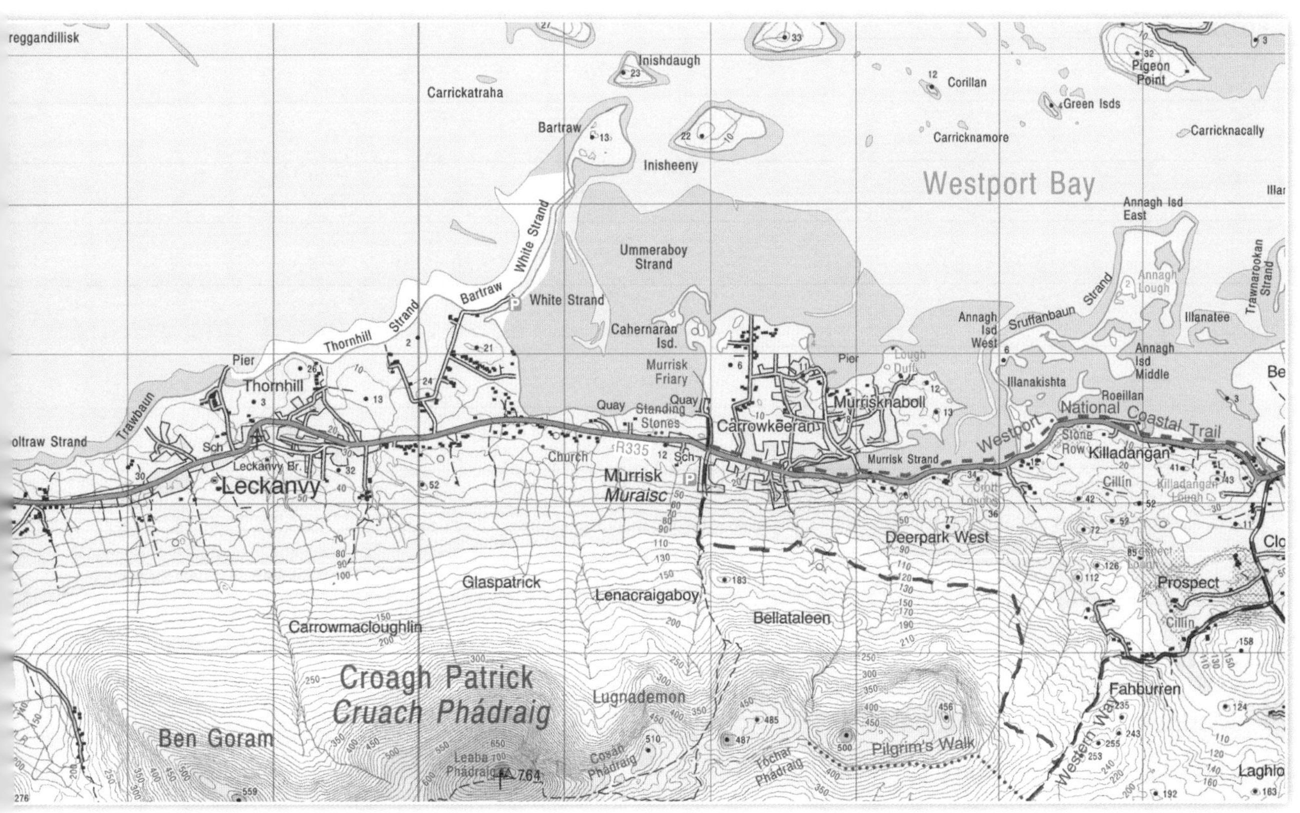

## GeoSkill

Here you are given an aerial photograph that corresponds to an area on the OS map.
By identifying a feature on the photograph, you can locate the same feature on the map.

**(i)** There is evidence of erosion and deposition in the photograph on page 133. **Circle** TWO examples of evidence from the photograph that support the statement above.

Waterfall    Beach    Meander    Sandbar

**(ii)** The photograph and map show evidence of glacial, weathering, marine and fluvial processes. Using THREE of these named processes, describe how the landscape has changed over time.

## Exam Hint

This question mentions glacial, weathering, marine and fluvial, so you can select any processes involved in those areas to answer this question. Look at the photograph and map – what features of these processes are visible to you? For example, how have marine processes had an impact? Can you see the sand spit or bay? As the question asks for evidence, make sure to give their position on the map/photograph.

Process 1: ______________________

______________________________________________

______________________________________________

______________________________________________

______________________________________________

Process 2: ______________________

______________________________________________

______________________________________________

______________________________________________

______________________________________________

Process 3: ______________________

______________________________________________

______________________________________________

______________________________________________

______________________________________________

## Remember!

Marine processes = Sea/Coastal
Fluvial processes = Rivers

## Question 2

You must set up an economic activity in the area shown in the photograph and map. What economic activity, i.e. business, industry, etc. would you set up? Use evidence from the photograph or map to explain the factors that would make this type of economic activity possible. [10 marks]

**Type of economic activity:** *Guided Hiking Business (Tertiary economic activity)*

*I have decided to set up a guided hiking business in Carrowkeeran, next to Murrisk Strand. The reasons for setting up this business and for selecting this location are:*

1. *The area of Carrowkeeran is flat land with a small town already established here. I could set up a small office here that would be used to book the hiking tours. There is a regional road, the R335, that travels right past this location. I could advertise my business along this route.*
2. *The Murrisk Strand area is a coastal site that tourists visit, so if I am located close by, I can meet tourists to make bookings. The aerial photograph was taken from high up on Croagh Patrick and the scenery below is beautiful. I can use images like this to promote my business to tourists who would enjoy this beautiful view.*
3. *Very importantly, I am selecting the location and business because of how close I will be to Croagh Patrick. This is the perfect upland area to bring tourists on hikes. The contour lines are tightly spaced and show a steep gradient with a peak of 764 m shown on the map.*
4. ________________________________________________________________

**Marks Awarded**

Name of economic activity = 2 marks

Explanation – statement of location = 2 marks

Development of reasons why, giving evidence = 2 + 2 + 2 (6 marks)

Total = 10 marks

This answer requires you to name the economic activity that you would set up. As it is a coastal region with an upland area close by, there are plenty of options. 2 marks are awarded for naming the activity.

We are awarded 2 marks for stating the location of where we would locate our business.

We then must give reasons with evidence for our business and location. It is important when you state the reason for your choice of site that it is always supported by specific evidence that can be seen on the map or photo. By looking closely at the map, we can see a grey shaded area to indicate a town. We can also see the brown shaded upland area for Croagh Patrick and the road network close by. Remember to use the map key to identify features if unsure.

Can you come up with another reason for setting up in this location?

# 13 Glaciation

In this section, the Learning Outcomes we will look at are: **1.5**, **1.10**, **2.7**, **2.9**

**Learning Checklist:**

- ☐ I can explain the main processes of glacial erosion – plucking, abrasion.
- ☐ I can discuss how people interact with glacial landscapes using an example that I have studied.
- ☐ I can describe how the processes of glacial erosion have formed unique features on the landscape such as U-shaped valleys, cirques (corries) and truncated spurs.
- ☐ I can read six-figure grid references and measure straight-line distance between two points on OS maps. I can identify physical features and recognise contour lines. I can identify features of glacial landscapes from photographs. I can draw a sketch map of an OS map at a scale of 1:50 000.
- ☐ I can describe how glaciers transport and deposit their load, resulting in the formation of features such as drumlins, erratics and moraines.

## Erosion by Glaciers

**1. (i) (a)** Below is a sketch of a cirque. Label the empty boxes, stating the erosional process that is occurring at each point.

Plucking | Abrasion | Freeze-thaw action

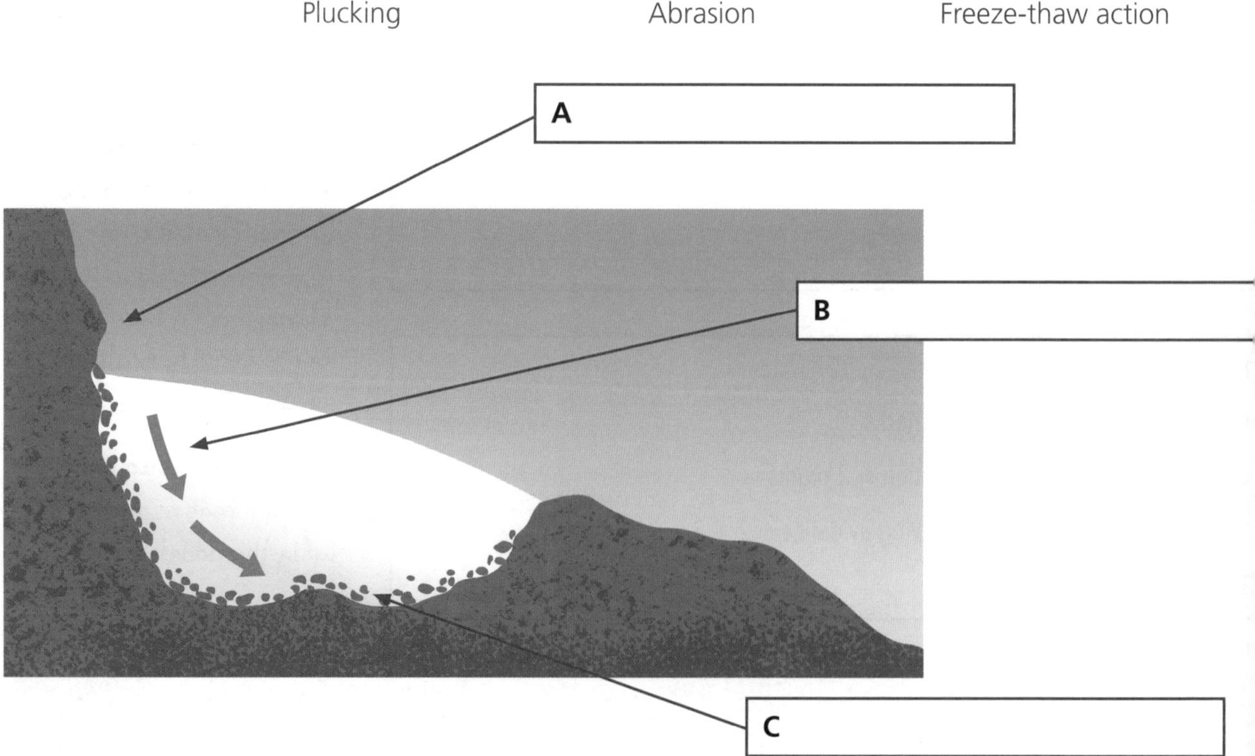

**(b)** Explain the difference between the processes occurring at B and C.

______________________________________________

______________________________________________

______________________________________________

______________________________________________

______________________________________________

______________________________________________

**(ii)** The diagram below shows a number of features of glacial erosion. Place the correct number for each feature next to its name on the table provided.

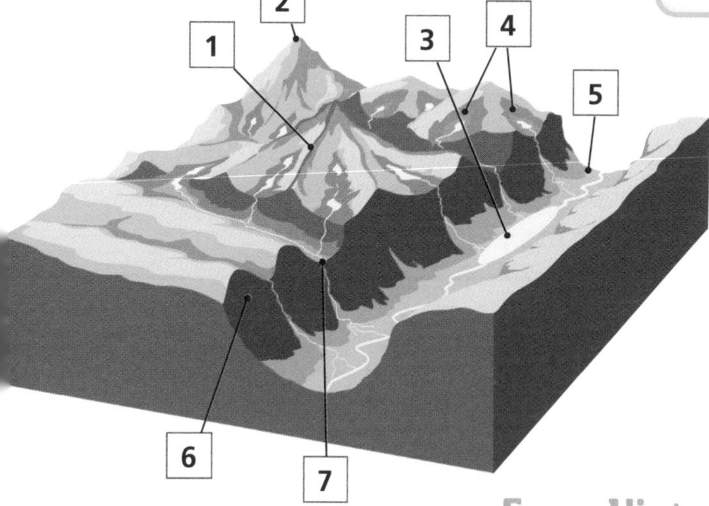


### Remember!

It is important to be able to label features from diagrams in your exam. Practise doing this as often as you can.

| No. | Feature |
|---|---|
| | Arete |
| | Truncated spur |
| | Pyramidal peak |
| | Glaciated valley (U-shaped) |
| | Ribbon lake |
| | Corrie |
| | Hanging valley |

**(iii)** Explain each of the following terms. The first one has been completed for you:

### Exam Hint

Prepare brief definitions for physical features. Read over these as you look at the features before the exam.

| Term | Explanation |
|---|---|
| Pyramidal peak | A steep-sided, pyramid-shaped mountain that was eroded on all sides by many cirques. Freeze-thaw action is also very active here. |
| Arete | |
| Truncated spur | |
| U-shaped valley | |

Continued on the next page →

| Term | Explanation |
|---|---|
| Paternoster lake | |
| Hanging valley | |
| Cirque | |

**(iv)** The OS map below shows an area of the MacGillycuddy's Reeks, Co. Kerry, that has been shaped by the processes of glacial erosion. Look at the map and answer the questions that follow.

**GeoSkill**

When given an OS map, make sure to use the legend provided. Here we see contour lines very closely spaced together and brown shading. What does this tell us?

Look at the names of features located on the map.

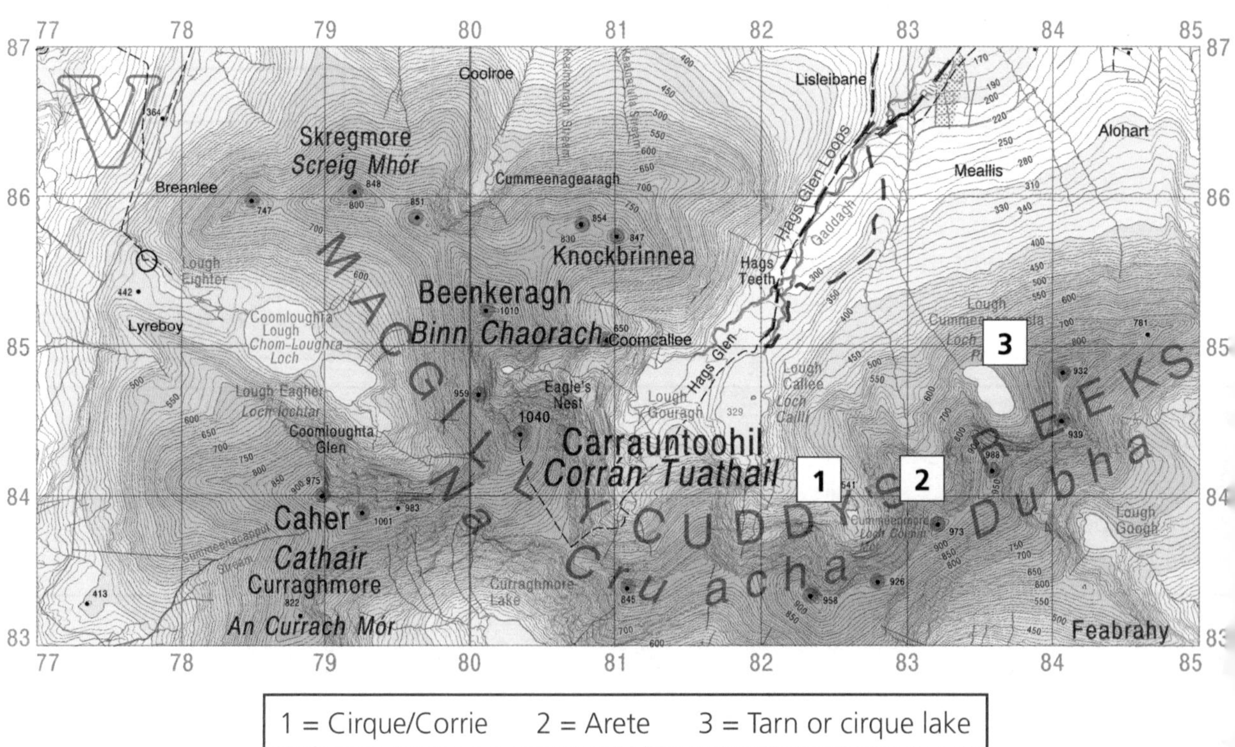


1 = Cirque/Corrie 2 = Arete 3 = Tarn or cirque lake

**(a)** There are three features of glacial erosion numbered 1, 2, 3 on the map above. Select one of these features and provide its six-figure grid reference below.

Feature: ________________________________

Six-figure grid reference: ________________________

**Remember!**

**L** Letter

**E** Easting →

**N** Northing ↑

**(b)** Describe how the processes of glacial erosion helped in the formation of your named feature in part (a) above. You may use a diagram to support your answer.

**Remember!**

**F E E D**

**Exam Hint**

There are important key terms that you can include here.

- Plucking
- Abrasion
- Friction
- Freeze-thaw action

Remember to describe how they have helped to form this feature.

**Diagram:**

**2.** **Image A** **Image B**

## Remember!

Here you are comparing two images to identify the signs of glacial erosion.

**(i)** Which of the images above are taken in an area that has been impacted by glacial erosion? Tick (✓) the correct box.

Image A ☐ Image B ☐

**(ii)** Name the feature of glacial erosion shown in part (i) above.

_______________________________________________

**(iii)** Review the image opposite of a glacial feature and answer the questions that follow.

**(a)** Name the glacial feature shown in the photograph.

_______________________________________________

_______________________________________________

**(b)** Look at the rocks closest to you in the foreground of the image. What processes may be at work on these rocks?

_______________________________________________

_______________________________________________

## Exam Hint

Look at the location and shape of the rocks in the foreground. What processes are likely to be taking place in this upland area?

# Transport and Deposition by Moving Ice

**3.** **(i)** Name the features of glacial deposition A, B, C and D in the diagram below and, in the space provided on the opposite page, write a description of each feature. One has been completed for you.

Medial moraine Terminal moraine Recessional moraine Lateral moraine

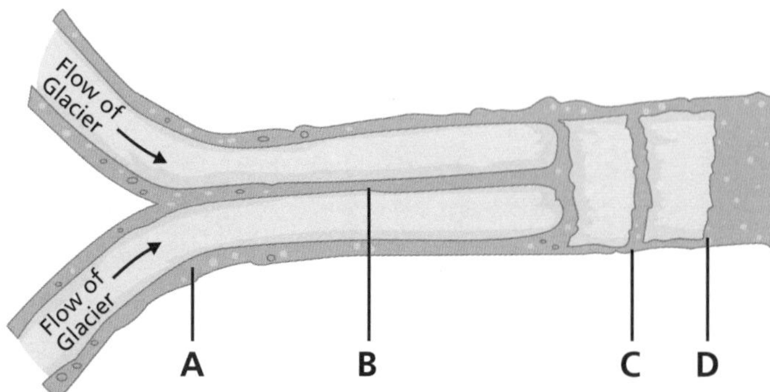


## Remember!

To help you remember the location of each moraine, break up the work. Example: Medial = in the middle. What might terminal be? What about lateral? Look up the words in a dictionary.

| Feature | Name | Description of feature |
|---|---|---|
| A | | |
| B | Medial moraine | This is found in the middle of a glacier when two glaciers have merged. The two lateral moraines on each glacier met and combined. |
| C | | |
| D | | |

**(ii)** Drumlins are oval-shaped hills that are formed from deposits of boulder clay. They are a feature of glacial deposition.

**(a)** Place an arrow on the image below to show the direction of glacial flow as the drumlin was being formed.

**(b)** Drumlins occur in swarms known as: ______________________________

**(c)** Below are the steps involved in the formation of a drumlin. Place the steps in the correct order of formation by numbering them 1, 2, 3, etc.

| Steps in the formation of a drumlin | Number |
|---|---|
| The gentle slope of the drumlin points to the direction in which the ice was travelling. The steep side is the side from which the glacier advanced. | |
| The glacier retreats, but then it advances again. | |
| Glacial ice drops and deposits boulder clay in large irregular heaps on the land. | |
| As the glacier advances again, it begins to shape and smooth the boulder clay into more rounded, oval-shaped hills. | |

**(iii)** You are on a walk with friends in the Burren and you come across a large granite boulder that is out of character for the area. Explain to your friends what this boulder is and how it made its way to this limestone area.

_______________

_______________

_______________

_______________

_______________

_______________

_______________

**4.** Read the article below and answer the questions that follow.

**Glaciers Melting at Increasing Rate**

Scientists say human-driven global warming is the cause of the increasing loss of glaciers. Rising temperatures have nearly doubled the speed at which the world's glaciers are melting, which will impact coastal regions across the globe and create flows of meltwater, affecting hundreds of millions of people who live downstream.

Melting glaciers add to rising sea levels, which in turn increase coastal erosion and raise storm surges as warming air and ocean temperatures create more frequent and intense coastal storms, like hurricanes and typhoons.

As sea ice and glaciers melt and oceans warm, ocean currents will continue to disrupt weather patterns worldwide. Local economies that thrive on the fishing industry will be affected as warmer waters change where and when fish spawn. Coastal communities will continue to face huge disaster recovery bills as flooding becomes more frequent and storms become more intense.

People are not the only ones impacted. In the Arctic, as sea ice melts, wildlife like walruses are losing their home and polar bears are spending more time on land, causing higher rates of conflict between people and bears.

**Adapted from World Wildlife Fund**

**Exam Hint**

You may be given short articles to read in the exam. It is useful to use a highlighter to highlight key points connected to the questions asked.

**(i)** What do scientists say is behind the increasing loss of glaciers?

_______________

**(ii)** Describe two potential economic impacts on humans due to the increased melting of glaciers.

**(iii)** According to the article, explain one environmental impact that this continued loss of glacial ice will have.

**(iv)** Describe one measure that your family could take to help reduce their carbon footprint.

### xam Hint

In the exam, you may be given a question in a reading comprehension that is not directly linked to the article given (such as part (iv) above). You must use your geographical knowledge to answer these questions.

## laciation and People

Glendalough, Co. Wicklow, is a glacial valley. Review the OS map extract of the area on the following page and answer the questions that follow.

**(i)** Draw a sketch map of the area shown on the map. On your sketch, include the following:

- A nature reserve
- An area of forestry
- The Glenealo River and upper lake
- An area suitable for tourists
- The route of the R755

### Remember!

Drawing a sketch map:

- Always place a title and north arrow on your sketch.
- Place all items asked in the question into the key.
- Sketch in pencil.

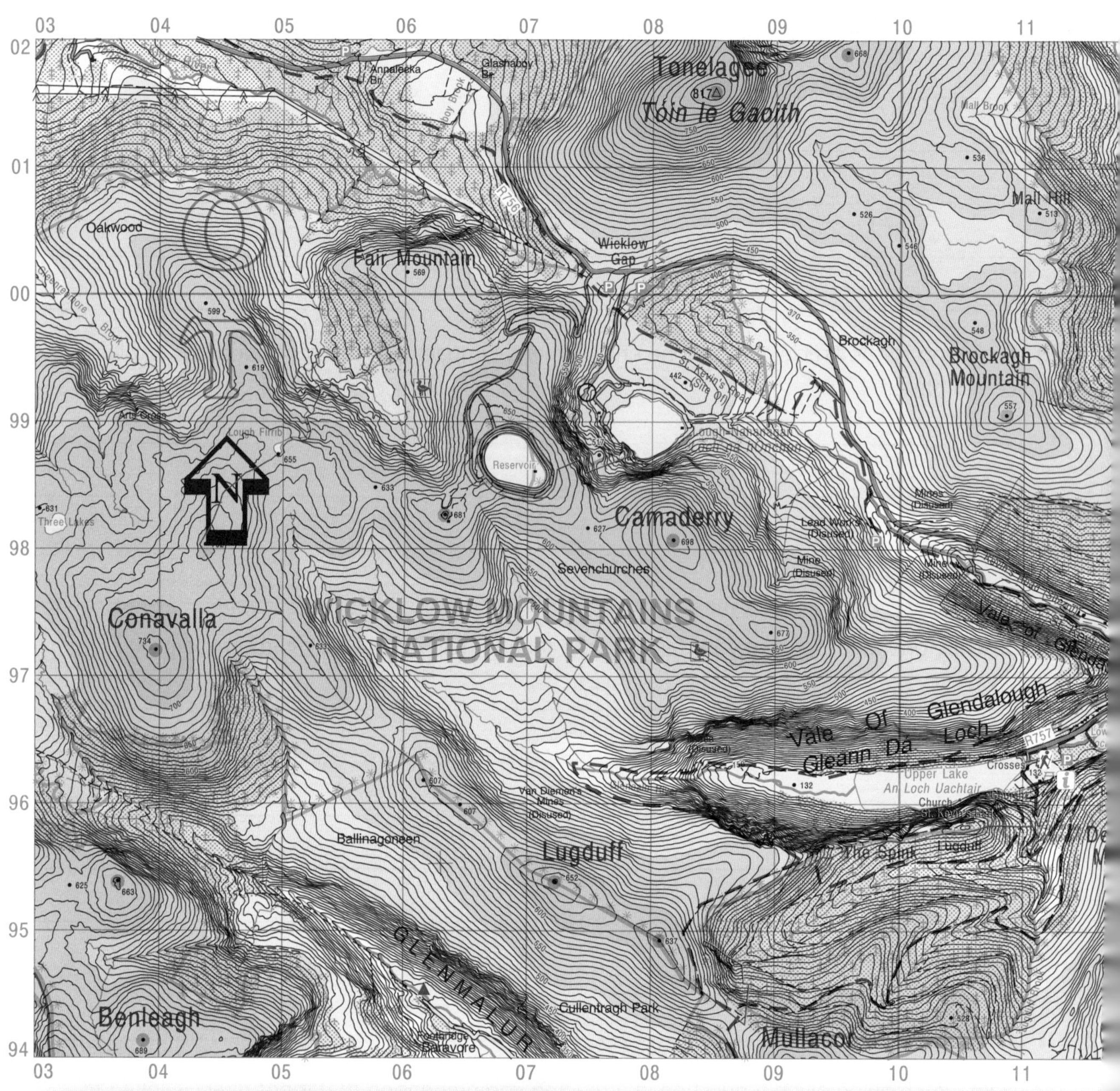

Tonelagee
Toin le Gaoith
Fair Mountain
Oakwood
Wicklow Gap
Brockagh
Brockagh Mountain
Mall Hill
Camaderry
Sevenchurches
Reservoir
Conavalla
WICKLOW MOUNTAINS NATIONAL PARK
Three Lakes
Vale of Glendalough
Gleann Dá Loch
Upper Lake
An Loch Uachtair
Ballinagoneen
Lugduff
Van Diemen's Mines (Disused)
Benleagh
GLENMALURE
Cullentragh Park
Mullacor
The Spink
Lead Works (Disused)
Mines (Disused)
R756
R757

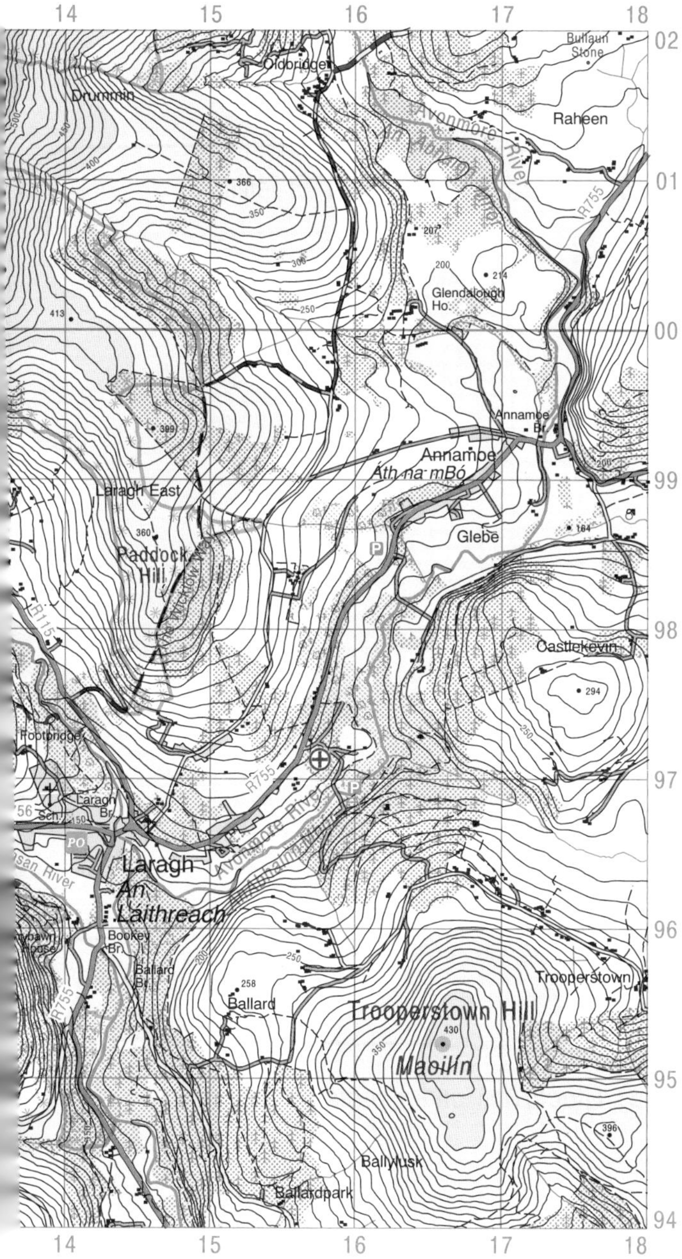

**(ii)** Using evidence from the map, describe two ways that this glaciated valley has been used by locals or visitors to the area.

Use 1:

Use 2:

**GeoSkill**

When asked for evidence, give a grid reference to highlight your point.

**(iii)** The glacial lakes in Glendalough provide natural reservoirs for the generation of hydroelectric power. Explain two advantages of hydroelectric power.

**Exam Hint**

Consider sustainability here!

**1.**

**2.**

**v)** Describe two objections that might be made to the development of a hydroelectric power station.

**1.**

**2.**

**Remember!**

When asked for evidence, give a grid reference to highlight your point.

**Answer the questions to complete the mind map. This will support your revision.**

## Prompt Questions for Mind Map

**(a)** Describe the two main processes of glacial erosion.

Draw a mini sketch to show these at work.

**(b)** Name the features of glacial erosion.

Where can examples of each be found?

**(c)** Name the features of glacial deposition and transportation.

Where can examples of each be found? What do they look like on the landscape?

**(d)** How might melting glaciers have an impact on the environment? On humans? On the economy of areas impacted by melting glaciers?

**(e)** How do people use and interact with areas that were glaciated or still are glaciated?

Discuss tourism, hydroelectric power and agriculture. Use a case study.

(a) Processes of Glacial Erosion

(e) Glaciation and People

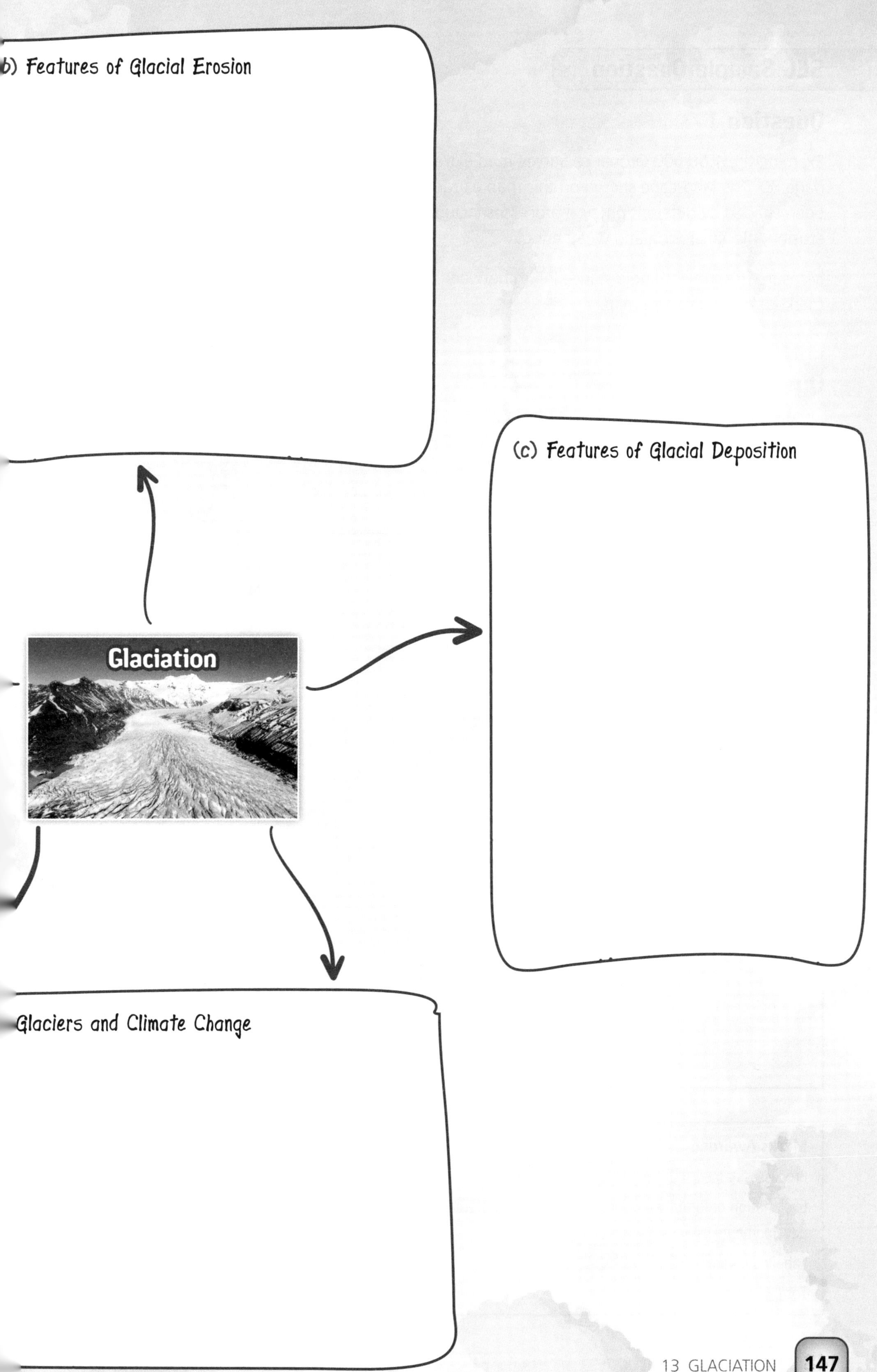
b) Features of Glacial Erosion
(c) Features of Glacial Deposition
Glaciation
Glaciers and Climate Change

## SEC Sample Question

### Question 1

Examine the 1:50 000 Ordnance Survey map extract on page 80. The landscape shown on this map extract has been shaped by different physical processes including river erosion, glacial erosion and weathering.

Measure the straight-line distance in km between the points marked A and B on the map.

**GeoSkill**

To measure the straight-line distance between two points, use a piece of paper to mark the distance between point A and B. Then place the marked piece of paper onto the scale bar on the map legend to read the measurement in km.

---

### Question 2

On a hike through the area shown on the map extract on page 80, your friend asks you how this landscape was formed. Write the answer you would give to explain how the processes of glacial erosion or the processes of river erosion shaped the landscape shown on the map extract. Use a diagram to support your explanation. Refer to the map extract in your answer. [10 marks]

**Chosen processes:**

*I have chosen the processes of glacial erosion.*

**Diagram:**

*The answer requires you to describe how the processes of glacial erosion OR river erosion have helped in the formation of this landscape. Here we will select glacial.*

*Begin by stating the processes of glacial erosion that have had an impact on this landscape (e.g. plucking, abrasion).*

*Next, you must develop you answer by explaining, using map evidence, the features of this type of erosion that are visible on the OS map. Can you identify a corrie, tarn, arrete, etc.?*

*Finally, describe how the processes of erosion have created the features that you have identified on the landscape.*

*Space has been left for you to draw a diagram to illustrate your answer.*

**Marks Awarded**

Processes named = 1 mark

Explanation of formation using map evidence (statement = 2 marks + development [1 + 1 + 1 + 1 + 1])

Labelled diagram = 2 marks

Total = 10 marks

# 14 Measuring and Forecasting Weather

In this section, the Learning Outcome we will look at is: **1.8**

**Learning Checklist:**

- ☐ I can name the different conditions recorded to produce a weather forecast.
- ☐ I can interpret information from weather maps, charts and graphs.
- ☐ I can name and describe the different instruments used to measure these conditions.

## Conditions Recorded to Produce a Weather Forecast

1. (i) Examine the weather maps below labelled A–D. In the space provided below, identify each type of weather and state if it is mild or severe for the country of Ireland.

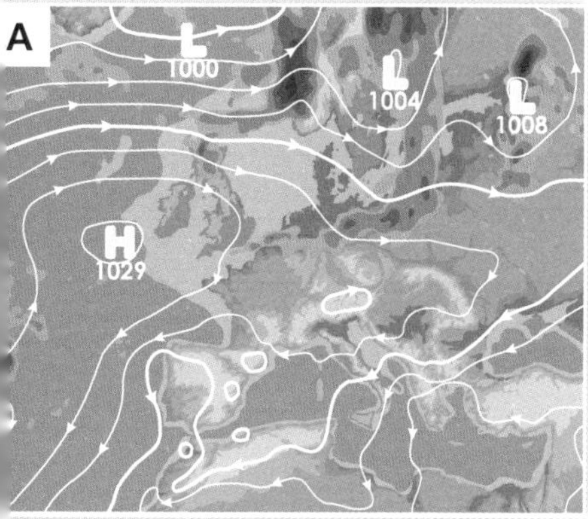

A

L 1000
L 1004
L 1008
H 1029

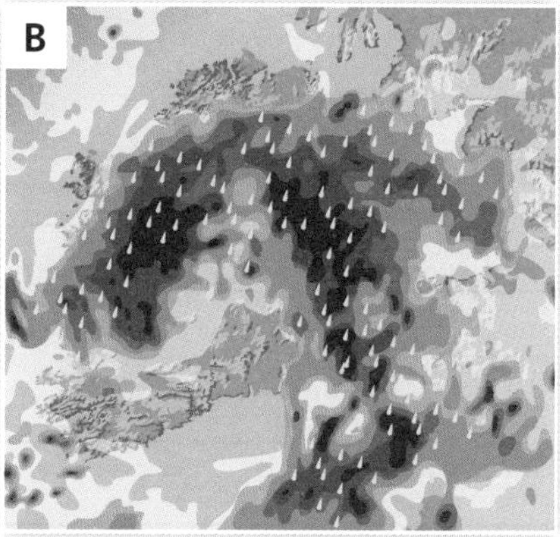

B

**Remember!**

This question is checking your knowledge of another Learning Outcome – Severe Weather. Do you remember its definition?

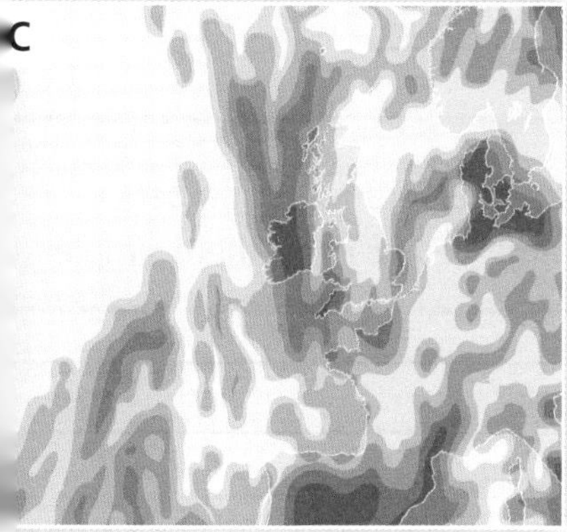

C

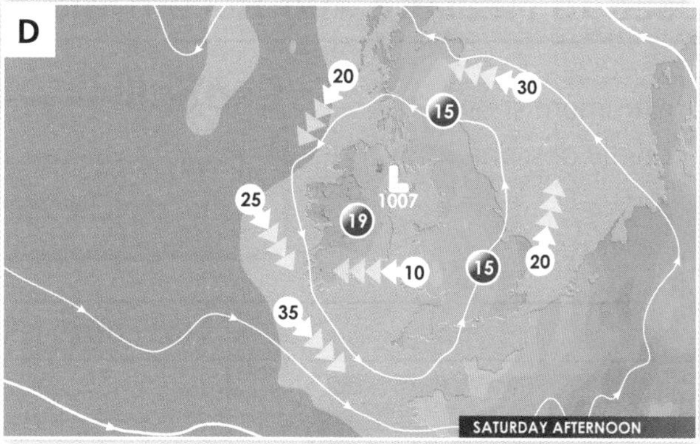

D

20
30
15
25
L 1007
19
10
15
20
35
SATURDAY AFTERNOON

| List types of weather here | Mild or severe? |
|---|---|
| A: ______ | ______ |
| B: ______ | ______ |
| C: ______ | ______ |
| D: ______ | ______ |

**(ii)** Answer the following short questions.

**(a)** What is weather?

______________________________________________

______________________________________________

______________________________________________

**(b)** What facility is used to observe and gather data on weather conditions?

______________________________________________

**(c)** List any three types of weather data or information gathered at these facilities.

- ______________________________
- ______________________________
- ______________________________

**(d)** List three jobs that are very dependent on the weather forecast.

- ______________________________
- ______________________________
- ______________________________

**Exam Hint**

Short questions are common in your exam papers.

Remember to answer the question asked. Only give relevant information and use examples where possible.

**(e)** Explain the term 'climate' using the key words below.

Long-term pattern    Area/region    30 years    Average weather

______________________________________________

______________________________________________

______________________________________________

______________________________________________

**(f)** What is Ireland's climate?

______________________________________________

## Instruments Used to Measure and Record the Weather

**2. (i)** Name the instrument shown below and briefly describe how it works.

**GeoSkill**

Always attempt sketches/diagrams with a pencil. Label sketches/diagrams clearly. Keep them simple.

| **Instrument:** | **How does it work?** |
|---|---|
| | |

## Exam Hint

The following questions are asking to sketch a suitable diagram to accompany the explanation and to explain how an instrument works. Keep your explanations simple and use bullet points.

**(ii)** Sketch, label and name the instrument in the space below based on the description provided.

| **Instrument:** | **How does it work?** |
| --- | --- |
| | • This instrument is used to measure precipitation.<br>• It is buried in the ground in an open area.<br>• This instrument consists of an overflow cylinder with a graduated funnel inside. |

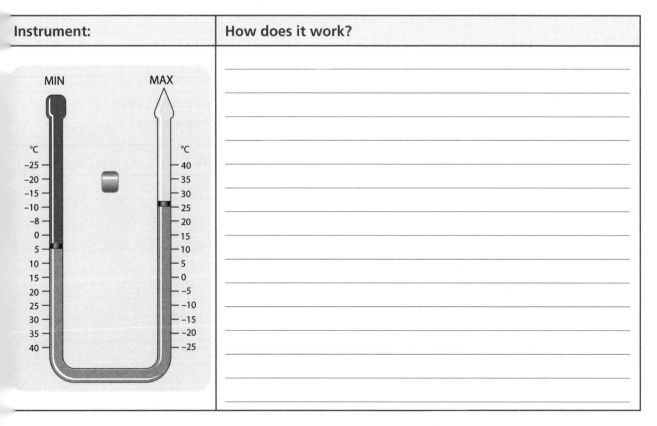

**(iii)** Name the instrument shown below and briefly describe how it works.

| **Instrument:** | **How does it work?** |
| --- | --- |
| MIN MAX<br>°C °C<br>-25 40<br>-20 35<br>-15 30<br>-10 25<br>-8 20<br>0 15<br>5 10<br>10 5<br>15 0<br>20 -5<br>25 -10<br>30 -15<br>35 -20<br>40 -25 | |

**(iv)** Label Instrument 1 below and give a brief description of how it works and what weather it records. Sketch and label Instrument 2 based on the description provided below.

| Instrument 1 | Instrument 2 |
|---|---|
| W N S E | |
| **How does it work?** | **How does it work?** |
| | • This instrument has three cups that catch the wind as they spin atop a long poll.<br>• The faster the wind, the faster the cups move.<br>• The number of times the cups rotate fully is used to calculate the speed of the wind. |

**(v)** A wet and dry bulb hygrometer is used to measure temperature and humidity. In the space below sketch and label this instrument and briefly describe how it works.

| Wet and Dry Bulb Hygrometer | How does it work? |
|---|---|
| | |

**(vi)** This paper is part of an instrument called a Campbell-Stokes Recorder.

**(a)** Briefly explain how this instrument records daily sunshine.

______________________________

______________________________

______________________________

______________________________

______________________________

______________________________

______________________________

______________________________

**(b)** Approximately how many hours of sunshine has this piece of paper recorded for this particular day? ______________________________

## Cloud Formations

Examine the three types of cloud formation in the image below. Describe the look of each cloud and the type of weather they usually bring in the space below.

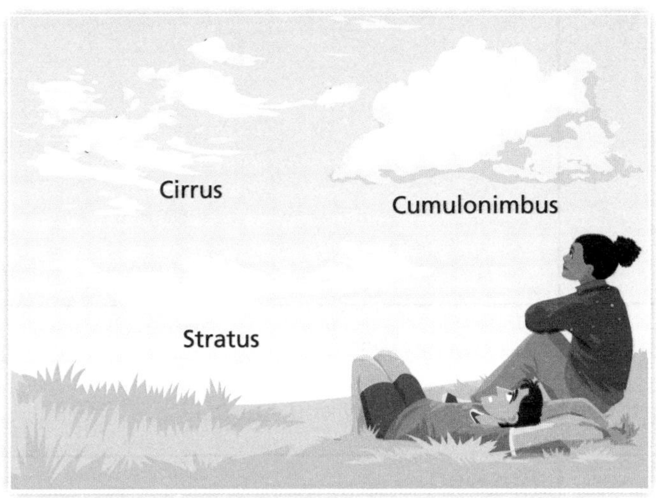


**GeoSkill**

Use the images of each cloud as evidence to support your explanation of each cloud type.

| | |
|---|---|
| Cirrus clouds | |
| Cumulonimbus clouds | |
| Stratus clouds | |

# Climate Graphs

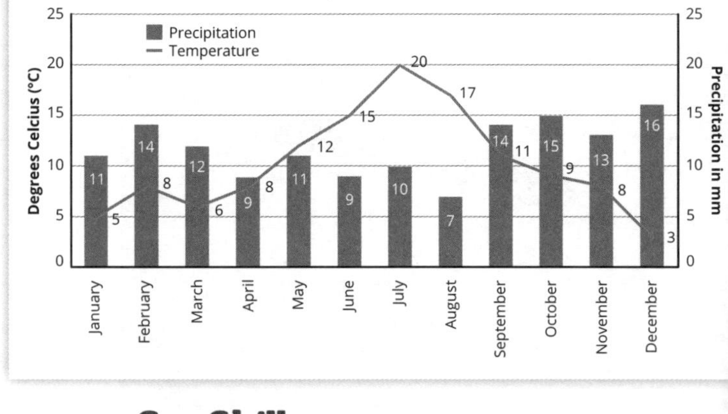


**4.** Climate graphs are used to illustrate the average precipitation and average temperature of an area over the 12 months of the year.

Answer the short questions below.

**(i)** Which month had the highest precipitation?

______________________________

**(ii)** Which month had the lowest precipitation?

______________________________

**(iii)** Calculate the average precipitation for Ireland for the months of January, February and March.

## GeoSkill

When reading weather charts, look at the labels of the x-axis and both y-axes. Look for information on both precipitation and temperature for your answer.

| **Workings** | **Answer:** |
| --- | --- |
| | |

**(iv)** Which month recorded the highest temperature and what was it? ______________________________

**(v)** Calculate the average temperature for the months of June, July and August.

| **Workings** | **Answer:** |
| --- | --- |
| | |

**(vi)** The table below shows average temperature and precipitation for a 12-month period. Use this information to model your own climate graph, similar to the one above.

| **Month** | Jan | Feb | Mar | Apr | May | June | July | Aug | Sept | Oct | Nov | Dec |
| --- | --- | --- | --- | --- | --- | --- | --- | --- | --- | --- | --- | --- |
| **Temperature** | 3 | 5 | 8 | 10 | 18 | 22 | 20 | 14 | 7 | 9 | 7 | 5 |
| **Precipitation** | 15 | 15 | 10 | 12 | 9 | 12 | 10 | 9 | 14 | 15 | 12 | 19 |

### Exam Dictionary

**Model:** Generate a mathematical representation. In this question, you must draw a graph.

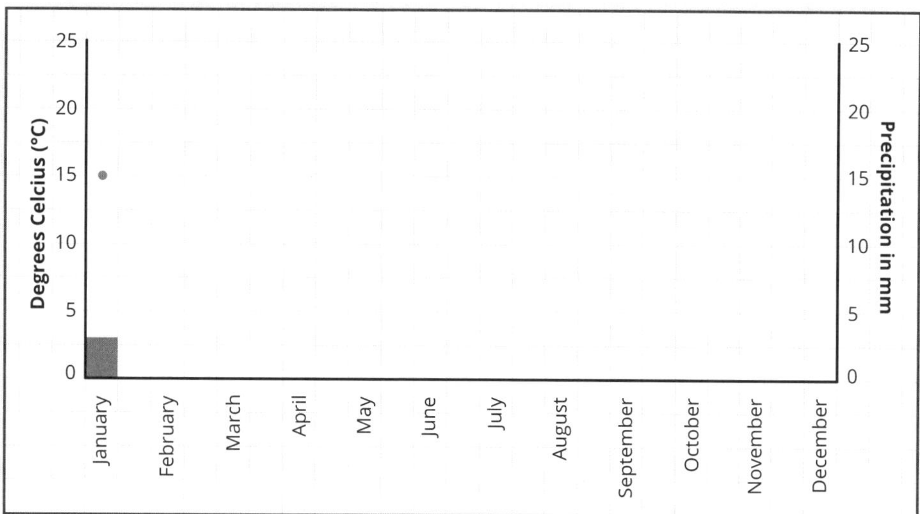


## Reading Weather Maps

### Exam Hint

To answer this question, write short detailed points on each weather type. Use the information on each weather map to help your answer.

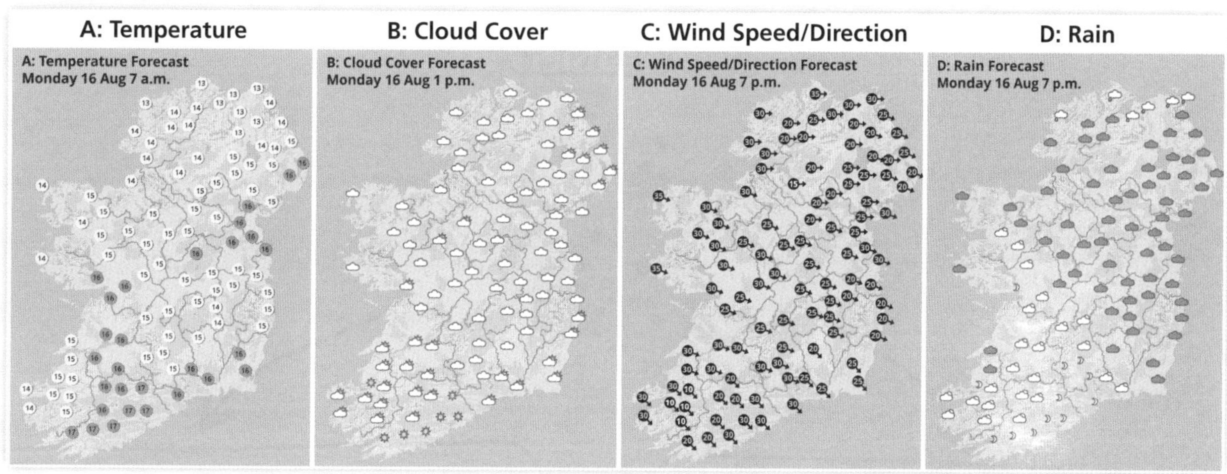


(i) Weather maps A–D show the weather forecast for Ireland on 16 August from 7 a.m. to 7 p.m. Study each image carefully. Write a detailed account of what the weather was like on this particular day, focusing on **temperature, cloud cover, wind speed/direction** and **rain.**

(ii) Write a smaller report here on the weather specific to your local area. Mention two pieces of equipment used specifically to record the weather in your local area.

**Answer the questions to complete the mind map. This will support your revision.**

**Prompt Questions for Mind Map**

**(a)** Can you recall **how** conditions are recorded to create a weather forecast?

**(b)** Are you able to list three instruments used to record weather and what they measure?

**(c)** What are the differences between weather and severe weather?

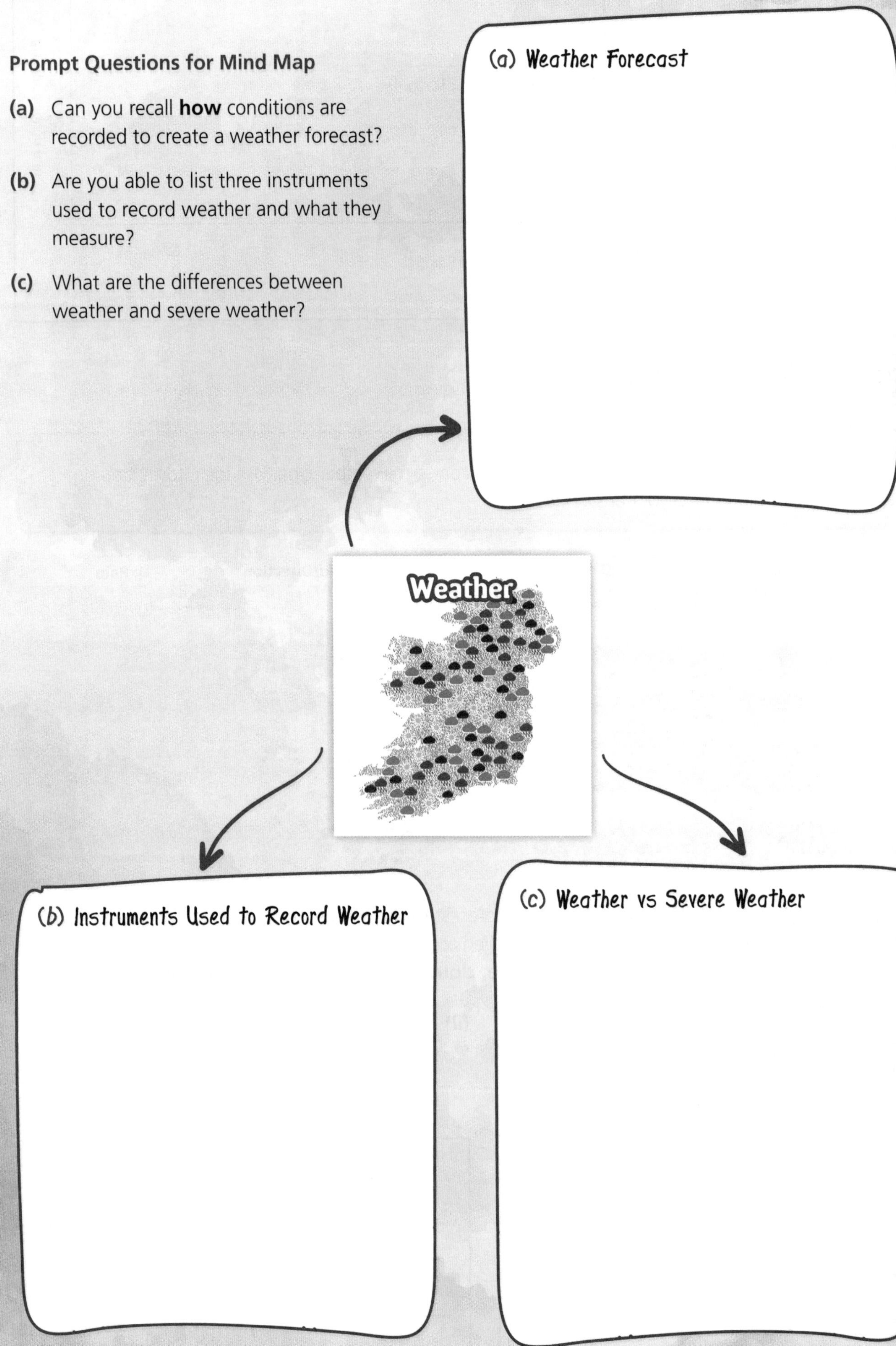

## SEC Sample Question 2021

### Question 1

Examine the table below showing monthly rainfall at Malin Head in the first six months of 2019 and answer each of the following questions.

| | Jan | Feb | Mar | Apr | May | June |
|---|---|---|---|---|---|---|
| **Rainfall (mm)** | 83 | 60 | 139 | 50 | 80 | 68 |

**i)** Complete the bar chart below using the information from the table for February, April and May.

**ii)** How much rain fell in March 2019 at Malin Head? Use the correct unit in your answer.

_______________________________________________

**Exam Hint**

When completing a bar chart/graph, always use a pencil, and draw carefully.

Read the questions/ information carefully.

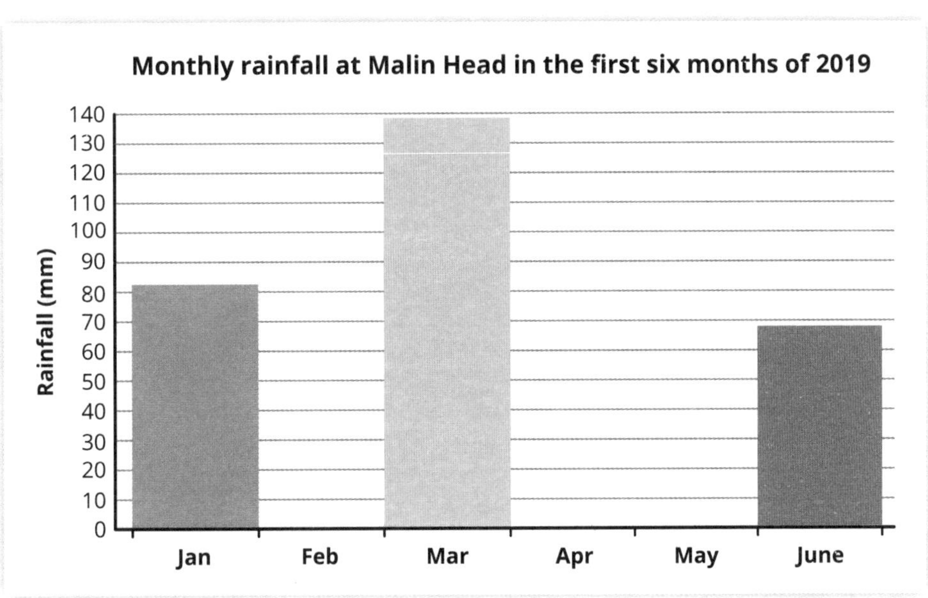


**iii)** In which month did the lowest amount of rain fall at Malin Head?

_______________________________________________

**iv)** Calculate the mean monthly rainfall at Malin Head for the first six months of 2019. Use the correct unit in your answer.

**Exam Hint**

Take your time with your rough work.

**Optional rough work:**

**Answer:** _______________________________________________

# 15 Severe Weather

In this section, the Learning Outcomes we will look at are: **1.7**, **2.8**

**Learning Checklist:**

- ☐ I understand what severe weather is.
- ☐ I can explain how hurricanes form and how they are categorised.
- ☐ I can describe the impacts of hurricanes on an area.
- ☐ I can interpret information from OS maps and images.
- ☐ I can draw graphs.

## What Is Severe Weather?

**Remember!**

This question is asking for information on another Learning Outcome – Weather.

**1.** **(i)** Can you explain the key differences between weather and severe weather in the space below?

Weather: ______________________________

______________________________

______________________________

Severe weather: ______________________________

______________________________

______________________________

**(ii)** List four examples of weather you are familiar with.

**1.** ______________________________

**2.** ______________________________

**3.** ______________________________

**4.** ______________________________

**(iii)** Tropical storms are known by three separate names in three different regions of the world. Complete the table below. One name and region has been completed for you.

| Name | Region |
|---|---|
| Hurricane | USA/Caribbean |
| | |
| | |

**(iv)** A Category 3 hurricane, with wind speed of 178–200 km/hr, has made land on the Galway coastline at the X on the map below. The hurricane is predicted to travel in a north-east direction. Make a list of three facilities/ amenities that may be impacted by this hurricane, ensuring to give a six-figure grid reference for each.

> **GeoSkill**
>
> **LEN** for the grid reference:
> **L**etter
> **E**asting
> **N**orthing

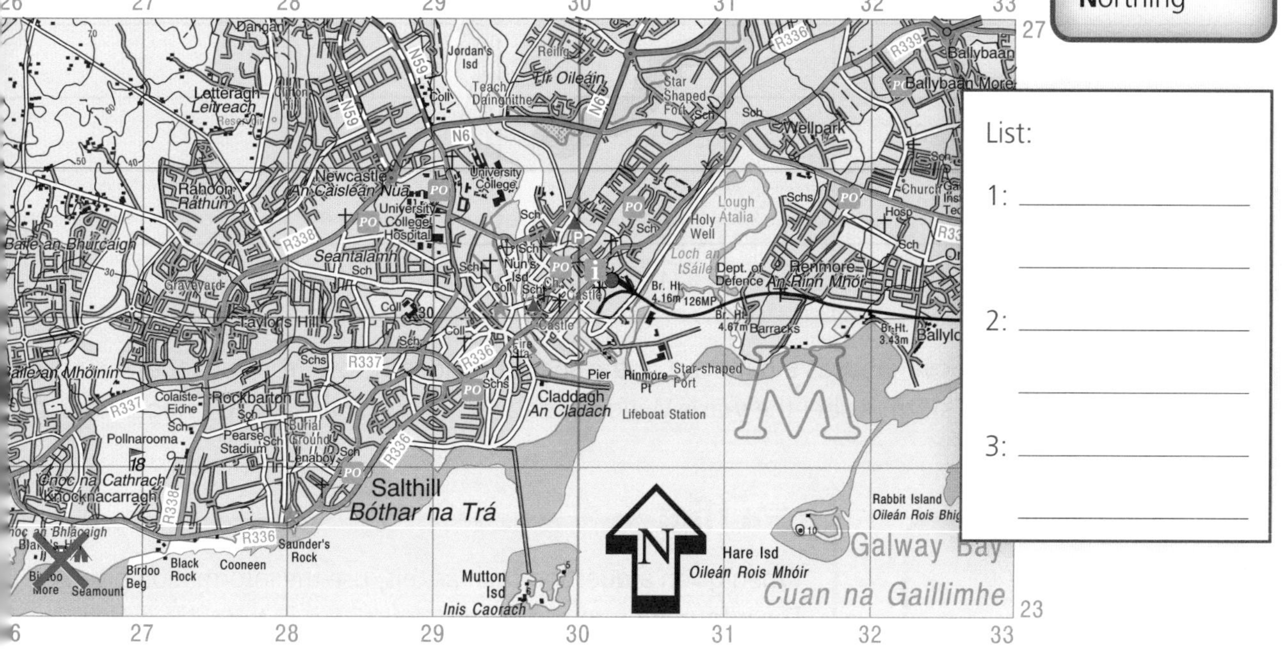


List:

1: ______________________

______________________

2: ______________________

______________________

3: ______________________

______________________

## Hurricane Formation and Categorisation

**(i)** Use the blank space below to explain how hurricanes form. Use as many of the key words below as you can. You can sketch diagrams with labels to help. You do not have to use all of the space provided.

Eye | Warm ocean water | Air condenses | Wind speed increases | Coriolis effect

> **GeoSkill**
>
> Always use a pencil for sketching. Keep pens for colouring or shading. Label diagrams. Draw them neatly.

**(ii)** The table below shows five hurricanes, the years they hit and their speed.

Fill in the category of each hurricane based on your understanding of the Saffir–Simpson scale.

| Name of Hurricane | Year | Speed of Wind km/h | Category |
|---|---|---|---|
| Hurricane Donna | 1960 | 241 | |
| Hurricane Charley | 1998 | 163 | |
| Hurricane Meredith | 2005 | 120 | |
| Hurricane Aladdin | 2010 | 194 | |
| Hurricane Benedict | 2017 | 211 | |

**(iii)** Represent the above table as a bar chart in the space provided below. You can label the x-axis the name of the storm. Label the y-axis Wind Speed. Within each bar say the category of each storm 1–5.

**GeoSkill**

When completing or drawing graphs, always use a pencil. Label each axis clearly.

**Exam Hint**

When given a question such as this, use the information given. The information to answer this question is in the table above. Use all the information provided, including the information you filled in yourself.

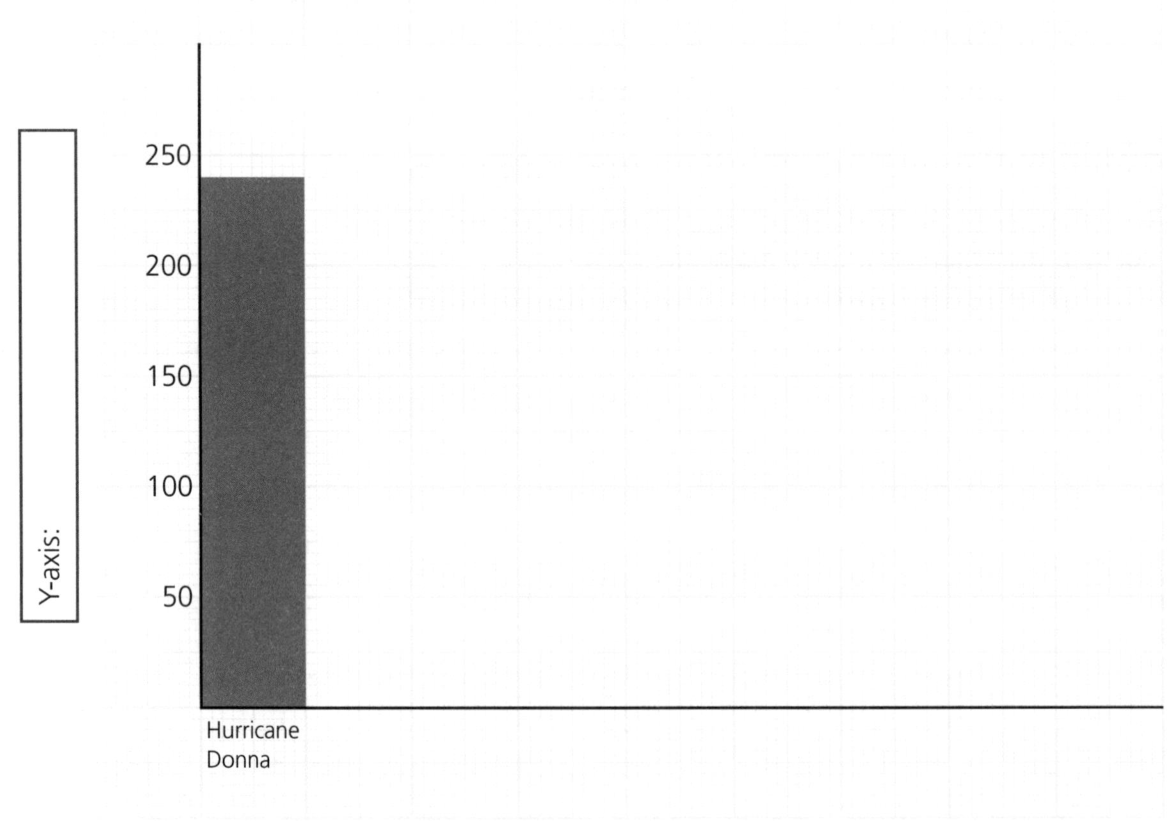

## The Impacts of Hurricanes on an Area

3. Use the space below to complete a report on a hurricane you have studied.

**Exam Hint**

Use the prompts in each heading to help.

### Case Study

The origins of the hurricane: where was it formed?

Economic impacts of the hurricane on the area it made land:

Where did it do most damage?

Wind speed and category:

Hurricane name here:

Social impacts:

Emergency response to the hurricane: what organisations (government and non-government) helped?

**Answer the questions to complete the mind map. This will support your revision.**

**Prompt Questions for Mind Map**

**(a)** Define the terms 'weather' and 'severe weather' and explain the difference between them.

**(b)** How are hurricane formed? How are hurricanes categorised?

**(c)** Name a case study that shows the impact of a hurricane on an area. Where and when did it take place?

(a) Weather and Severe Weather

(b) Hurricane Formation and Categorisation

(c) Impact of a Hurricane on an Area

## SEC Sample Exam Question with Answers

### Question 1

**(a)** Name **one** example of a significant weather event you have studied. [3 marks]

*Hurricane Matthew*

**(b)** When did the weather event happen? [3 marks]

*2016*

**(c)** Name a location that was affected by this weather event. [3 marks]

*Haiti and Cuba*

**(d)** Name a weather instrument that was used to gather data during this event and say what it measures. [3 marks each]

Weather instrument: *Anemometer*

What it measures: *Wind speed*

**(e)** Explain how the weather event you named in part (a) was formed. Use at least one diagram in your answer. [9 marks]

**Exam Dictionary**

**Explain:** Give a detailed account, including reasons or causes.

*urricanes form over warm ocean water found in the tropical reas of the world. Warm, moist air rises; as it rises, it begins to ool. The air begins to change back into a liquid.*

*s the air condenses, it releases heat which powers the hurricane. hen the wind speed reaches 120 km/h, the storm is officially belled a tropical storm.*

*everal of these storms can join together. This draws even more ater up from the ocean. The storm develops an 'eye' in its iddle where it is calm.*

*he storm is carried across the ocean by winds, getting stronger it moves.*

There are 6 marks going for your explanation. Give as much detail as you can. The examiner will read your answer as if reading about hurricanes for the first time. Your diagram(s) should be drawn in pencil and labelled clearly to achieve the full 3 marks.

**Diagram:**

Attempt to draw how a hurricane is formed based on the description above. Remember to label your diagrams clearly. Use only pencil to draw.

# 16 Global Climates

In this section, the Learning Outcome we will look at is: **1.8**

**Learning Checklist:**

- ☐ I can explain what climate is.
- ☐ I can list and explain the factors affecting Ireland's climate.
- ☐ I can organise global climates into their three main types.
- ☐ I can interpret information from charts and images.

## What Is Climate?

**1.** **(i)** Explain the term 'climate'.

______________________________

______________________________

______________________________

**(ii)** List the weather conditions that must be recorded to determine the climate of an area.

**1.** ______________________________

______________________________

**2.** ______________________________

______________________________

**3.** ______________________________

______________________________

**Remember!**

Think back to the Learning Outcomes on weather. What conditions are measured for weather to be recorded over a period of time?

**(iii)** Climate and weather are not the same. Explain the key difference between the two.

**Exam Hint**

**S: State** clearly what weather and climate are.

**E: Explain** the differences.

**E:** Give an **example** of weather and an example of climate.

______________________________

______________________________

______________________________

______________________________

______________________________

______________________________

______________________________

## Global Climates

**2.** **(i)** Fill in the table on the following page with the missing terms provided.

Cold climates　　Savanna　　Warm temperate/Mediterranean　　Hot climates　　Tundra

| Type of climate | | Temperate climates | |
|---|---|---|---|
| Examples of climate | Equatorial | | |
| | | Cool temperate oceanic | Boreal |
| | Hot desert | | |

**(ii)** Global climates are categorised by measuring a number of characteristics. Circle **three** characteristics from the list below.

Wind speed    Temperature    Hours of sunshine    Cloud type    Acidic rain levels

Levels of precipitation    Location    Air pressure    Wind direction

**(iii)** On the world map below, locate a hot climate you have studied. Fill in the table below with information on each characteristic of your chosen climate.

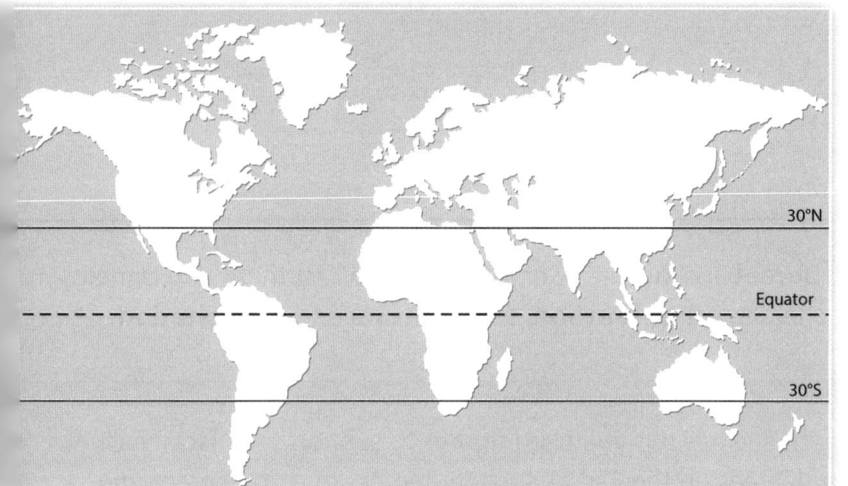


**Exam Hint**

**Location:** Where is it found on the Earth's surface in relation to the equator (degrees north or south)?

**Temperature:** What is the temperature range in summer and winter?

**Precipitation:** How much precipitation falls in a year?

## Case Study

| Characteristic | Climate: |
|---|---|
| **Location** | |
| **Temperature** | |
| **Precipitation** | |

**(iv)** You are on holiday in a country with a temperate climate and you must write a postcard to a friend describing the **climate type, the location, the temperature** and **precipitation levels**. Give the latitude where temperate climates can be found. Name another country that experiences this climate.

POSTCARD

**(v)** There are two cold climates, **boreal** and **tundra**. Compare and contrast these two climates under **two** of the following characteristics: **location, temperature** and **precipitation**.

**Exam Hint**

To properly answer questions such as this you need figures to support your facts. Include figures such as location in degrees on the Earth's surface, temperature in degrees and annual rainfall.

| Characteristics | Boreal | Tundra |
|---|---|---|
| 1. ______ | | |
| 2. ______ | | |

## Ireland's Climate: Cool Temperate Oceanic

**3. (i) (a)** Using your pencil, sketch the location and direction of the North Atlantic Current (NAC) on this map of the world.

**(b)** On your sketch, mark where the current is warmest and where it is coldest.

**Exam Hint**

For this question use the evidence supplied by the map.

Where is the Earth at its warmest? What will it do to water in this area? How might transferring this water to North Europe prevent freezing temperatures?

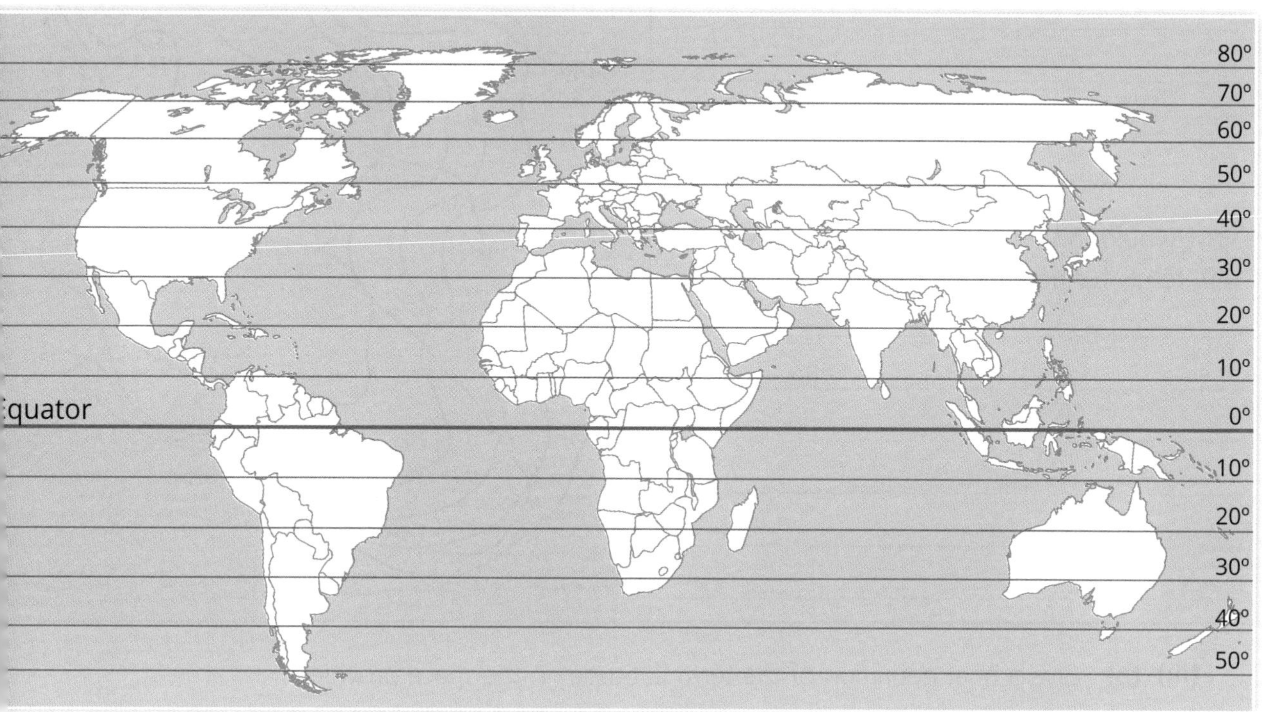


**(c)** Examine the map above that shows the equator and lines of latitude. Explain how the NAC keeps parts of Europe from freezing over by moving warm and cold water across the Atlantic Ocean.

**(ii)** Examine the map below, which shows the mean daily temperature across Ireland in July. In the space provided, explain how and why distance from seas and oceans affects Ireland's climate.

## GeoSkill

Map interpretation: Read the key supplied with this map carefully. Note the different colour of each line and the information it represents.

| **Explanation** | **Map of Ireland** |
|---|---|
| How does distance from seas and oceans affect heating and cooling of land?<br><br><br><br>Why would this affect temperature ranges differently further inland? | KEY<br>— Daily January Temperature in Ireland<br>— Daily July Temperature in Ireland<br>5.5°C, 5°C, 4.5°C, 14.5°C, 4°C, 4°C, 5°C, 6°C, 15°C, 4.5°C, 14.5°C, 5°C, 15.5°C, 4.5°C, 15°C, 5.5°C, 15°C, 15.5°C, 5.5°C, 16°C, 4.5°C, 15°C, 15.5°C, 6°C, 6.5°C, 5°C, 15.5°C, 6°C, 7°C, 5.5°C, 6°C, 16°C, 6.5°C, 6.5°C, 7°C |

**(iii) (a)** Give a brief definition of the term 'latitude' in the space provided.

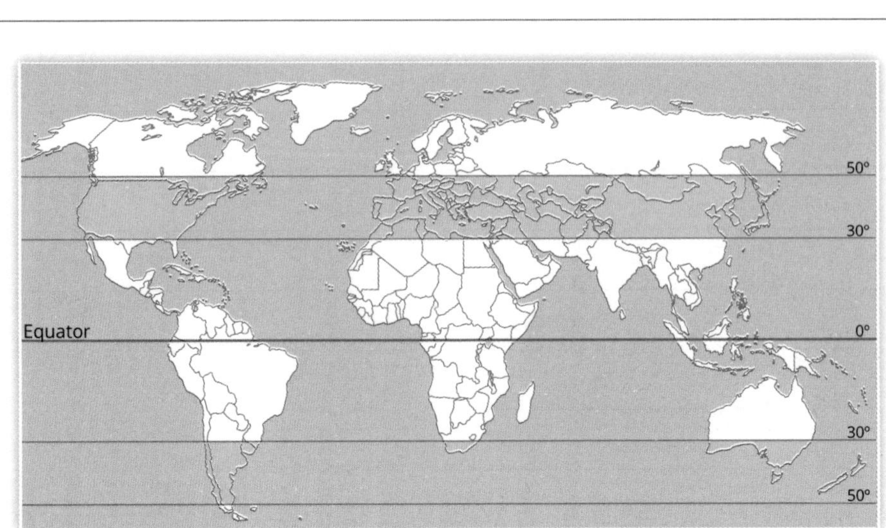

**(b)** What distance, roughly, is Ireland from the equator in degrees? ______________________

**(c)** Complete the diagram below. Include the following:

- The equator
- An area (label it A) where the sun's rays would be almost directly overhead and concentrated
- A second area (label it B) where the sun's rays are curved or slanted and less concentrated

**(d)** Explain how distance from the equator can affect the strength of the sun's rays on the areas you have marked A and B on this map.

**Exam Hint**

The larger the surface area covered by the sun's rays, the lower the temperature. When directly overhead, the sun's rays are concentrated and temperatures are at their highest.

## revailing Winds/Air Masses

**(i)** Briefly explain how winds, such as northerly winds, get their names.

**(ii)** The map below shows the five prevailing winds/air masses that affect Ireland's climate. Write two points about each wind/air mass in the spaces below. Focus on where they come from and the types of weather they bring.

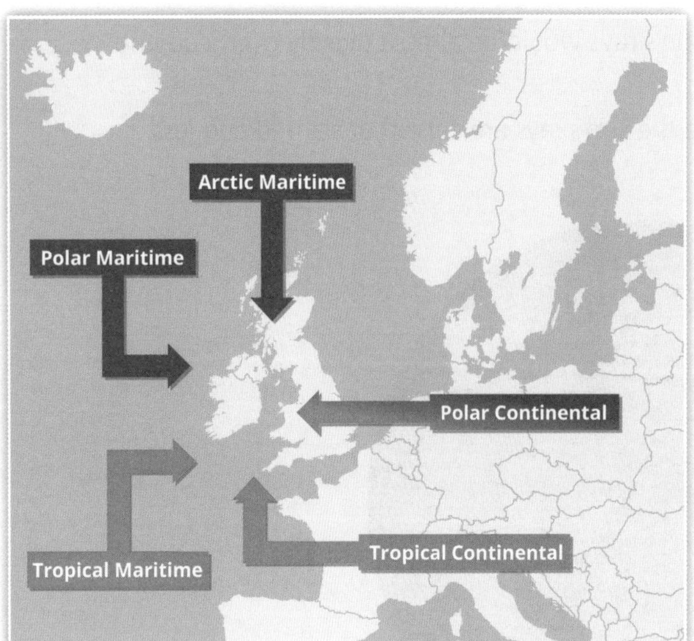


Arctic Maritime

- ____________________
- ____________________

Polar Maritime

- ____________________
- ____________________

Polar Continental

- ____________________
- ____________________

Tropical Maritime

- ____________________
- ____________________

Tropical Continental

- ____________________
- ____________________

## Altitude

**5.** The image below shows the location of Ireland's mountains (A) and the average temperatures experienced by the island of Ireland in a year (B).

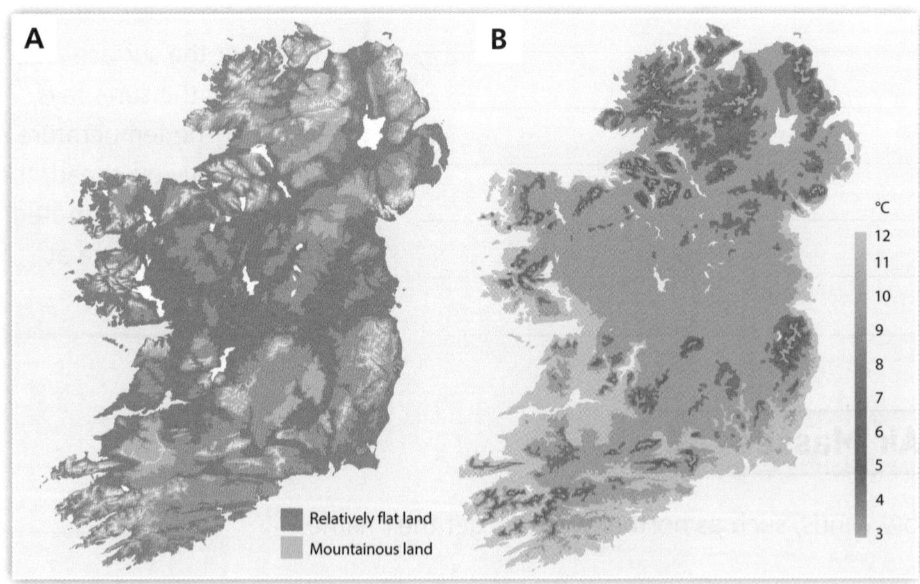


**(i)** By roughly how much does the temperature decrease for every 150 m climbed?

____________________

**(ii)** By how much does annual precipitation increase for every 100 m increase in height?

____________________

**Remember!**

For question (iii), remember the Learning Outcomes on Settlement. How can altitude affect location?

**(iii)** Think of the location of your town/village. How might altitude have affected its location?

## Aspect and Local Climate

**6. (i)** Below is a sketch of a hillside. Complete this sketch by doing the following:

- Choose which is the north-facing slope and which is the south-facing slope
- Sketch the sun on either of the slopes, based on your previous decision
- Sketch your house to indicate on which side you would place it
- Mark the leeward side with a capital 'L'

**GeoSkill**

When drawing or completing a diagram, always use a pencil. Label the diagram clearly. Only add information or features asked for. Draw neatly.

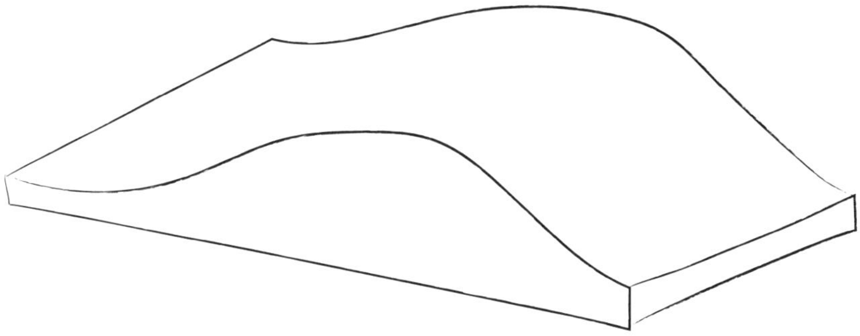

**(ii)** What does the term 'leeward side' mean?

**(iii)** Give an explanation of the term 'aspect'.

**(iv)** State which side of the slope you placed your house in the sketch above and explain your reasons.

**Answer the questions to complete the mind map. This will support your revision.**

**Prompt Questions for Mind Map**

**(a)** Can you name the three main climate types?

**(b)** Can you classify each climate according to location, precipitation and temperature?

**(c)** How does distance from seas and oceans affect climate?

**(d)** How does latitude affect Ireland's climate?

**(e)** How do altitude and aspect affect Ireland's climate?

**(f)** How do prevailing winds affect Ireland's climate?

**(g)** What are local climates?

(a) Climate Types

1.

2.

3.

(g) Local Climates

(f) Irish Climate – Prevailing Winds

(b) Climate Characteristics

| Climate Type | Location | Precipitation | Temperature |
|---|---|---|---|
| | | | |
| | | | |
| | | | |

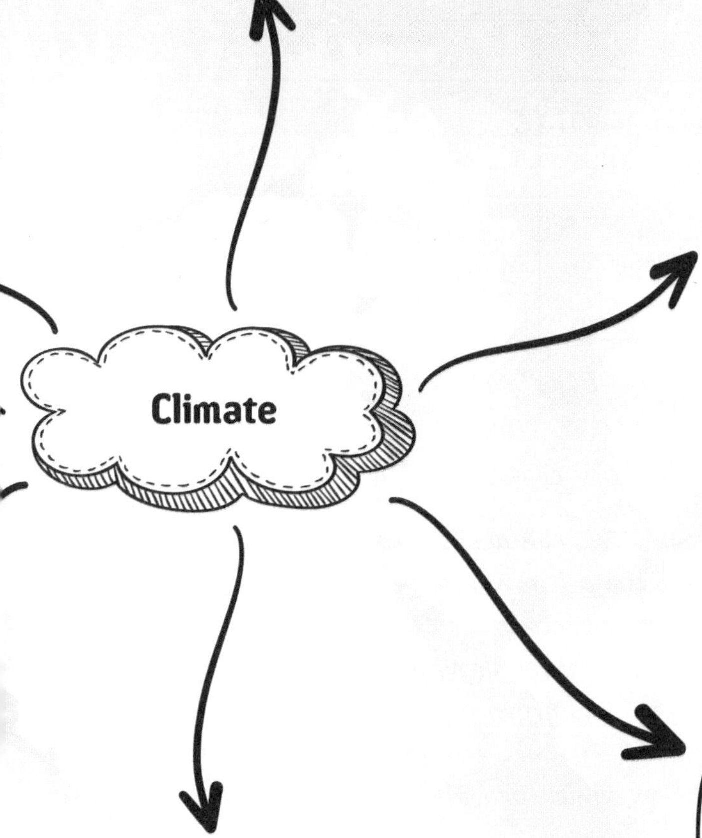


(c) Distance from Sea/Ocean

(d) Irish Climate – Latitude

Irish Climate – Altitude and Aspect

## NCCA Sample Question and Answer

### Question 1

Choose **ONE** of the following and describe how they affect climate in Ireland. [5 marks]

(a) Latitude (b) Air masses

**Exam Hint**

Choose one factor only.

**S: State** Ireland's climate and the factor you have chosen.

**E: Explain** the factor clearly and how it affects Ireland.

**E:** Give **evidence** of this.

**Marks Awarded**

2 marks for explaining whichever factor you choose

3 marks for explaining how this factor affects Ireland specifically

Total = 5 marks

### Question 2

List **TWO** ways Ireland's economic activity is related to its climate. [8 marks]

1. *Ireland's climate is cool temperate oceanic. This climate is ideal for both primary and tertiary economic activities. Farming in Ireland is a mix of arable and pastoral farming. Rainfall of 400 mm a year and average temperatures of 30 degrees in summer and 8 degrees in winter means the conditions are ideal for growing grass for rearing dairy cows and beef calves. This weather also provides ideal growing conditions for market gardening north Dublin and barley growth in Wexford. Primary economic activities offer employment to roughly 10% of the country's population, which provides income for the government from taxes.*
2. *The climate is ideal for year-round tourism …*

For the second part of thi[s] question, focus on tourism

How does Ireland's clima[te] contribute to year-round tourism?

How does the climate len[d] itself to particular tourist activities?

What percentage of peopl[e] are employed in tourism?

**Marks Awarded**

2 marks for choosing an economic activity

4 marks for explaining how Ireland's climate is linked to the activity directly

2 marks for including any facts and figures to support the link

Total = 8 marks

# 17 Climate Change

In this section, the Learning Outcome we will look at is: **2.6**

## Learning Checklist:

- ☐ I can explain how we know that our climate is changing.
- ☐ I can describe human impact on climate change.
- ☐ I can explain the greenhouse effect and its impact on climate.
- ☐ I can outline and explain some implications of climate change.
- ☐ I can read information from graphs, infographics and media images.
- ☐ I can draw conclusions based on information presented to me in articles and photographic images.

## Our Changing Climate

1. Answer all of the questions below.

   **(i)** What is meant by the term 'climate change'?

   ______________________________________________

   ______________________________________________

   ______________________________________________

   **(ii)** Review the chart below, showing the history of global surface temperatures from 1880 to 2020, and answer the questions that follow.

**GeoSkill**

Here you are given a graph and you must carefully examine the x- and y-axes. The title on the graph will tell you what is being displayed.

   **(a)** If we consider the average temperature records from 1880 to 2020, in which decade do we see the most significant increase in global temperatures begin to occur? Tick the correct box below.

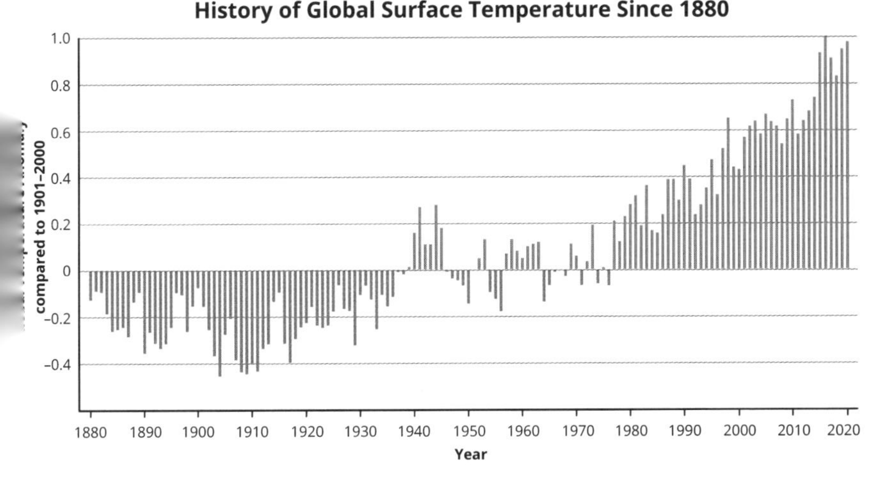


**Remember!**

What happened in the developed world to cause this temperature increase?

- 1890s ☐
- 1910s ☐
- 1970s ☐

**(b)** Suggest one reason why we begin to see this significant increase in temperature at the time period selected in (a) above.

___

___

**(c)** In what year do we see the highest average temperature recorded?

___

___

**(iii)** Name one greenhouse gas that is having a direct impact on climate change.

___

**(iv)** Tick (✓) the correct answer below. Deforestation results in:

**(a)** Increasing the amount of carbon dioxide in the atmosphere ☐

**(b)** Increasing the level of oxygen in the atmosphere ☐

State one other impact that deforestation can have on an area.

___

___

**Remember!**

Think back to mass movement and soil for this answer.

**(v)** List two human activities that can contribute to climate change.

**1.** ___

___

**2.** ___

___

**(vi)** Circle the correct answer in each of the statements below:

**(a)** **Gas / wind power** is a renewable source of energy.

**(b)** Ice cores can be used **to tell us about past temperatures / to predict sea level rise**.

**(c)** The greenhouse gases that human activities emit in large quantities are **carbon dioxide and methane / oxygen and nitrogen**.

**(d)** Global sea levels are predicted to **rise / fall** due to climate change.

**(e)** The level of carbon dioxide in the atmosphere is increased by using fossil fuels such as **oil** / **solar power**.

**(vii)** State two possible consequences of climate change.

**1.** ___

___

**2.** ___

___

**(viii)** Evidence for climate change is found using data collected from ice core samples. How do ice cores provide evidence that our climate is changing?

**Remember!**

The layers of ice alternate like tree rings.

**Age of Ice Cores**

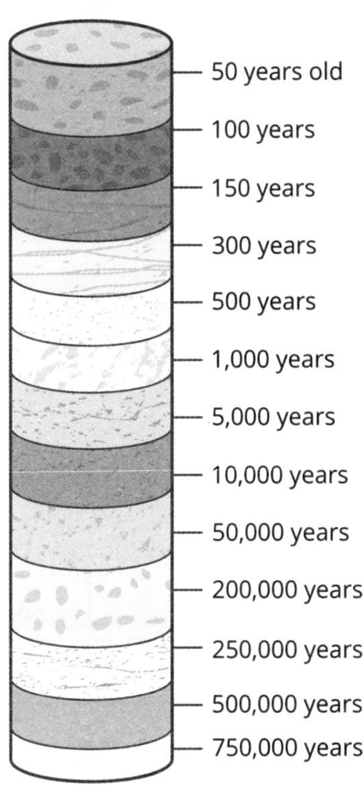


____________________

____________________

____________________

____________________

____________________

____________________

____________________

____________________

____________________

____________________

____________________

____________________

____________________

____________________

## reenhouse Effect

**(i)** Fill in the blanks using the following terms:

| Carbon dioxide | Greenhouse gases | Methane | Greenhouse effect |
|---|---|---|---|
| Warmer | Strong | Solar | Paris Climate |

Since the start of the Industrial Revolution in 1780, human activity and industries have released large quantities of ________________ ________________ into the atmosphere. Examples of these gases are ________________ ________________, ________________ and nitrous oxide. These have had a negative impact on the environment. The ________________ ________________ is the warming of the Earth's surface from the air above it. It is caused by these gases trapping the sun's ________________ energy within our atmosphere. The greenhouse effect is now too ________________ and the Earth is becoming ________________. In 2015, the international community of 195 countries agreed a new programme to tackle climate change known as the ________________ ________________ Agreement.

**(ii)** Use the terms to correctly label the sketch of the greenhouse effect below.

Sun — Atmosphere containing greenhouse gases

Incoming energy — Outgoing energy — Trapped energy

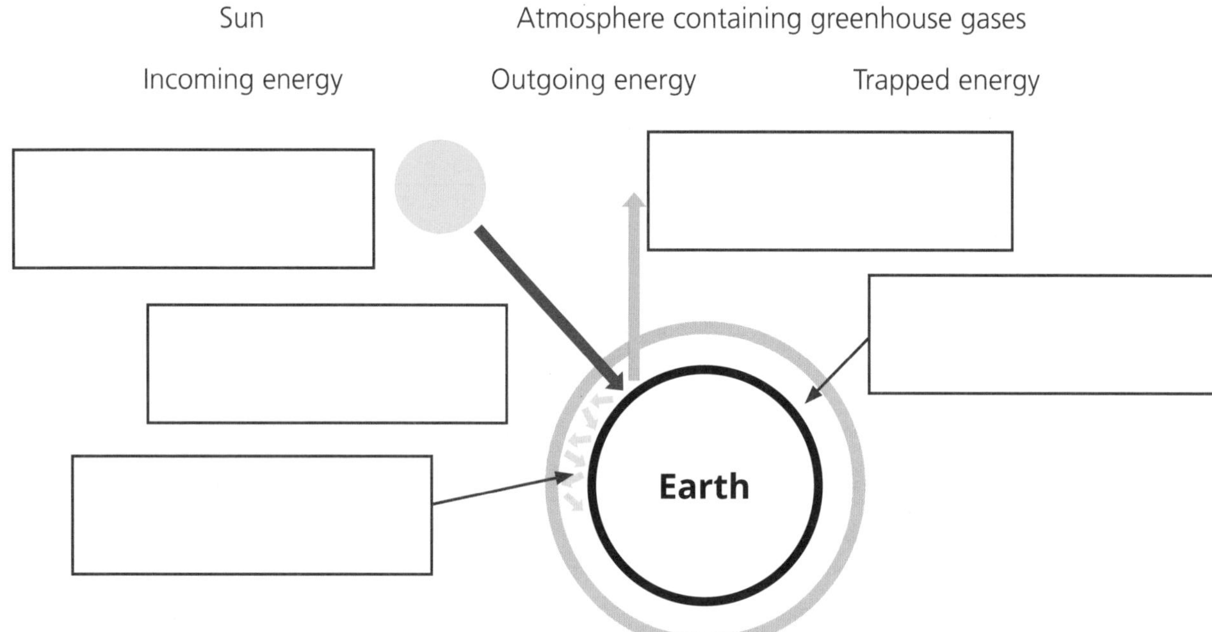


**(iii)** Number the statements below to place them in the correct sequence (1–7) to explain how the greenhouse effect occurs. The first one has been numbered for you.

| Statement | Number |
|---|---|
| Large areas of forest are cleared; fossil fuels are burned to power industry. | 1 |
| Increased amount of solar energy gets trapped in the atmosphere now. | |
| Global average temperatures continue to rise. | |
| The levels of greenhouse gases in the atmosphere rise due to the burning of fossil fuels. | |
| Increase in severe weather events: flooding, drought and storms occur. | |
| The atmosphere continues to get warmer due to the heat-trapping gases. | |
| Large ice caps begin to melt, and sea levels can rise. | |

**(iv)** Below is an infographic showing Ireland's greenhouse gas projections from 2020 to 2030.

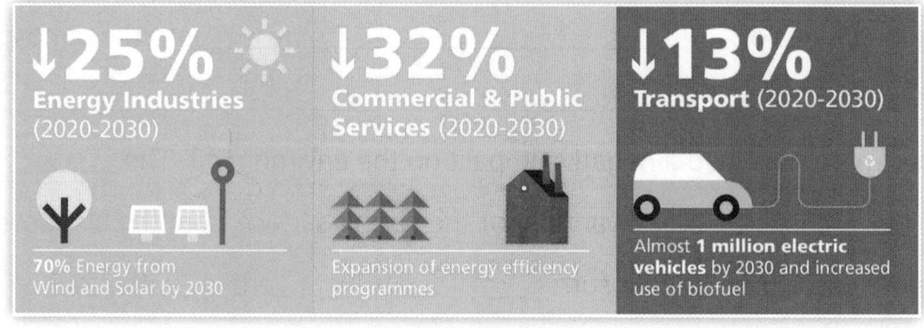


## Exam Hint

**RHA**

**R: Read** the information. **H: Highlight** what's important. **A: Answer** the questions.

(a) There will be a 13% decrease in greenhouse gases from transport between 2020 and 2030. What is being proposed to help achieve this?

___

___

___

(b) What percentage of energy will come from wind and solar power by 2030?

___

___

(c) What advice would you give to your family on two things that you can do in your home to limit greenhouse gas emissions?

___

___

___

## mplications of Climate Change

(i) Read the article below and answer the questions that follow.

**Climate Scientists Shocked by Scale of Floods in Germany and China**

Both Germany and China have been devastated by deadly floods, sending a worrying reminder that climate change is making weather more extreme around the world.

In China, at least 33 people in the central province of Henan were killed as floodwater ripped through the region after several days of very heavy rainfall. This occurred only days after flooding in Europe killed at least 165 people in Germany and another 31 in Belgium. The floods have highlighted the need for significant changes to be made to be better prepared, as disasters like these begin to happen more often.

Evidence suggests that in Europe, climate change means more large, slow-moving storms that can stay longer in one area. Scientists are predicting that these storms could become 14 times more common by the end of the century.

(a) According to the article, what worrying reminder has the recent floods in Germany and China given to people?

___

___

___

**Remember!**

**R: Read**
**H: Highlight**
**A: Answer**

(b) Describe one impact that these floods had in China or Germany.

___

___

___

**(c)** State one way that climate change is predicted to impact Europe by the end of the century.

______________________________________________

______________________________________________

**(d)** Other than the impacts of climate change mentioned in the article, explain one further implication of climate change for our planet.

______________________________________________

______________________________________________

______________________________________________

**Remember!**

Think back to the topics of extreme weather, mass movement, rivers and the coast.

**(ii)** Complete the fact file below, showing some of the main implications of climate change. In the spaces provided, briefly explain each implication. Use the prompts on the next page to help you

## Implications of Climate Change

1. Extreme weather events

______________________________________________

2. Desertification

______________________________________________

3. Sea levels rising and melting ice

______________________________________________

CLIMATE CHANGE

4. Threats to wildlife

______________________________________________

**Prompts to complete infographic:**

**Weather** = What types of severe weather do we expect to see more of? How might these events impact humans, animals and local environments?

**Desertification** = What does this term mean? What impact will the loss of fertile land have on farmers, communities and economies?

**Sea level** = If sea levels rise, how will this impact coastal areas? As glaciers and ice sheets melt, they add water to oceans. How will this impact on coastal erosion, flooding and freshwater contamination?

**(iii)** Review the two images below and answer the question that follows.

**A**

News

**B**

**Remember!**

**RHA**

**xam Hint**

You may be given cartoon or magazine images in the exam that you are asked to explain the meaning of. Always read any text in the image, then look carefully at the picture. Make connections between the text, image and the topic that you are being asked about.

Select either image A **or** B above and explain the message that you feel is being portrayed.

**Thing to consider in your answer:**

- What is shown in the image?
- If there is text, what is it telling us?
- Have you seen anything like this before?
- Do you think there is a key message?
- What topic is it telling us something about?

Image A ____________ or B ____________

## Solutions to Climate Change

**4.** **(i)** There are many ways that we can manage and reduce the risk of climate change. Below is an infographic outlining some low-, moderate- and high-impact changes that can be made.

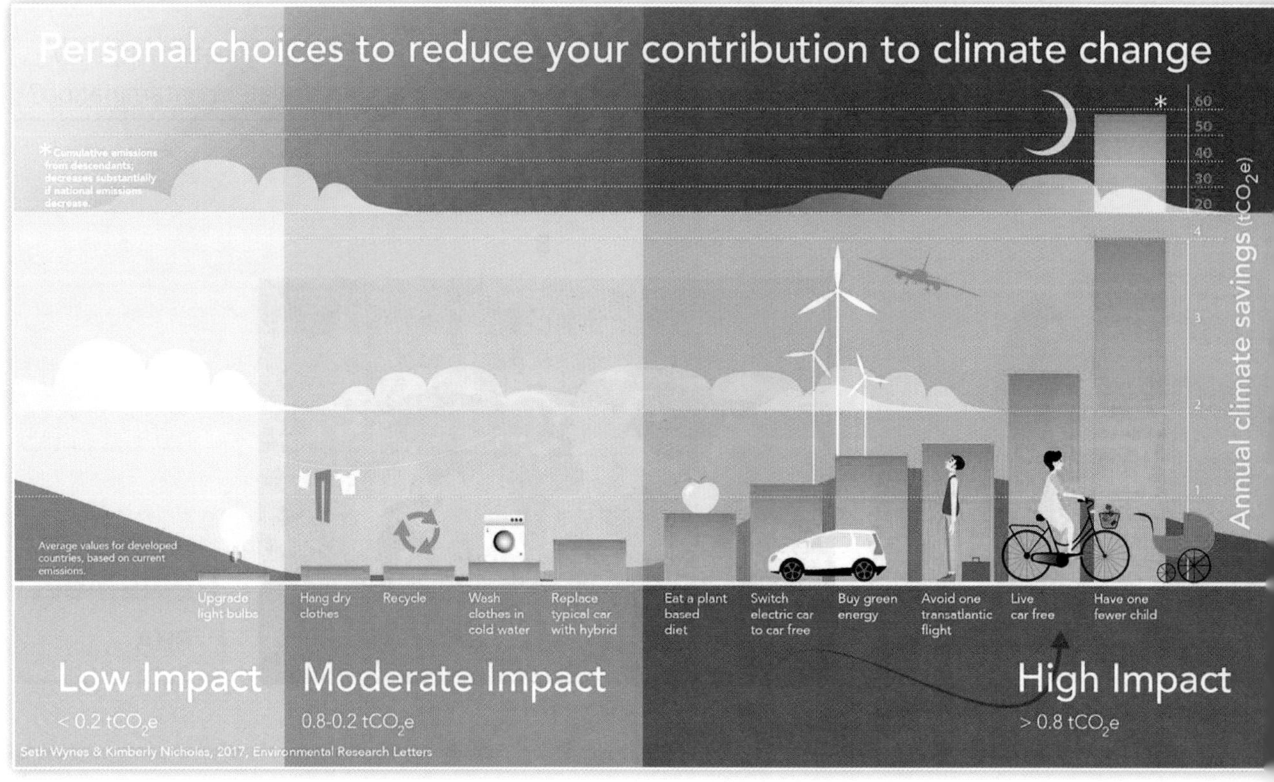


Select one of the high-impact ways of reducing our contribution to climate change and explain how its reduction can support this.

High impact: ____________________

______________________________________________

______________________________________________

______________________________________________

______________________________________________

**(ii)** You live in an area that has experienced flooding in recent times. Your home is located in an estate close to the river's floodplain. It has been stated that climate change will have a big impact on your location, causing flood events to become more frequent and intense.

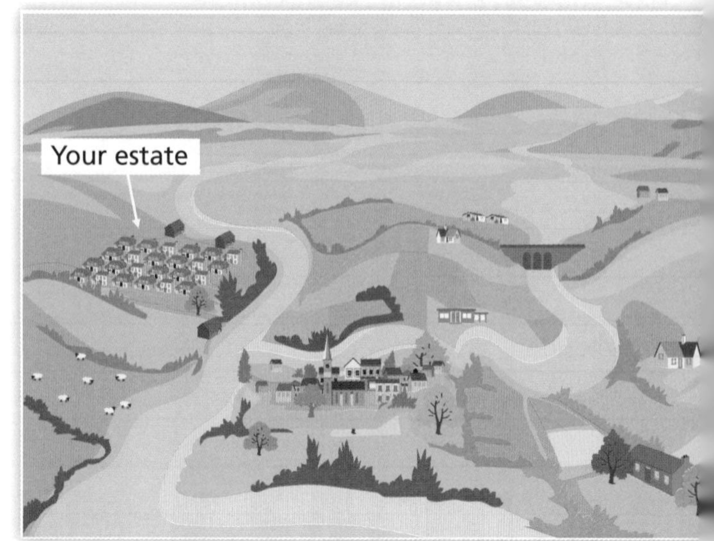

dentify **one adaption strategy** that your local or ıational government can take to help to reduce the mpact of climate change in your local area. Write a brief etter to a local TD to outline the adaption measure that ou feel should be implemented, and describe the proposed impact that you think it will have in your area.

**Exam Dictionary**

**Adaption strategy:** Taking action to prepare for and adjust to both the current effects of **climate change** and the predicted impacts in the future.

**Things to include:**

- State one adaption strategy that you have selected (examples include flood barriers, altering river's course, deepening channel, advance flood warning system and preventing further building on the floodplain).
- Describe why you feel this measure is needed. What problem are you hoping that it will help to resolve?
- Explain what impact you hope the measure will have.

Adaption measure:

Dear

## CCA Sample Question and Answer

### uestion 1

e following table has been sourced from data shared by NASA.

| Carbon Dioxide | Global Temperature | Arctic Ice | Ice Sheets | Sea Level |
|---|---|---|---|---|
| Carbon dioxide levels in the air are at their highest in 650,000 years. | 19 of the 20 warmest years on record have occurred since 2001. | In 2012, Arctic summer sea ice shrank to the lowest extent on record. | Satellite data show that Earth's polar ice sheets are losing mass. | Global average sea level has risen nearly 7″ (178 mm) over the past 100 years. |

**(a)** Choose **two** of the following and outline possible causes for the change in record over time.

Carbon dioxide/Global temperature/Arctic ice/Ice sheets/Sea level [8 marks]

1. Sea Level

Sea level has risen 7 inches in the past 100 years. This is possibly caused by the increase in global temperatures over this time. We know that global average temperatures have risen steadily since the 1970s. A rise in temperature will melt polar ice caps. The Greenland ice sheet has lost over 30% of its volume since 1980.

**2.** ______________________

___________________________________________

___________________________________________

___________________________________________

___________________________________________

___________________________________________

You must outline the causes for the change in the record over time for two of the headings you have been given. We have completed the first one using sea level and described how it has risen due to rising temperatures. This would be awarded 4 marks. You should now complete the second one by selecting another heading from the list and outlining its impact, using your knowledge of the topic.

**Marks Awarded**

**(a)** Named causes (1 + 1 = 2 marks)

Outline of causes for each selected change, plus development (3 + 3 = 6)

**(b)** What are the consequences of climate change in your local area? [6 marks]

1. One consequence of climate change in my local area is flooding. I live in a housing estate that was built on an old floodplain. The land is low and flat. Due to climate change, it is becoming more likely that we will have heavier storms and rainfall events in the future. This water will drain into the local river and may come over the levees and flood the areas around my home.

**2.** ___________________________________________

___________________________________________

___________________________________________

___________________________________________

___________________________________________

In question (b), you must discuss two consequences of climate change in your local area. We have discussed flooding, so you should think of another consequence for where you live. 'Local' can mean your town, county or country. Consider the impact on agriculture, wildlife and so

**Marks Awarded**

1 mark for each named consequence (max. 2 marks) (1 + 1 = 2 marks)

2 marks for development of each consequence (2 + 2 = 4 marks)

# 18 Population

In this section, the Learning Outcomes we will look at are: **3.1**, **3.3**, **3.9**

## Learning Checklist:

- [ ] I can describe population change over time and make projections into the future.
- [ ] I can explain what is meant by birth rate and death rate, natural increase and natural decrease and can calculate each.
- [ ] I can describe population change in Ireland over time (developed country).
- [ ] I can explain seven factors that influence population change (food, globalisation, war, education, place of women in society, technology, health).
- [ ] I can explain what a population pyramid is showing and read information from it.
- [ ] I can explain three types of population pyramid – expansive, constrictive and stationary.
- [ ] I can describe what is happening in all five stages of the demographic transition model and can name a country that is currently found in each stage.
- [ ] I can describe population change in a developing country over time.
- [ ] I can read information from different type of graph; I can read population pyramids; I can read data from tables and make necessary calculations. I can calculate natural increase/decrease and percentage change.

## Population Change Over Time

Study the chart below, showing projected world population growth from 1750 to 2150. Answer all questions on the following page.

**GeoSkill**

Here we read information from the graph. The x-axis tells us the year, the y-axis tells us the population in billions. The graph shows us population figures from 1750 and makes projections on world population up to 2150.

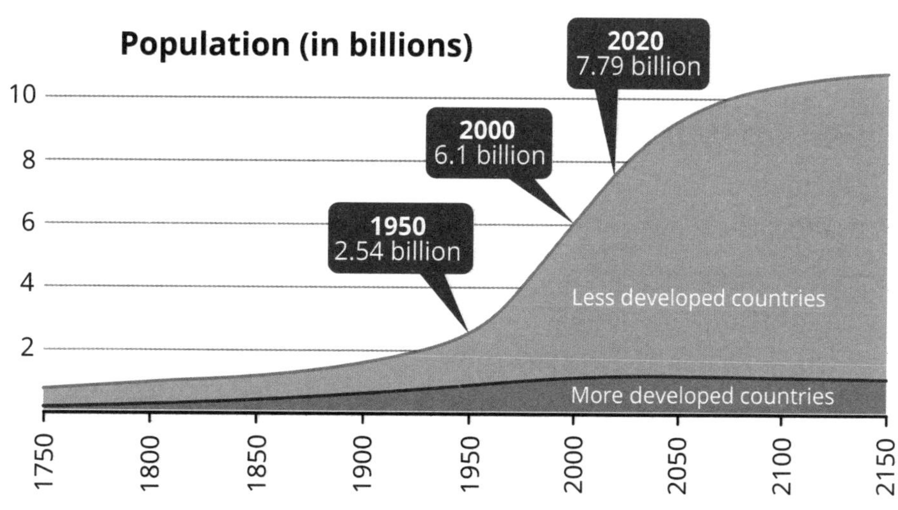

**(i)** Describe the trend of population growth from 1750 to the present day. Use information from the graph to support your answer.

## Exam Dictionary

**Trend:** A general direction in which something is developing or changing.

______________________________________________

______________________________________________

______________________________________________

______________________________________________

______________________________________________

**(ii)** Calculate the change in population from 1950 to 2020.

**Optional rough work:**

**Answer:** ______________________________________________

**(iii)** List two reasons for such a sharp rise in population between 1950 and 2020.

**1.** ______________________________________________

______________________________________________

**2.** ______________________________________________

______________________________________________

## Remember!

Think about the developments that occurred in the world between 1950 and 2020 that could impact on population.

**(iv)** Based on the graph, what can we expect the world population to be by 2150?

______________________________________________

______________________________________________

**(v)** Answer true or false to the statements below:

## Exam Dictionary

**Fluctuated:** To move up and down.

| | | True | Fal |
|---|---|---|---|
| **(a)** | Between 1750 and 1900, world population fluctuated. | ☐ | ☐ |
| **(b)** | The population of developed countries is growing much faster than that of less developed countries. | ☐ | ☐ |
| **(c)** | The world's population grew faster between 1900 and 2000 than any other time in history. | ☐ | ☐ |

**(vi)** Outline why population growth projections in more developed countries appear to dip slightly from 2050 to 2150.

## Exam Hint

Think economically and socially. What happens to the birth rate as a country becomes more economically developed?

## Exam Dictionary

**Projections:** An estimate of a future situation based on a study of present trends

## irth and Death Rates

The table below gives data on the birth and death rates for a number of countries in 2019.

| Country | Birth rate *Per 1,000 in population | Death rate | Natural increase | Natural decrease | Percentage change |
|---|---|---|---|---|---|
| Austria | 9.6 | 9.4 | 0.2 | – | 0.02% |
| Bulgaria | 8.8 | 15.5 | | | |
| Cyprus | 10.9 | 6.8 | | | |
| Ireland | 12.1 | 6.3 | | | |
| Japan | 7.3 | 10.7 | – | 3.4 | 0.34% |
| USA | 11.9 | 8.8 | | | |
| Nigeria | 37.4 | 11.6 | | | |

**(i)** Explain the terms 'birth rate' and 'death rate'.

Birth rate: ______

Death rate: ______

**(ii)** Complete the table above to calculate all missing natural increase/decrease and percentage change figures.

### GeoSkill

To calculate natural increase or decrease, you must take away (subtract) the birth rate and death rate from each other.

If birth rate is higher than death rate, then it is a natural increase. If death rate is higher than birth rate, then it is a natural decrease.

Example: Birth rate = 9.6 Death rate = 9.4 so, 9.6 – 9.4 = 0.2

This is then divided by 1,000 and multiplied by 100 to get the percentage change, e.g. 0.2 ÷ 1,000 = 0.0002

0.0002 × 100 = 0.02%

**(iii)** True or false? Look at the table on page 187 and tick (✓) the correct box in each case.

| | True | False |
|---|---|---|
| **(a)** The USA had a death rate higher than its birth rate. | ☐ | ☐ |
| **(b)** Japan is experiencing a natural decrease in its population. | ☐ | ☐ |
| **(c)** Bulgaria is experiencing a natural increase in its population. | ☐ | ☐ |
| **(d)** The natural increase experienced in Nigeria is 25.8. | ☐ | ☐ |

## Population Cycle

**3. (i)** Below is the demographic transition model with certain details left blank. You should fill in the blank spaces to complete the model.

**Demographic Transition Model**

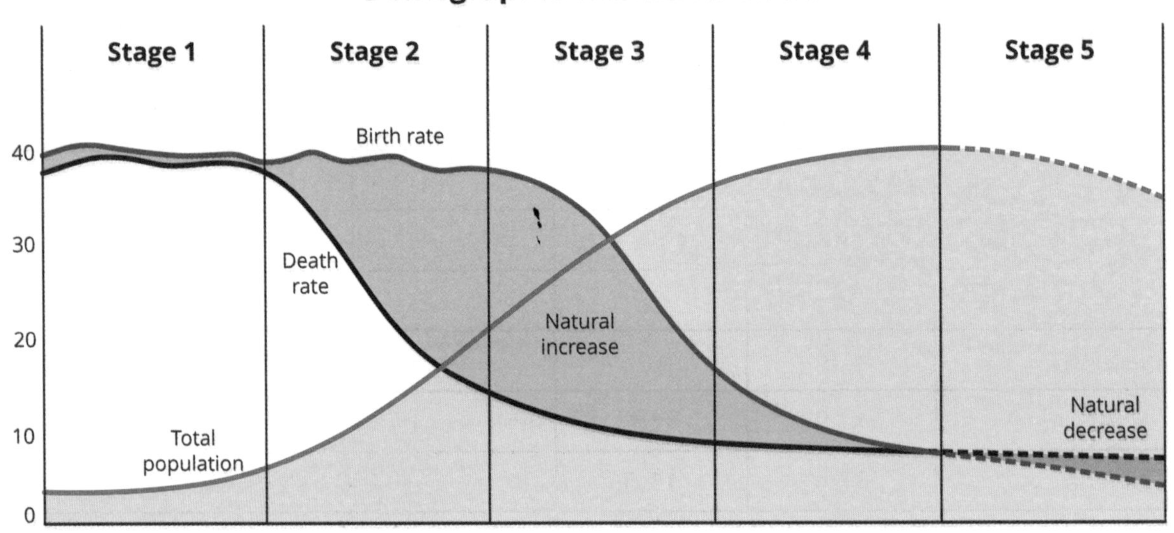


| Example of country in this stage | Somalia | | | Ireland | |
|---|---|---|---|---|---|
| **Birth rate** | | High | | | Low |
| **Death rate** | High | | Falling slowly | | |
| **Natural increase or decrease?** | | | Increase | | |
| **Description of economy** | Poorly developed. High levels of poverty. May experience war or famine. | | | Economy considered developed, with most people living long lives and having fewer children. | |

**(ii)** Circle the correct answer in each of the following statements:

**(a)** Stage 3 is known as **early expanding / late expanding**.

**(b)** This graph is known as a **demographic transition model / population pyramid**.

**(c)** In Stage 2 the birth rate is **higher / lower** than the death rate.

**(d)** The overall population **increases / decreases** in Stage 4.

**(e)** In Stage 5, there is a natural **increase / decrease** in population.

**(iii)** Why, do you think, has Stage 2 of the model been named early expanding?

______________________________

______________________________

______________________________

______________________________

**(iv)** In what stage of the model is the birth rate highest? Explain why this is the case.

Stage: ______________________________

Reason: ______________________________

______________________________

______________________________

______________________________

**(v)** Explain why the death rate decreases before birth rate as a country develops.

______________________________

______________________________

______________________________

______________________________

**(vi)** Outline two problems faced by governments of countries with a very low birth rate.

**1.** ______________________________

______________________________

**2.** ______________________________

______________________________

## ctors Influencing Population Change

**(i)** True or false? Tick (✓) the correct box in each case.

| | True | False |
|---|---|---|
| **(a)** The population in a country increases when it has access to improved medical care. | ☐ | ☐ |
| **(b)** The population increases when soldiers leave their family to go to war. | ☐ | ☐ |
| **(c)** The birth rate decreases when women achieve higher levels of education. | ☐ | ☐ |
| **(d)** The death rate increases when there is greater access to technology. | ☐ | ☐ |

**(ii)** Complete the mind map below, detailing the factors that influence population change. Use the prompt questions to support you.

**Prompt Questions for Mind Map**

**(a)** What was the impact of the Agricultural Revolution? When people have access to more and better food, how does that impact population growth? What is the impact of famine?

**(b)** What is the impact of globalisation on population? How can increased trade, sharing of ideas and greater access to travel all impact on population?

**(c)** When soldiers leave to go to war, how does this impact population? When they return and are reunited with their partners, how does this then impact birth rates?

**(d)** Describe the impact that higher levels of education have on population. Discuss family planning, diet, hygiene and sanitation.

**(e)** How does the role of women in society impact population? Think of the traditional role vs modern society. How does family planning change? Family size? Maternal age?

**(f)** How do new technologies such as medical equipment, mechanised farming, water treatment, motorised transport, the internet and technology in the home (washing machine, fridge) impact on population?

**(g)** How do improved medical care and access to doctors, vaccinations and antibiotics impact on population?

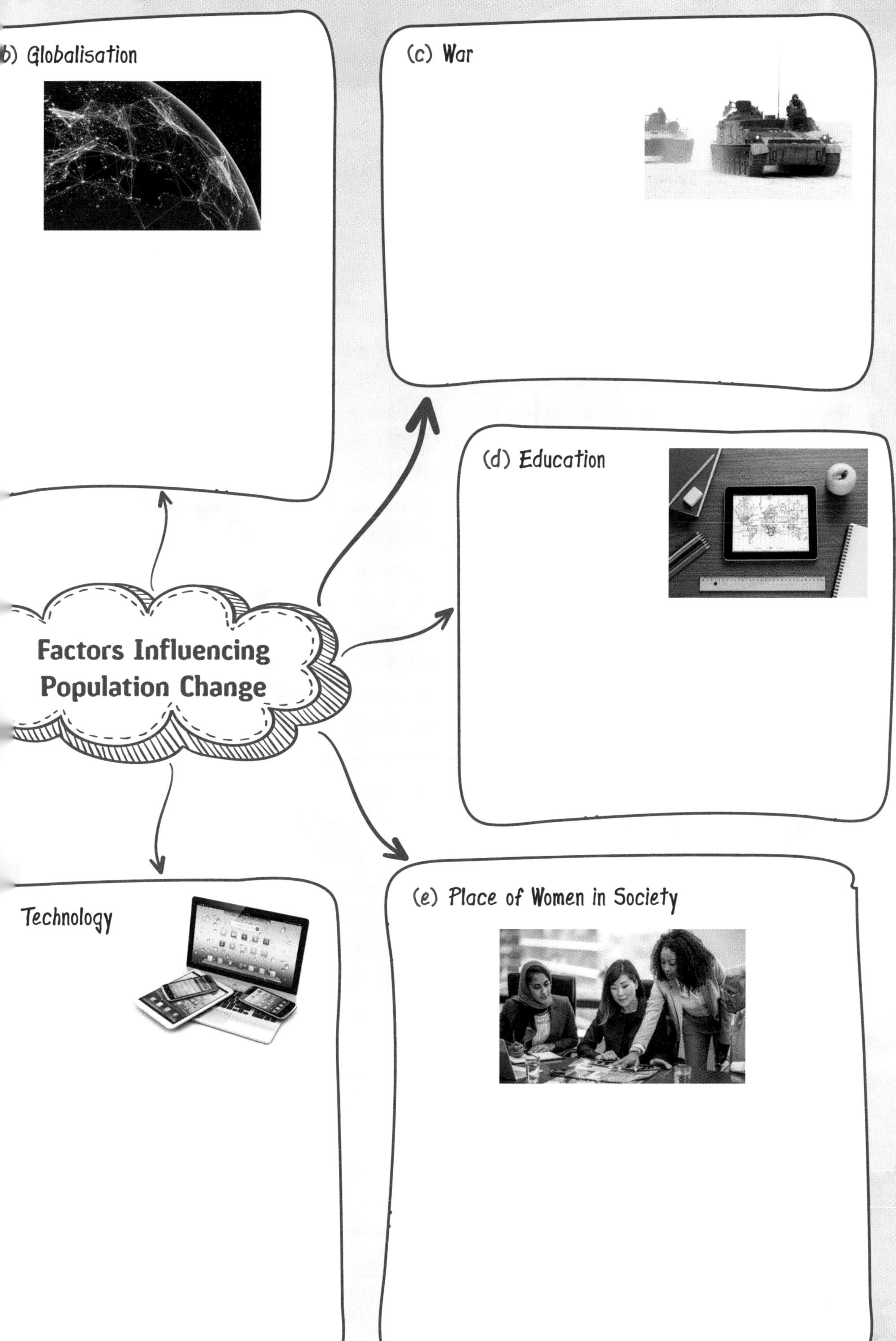
b) Globalisation
(c) War
(d) Education
Factors Influencing Population Change
Technology
(e) Place of Women in Society

## Population Graphs

**5.** Review the graph below and answer the questions that follow.

### GeoSkill

On the left we are shown males; on the right, females.

Each section of the graph is broken up into age brackets (0–4 years, 5–9 years, etc.).

The axis showing ages is on the left side but can also sometimes be in the middle.

The percentage of people found in each age range is written next to it on the graph (e.g. male 0–4 years = 3.1%).

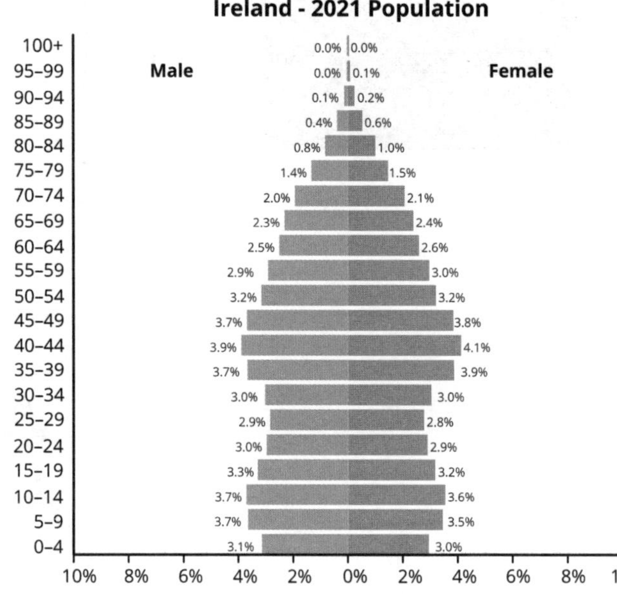


**(i)** What is the name given to the graph above?

______________________________

**(ii)** What information does this graph tell us about the Irish population?

______________________________

______________________________

______________________________

**(iii)** Outline two ways that information on this graph is useful to local and national governments.

**1.** ______________________________

______________________________

______________________________

______________________________

______________________________

**2.** ______________________________

______________________________

______________________________

______________________________

______________________________

### Exam Hint

What do governments use population data for?

- Schools for children
- Hospitals
- Nursing home care
- Housing

**(iv)** The graph shown above is __________. Tick (✓) the correct answer.

Expansive ☐ Constrictive ☐ Stationary ☐

**(v)** Calculate the percentage of the Irish population between the ages of 0 to 14 years in 2021.

**Optional rough work:**

**Answer:** ______________________________

**(vi)** Which age group and sex has the highest percentage of population across all groups?

Age group: ______________________ Sex: ______________________

**(vii)** Review the population pyramids below and answer the questions that follow.

### (A) Somalia 2020

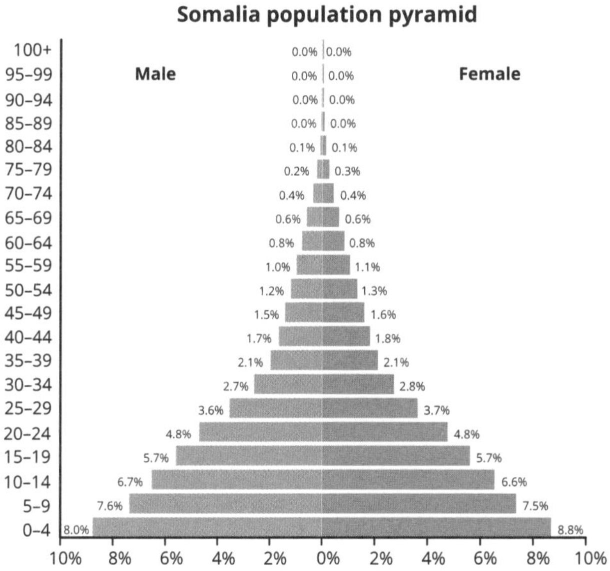

**Somalia population pyramid**

| | Male | Female |
|---|---|---|
| 100+ | 0.0% | 0.0% |
| 95–99 | 0.0% | 0.0% |
| 90–94 | 0.0% | 0.0% |
| 85–89 | 0.0% | 0.0% |
| 80–84 | 0.1% | 0.1% |
| 75–79 | 0.2% | 0.3% |
| 70–74 | 0.4% | 0.4% |
| 65–69 | 0.6% | 0.6% |
| 60–64 | 0.8% | 0.8% |
| 55–59 | 1.0% | 1.1% |
| 50–54 | 1.2% | 1.3% |
| 45–49 | 1.5% | 1.6% |
| 40–44 | 1.7% | 1.8% |
| 35–39 | 2.1% | 2.1% |
| 30–34 | 2.7% | 2.8% |
| 25–29 | 3.6% | 3.7% |
| 20–24 | 4.8% | 4.8% |
| 15–19 | 5.7% | 5.7% |
| 10–14 | 6.7% | 6.6% |
| 5–9 | 7.6% | 7.5% |
| 0–4 | 8.0% | 8.8% |

10% 8% 6% 4% 2% 0% 2% 4% 6% 8% 10%

### (B) Japan 2020

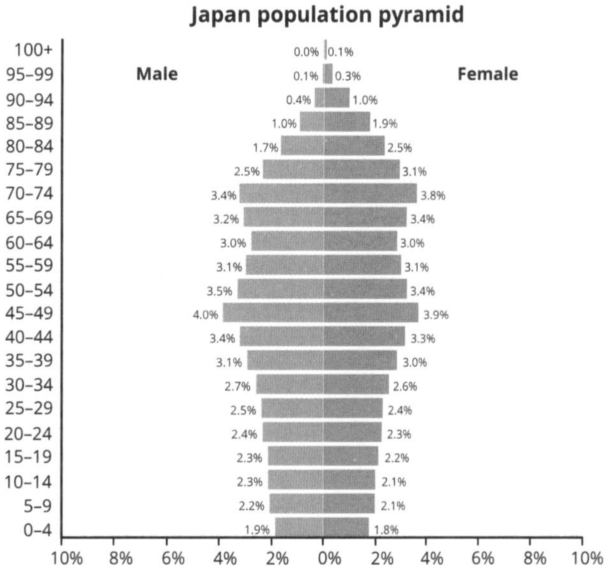

**Japan population pyramid**

| | Male | Female |
|---|---|---|
| 100+ | 0.0% | 0.1% |
| 95–99 | 0.1% | 0.3% |
| 90–94 | 0.4% | 1.0% |
| 85–89 | 1.0% | 1.9% |
| 80–84 | 1.7% | 2.5% |
| 75–79 | 2.5% | 3.1% |
| 70–74 | 3.4% | 3.8% |
| 65–69 | 3.2% | 3.4% |
| 60–64 | 3.0% | 3.0% |
| 55–59 | 3.1% | 3.1% |
| 50–54 | 3.5% | 3.4% |
| 45–49 | 4.0% | 3.9% |
| 40–44 | 3.4% | 3.3% |
| 35–39 | 3.1% | 3.0% |
| 30–34 | 2.7% | 2.6% |
| 25–29 | 2.5% | 2.4% |
| 20–24 | 2.4% | 2.3% |
| 15–19 | 2.3% | 2.2% |
| 10–14 | 2.3% | 2.1% |
| 5–9 | 2.2% | 2.1% |
| 0–4 | 1.9% | 1.8% |

10% 8% 6% 4% 2% 0% 2% 4% 6% 8% 10%

**(a)** Which of the population pyramids is showing a developed country? Tick (✓) the correct answer.

A ☐ B ☐

**(b)** The term used to describe the structure of Pyramid A is ________. Tick (✓) the correct answer.

Expansive ☐ Constrictive ☐ Stationary ☐

(c) Using the graphs provided, describe the population **characteristics** for the two countries shown on the previous page.

**Exam Hint**

In your answer, make sure to comment on:

- Width of the base – a wide base indicates a higher birth rate.
- Width at higher levels, which indicates the numbers living into old age.
- Any narrowing or widening in the centre.
- The age/sex breakdown of each population – are there more males or females in any particular group?

**Exam Dictionary**

**Characteristics** of population include things such as population size, age structure, birth rate, numbers living into old age and gender balance.

| A | B |
|---|---|
| ______________________ | ______________________ |
| ______________________ | ______________________ |
| ______________________ | ______________________ |
| ______________________ | ______________________ |
| ______________________ | ______________________ |
| ______________________ | ______________________ |
| ______________________ | ______________________ |
| ______________________ | ______________________ |
| ______________________ | ______________________ |

## Population Change

6. Complete the case study on the next page relating to population change in Ireland and any developing country that you have studied. You must provide a description of population under each of the headings given.

**Remember!**

It is very useful to consider some of the following in your answer:

- Impact of colonialism
- Joining the EU (Ireland)
- Changing role of women
- Role or influence of religion
- Events such as famine or war
- Periods of economic boom or downturn
- Education
- Infant mortality rates

**Exam Hint**

Having this information in one place will be extremely helpful exam preparation.

You must be able to show how population has changed in Ireland and in a developing country.

## Case Study

Name of developed country: **Ireland** Location: **Europe**

Birth rate: __________ Death rate: __________

Life expectancy: __________

Shape of population pyramid: __________

Stage on the demographic transition model: __________

Describe how Ireland's population has changed over time:

Future population projections for Ireland:

Name of developing country: __________ Location: __________

Birth rate: __________ Death rate: __________

Life expectancy: __________

Shape of population pyramid: __________

Stage on the demographic transition model: __________

Describe how population in __________ has changed over time:

Future population projections for __________:

## NCCA Sample Question and Answer

### Question 1

**(i)** Outline how the birth rate changes in Stage 3 and Stage 4 of the demographic transition model. [4 marks]

In Stage 3 of the Demographic Transition Model (DTM) we see birth rate drop from a high level. This is because the economy of the country is continuing to grow and people begin to plan their family size.

In Stage 4 of the DTM we see birth rates and death rates that are both low and population growth stabilises. Population growth in this stage can still be impacted by incidences of pandemic or environmental disasters.

This answer requires us to outline how birth rate changes in Stage 3 and 4. It is important to state what you see on the graph and then to use your knowledge of the topic to state why we see the drop. Marks are awarded for stating what we see and development marks are awarded as we provide more information.

**Marks Awarded**

**(i)** 1 mark for stating; 3 marks for development

(1 + 3 = 4 marks)

**(ii)** According to the demographic transition model, birth rates and death rates are decreasing in Stage 3. Outline **three** reasons for this possible decrease. [9 marks]

1. Family planning

   In Stage 3, the economy of the country is developing. People now begin to plan the size of their families and use contraceptives through better healthcare. There are increased levels of awareness and education around family planning.

2. Access to healthcare

   ______________________________

   ______________________________

3. Better food

   ______________________________

   ______________________________

(ii) The first one has been completed for you. 1 mark is awarded for stating 'family planning', 2 further marks are awarded for explaining this. You can now complete the next two.

**Marks Awarded**

**(ii)** 1 mark awarded for each stated reason (1 + 1 + 1 = 3 marks)
Further 2 marks for each for development (2 + 2 + 2 = 6 marks)
(3 + 6 = 9 marks)
Total = 13 marks

# 19 Migration

In this section, the Learning Outcomes we will look at are: **3.2**, **3.9**

## Learning Checklist:

- ☐ I can give a definition for the key words and terms associated with migration.
- ☐ I can explain what push and pull factors are and give examples.
- ☐ I can describe forced migration and use my case study to explain where it has happened.
- ☐ I can describe organised migration and use my case study to explain what occurred.
- ☐ I can explain how globalisation has an impact on migration.
- ☐ I can interpret information from graphs.
- ☐ I can identify trends in data and outline what I see.
- ☐ I can locate different locations on maps and draw conclusions based on evidence provided.

## Key Migration Language

1. (i) Match each key term in Table A with its definition in Table B below. The first one has been completed for you.

| A | B |
|---|---|
| Refugee | When a person moves from one country or district to another. |
| Forced migration | An immigrant given special permission to live in another country because of war, natural disasters or persecution. |
| Migrant | A person who moves from one place to another to find work or better living conditions. |
| Individual migration | An immigrant looking to be accepted as a refugee in another country. |
| Emigrant | A person who comes to live in a foreign country. |
| Asylum seeker | When a person is forced to move due to war or famine. |
| Organised migration | A person who leaves their own country to live in another. |
| Immigrant | Planned migrations of people carried out by governments or other organisations. |

**(ii)** Review the tweet below and answer the question.

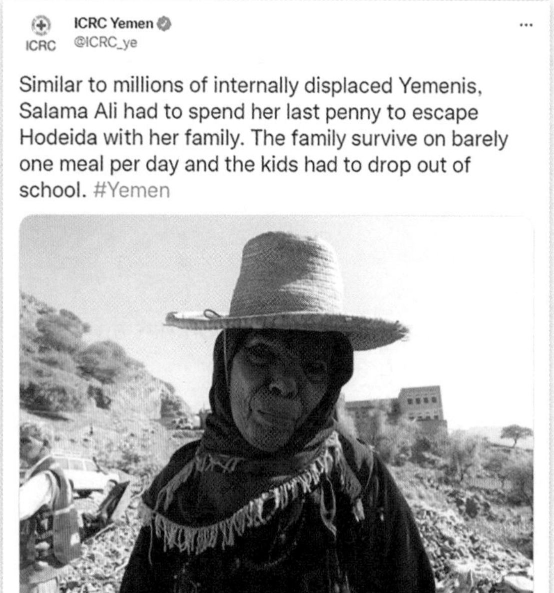
ICRC Yemen
@ICRC_ye

Similar to millions of internally displaced Yemenis, Salama Ali had to spend her last penny to escape Hodeida with her family. The family survive on barely one meal per day and the kids had to drop out of school. #Yemen

Salama Ali is an **internally displaced person** in Yemen. Explain what is meant by this term.

___

___

___

___

___

___

___

___

## Exam Hint

If you are presented with a term in the exam that is unfamiliar to you, break it down into parts. For example, here we can break down the term **'internally displaced person'** into a **person** who has been **'displaced'** (forced to move from their original **place**/home), and this has happened **'internally'** (**inside** their own country).

**(iii)** The people in the images below have all left their home country to move elsewhere. Select the appropriate terms from the list below to describe each situation and place them underneath the correct image.

| Organised migration | Refugee | Individual migration |
|---|---|---|
| Emigrant | Forced migration | Internally displaced person |

Sarah O'Connor is an Irish person who decided to move to Sydney, Australia, in search of greater job opportunities.

___

___

___

___

Abbas Khaled fled to Germany from Syria when civil war broke out in his home country. He was given permission to stay.

___

___

___

___

Piotr and Anna Nowak came to live in Ireland from Poland. They came to find employment and to save up to refurbish a family business back home.

___

___

___

___

## Push and Pull Factors

2. **(i)** Match each term to its correct definition and place the answer in the answer box.

| Term |
|---|
| A. Push factor |
| B. Pull factor |
| C. Barrier to migration |

| Definition |
|---|
| 1. Something that encourages a person to leave an area. |
| 2. Something that prevents or discourages a person from migrating. |
| 3. Something that encourages a person to come to an area. |

| Answer | |
|---|---|
| A | |
| B | |
| C | |

**(ii)** For each of the factors in the table below, state if it is a push factor, a pull factor or a barrier to migration. You must then explain why. The first one has been completed for you.

| Factor | Push factor/Pull factor/Barrier to migration | Why? |
|---|---|---|
| War | Push factor | War in a country can make it unsafe for people to remain. They may flee their homes in search of safety. |
| Natural disasters | | |
| Lack of employment | | |
| Climate change | | |
| Leaving family behind | | |
| Improved quality of life | | |
| Desertification | | |
| Safety | | |

Continued on the next page →

| Factor | Push factor/Pull factor/Barrier to migration | Why? |
|---|---|---|
| Education opportunities | | |
| Improved healthcare | | |
| Cost of travel | | |
| Famine | | |

**(iii)** The graph below shows migration data in Ireland from 2009 to 2020.

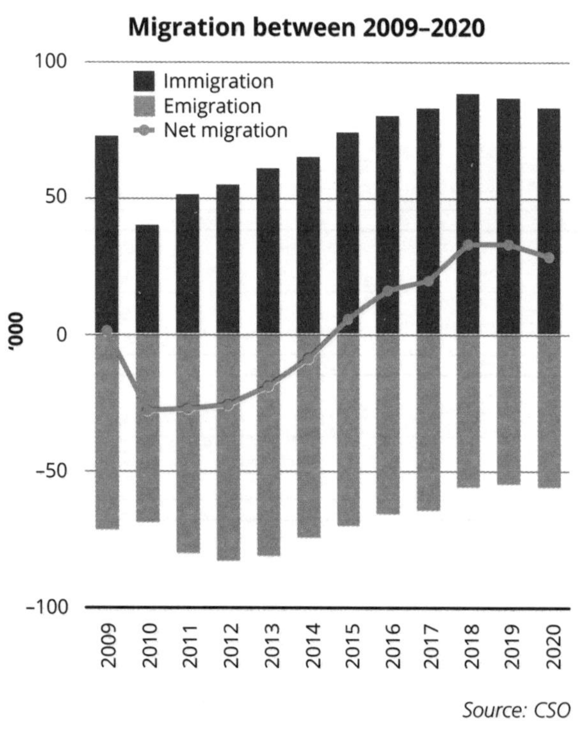


## GeoSkill

This graph is showing the numbers of people who have immigrated to Ireland and the number who have emigrated from Ireland between 2009 and 2020. Use the key to help you.

**(a)** In what year was emigration highest?

______________________

**(b)** State two push factors that could cause a young person to leave Ireland to live elsewhere.

**1.** ______________________

**2.** ______________________

**(c)** Describe the trend shown on the graph above for immigration and emigration from 2009 to 2020.

______________________

## Exam Hint

When describing trends from a graph, you are looking at any pattern shown in the results. Is there any change in the figures shown?

**(d)** Can you think of one possible reason (push or pull factor) behind this trend?

______________________________________________

______________________________________________

______________________________________________

______________________________________________

## Forced Migration

**3. (i) (a)** Read the article below which outlines the experience of refugees who are fleeing civil war in Cameroon in search of safety.

**8,000 Cameroonian refugees have fled to Nigeria's eastern and southern states, bringing the total Cameroonian refugee population in the country to nearly 60,000 people**

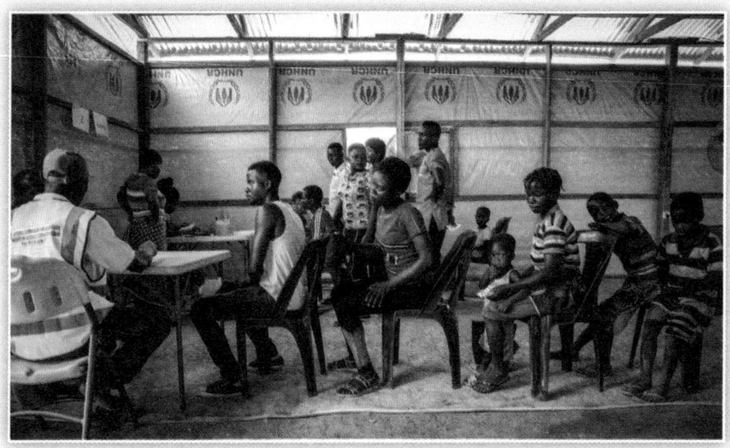

Refugees reported fleeing violence and some even arrived across the border with gunshot wounds. According to new arrivals, most come from areas near the border and have trekked across savannah and forests to reach Nigeria.

Local communities and governments are the first responders to this latest influx, providing food, shelter and household items that are desperately needed for those who have left everything behind.

Refugees who just arrived are currently being sheltered in public schools and health facilities or with local families.

*Source: www.unchr.org*

**(b)** This is an example of what type of migration? Tick (✓) the correct box.

Organised ☐ Individual ☐ Forced ☐

**(c)** How many Cameroonian refugees in total have fled to Nigeria?

______________________________________________

**(d)** What push factors forced the refugees to flee?

______________________________________________

______________________________________________

**(e)** Describe the response of local government and people to the arrival of the refugees.

## Case Study

**(ii)** Forced migration is occurring in many places across the world.

**(a)** Other than the named example of forced migration mentioned on the previous page, name an example of forced migration that you have studied and state where and when it occurred.

Forced migration studied:

Where and when it occurred:

### Exam Hint

Having some key information from case studies prepared is very helpful for your exam. This will also help you to revise key migration terms!

**(b)** Outline the reasons for the forced migration and any consequences.

In your answer, include any push factors (to leave their home country), pull factors (to their destination country) and barriers that the migrants faced.

### Remember!

The consequences can include any effects that the migration had on those moving and also on the place/people in the place where they migrated to.

## )rganised Migration

### Case Study

**4. (i)** Complete the paragraph below using the terms provided.

England Scottish Organised Ulster Estates Undertakers

The Plantation of ________________ took place in 1609. King James I of ________________ confiscated land from the native Irish. Almost four million acres of land was divided up into ________________ and rented cheaply to the English and ________________ planters. These new planters were known as ________________ who undertook to plant the new settlers onto the land to make it easier for the English to rule. This was an ________________ migration.

**(ii)** State one pull factor that pulled the new English and Scottish settlers to Ulster.

________________________________________

**(iii)** Explain two consequences of the organised plantation of Ulster.

**1.** ________________________________________

**2.** ________________________________________

**(iv)** State one barrier to migration that the English and Scottish planters faced.

________________________________________

## ligration and Globalisation

Migration is a powerful driver of sustainable development.

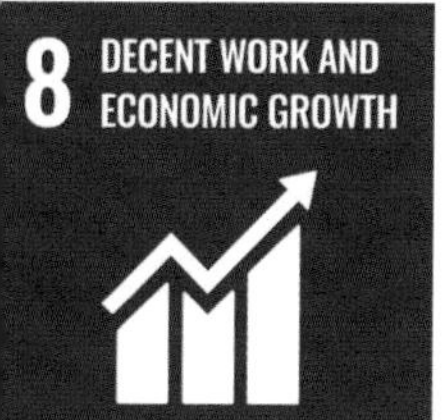


- Promoting decent work
- Working to combat (resolve) issues of child labour
- Working to resolve issues of trafficking people for forced labour
- Working to address the increasing issue of women being forced to migrate in search of employment
- Working on improving the laws that protecting those who migrate for employment

**(i)** Sustainable Development Goal number 8 shown above has many targets to help promote safe, fair and sustainable migration. Select one of the targets and describe how this would help migrants.

________________________________________

________________________________________

________________________________________

________________________________________

________________________________________

**Answer the questions to complete the mind map. This will support your revision.**

## Prompt Questions for Mind Map

**(a)** Can you give definitions of all key terms related to migration?

**(b)** List all of the push and pull factors that you can think of. Are you clear on the definition of each term? What is a barrier to migration? Can you give an example?

**(c)** Outline what forced migration is. What is your case study on this topic? Can you outline this case study to describe push/pull factors and barriers? Do you know the consequences of this migration?

**(d)** What is individual migration? What is your case study on this topic? Can you outline this case study to describe push/pull factors and barriers? Do you know the consequences of this migration?

**(e)** What is organised migration? What is your case study on this topic? Can you outline this case study to describe push/pull factors and barriers? Do you know the consequences of this migration?

**(f)** Can you outline how globalisation has an impact on migration?

(a) Key Migration Language

(f) Globalisation and Migration

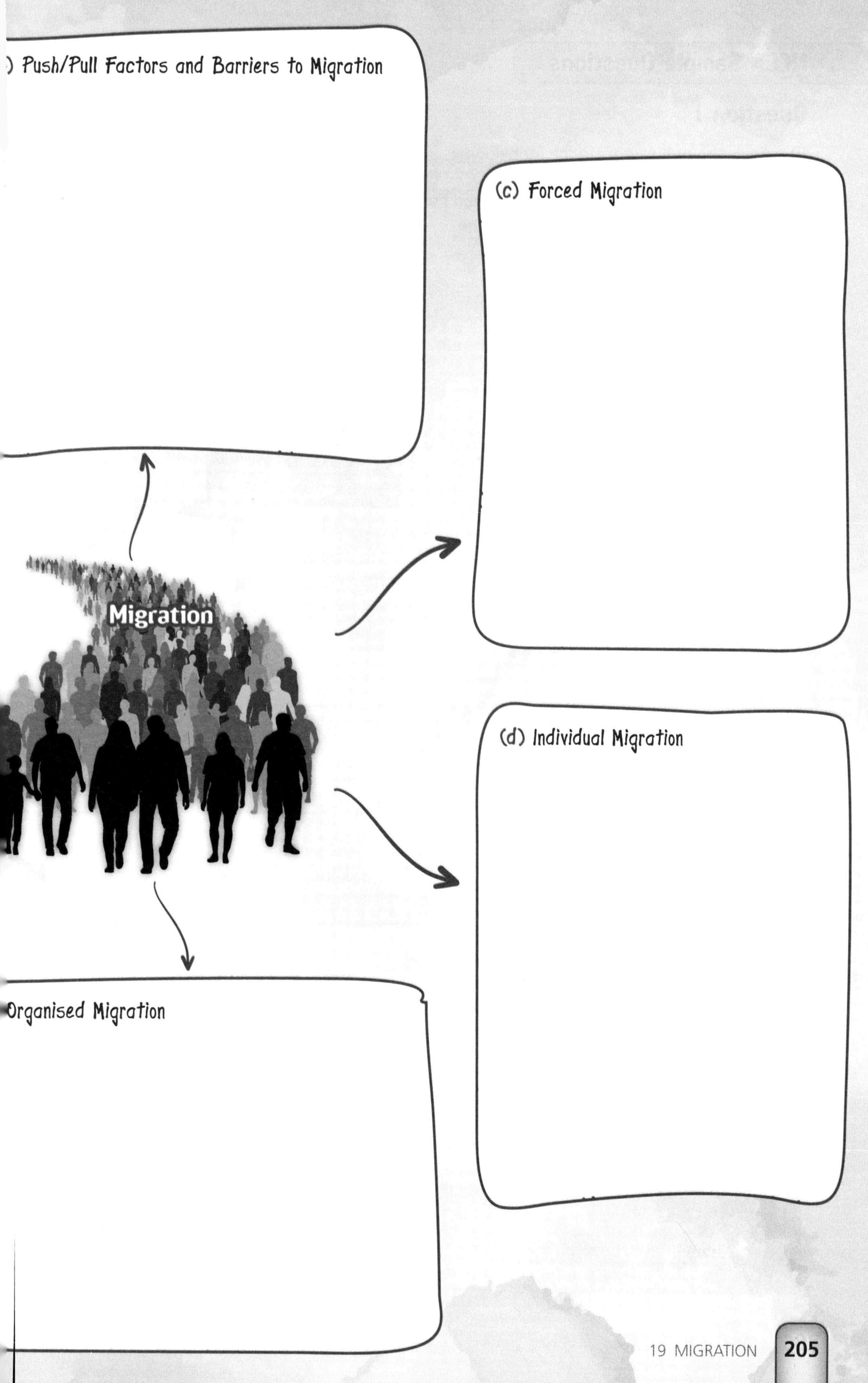
) Push/Pull Factors and Barriers to Migration
(c) Forced Migration
Migration
(d) Individual Migration
Organised Migration

## NCCA Sample Questions

### Question 1

**(i)** Circle the **pull factors** in the list below:

War    Employment    Good healthcare    Famine    Access to schools

**(ii)** Read the article below.

This Syrian refugee family fled their home in Aleppo in 2012. When bombing struck their town, 'within 24 hours the city was destroyed,' Ahmad recalls. They fled to Lebanon, where they shared a small flat with Ahmad's three siblings and their children. Ahmad was able to find some work from time to time, but knew his future was bleak, especially as his six-year-old son Abdullah had developed hearing problems. The family was eventually accepted to resettle in Germany under the government's Humanitarian Assistance Programme. They travelled to Germany in September 2013 and were among the first group of Syrians to arrive in the country under this programme.

*Source: The UN Refugee Agency*

**Exam Hint**

Underline key words or figures as you read the passage.

Define the term 'refugee'.

________________________________________

________________________________________

________________________________________

**(iii)** Describe **two** possible **reasons** why the family would have originally migrated to Lebanon. Refer to the snapshot of the map below to inform your answer.

**GeoSkill**

Look closely at the map and locate Aleppo and then Lebanon. Use evidence from the map in your answer here.

1. ________________________________________

________________________________________

________________________________________

________________________________________

________________________________________

2. ________________________________________

________________________________________

________________________________________

________________________________________

________________________________________

**(iv)** What is the impact of families like Ahmad's relocating to host countries such as Germany?

______________________________

______________________________

______________________________

**(v)** List **two** positive impacts of families like Ahmad's locating to your local area.

1. ______________________________

2. ______________________________

## Question 2

**(i)** The data presented below represents child migrants hosted in a country. Use the data in the table to draw a bar chart. (In this data set, 'child migrants' are persons aged 19 and under). [8 marks]

| Year | 1990 | 1995 | 2000 | 2005 | 2010 | 2015 |
|---|---|---|---|---|---|---|
| Percentage of migrants | 21% | 20% | 19% | 15% | 14% | 14% |

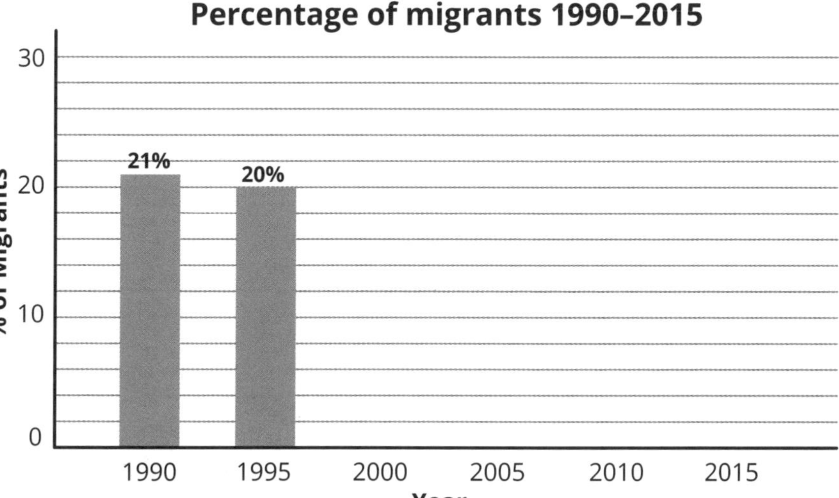


*In this question you are expected to draw your own bar chart to display the data. You need to use a ruler and pencil to do this. Each bar should be equally spaced.*

**(ii)** Outline **one** pattern that the table demonstrates. [4 marks]

*From reviewing the data I can see that the percentage of migrants has decreased between the period 1990 and 2015. Between 1990 and 2000 the numbers are dropping by only 1% every five years. However, over the period 2000 to 2010 we see a much larger drop of 4% and then 1%. This appears to stabilise between 2010 and 2015.*

*Here we must state the pattern that we see in the graph/table. We must then further develop our answer by outlining the pattern across the years shown. It is important to quote the data displayed on your graph or from the table to provide evidence to develop your answer.*

**Marks Awarded**

**(i)** Correctly drawn axis – 2 marks
1 mark for each % correctly shown on the graph – 6 marks
(2 + 6 = 8 marks)

**(ii)** Pattern stated = 1 mark
Development = 3 marks
(1 + 3 = 4 marks)

Total = 10 marks

# 20 Rural and Urban Settlement in Ireland

In this section, the Learning Outcome we will look at is: **3.4**

## Learning Checklist:

- ☐ I can explain the difference between rural and urban settlement.
- ☐ I understand how historical factors influenced settlement in Ireland.
- ☐ I can describe how the physical landscape influenced the origin of settlement in Ireland.
- ☐ I understand how Dublin city has influenced the location of settlement in Ireland.
- ☐ I can interpret information from maps and infographics.

## What Is a Settlement?

**1.** **(i)** Write a brief description highlighting the differences between urban and rural settlement. You may use the images below to help you.

| **Urban** | **Rural** |
|---|---|
|  | 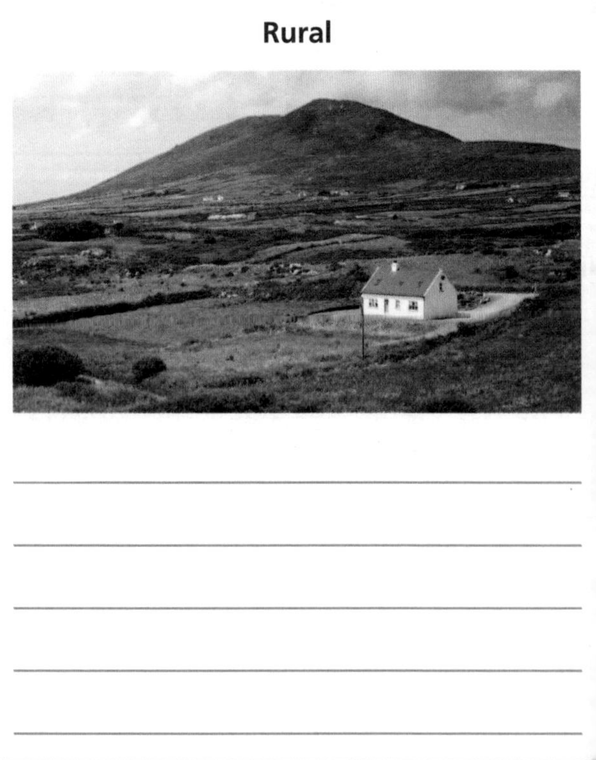 |

**Exam Hint**

Use both your understanding of the difference between urban and rural settlement and the evidence in the pictures. Bullet points would suffice here.

**(ii)** Examine the map of Ireland below which shows the location of urban and rural settlement in Ireland. Answer the accompanying questions.

**Remember!**

What physical features are found along Ireland's coasts? These can make settlement difficult.

**GeoSkill**

Interpreting maps: carefully examine the legend with the map.

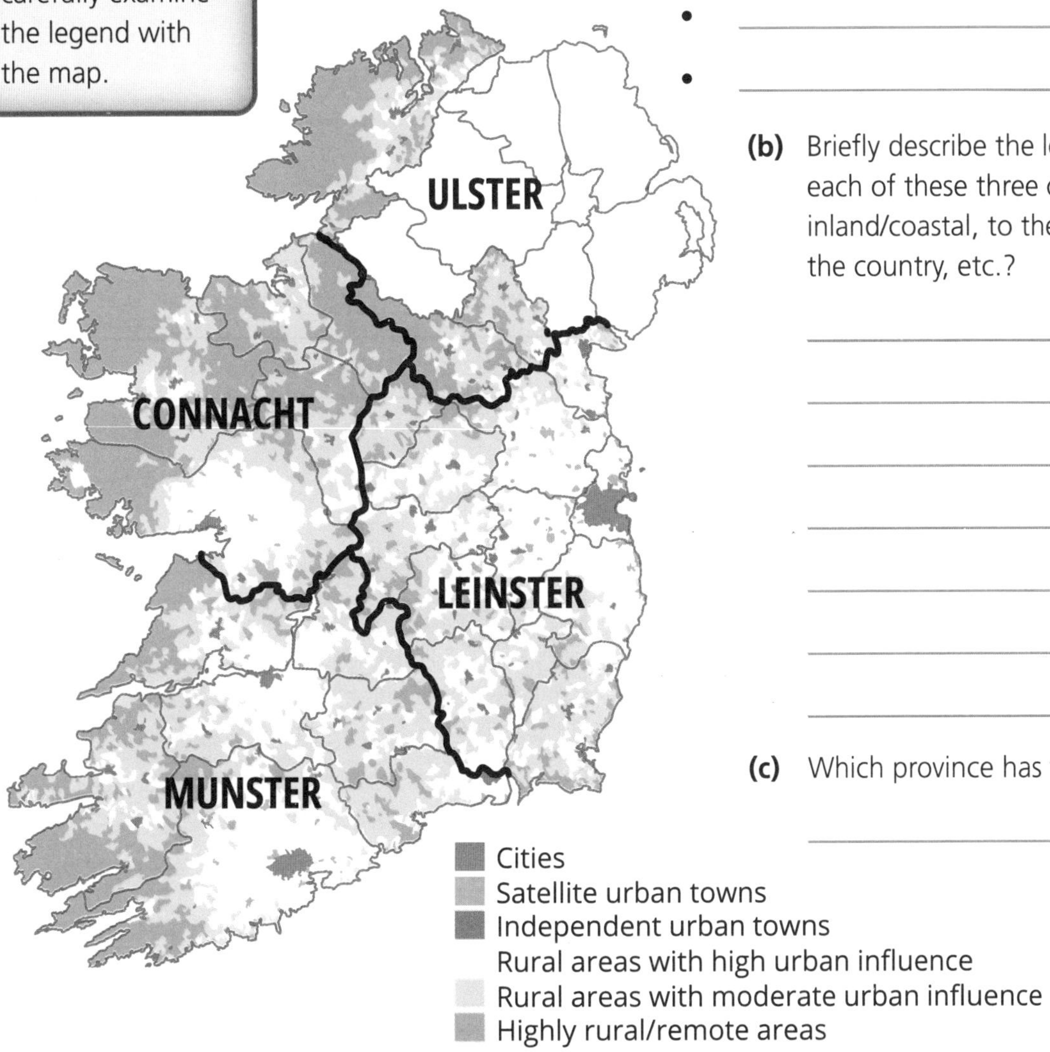

**(a)** Name three Irish cities shown on this map.

- __________
- __________
- __________

**(b)** Briefly describe the location of each of these three cities. Are they inland/coastal, to the east/west of the country, etc.?

**(c)** Which province has the most cities?

**(d)** Describe where the highly rural areas of Ireland are located on the map. Suggest reasons why these areas are highly remote.

**(e)** Which province has the least number of cities according to this map?

2. Examine the three images below showing three different settlement periods in Ireland. Use these images to help you complete the Settlement in Ireland Timeline on the next page.

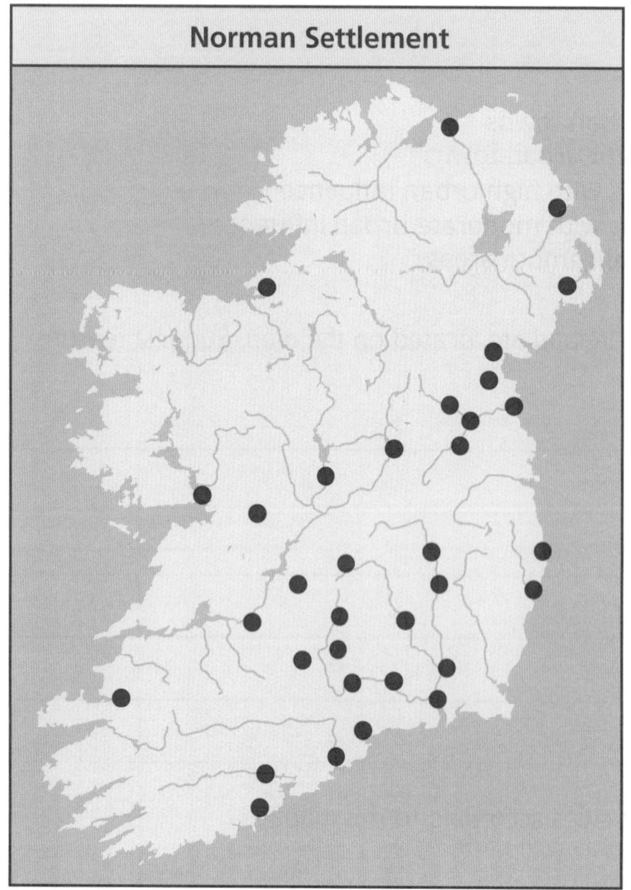

# SETTLEMENT IN IRELAND TIMELINE

| Viking | Norman | ______________ |
|---|---|---|
| When did these settlers arrive? | When did these settlers arrive? | |
| What cities can trace their origins to these settlers? | What cities can trace their origins to these settlers? | |
| Why did they choose these locations? | Why did they choose these locations? | |
| Describe their type of settlement. | Describe their type of settlement. | |

**Exam Hint**

The last piece of the timeline is blank. What type of settlement is left from the options above? Why would the questions used in each of the other sections not be suitable to use here?

When you've chosen which settlement to put here, write about the factors you are most familiar with:

- What have you studied about this type of settlement?
- What topics are dominating the news today regarding settlement in Ireland?

3. **(i)** The town of Drogheda is situated on the east coast of Ireland. Based on your understanding of the influence of the physical landscape on settlement, complete the boxes below, using the OS map on the following page. You must provide map evidence to support your answers.

**Rivers:** What did they provide in terms of direction, bridging points, etc.?

**Drainage:** Why is dry land important and what maintains this?

**Fertile soil:** What economic activities does this support?

**Altitude and relief:** What influence do flat land and weather exposure have on settlement?

**Remember!**

**LEN** for the grid references:

- **L**etter
- **E**asting
- **N**orthing

**Exam Hint**

Use four- or six-figure grid referencing to highlight evidence to put in each box. Keep each point short.

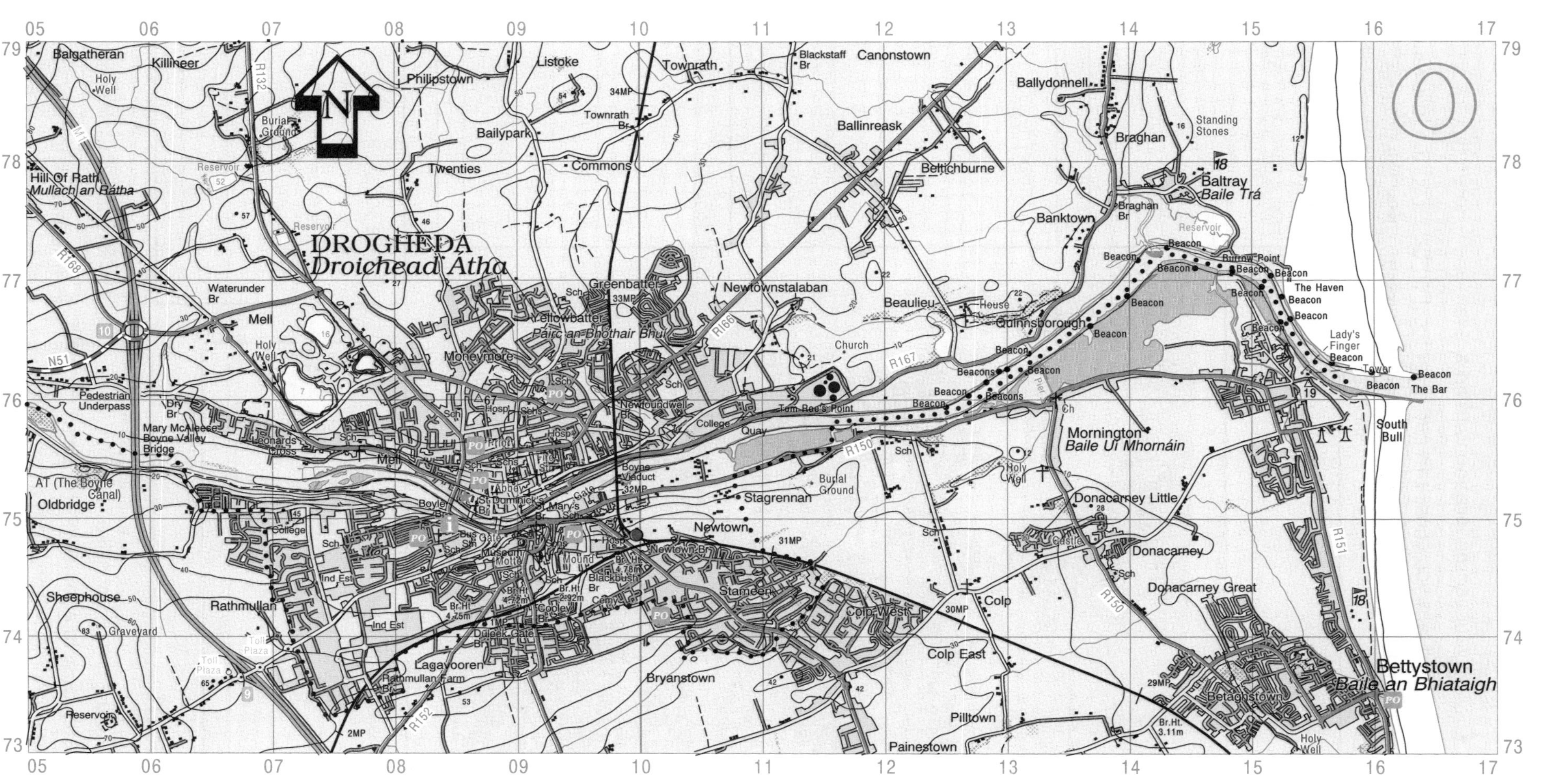

**(ii)** Examine the map below showing Ireland's rivers, mountains, lakes, towns and cities.

The Irish Government has tasked you with choosing the location for a new rural **or** urban settlement.

- Mark your chosen location with an X. State your chosen type of settlement.
- Explain why you chose this particular location based on the following factors: drainage, altitude/relief, rivers, fertile soil and closeness to other towns/cities.

Type of settlement:

_______________________________________________

Drainage:

_______________________________

_______________________________

_______________________________

_______________________________

Altitude/Relief:

_______________________________

_______________________________

_______________________________

_______________________________

_______________________________

Rivers:

_______________________________

_______________________________

_______________________________

_______________________________

_______________________________

Closeness to other towns/cities:

_______________________________________

_______________________________________

_______________________________________

Fertile soil:

_______________________________________

_______________________________________

_______________________________________

_______________________________________

**Exam Hint**

Why would a city or town like to be reasonably close to another city or town? Think of economic factors, such as work, and social factors, such as lifestyle.

**Remember!**

Check back to the Learning Outcome on soil. Where is Ireland's most fertile soil located?

## The Importance of Dublin City

4. (i) Dublin is Ireland's **primate city**. Explain the term in bold.

(ii) Look at the maps below.

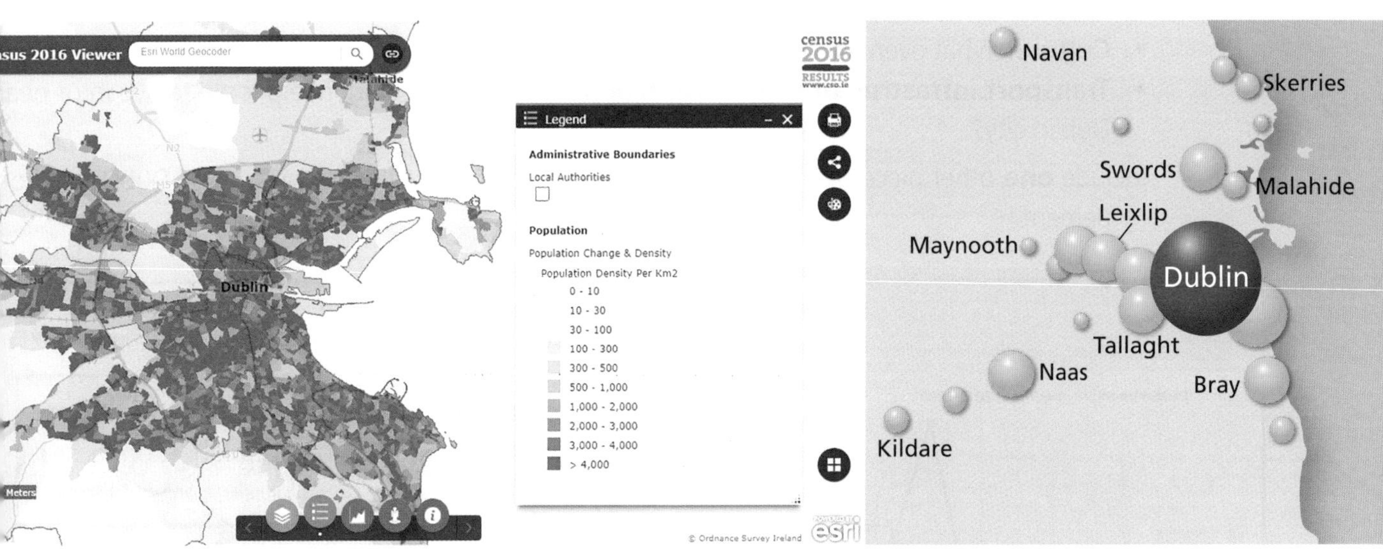


*Population density of Dublin per km²*

*Map of urban settlement around Dublin city*

(a) Where is the population density of Dublin higher – north or south?

**Exam Hint**

Why might Dublin city have a wider choice of jobs? What cultural events, e.g. sporting events, might Dublin attract that other towns might not?

(b) What infrastructure/service located in the north of County Dublin might deter people from living there?

(c) In which counties are the settlements of Bray, Navan and Maynooth located?

Bray:

Navan:

Maynooth:

(d) Explain **two** reasons why people from the towns of Kildare and Bray may rely on Dublin city for things such as employment and services.

Reason 1:

Reason 2:

**(iii)** Being Ireland's primate city means that:

- Dublin has employment opportunities in many different areas, such as secondary and tertiary economic sectors.
- Cultural events happen all year round exclusively in Dublin, e.g. sporting events and musicals.
- Getting to the city and around it can be easier than many other large towns/cities in the country. What type of roads lead to and from our country's capital? What types of transport are found here that other large towns or cities wouldn't have on such a similar scale?

Write **one** piece of information to complete the infographic below on how each factor could influence settlement in Dublin city. You may use information from the text below, such as:

- **Employment:** The graph shows unemployment in Dublin between 2018 and 2020. The headline refers to country-wide unemployment in May 2021.
- **Culture:** What events are held annually in Dublin only?
- **Transport infrastructure:** What types of transport might influence people to live in or near Dublin city?

Include **one** other piece of information you believe highlights the importance of Dublin city for settlement.

## Why Live in Dublin?

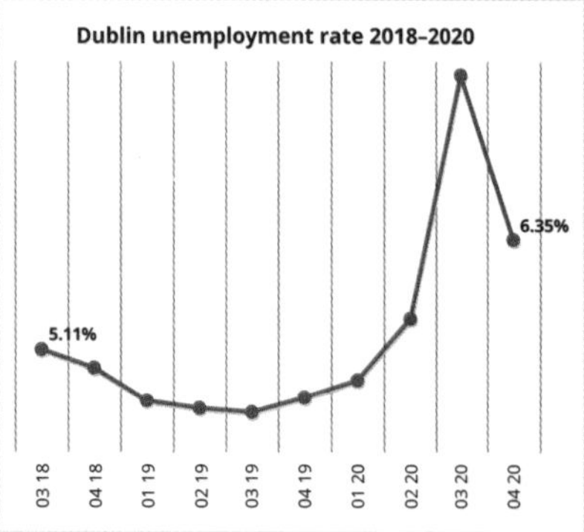

**Dublin unemployment rate 2018–2020**

5.11%
6.35%
03 18
04 18
01 19
02 19
03 19
04 19
01 20
02 20
03 20
04 20

**State's unemployment rate stays high at 21.9% in May**
Youth unemployment rate of 58.8% is one of highest on record
*Source: Irish Times*

Employment:

________________________________________

________________________________________

**Dublin Airport welcomed 32.9 million passengers in 2019**
*Source: Dublin Airport website*

**Trip Advisor: 7 out of Ireland's top 10 museums are found in Dublin**

Culture (GAA/concerts/museums):

________________________________________

________________________________________

Transport (airports/ports):

________________________________________

________________________________________

What else can you tell us about Dublin?

________________________________________

________________________________________

**Answer the questions to complete the mind map. This will support your revision.**

(a) Describe three main differences between urban and rural settlement in Ireland as you understand it.

(b) List the three main factors that influence urban settlement in Ireland.

(c) What influence did the Vikings have on settlement in Ireland?

**Urban/Rural Settlement**

(d) How did Norman settlement develop Viking settlement?

(e) The physical landscape plays a major role in the location of settlements. Write a brief paragraph explaining this statement.

(f) What is a primate city? Explain the influence Ireland's primate city has on settlement.

## NCCA Sample Questions and Answer

### Question 1

Discuss **two** factors that would have influenced the origin of settlement below. The first factor has been provided. [8 marks]

With the action verb 'discuss', this question wants you to support your chosen factors with evidence. You should choose two clear factors. Explain each factor, then use evidence from both images to support each one.

- What physical feature is the settlement located on and near? Why is this important to first-time settlers?
- What physical feature is offering protection from storms?
- What does the altitude of the settlement appear to be?

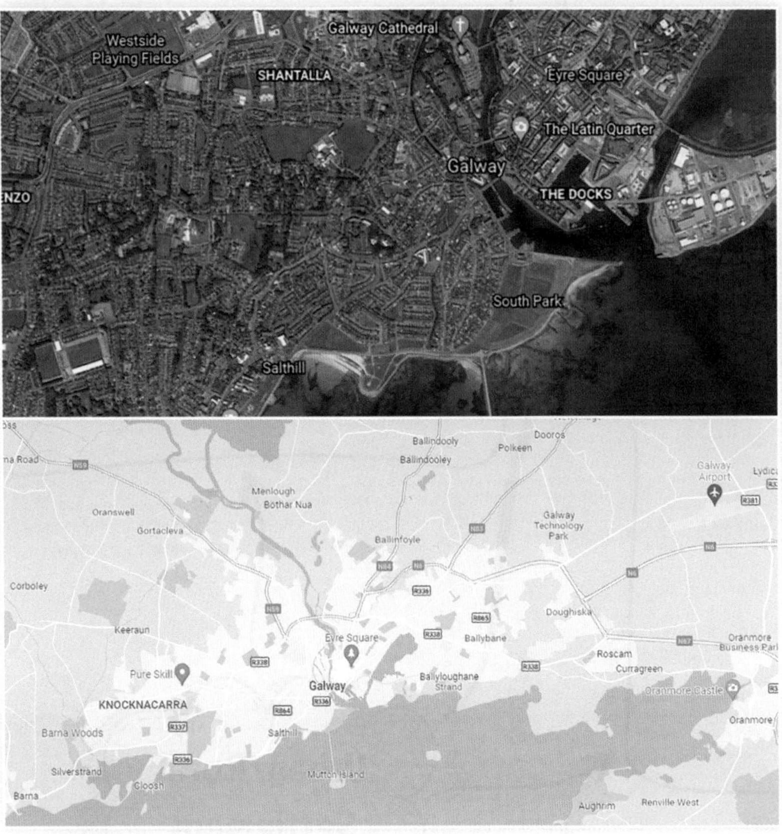


1. The settlement is located on a river. When settlers first arrived on the shores of what is now Galway they would have used the river, seen in the second image, as a means of transport. As there were no roads, this river would have allowed settlers to travel further inland. The river would have also meant potentially fertile soil for agricultural purposes. Lastly, the settlement built very close to the river in the photograph means that flooding would not have been a potential threat to settlers when they first arrived here.

2. ______________________________

______________________________

______________________________

______________________________

______________________________

**Exam Hint**

For your second factor, use the **SEE** method:

**S: State** it clearly

**E: Explain** it

**E:** Give **evidence** from both maps

**Marks Awarded**

4 marks per factor:

- 1 mark for clearly stating your factor
- 3 marks for developing it and giving evidence to support it

Total: 4 × 2 = 8 marks

## Question 2

**(i)** Using the snapshot of the two Google map images on page 218, would you classify this settlement as **A) rural** or **B) urban**?

___

**Exam Hint**

Use the **SEE** method:

**S: State** clearly your understanding of both rural and urban settlements and their differences

**E: Explain** each piece of evidence you have chosen

**E:** Give **evidence** from both maps

**(ii)** Use **three** pieces of evidence to explain your answer. The first one has been provided.

1. *In Ireland, urban settlement is any built-up settlement with a population over 1,500 people. There are several housing estates clearly visible in the first Google image. Each estate has many homes and I believe the population of this area exceeds 1,500 people.*

2. The number of national roads: N6, N59, N83 and N18

*Would a rural area have as many national roads converging on it?*

*Why would a large urban area need national roads converging on it?*

3. Green fields vs built-up areas

*Which is more obvious in each Google image? Which would you expect to find more of in a rural settlement and for what potential purposes?*

**Marks Awarded**

**(i)** 2 marks

**(ii)** 12 marks

- 1 mark for stating the evidence
- 3 marks for developing it and using evidence from both images

(4 × 3 = 12 marks)

Total = 14 marks

# 21 Urban Change

In this section, the Learning Outcome we will look at is: **3.4**

**Learning Checklist:**

- ☐ I can explain the term 'urban change'.
- ☐ I can describe the causes of urban change in an Irish city.
- ☐ I can explain the effects of urban change in an Irish city.
- ☐ I will practise the geographical skills of map reading (four- and six-figure referencing), examining an aerial photograph (identifying land use and locating it) and infographic interpretation (reading and answering questions on an infographic).

## What Is Urban Change?

**1.** Read the article below and answer each of the following questions.

**Cork 2050 Regeneration**

CORK 2050
REALISING THE FULL POTENTIAL

Taoiseach Micheál Martin announced that more than €400 million is being made available for regeneration projects in Cork city and county as part of the Cork 2050 Planning Framework.

The package includes more than €300 million to redevelop Cork's docklands beside the city centre, to allow for the construction of thousands of homes, and to develop public parks, leisure and cultural facilities.

For Cork's docklands the project will involve the redevelopment of the area, with many old buildings and factories removed to make way for new amenities. The city centre has a significant number of medieval sites and attractions and the plan looks to maintain the link Cork has with its past.

Why Cork? Cork is Ireland's second-largest city. It is estimated that Cork city and its surrounding areas will have a population of over 500,000 by 2050. It has Ireland's second-largest airport. Cork shipping port handles over 19% of all goods imported into Ireland by sea.

**Information adapted from RTÉ, Cork County Council and Cork City Council**

**Exam Hint**

- Read any article/headline carefully.
- Read the questions carefully.
- Underline any key terms/important facts you feel will help you to answer questions.
- Answer the questions asked.
- When using facts/information from articles/headlines, give the exact quote.
- Give as much relevant detail in your answers as you can.

**Remember!**

Always attempt the question in full. Even if you're unsure of the answer, you should never leave anything blank in the exam.

**(i)** **(a)** How much money is being made available for this project to Cork county as a whole?

**(b)** How much money is being made available specifically to Cork's docklands?

### Exam Hint

Short questions: These types of questions need specific answers, which can usually be found directly in the text/headline.

**(ii)** Why was Cork chosen to receive funding for a project of this size?

**(iii)** The Cork 2050 project has elements of **urban redevelopment** and **regeneration** in its plan. **Explain** both of these terms and find an example of each from the article.

### Exam Dictionary

**Explain:** Make clear by describing in more detail.

### Remember!

Highlight the **action verb** in the question to be sure of what you are being asked to do.

**Urban redevelopment:**

Example:

**Urban regeneration:**

Example:

**(iv)** 'This project will have a significant impact on the social, economic and environmental development of Cork city and county.'

Choose any two potential social, economic or environmental impacts of the Cork 2050 project mentioned in the article. Consider how they will impact Cork now and in the future.

### Exam Dictionary

**Consider:** Think carefully about something before making a decision.

Impact 1:

Impact 2:

## Urban Change: Causes and Consequences

2. (i) **Examine** the statements below and **classify** them as either a cause of urban change or an effect of urban change/urbanisation for Dublin city.

### Exam Dictionary

**Examine:** Consider an idea in a way that uncovers the assumptions and relationships of the issue.

**Classify:** Group things based on common characteristics.

**Cause and effect:** The relationship between two things when one thing makes something else happen.

| Statements | Cause or Effect? |
|---|---|
| Dublin's population is expected to grow by 400,000 in the decades ahead. | |
| Dublin is home to nearly 200,000 non-Irish nationals, more than any other part of the country. | |
| Dublin residential property prices rose by 0.6% in the year to May 2019, with house prices up 0.4% and apartments rising by 0.8%. | |
| Dublin urban sprawl has seen the creation of new towns such as Adamstown and Clonburris. | |
| Dublin is home to four universities and three institutes of technology. | |
| Dublin saw Ireland's highest number of new residential properties in 2019 at 1,546. | |

**(ii)** Choose two factors from those highlighted below. Using a city that you have studied, explain how each factor has had an impact on population change in that city.

**Immigration** (people moving to Ireland from other countries)

**Migration within cities** (people being rehoused)

**Natural population increase** (birth rate higher than death rate)

**Remember!**

If you are unsure of the meaning of any of the words here, now is the time to look it up and write out the definition.

Name of city: ______________________________

Factor 1:

_______________________________________________

_______________________________________________

Factor 2:

_______________________________________________

_______________________________________________

## Rural to Urban Migration

3. **(i)** From the table below, what trend can you **interpret** between urban and rural migration across Ireland in 2016?

**Exam Dictionary**

**Interpret:** Look at information and make conclusions.

**Percentage of people who moved to another county in 2016**

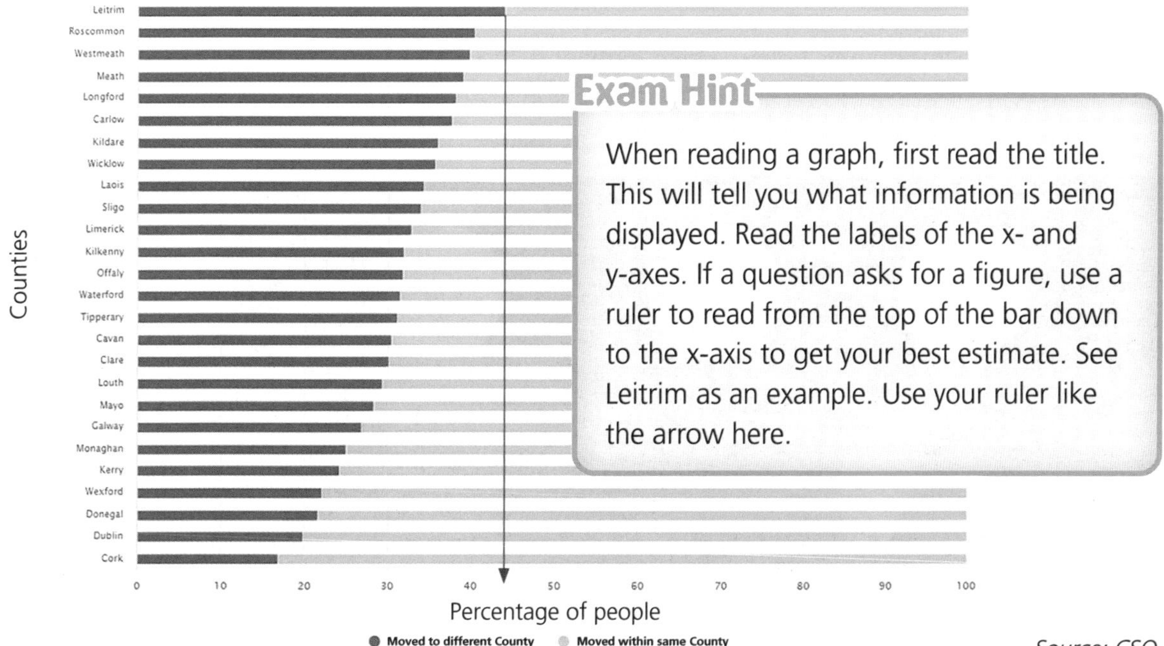


**Exam Hint**

When reading a graph, first read the title. This will tell you what information is being displayed. Read the labels of the x- and y-axes. If a question asks for a figure, use a ruler to read from the top of the bar down to the x-axis to get your best estimate. See Leitrim as an example. Use your ruler like the arrow here.

*Source: CSO*

**It's a Fact!**

**14,330 – The number of people who moved to Dublin from another county from January to April 2016**

## Exam Hint

Include information from the chart on the previous page to support your answer. Look at where Ireland's two largest cities (Dublin and Cork) are on the table.

(ii) The government has announced its Rural Development Policy 2021–2025. Opposite are some of the aims this policy hopes to achieve.

Can you list one economic, one social and one environmental benefit of this policy?

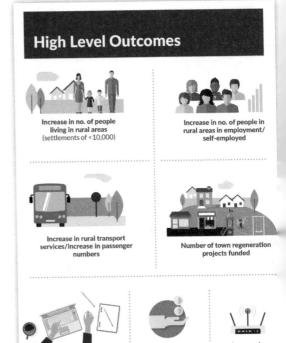

Economic:

Social:

Environmental:

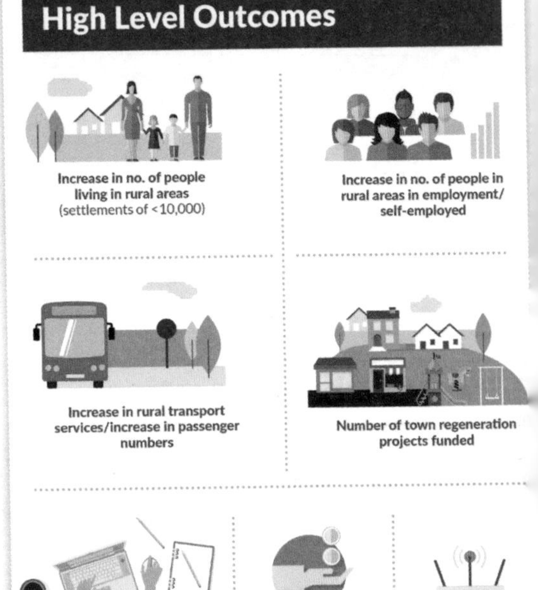

High Level Outcomes
Increase in no. of people living in rural areas (settlements of <10,000)
Increase in no. of people in rural areas in employment/ self-employed
Increase in rural transport services/increase in passenger numbers
Number of town regeneration projects funded
Number of hubs in the national remote working hub network
Reduction in regional income disparity
Increase in broadband coverage in rural areas

Source: Government of Irelan

## Urban Problems: Sprawl and Decay

4. Examine the infographic below which highlights the reasons why people would and would not live in Dublin city centre. Answer the questions that follow.

Source: dublinchamber.i

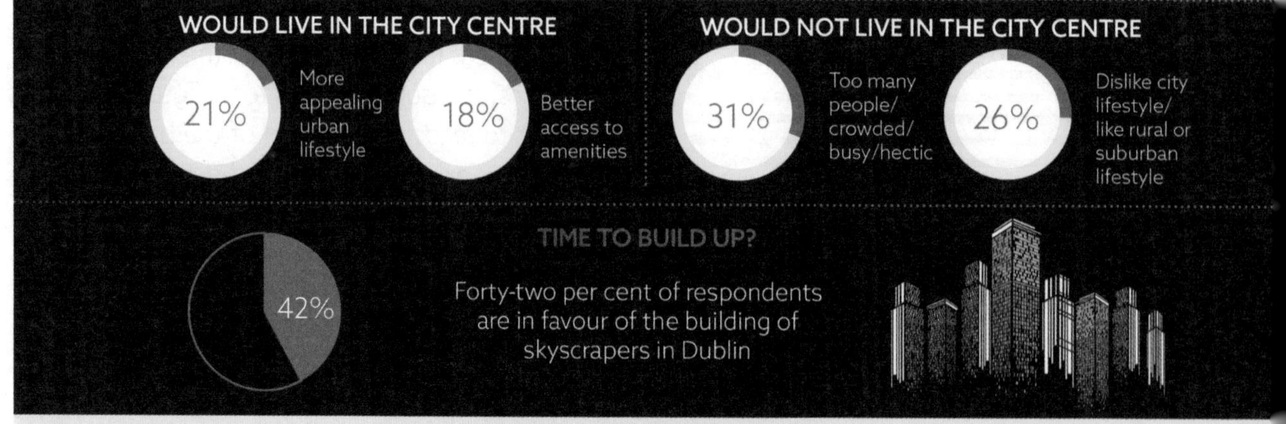

WOULD LIVE IN THE CITY CENTRE
21% More appealing urban lifestyle
18% Better access to amenities
WOULD NOT LIVE IN THE CITY CENTRE
31% Too many people/ crowded/ busy/hectic
26% Dislike city lifestyle/ like rural or suburban lifestyle
TIME TO BUILD UP?
42%
Forty-two per cent of respondents are in favour of the building of skyscrapers in Dublin

### Dublin City Population Density

The Dublin region accounts for more than 25% of the country's total population, with a population density of 4,588 people per square kilometre in the city.

Source: worldpopulationreview.com

**(i)** What are the two reasons why people would choose to live in the city, according to the infographic on the previous page?

______________________________

______________________________

**(ii)** What are the two reasons why people would choose not to live in the city, according to the infographic?

______________________________

______________________________

**(iii)** What issue would the building of more skyscrapers in Dublin city resolve?

______________________________

______________________________

**(iv)** Discuss one advantage and one disadvantage of building skyscrapers in a city.

Advantage: ______________________________

______________________________

Disadvantage: ______________________________

______________________________

**(v)** Name a city that you have studied. List two reasons why a person would choose to live in this city and two reasons why they would not.

Name of city: ______________________________

| Would live in the city | Would not live in the city |
|---|---|
| 1. | 1. |
| 2. | 2. |

Explain one reason from each of your choices above in greater detail below.

Would live in the city: ______________________________

______________________________

______________________________

______________________________

______________________________

______________________________

Would not live in the city: ______________________________

______________________________

______________________________

______________________________

______________________________

______________________________

**5.** Examine the infographic below which highlights the problems associated with urban sprawl in Dublin, and answer the question that follows.

### House Prices 2020

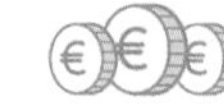

| **LEAST** EXPENSIVE | | **MOST** EXPENSIVE | |
|---|---|---|---|
| Leitrim | **€131,904** | Sth Co. Dublin | **€578,776** |
| Longford | **€135,622** | Sth Dublin City | **€408,371** |
| Roscommon | **€140,466** | North Dublin City | **€344,416** |
| Donegal | **€149,334** | Dublin City Centre | **€327,379** |

daft.ie

*Source: Daft.ie*

### Dublin is Europe's sixth most congested city

*Headline and photo source: thejournal.ie*

### Dublin is the county with the highest number of people who are receiving the Covid Pandemic Unemployment Payment this week at 14,305

*Source: www.gov.ie*

## Exam Hint

- When presented with a poster or infographic, take a minute to read the information on it.
- Use the information (facts and figures) from the infographic to back up your answer.

Using an image or headline from the infographic, discuss two problems associated with urban sprawl and explain how each problem may be overcome in a city you have studied.

## Remember!

State your chosen problems clearly. Use the 4 Ws approach: **W**hat is the problem? State clearly. **W**ho is impacted by it? **W**hy are they affected? **W**here is it happening? Lastly, suggest one possible solution to each problem.

Name of city: ______________________________

Problem 1: ______________________________

______________________________

______________________________

______________________________

______________________________

Problem 2: ____________________

____________________

____________________

____________________

____________________

**Exam Hint**

Longer questions are testing your understanding of Learning Outcomes. You are not limited to what information is given in the text. Show what you know!

6. Examine the tweets below and answer the questions that follow.

**A**

Frank O'Connor
@frank_oconnor

another historic empty property in #cork city centre with so much character, someone's home, be lovely see it restored, lived in, life, play, families, children #Homeless #socialcrime #Ireland #inequality #programmeforgovernment @CorkHealthyCity @corkcitycouncil #citiesforpeople

**B**

Noel Hogan
@noelahogan

Where is the sense in allowing these wonderful town centre buildings in #Drogheda to decay? They could be homes, or businesses, or something - anything - useful. #DerelictIreland #DerelictDrogheda

11:47 AM · Jul 12, 2021 · Twitter for iPhone

**(i)** What large urban areas are mentioned in each tweet?

A: ____________________

B: ____________________

**(ii)** Evidence of urban decay is visible in each image. Explain the term 'urban decay'.

____________________

____________________

____________________

____________________

**(iii)** List two other problems mentioned in the first tweet that are related to urban decay (hint: read the hashtags).

____________________

____________________

**(iv) Urban redevelopment** and **urban renewal** are two possible solutions to the urban decay described in the tweets on the previous page. Choose one solution and explain why you chose it.

Solution:

______________________________________________

______________________________________________

Reason:

______________________________________________

______________________________________________

## New Towns

**7.** The town of Clonburris is a new town located in Dublin West, near Lucan, Liffey Valley and Clondalkin. Examine the infographic below and answer the question that follows.

8,400 homes. It is hoped 4,000 will be sociably affordable.

Almost all residents will be able to access a bus stop within 400 metres or a train station within 800 metres.

Three primary and post-primary schools will be built and nearly all the houses will be located within 500 metres of a school.

90 acres of parks and open spaces.

*Sources: CSO, clonburris.ie, thejournal.ie*

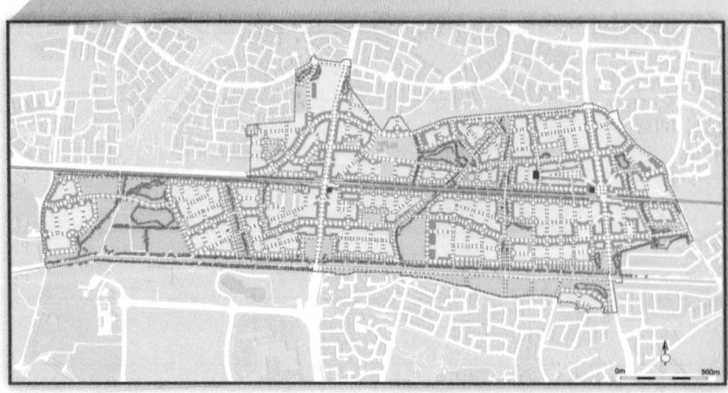

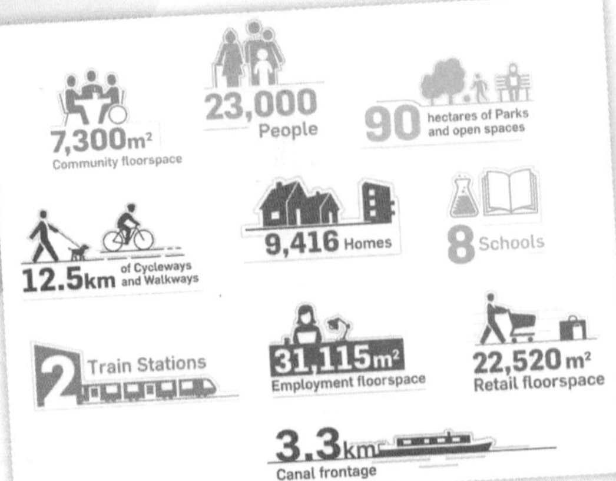


### Exam Hint

Use information from the infographic above to back up your answer.
Use terms such as 'urban renewal' and 'urban sprawl'.

A local TD has objected to this development on the grounds of potential increased traffic in the area. Write a letter to this local TD to explain how this development will address that issue and also help reduce overcrowding in Dublin county.

______________________________________________________________________

______________________________________________________________________

______________________________________________________________________

______________________________________________________________________

______________________________________________________________________

______________________________________________________________________

______________________________________________________________________

## Geography Skills Question: OS Maps and Urban Change

3. (i) The 2016 census showed that 'The biggest change in urbanisation occurred in Sligo county, where 40% of the population now live in the town compared with 37% five years ago'.

Study the Ordnance Survey map of Sligo town below. Identify (using four- or six-figure grid referencing) five services/amenities that you can see that would attract people from rural Sligo.

**Exam Hint**

Look for converging roads. Check the legend of an OS map to see the different types of roads running through Sligo. These roads will have differing amounts of traffic on them. Look for junctions where two different roads meet.

- Service/Amenity: ______________________ Grid reference: ______________________
- Service/Amenity: ______________________ Grid reference: ______________________
- Service/Amenity: ______________________ Grid reference: ______________________
- Service/Amenity: ______________________ Grid reference: ______________________
- Service/Amenity: ______________________ Grid reference: ______________________

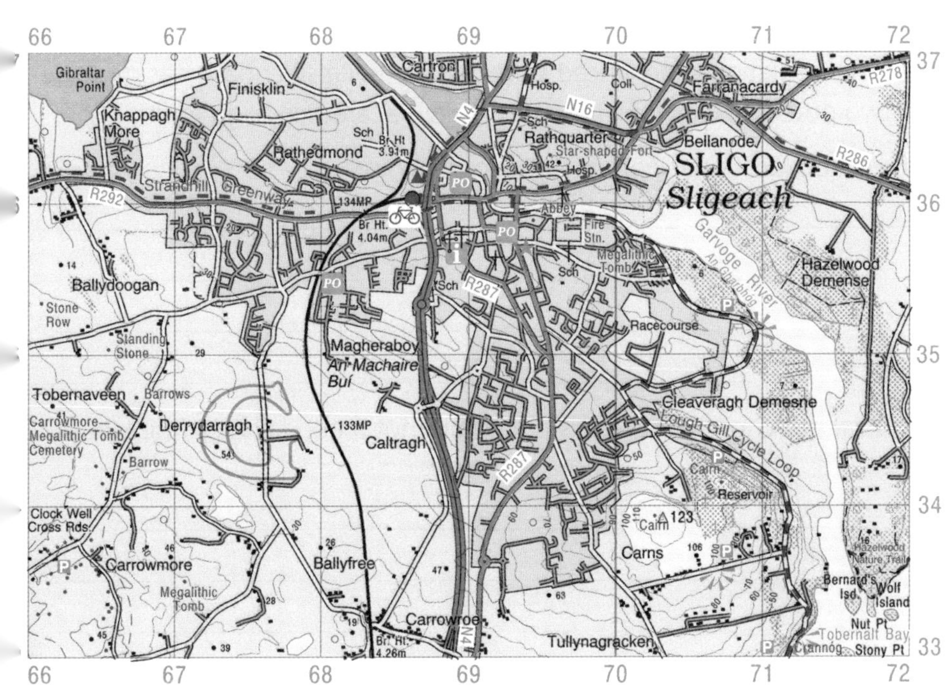


**Exam Hint**

Study the OS map carefully. Only use the evidence you can see. Include the subzone letter first. Make sure you use the correct coordinates: x-axis (eastings) followed by y-axis (northings).

(ii) Use six-figure grid referencing to locate one potential area where traffic congestion may occur in Sligo as a result of increased traffic in the area.

_______________

**Exam Hint**

When studying an aerial photograph, remember the correct directions to use. On vertical photographs, if there is a north arrow, the directions used can be seen on the vertical photograph below. When asked to identify land, your best estimate is allowed as nothing is certain from an aerial viewpoint.

## Geographical Skills: Aerial Photographs and Urban Change

**9.** Study the aerial photograph of Sligo town below and answer the questions that follow.

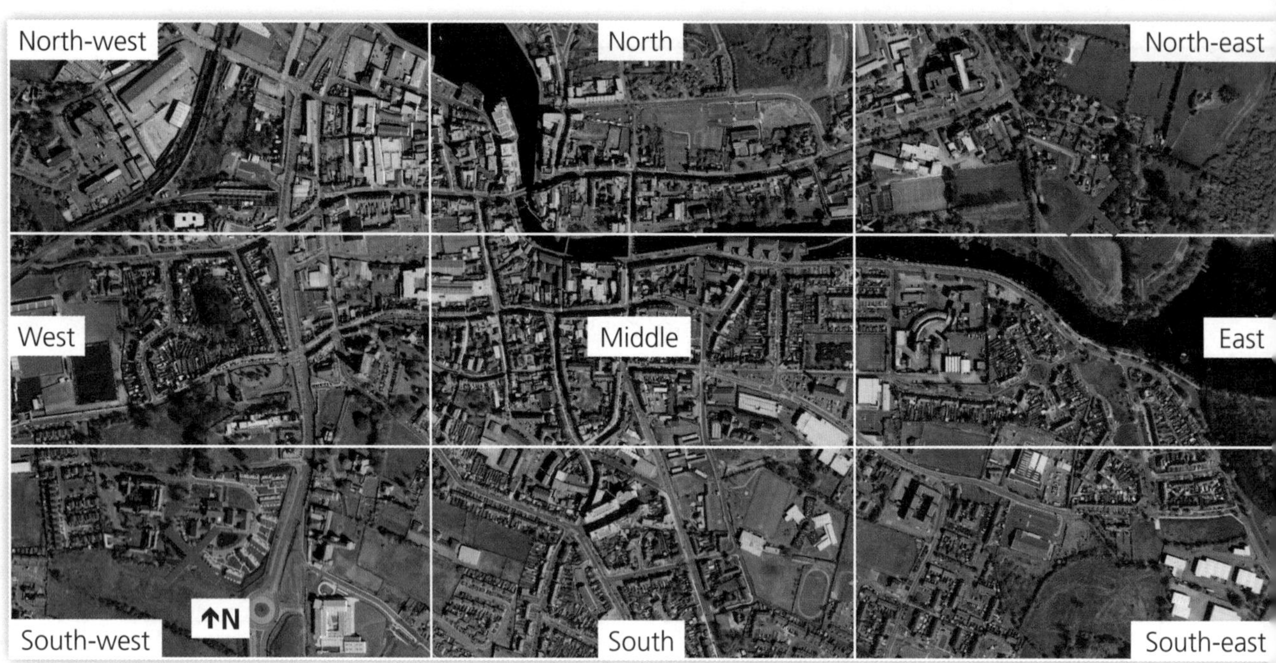


**(i)** List/name and give the location of three potential land uses in the photograph.

**1.** _______________ **2.** _______________

**3.** _______________

**(ii)** With the 40% increase in population experienced since 2016, new residential areas must be sourced. The Xs mark two potential locations for new residential areas in Sligo town.

**(a)** Explain why each chosen location is potentially a good choice.

_______________

_______________

_______________

_______________

**(b)** Explain a reason why each chosen location is potentially not a good choice (think back to urban problems).

_______________

_______________

_______________

_______________

**Answer the questions to complete the mind map. This will support your revision.**

**Prompt Questions for Mind Map**

**(a)** Can you explain the term 'urban change'?

**(b)** Do you know the difference between urban renewal and urban redevelopment?

**(c)** Can you describe the causes and explain the effects of urban change in an Irish city?

**(d)** An urban area (village, town or city) has experienced a large increase in population. What problems may this create for the area?

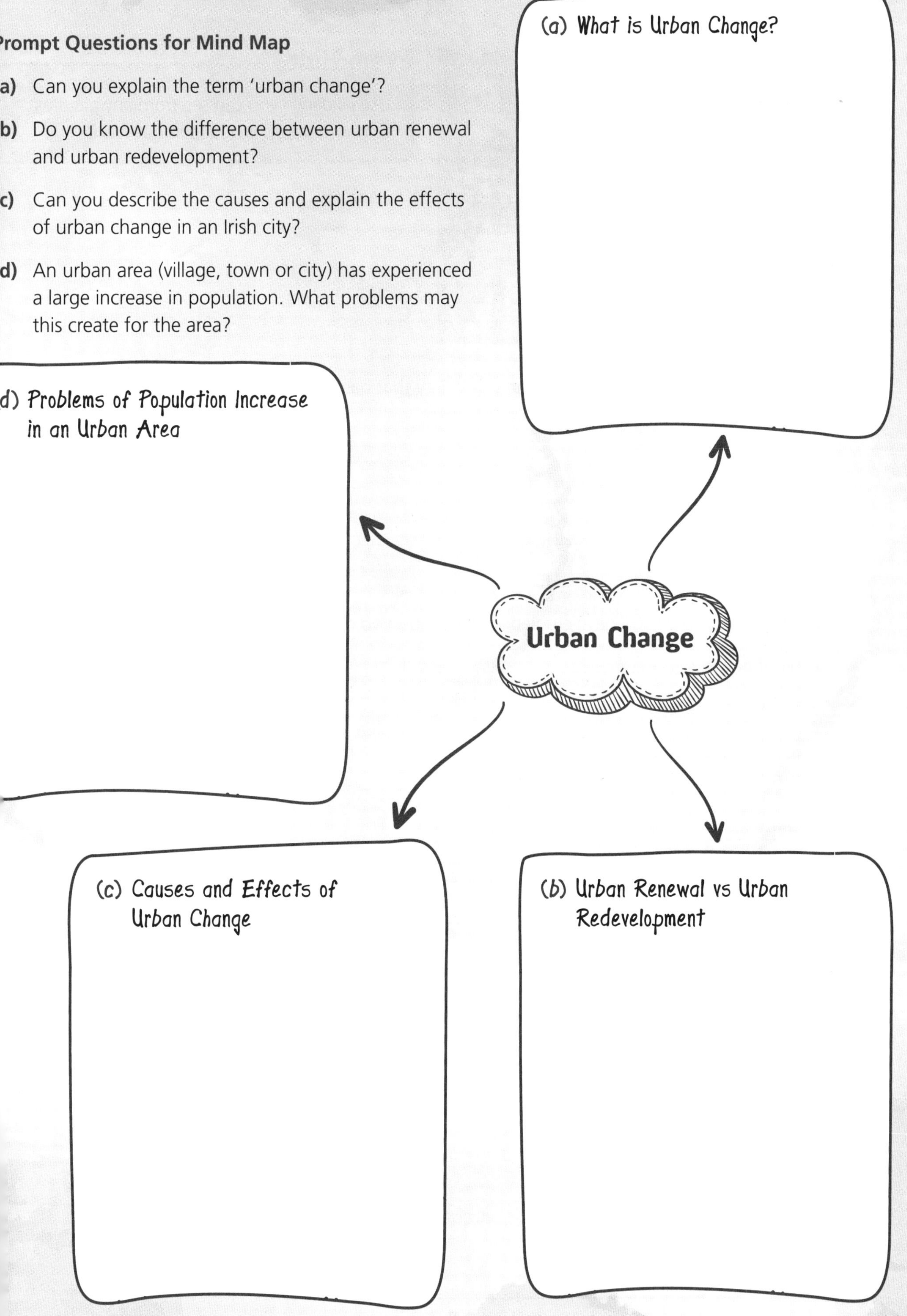

## Sample Questions

### Question 1

**Exam Hint**

Use evidence you can see from any pictures or photographs included in questions.

**(i)** The photograph above shows an area in Cork city that has undergone urban renewal. Explain what is meant by the term 'urban renewal'. [4 marks]

______________________________

______________________________

______________________________

______________________________

**(ii)** Name any new town you have studied and describe two characteristics of this new town. [10 marks]

Name of new town: ______________________________

Two characteristics:

______________________________

______________________________

______________________________

______________________________

______________________________

______________________________

______________________________

**Marks Awarded**

**(i)** 4 marks for correct explanation

**(ii)** 2 marks for naming town

4 marks for each characteristic:

- 1 mark for naming your characteristic
- 3 marks for explaining your characteristic and giving evidence

2 + (4 × 2) = 10 marks

Total = 14 marks

## Question 2

'Urban redevelopment brings many benefits to an area and its inhabitants.'

List one social, one economic and one environmental benefit it can bring to an area and briefly explain each benefit. [12 marks]

## Sample Answer

*Urban redevelopment is when old rundown houses and buildings are demolished. The original inhabitants are relocated to the suburbs and new shops and businesses are built on the valuable inner-city land.* ***An example of this would be Ballymun in Dublin, which was created in the 1960s to relocate Dublin's inner-city residents.***

***Social benefit:*** *A social benefit of urban redevelopment is that the people relocated can often move to better housing with more space. People may be moved from apartments to houses with gardens. This may improve quality of life as families with children have more room to socialise.*

***Economic benefit:*** *The valuable inner-city land once occupied with residential properties can be replaced with shops and businesses which generate income for the government with taxes and create jobs for that area.*

***Environmental benefit:*** *Old buildings in disrepair or near collapse can be replaced with energy-efficient buildings. Land that previously had buildings on it can be rezoned as recreational to have parks with trees, which will improve the local ecosystem.*

**Marks Awarded**

3 marks for a clear definition of urban development

3 marks each for a clear example of a social, economic and environmental benefit

- 1 mark for naming example
- 2 marks for explaining

3 + (3 × 3) = 12 marks

Total = 12 marks

# 22 Economic Activities – Primary, Secondary and Tertiary

## Primary Economic Activities

In this section, the Learning Outcomes we will look at are: **2.3**, **2.5**, **2.9**

**Learning Checklist:**

- ☐ I can explain the factors that influence the physical landscape.
- ☐ I can examine images to answer questions.
- ☐ I can describe the three types of economic activities.
- ☐ I can interpret information on OS maps and use it to support my answer.
- ☐ I can explain primary economic activities.

### The Physical Landscape

**1.** Sort the features below into one of the following categories: **natural** or **man-made**.

**M50**
**River Shannon**
**Lough Derg**
**Newgrange**
**Carrauntoohil Mountains**
**Croke Park**

| Natural | Man-made |
|---|---|
| | |

### What Are Economic Activities?

**2.** In the spaces on the next page, write a brief definition for the terms 'primary', 'secondary' and 'tertiary' in relation to economic activities, and list five jobs associated with each one.

**Exam Hint**

With this question it might help to think of a simple product such as a bag of your favourite crisps. How does it get from the farm to your house? Can this help you to write your definitions of each economic sector?

| Primary | Secondary | Tertiary |
|---|---|---|
| Definition: | Definition: | Definition: |
| Examples: | Examples: | Examples: |

## Primary Economic Activity: Farming

**GeoSkill**

Examining images: these images are here to be used. Write what you see.

. Answer the following short questions.

**(i)** State which of images A and B below is pastoral farming and which is arable farming. Write a brief definition of each type of farming in the spaces provided.

A

B

A: ____________________ B: ____________________

Arable:

Pastoral:

(ii) Mixed farming is a common practice in Ireland. What is mixed farming?

(iii) Soil can have an influence on farming. Give one example of a fertile soil and one example of a soil with poor fertility.

(iv) Relief influences the type of farming that can take place in a given area. Give a short explanation as to why. (Hint: growing crops or raising animals on steep slopes would be difficult – why?)

**Remember!**

When studying settlement, think about how relief influences it. How does relief affect weather, which, in turn, affects farming?

## Primary Economic Activity: Fishing

4. Killybegs is the premier fishing port of Ireland. It has one of the best natural harbours on the north-west coast. It is accessible day or night, in all weathers, and can accommodate vessels up to 40,000 tonnes.

**GeoSkill**

Examining images and maps: what evidence can you take from each map, e.g. location, physical features?

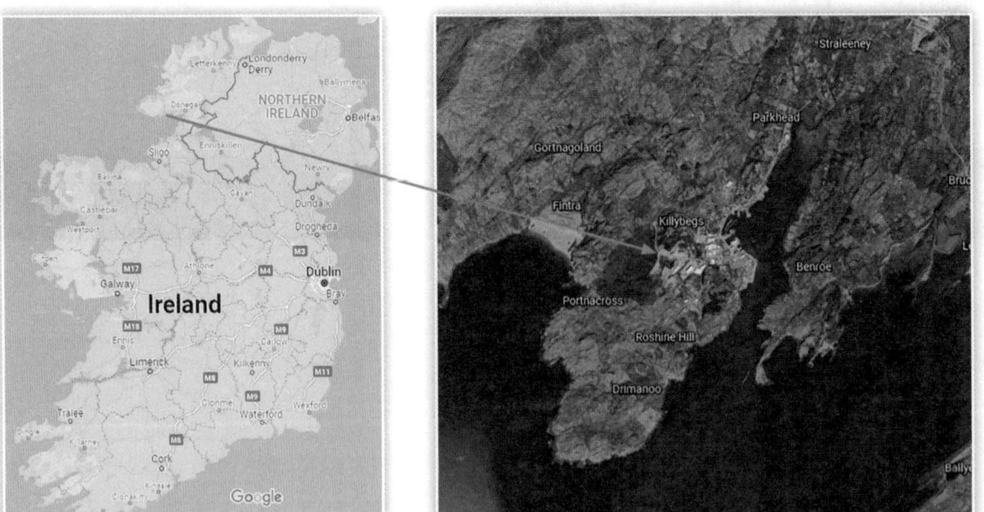


(i) What natural feature is providing shelter for Killybegs harbour and the boats that dock there to unload their catch?

**Remember!**

Both questions here are testing your knowledge of other Learning Outcomes (The Sea).

**(ii)** Describe how this natural feature may protect against stormy weather and also allow ships weighing up to 40,000 tonnes to dock there.

**(iii)** Relief and soils are factors that can influence the location of a fishing port. Using evidence from the OS map and soil map below, explain why Killybegs was a good choice of location.

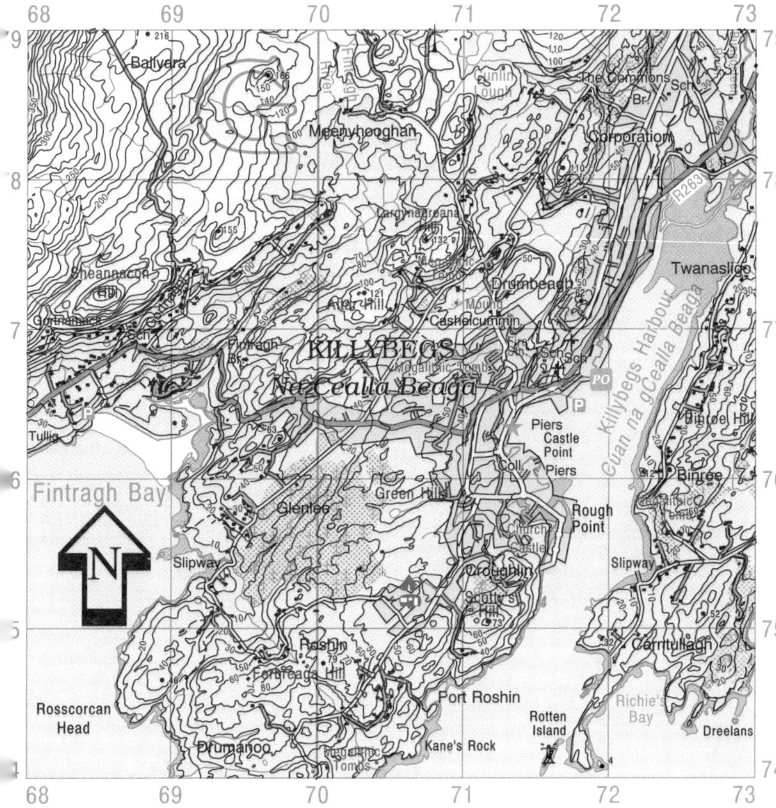

**Remember!**

Use four-figure or six-figure grid referencing.
Use **LEN** for the grid referencing.

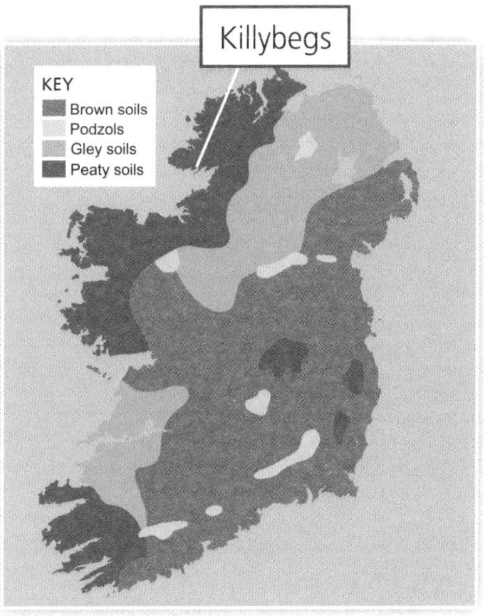

**Exam Hints**

What height are the contour lines on the OS map? Why might poor soil discourage farming and encourage alternate practices such as fishing?

# Secondary Economic Activities

## Learning Checklist:

- ☐ I can explain what a secondary economic activity is.
- ☐ I can explain the factors that influence the location of industry.
- ☐ I can describe an industry in its local area.
- ☐ I can explain why industries might change location over time.
- ☐ I can interpret information from images.

**1. (i)** What are secondary economic activities?

Explain using words/key terms such as **processing**, **inputs/outputs**, **raw materials** and **finished products**.

**Remember!**

If any of the words highlighted here are unfamiliar to you, now is the time to check their meanings.

**(ii)** Using an example you are familiar with, explain a system that takes raw materials from inputs through to finished products. It can be as simple as you like.

| Input → | Processes → | Output |
|---|---|---|
| | | |
| | | |
| | | |
| | | |
| | | |
| | | |

**Exam Hint**

Keep your example simple. Think about making a cup of tea – how is it done?

## Case Study

**(iii)** Think of a secondary economic industry (e.g. a factory) you have read about or studied. Fill in the spaces below with this industry's inputs, the processes involved and, lastly, its finished outputs.

Name of industry: ______________________________

Location: ______________________________

Inputs:

- ______________________________
- ______________________________
- ______________________________

Processes occurring in this secondary economic activity:

______________________________

______________________________

______________________________

______________________________

______________________________

Outputs:

- ______________________________
- ______________________________
- ______________________________

. Examine the aerial photograph below and answer the questions on the following page.

**xam Hint**

What does the physical landscape in the background of this photo consist of? What might this land be used for instead? Think of primary economic activities.

**(i)** In the background of the photograph there is little evidence of infrastructure. Explain two reasons why secondary economic activities might not be keen to set up here.

Reason 1: ______________________________

______________________________

______________________________

Reason 2: ______________________________

______________________________

______________________________

**(ii) (a)** The X in the photograph is the proposed site for a new business park. Explain the term 'business park'.

______________________________

______________________________

______________________________

**(b)** Why might the site marked X be unsuitable for building a business park?

______________________________

______________________________

______________________________

**3.** Examine the OS map below and answer the questions on the next page.

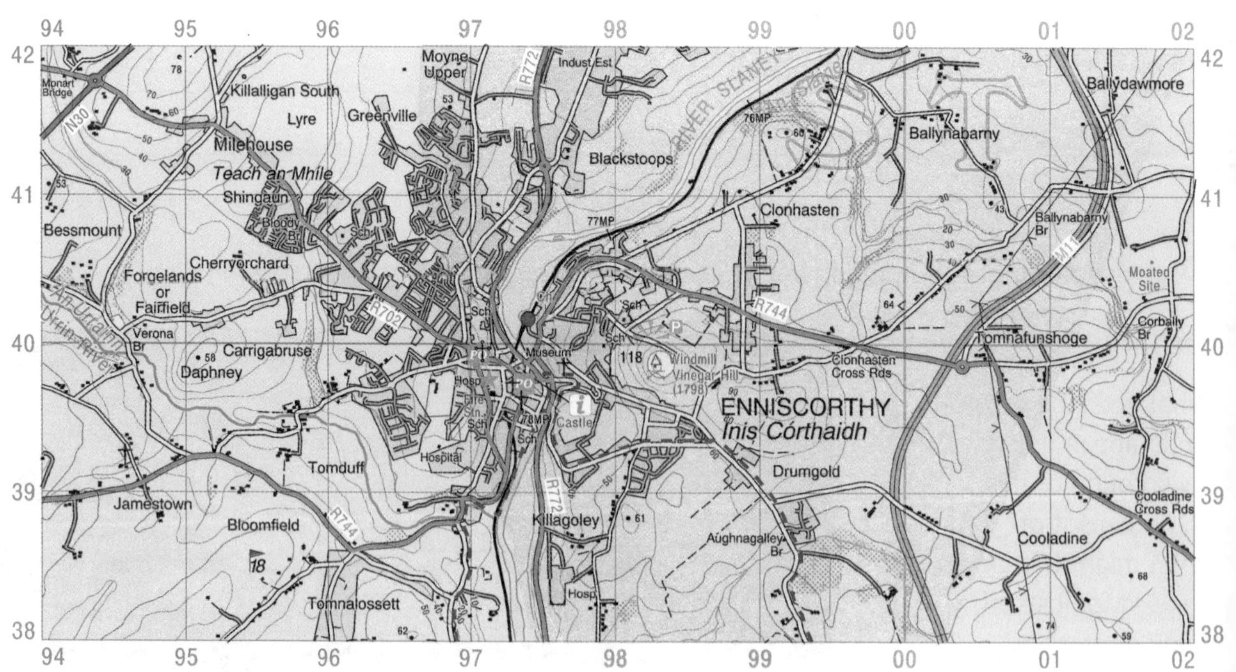


**Remember!**

Use **LEN** for the grid referencing.

**(i)** You have been given planning permission to build a new car manufacturing plant on the outskirts of Enniscorthy at S 99 4, 40 2, creating 600 new jobs. Choose **two factors** from the list below and explain why this particular choice of location is a good or bad location for this new factory.

| | | | |
|---|---|---|---|
| Raw materials | Transport services | Labour | Market |
| Linkages | Capital | Government and EU policy | Personal preferences |

Factor 1: ____________________

Factor 2: ____________________

**Exam Hint**

For questions with options given, you can explain one positive factor and one negative factor.

**(ii)** Explain one economic and one social benefit the new car manufacturing plant would bring to Enniscorthy.

Economic benefit: ____________________

Social benefit: ____________________

**(iii)** The new car manufacturing plant in Enniscorthy may have several environmental impacts on the local area. Describe one potential environmental impact it may have.

**Exam Hint**

Think of pollution: what kinds? How can it affect the climate?

# Tertiary Economic Activities

## Learning Checklist:

- ☐ I can explain what tertiary economic activities are.
- ☐ I will examine the connection between tourism, the physical landscape and transport.
- ☐ I can describe what tourism is and understand what is meant by sustainable tourism.

1. (i) What are tertiary economic activities?

(ii) The pie chart below shows the number of people employed in primary, secondary and tertiary economic activities in Ireland. Based on this pie chart, explain one reason why tertiary economic activities are important to the Irish economy.

**Number of people employed in each economic sector, Ireland**

| Sector | Number of people employed |
|---|---|
| Tertiary economic activities | 1,320,500 |
| Secondary economic activities | 406,300 |
| Primary economic activities | 107,700 |

## The Physical Landscape and Tourism

2. Examine the OS map of Kenmare on the next page and answer the questions below.

Hiking has become a hugely popular activity for both the local people of Kenmare and tourists visiting the area. Suggest a route for a new hillwalking trail that would take people from the town of Kenmare into any of the mountains located on this OS map.

(i) Mark the starting point of the trail on the map (it can be anywhere on the map).

**Exam Hint**

Is your route 'as the crow flies' or will it follow a feature, such as a river or road?

(ii) Give the six-figure grid reference of the starting point.

(iii) Give a rough guide of the direction your trail will take. Use directions such as north, south-west, etc.

## GeoSkill

Reading grid references: **LEN** – **L**etter, **E**asting, **N**orthing

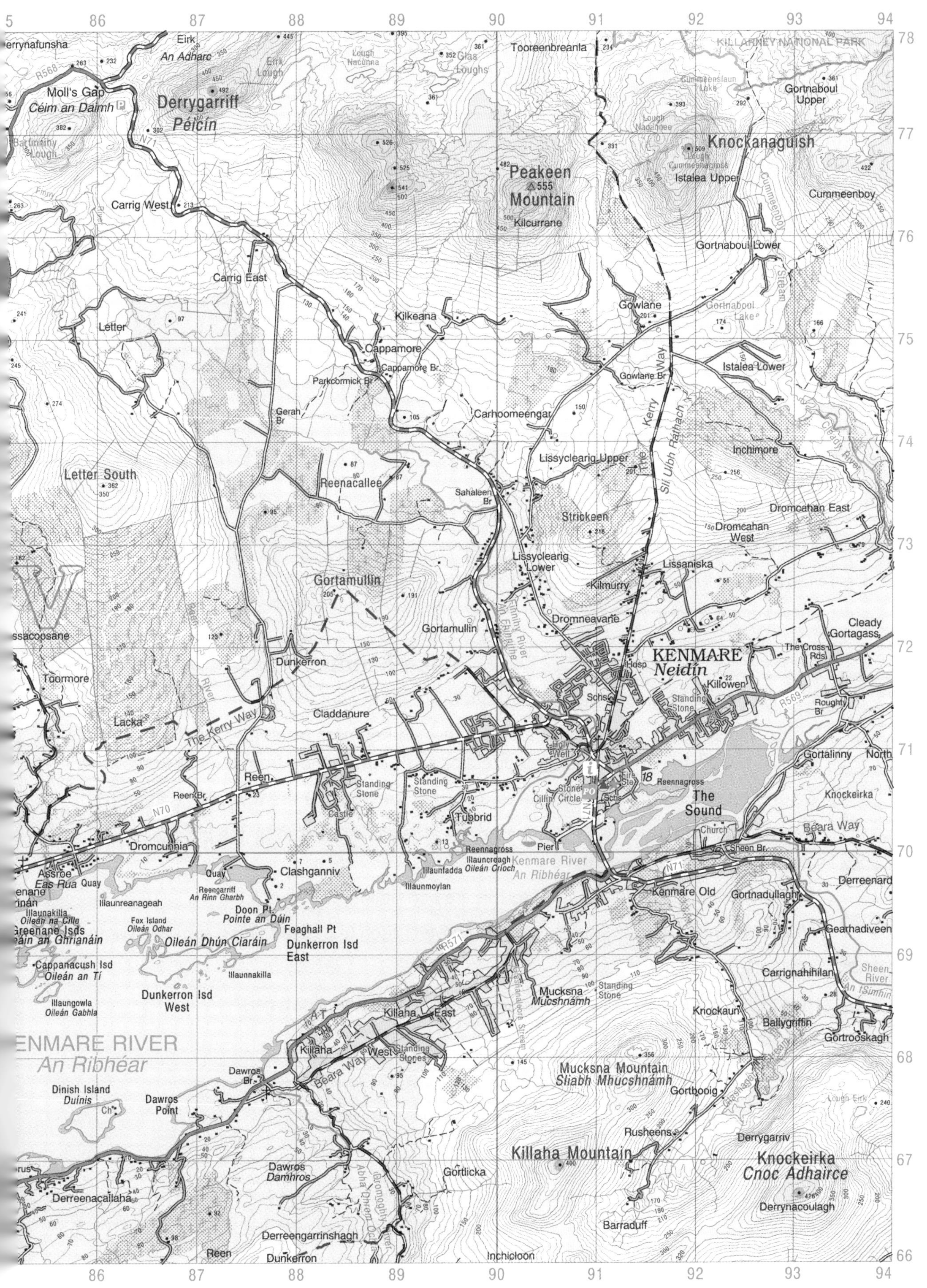

**(iv)** List two physical features your trail will take you to (e.g. lakes, rivers, bays, mountains, forest areas, valleys) and give a grid reference for each (using four or six figures).

| Feature | Grid reference |
|---|---|
| 1. ____________ | ____________ |
| 2. ____________ | ____________ |

**(v)** Sustainable tourism is important. Can you explain how the route of your new hillwalking trail will not damage the natural environment?

**Exam Hint**

What steps would you take to ensure the environment is not damaged by the route?

______________________________

______________________________

______________________________

______________________________

**(vi)** What distance (approximately) will your proposed route cover?

______________________________

**Exam Hint**

To help, lightly draw an outline (using pencil) of your route and use the methods you learned for measuring curved line distance on a map.

**Remember!**

Don't forget to include the unit of measurement in your answer!

## Case Study

**3.** 'The physical landscape influences the tourism of an area.'

Discuss this statement with reference to tourism in Kenmare **or** an area you have studied. Tick (✓) the boxes each time you include a piece of information from the hints below.

**Where:** Is the area you have chosen to discuss? (You may use the town of Kenmare.) ☐

**What:** What kind of tourist attractions in the area are influenced by the physical landscape? ☐

**Who:** Who are the people that go to this area on holidays? ☐

**When:** When do tourists visit the area you have chosen (e.g. peak times, summer, winter)? ☐

Additional information:

**How:** How do tourists get to your chosen area (e.g. plane, boat, car)?

**Your tourist area:**

______________________________

______________________________

______________________________

______________________________

______________________________

______________________________

**Answer the questions to complete the mind map. This will support your revision.**

| Primary | Secondary | Tertiary |
|---|---|---|
| • Are you aware of the influence of the physical landscape on economic activities?<br>• Can you define primary economic activities?<br>• Are you able to explain how farming/fishing are examples of primary economic activities? | • What are secondary economic activities?<br>• What factors affect the location of an industry?<br>• Where do industries like to set up and why? | • What are tertiary economic activities?<br>• What is sustainable tourism?<br>• Can you connect tourism and transport to the physical landscape? |

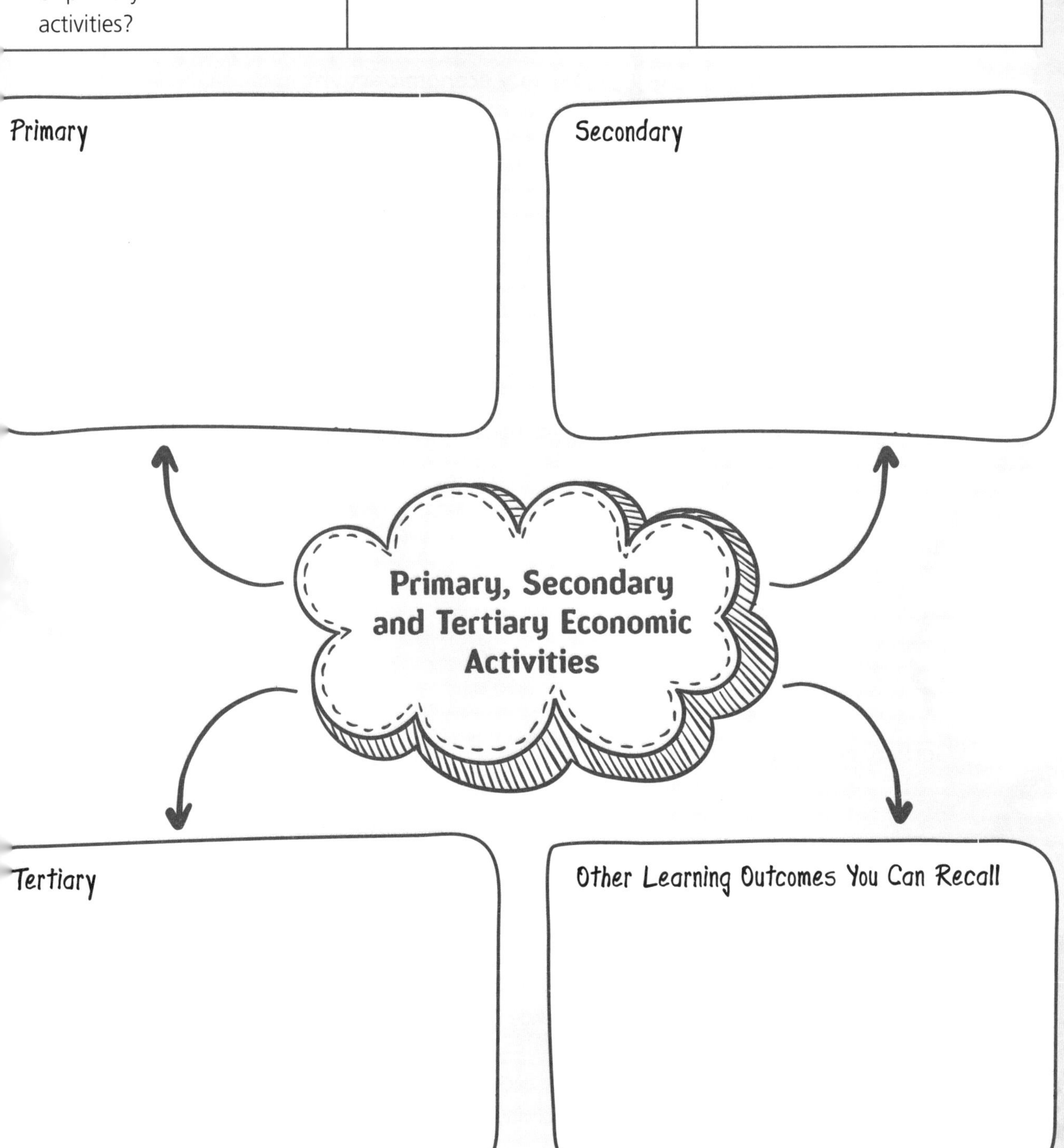

## NCCA Sample Questions

### Question 1

Below are two snapshots taken of the same area of Co. Galway from Google Maps.

There is evidence of **primary**, **secondary** and **tertiary economic activity** in the settlement above.

**(i)** Identify evidence from the two Google Maps snapshots to support the statement above. The first one has been completed for you. [12 marks]

**Primary economic activities:** *Fishing – there is a pier located to the middle right/east of first image (the docks). The pier here could potentially be used to allow boats to dock and unload their catch. The pier is located in a bay which would provide protection from storms as boats unload their catch.*

**Exam Hint**

Secondary economic activities: business park/the docks
Tertiary economic activities: sportsground/racecourse/caravan park

**Secondary economic activities:**

______________________________

______________________________

______________________________

**Tertiary economic activities:**

______________________________

______________________________

______________________________

**Marks Awarded**

**1. (i)** 4 marks for identifying each piece of evidence

- 1 mark for stating evidence
- 3 marks for explaining evidence and backing up with where it is located on images (do so for each economic activity)
  (4 + 4 + 4 = 12 marks)

**(ii)** Outline the environmental considerations of **one** of the economic activities you have identified on the previous page. [6 marks]

Choose one economic activity: ______________________________

Pollution (air, $CO_2$, noise):

______________________________

______________________________

______________________________

Soil (potential damage to soil from activity):

______________________________

______________________________

______________________________

Sustainable exploitation (are all resources being used sustainably?):

______________________________

______________________________

______________________________

______________________________

______________________________

> **Marks Awarded**
>
> **1. (ii)** Choose one economic activity:
> - 2 marks for stating the environmental considerations the economic activity would take to set up in these images
> - 4 marks for summarising the considerations taken
>
> (2 + 4 = 6 marks)
>
> Total = 18 marks

## Question 2

List **THREE** factors that influence the development of secondary economic activities. [6 marks]

- ______________________________
- ______________________________
- ______________________________

> **Marks Awarded**
>
> **2.** 2 marks for listing each factor
> Explanations not needed
>
> Total = 6 marks

## Question 3

Starting in 1970, Cancún in Mexico transformed from an impoverished town of about 100 people into a vacation destination with a permanent population of 740,000 and two million visitors per year. Cancún accounts for one quarter of Mexico's tourism revenue. [16 marks]

**Cancún 1985**

**Cancún 2019**

*Source: earthobservatory.nasa.gov*

**(i)** Housing, transport and services were developed in Cancún. Choose **one** example from the list below and, based on the information on the previous page, explain in detail what type of development occured.

Focus on transport for this question. Look at the road network. How has it evolved between 1985 and 2019? There is a pier visible in the picture. How might that help tourism?

**Housing Transport Services**

**Marks Awarded**

**3. (i)** 3 marks for each piece of information given

- 1 mark for stating
- 2 marks for developing

**(ii)** Describe **two** possible social implications of the increase of international visitors per year to this area.

Discuss how increased employment from increased tourism will lead to happier families with a higher income, and more taxes for government to spend on education. Think about urban regeneration/renewal; how will increased wealth in the area lead to better buildings?

**1.** Increased employment

**2.** Urban regeneration/renewal

**Marks Awarded**

**3. (ii)** 4 marks for each social implication

- 1 mark for stating social implication
- 3 mark for developing

(4 + 4 = 8 marks)

**(iii)** What is the relationship between the growth of tourism and the environment in Cancún? Refer to one positive **or** one negative relationship in your answer.

Look at aspects of increased coastal erosion due to human interaction for negatives.

Tourism can be done in a sustainable manner. Explain how money generated from tourism can help the environment.

**Marks Awarded**

**3. (iii)** 5 marks

- 2 marks for identifying relationship between tourism and environment
- 3 marks for developing the positive or negative impact and referring to evidence from the images

Total = 16 marks

# 23 Economic Development and Inequality

In this section, the Learning Outcome we will look at is: **3.6**

**Learning Checklist:**

- ☐ I can explain the economic divide that exists in the world today.
- ☐ I can examine the patterns of development of countries around the world.
- ☐ I can describe how to measure economic development.
- ☐ I can interpret information from maps, articles and infographics.
- ☐ I can explain the causes of economic development around the world.
- ☐ I can analyse charts.
- ☐ I can explain how the economic development of countries can improve.

## The Economic Divide in the World Today

1. 'There is a divide in our world today based on the economic development between countries. There are rich and there are poor countries. Generally, these countries are defined as the affluent North and less affluent South.'

**Exam-Dictionary**

**Affluent** means wealthy.

**The World by Region and Income, 2020**

Low income | Lower-middle income | Upper-middle income | High income

**GeoSkill**

Map interpretation. Read the legend carefully to better understand the information on this map.

**(i)** Draw a line on this map that divides (approximately) the world into the affluent North and less affluent South.

**(ii)** Name a high-income country found above the line you have drawn: ______________________

**(iii)** Name a low-income country found below the line you have drawn: ______________________

**(iv)** Name a high-income country found below the line you have drawn: ______________________

2. Examine the two maps below which show the changes in income levels in countries between 1990 and 2020. Using the information from the maps, answer the questions below.

**The World by Region and Income, 1990**

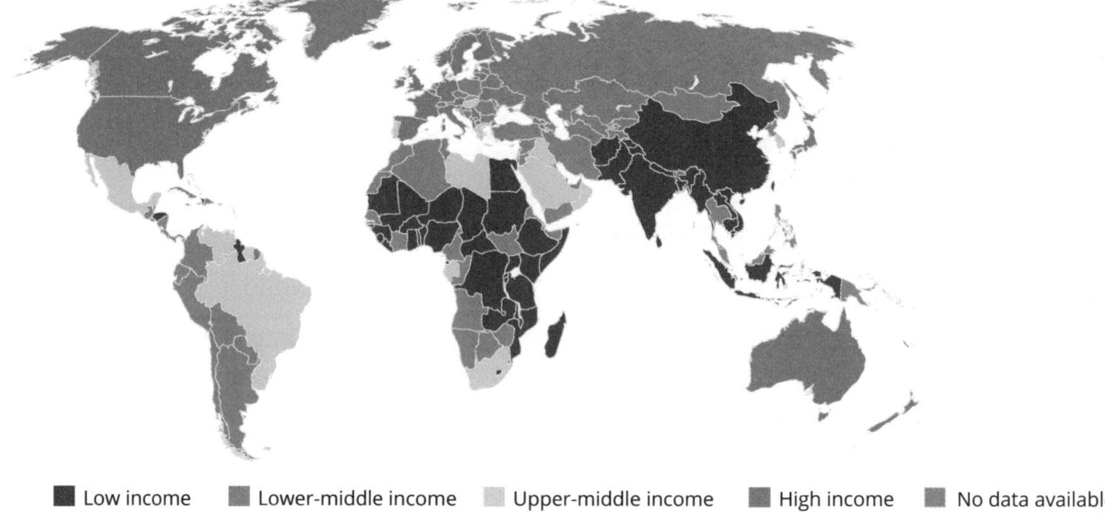


**The World by Region and Income, 2020**

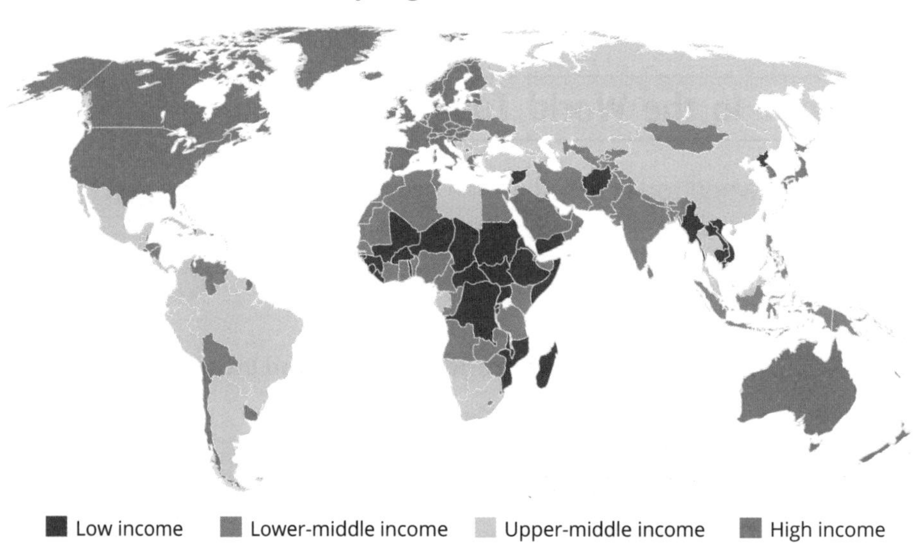


**(i)** Place a tick (✓) beside the two continents that experienced the greater change in income level according to both maps between 1990 and 2020.

| | | | | | |
|---|---|---|---|---|---|
| North America | ☐ | Europe | ☐ | Asia | ☐ |
| South America | ☐ | Africa | ☐ | Australasia | ☐ |

**(ii)** Aid played a significant part in helping countries' levels of income improve between 1990 and 2020. Select **one** type of aid from the list below which you believe may have contributed to this and explain why.

Emergency aid    Long-term developmental aid    Tied aid    Untied aid

**Exam Hint**

This question is testing your knowledge of other Learning Outcomes. What can you remember about the different types of aid?

Type of aid:

______________________________________________

______________________________________________

______________________________________________

______________________________________________

______________________________________________

______________________________________________

## Measuring Economic Development

**Exam Hint**

Attempt every question. Leave no space unfilled.

. **(i)** Read the indicators listed in the box below and write whether they are a characteristic of a developed country/more economically developed country or those of a developing country/less economically developed country.

| **Indicators** | **Economic Development** |
|---|---|
| High income per person | |
| Guaranteed health provision | |
| Inadequate technology and capital | |
| Security is guaranteed | |
| Unskilled labour force | |
| Low literacy and school enrolment rates | |
| Varying dependence on international trade | |
| Mastering science and technology | |
| Rapid population growth | |
| Low unemployment rate | |
| Low levels of saving | |
| Level of exports is higher than imports | |

**(ii)** The image below shows the United Nations Sustainable Goals. Choose **three** that you think are used to measure the economic development of a country directly.

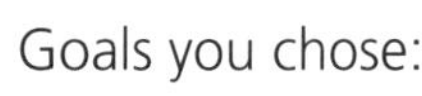

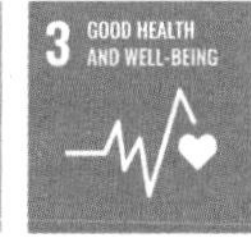

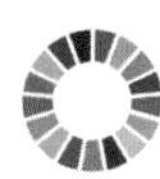


Goals you chose:

- ______________________
- ______________________
- ______________________

**(iii)** Explain how **two** of the goals you have chosen relate to the economy.

**Exam Hint**

Keep the explanation of each goal you have chosen short. You must explain why you think they affect an economy directly.

| Goal | Explanation |
|---|---|
| | |
| | |

**(iv)** The most common indicators used to measure economic development are listed on the incomplete poster below. Complete the poster by giving brief explanations of each indicator and how it is used to indicate economic development.

## Indicators of Economic Development



Employment:

Education:

Life Expectancy:

Literacy:

______________________________________________

______________________________________________

______________________________________________

Gross Domestic Product (GDP):

______________________________________________

______________________________________________

______________________________________________

Education Rate:

______________________________________________

______________________________________________

______________________________________________

The G20 is made up of 19 singular countries. The twentieth member is the entire European Union. It works to tackle major issues related to the global economy.

The bar chart below shows the GDP of each country of the G20 group. Examine the bar chart and answer the questions that follow.

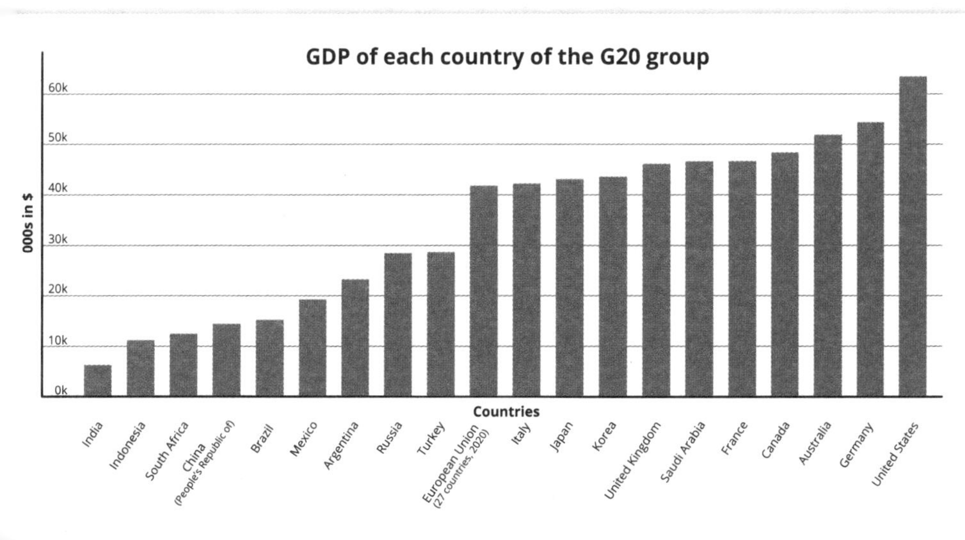


P of each country of the G20 group

**GeoSkill**

Chart analysis. To read this chart, look at the labels of the x- and y-axes. Look at the title as well.

**(i)** Which G20 country has the highest and lowest GDP according to this graph?

Highest: ______________________ Lowest: ______________________

**(ii)** Which is better represented on this graph, countries from the affluent North or less affluent South?

______________________________________________

**(iii)** Explain **one** reason why GDP might not be the best indicator of economic development of a country.

______________________________________________

______________________________________________

______________________________________________

______________________________________________

______________________________________________

## Causes of Unfair Trade

**5.** **(i)** Examine the terms below. Each is a contributing factor to unequal economic development, either past or present.

Place each term under the correct heading in the table below.

**Remember!**

You have used some of these terms before. If you cannot remember their definitions, now is the time to look them up and write them out.

| Climate | Colonialism | Overpopulation |
|---|---|---|
| Exploitation of natural resources | Unfair trade | Globalisation |
| Severe weather | Tied aid | Location (Rich North/Poor South) |

| Physical Factor | Historical Factor | Social Factor |
|---|---|---|
| | | |
| | | |
| | | |
| | | |
| | | |

**(ii)** Severe weather like the flooding in western Europe mentioned in the news bulletin below can hinder the economic growth of even the most well-developed economies.

**Enormous scale of destruction is revealed as water drops after historic flooding in western Europe**

The number of people who lost their lives in the heavy floods in the western part of Germany increased to at least 81. Around 200,000 households lost power due to the floods.

*Source: www.independent.ie*

Cars are nearly submerged as floodwaters run down a main street in Pepinster, Belgium, Thursday, 15 July 2021

**(iii)** Explain how levels of flooding like this can negatively affect the economic development of even a well-developed region.

________________________________________

________________________________________

________________________________________

________________________________________

________________________________________

**Exam Hint**

Which indicators of economic development would be best used to answer question 5? Some are more relevant than others.

6. **Map A** shows the types of natural resources each African country produces. **Map B** shows the income of each African country. **Map C** shows what areas were colonised by European countries in 1884.

**GeoSkill**

Map interpretation. Look at each legend from Map A and Map B carefully. Both show the continent of Africa but display different information.

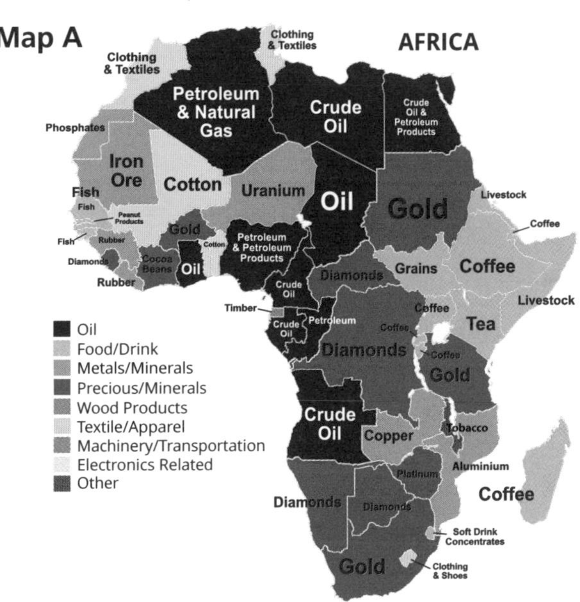


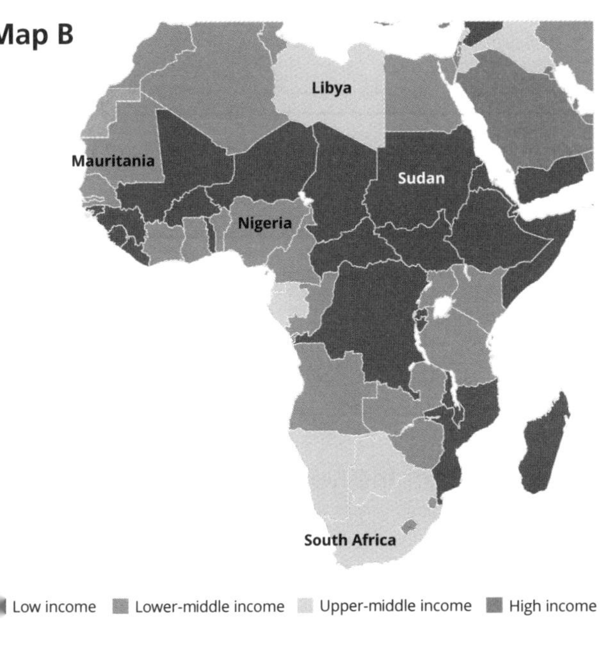

**(i)** Fill in the table below with the coloniser of each African country and the resource they gained access to.

| African Country | Coloniser | Resource |
|---|---|---|
| Sudan | | |
| South Africa | | |
| Libya | | |
| Nigeria | | |
| Mauritania | | |

**(ii)** List two renewable and two non-renewable resources found on the continent of Africa.

| Renewable | Non-renewable |
| --- | --- |
| | |
| | |

**(iii)** Briefly explain how losing control of a natural resource may slow down the economic development of a county.

## Case Study

**(iv)** Using a food product you have studied, complete the report below on how unfair trade has helped increase or decrease the gap between well-developed and less-developed economies of countries.

**Exam Hint**

3 Ws approach:
**W**hat is the product?
**W**here is it produced?
**W**ho produces it?

| What is unfair trade? |
| --- |
| Name the product you have studied: |
| Is your chosen product traded fairly or unfairly?<br>Give some background information on your chosen product:<br>• Its history of trading – fair or unfair?<br>• What countries are affected?<br>• Are the countries affected positively or negatively?<br>• Explain the economic, social and environmental effects of the type of trading you have studied. |

## Developing an Economy

7. The graph below shows how countries can improve their economic development. Slight improvements made to each indicator can have a dramatic effect on a country's development. Complete the graph. One indicator has been completed for you already.

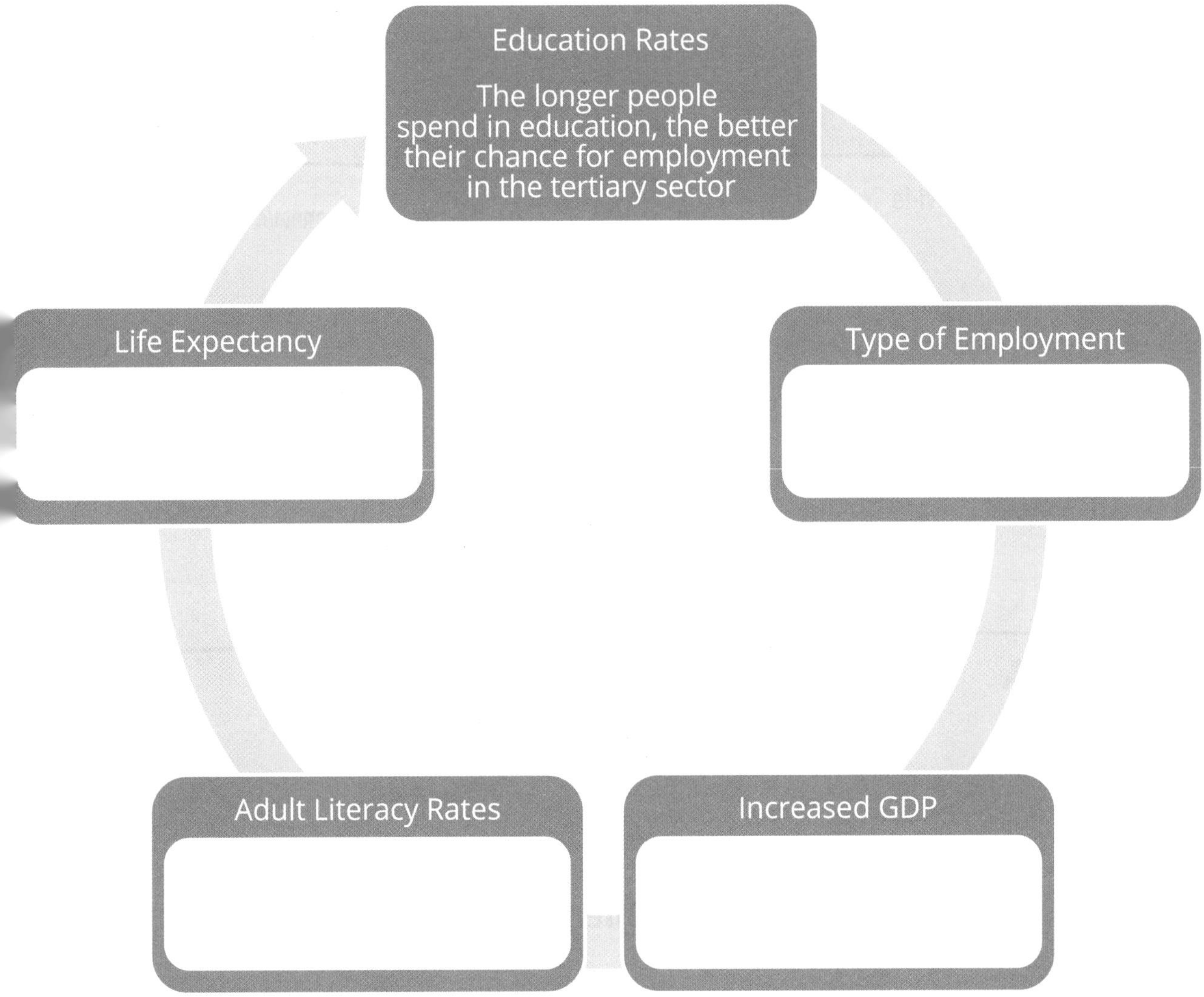

**Education Rates**

The longer people spend in education, the better their chance for employment in the tertiary sector

**Type of Employment**

**Increased GDP**

**Adult Literacy Rates**

**Life Expectancy**

### xam Hint

When answering this question, think of your understanding of each indicator mentioned, then think about how improving each could improve a country's economic development.

**Answer the questions to complete the mind map. This will support your revision.**

**Prompt Questions for Mind Map**

**(a)** Can you list three countries found in the rich North and three found in the poor South?

**(b)** Can you explain the terms 'more economically developed' and 'less economically developed'?

**(c)** Certain indicators are monitored continuously to determine the economic development of a country. Can you list and explain them?

(a) The Economic Divide in the World Today

(b) Measuring Economic Development

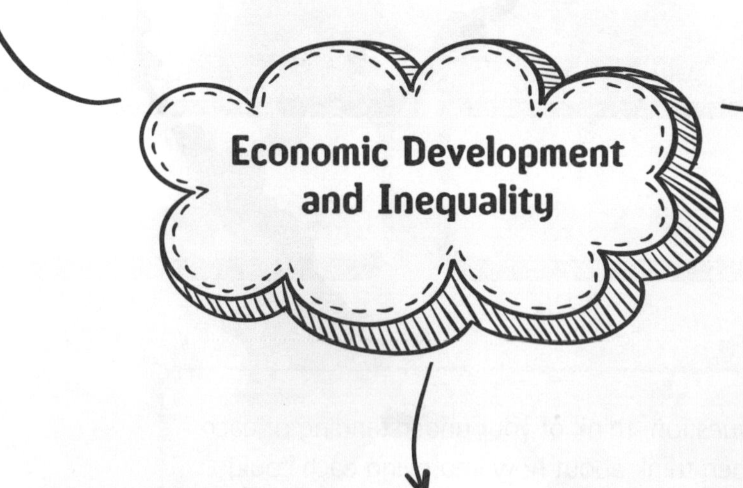


(c) Developing an Economy

## NCCA Sample Questions

### Question 1

Ireland is categorised as a developed/high-income country. Describe your access to:

**(i)** Education:

______________________________

______________________________

______________________________

**(ii)** Healthcare:

______________________________

______________________________

______________________________

[10 marks]

> **Marks Awarded**
>
> **(i)** 5 marks for describing your experience of education so far. Was it paid for or free? Was there any difficulty in accessing second-level education?
>
> **(ii)** 5 marks for discussing how close both your family doctor and the nearest hospital is to your home.
>
> Total = 10 marks

### Question 2

Explain how any two of the following indicators have slowed economic development in a country/countries you have studied. [10 marks]

Colonialism is when a country or a nation takes control of other lands, regions, or territories outside of its borders.

- Climate change
- Population growth
- Unfair trade
- Colonialism

Indicator 1:

______________________________

______________________________

______________________________

______________________________

Indicator 2:

______________________________

______________________________

______________________________

______________________________

> **Marks Awarded**
>
> - 5 marks for each indicator, broken down as follows:
>   - 3 marks for explaining each indicator you chose (3 + 3 = 6 marks)
>   - 2 marks each for naming the different countries affected (2 + 2 = 4 marks)
>
> Total = 10 marks

# 24 Exploitation of Natural Resources

In this section, the Learning Outcome we will look at is: **2.4**

**Learning Checklist:**

- ☐ I can explain what natural resources are.
- ☐ I can explain the term 'exploitation'.
- ☐ I can describe the impact of using natural resources in a sustainable way.
- ☐ I can interpret images.
- ☐ I can read maps and interpret information from them.

## Natural Resources

**1.** Attempt all the short questions below.

**(i)** Write a brief explanation for the words on each of the flashcards below.

Natural resources

Renewable

**Exam Hint**

For questions that ask for the definition of a word or phrase, try and add examples to strengthen your explanation.

Non-renewable

Infinite

Finite

**(ii)** Place each resource under the correct heading in the table below (remember your explanations in the previous answer).

Water   Peat   Wood   Gas   Coal   Animals   Minerals   Soil

| Renewable | Non-Renewable |
|---|---|
| | |
| | |
| | |
| | |

**(iii)** Complete the following sentence.

Exploitation is ... ______________________________

______________________________

______________________________

______________________________

**(iv)** Read the tweet below and explain the words in bold.

> **The Geography Times** @geogtimes
>
> The **overexploitation** of the world's natural resources may have serious consequences. Overexploitation may lead to resources becoming **depleted** or exhausted. **Sustainable exploitation** is the only way to make sure our resources are still available for use in the future!
>
> 2:24 PM · Oct 26, 2021 · Twitter for Web
>
> 37 Retweets   8 Quote Tweets   102 Likes

| Word | Explanation |
|---|---|
| | |
| | |
| | |

## Sustainable Exploitation of Water

**GeoSkill**

Interpreting information from an article, graph or infographic.

**2.** Read the newspaper article below and attempt the question that follows.

### Ireland's Daily News

**South of Ireland faces worst drought in history as no rain in the country for a record 100 days!**

After a record-setting 100 days with no rainfall, the counties of Cork, Kerry, Limerick and Tipperary face a drought like never experienced before.

Rain levels remain normal in the rest of the country.

Rivers in the region such as the Three Sisters and the Blackwater are almost down to a trickle.

The natural and man-made reservoirs are also dangerously low, with no sign of being refilled any time soon.

Farmers in the region are concerned as their sugar beet and maize crops will die in the fields. Dairy animals have faced days with no water and will suffer soon.

The last chance to end this emergency may lie in an ambitious irrigation scheme carried out by Irish Water.

Copying schemes seen in the likes of New Zealand, France and many African countries, Irish Water will attempt to bring water from the rest of Ireland to the southern region.

Irish Water are in the final stages of completing a report on the project. Should the government approve it, it is hoped to begin almost immediately in the hopes of bringing much-needed water to the region.

**Exam Hint**

Read the article carefully. Underline key words. Highlight sentences.

You are an engineer for Irish Water. You have extensive knowledge of irrigation schemes of this scale from around the world. Complete the report below to give to the Irish government for approval.

**Exam Hint**

The scheme you choose can be from your local area or another scheme from somewhere in the world. Fill in each section. Don't leave any parts blank.

### Case Study

| Ireland's Sustainable Irrigation Scheme for the South | |
|---|---|
| Name the irrigation scheme you studied on your travels. | |
| What is irrigation? | |
| Was the irrigation scheme you studied carried out in a sustainable way – yes/no? | |

| | |
|---|---|
| Why was the irrigation scheme needed? | |
| How was the water in your chosen irrigation scheme sustainably exploited? How can it be applied to the issue facing the south of Ireland? | |
| List and explain two positive effects of the irrigation scheme you have chosen. Can they be applied to this issue? | **Remember!** Think social, economic and environmental for these parts of the report. |
| Explain one potential negative impact of the irrigation scheme you studied that Irish Water should be aware of. | |

## Sustainable Exploitation of Fish

**3.** Study the infographic below and answer the questions that follow.

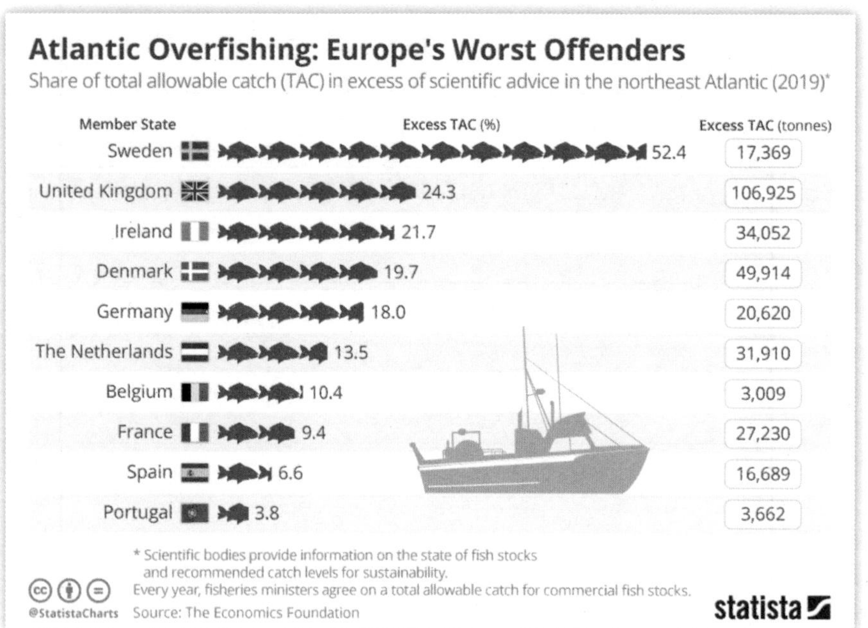


**Exam Hint**

The figures here refer to the extra fish each country caught, exceeding the amount it was allowed. It is measured in tonnes and %. So, Belgium caught 3,009 tonnes, or 10.4% more fish than allowed.

**GeoSkill**

Interpreting information from an article, graph or infographic. Read this infographic carefully. Check the title. Also read the advice given.

**(i)** What governing body sets the total allowable catch for these European countries in 2019?

______________________________

**(ii)** What percentage did Ireland exceed its allowed catch by in 2019, according to this infographic

______________________________

**(iii)** What was the difference in excess tonnes of fish caught between Portugal and Sweden?

______________________________

**(iv)** The United Kingdom caught 106,925 tonnes or 24.3% of extra fish in 2019. Sweden caught 17,369 tonnes of extra fish but this was 52.4% over its allowed limit. This means Britain is permitted to catch more fish than Sweden.

Explain one reason why the United Kingdom might be allowed to catch more fish than Sweden.

______________________________

______________________________

______________________________

**4.** Individual member states of the EU are responsible for monitoring and enforcing the regulations se out in the Common Fisheries Policy. The policy has been updated to encourage a more sustainable exploitation of fish. It is called The New Common Fisheries Policy: Sustainability in Depth.

A summary of the new guidelines is as follows:

- Total allowable catches
- Boat capacity management
- Reducing environmental impact
- Minimum fish and mesh sizes
- Design and use of gears
- Closed areas or seasons

**(i)** Choose **two** of the rules listed above and explain how ignoring each has contributed to overfishing in the past.

| Rule | Cost of Ignoring This Rule |
|---|---|
| 1. | |
| 2. | |

**(ii)** Choose any **one** of the rules mentioned and explain how observing them can lead to a more sustainable exploitation of fish.

| Rule | Result of Obeying This Rule |
|---|---|
| 1. | |

## Sustainable Exploitation of Forestry in Ireland

The diagram opposite explains how Coillte (the organisation responsible for maintaining Ireland's forests) manages a forest sustainably.

**(i)** In the boxes provided, correctly label each Stage 1 to 4 with the following labels: old forest, young forest, planting and middle-aged forest.

Also write a short bullet point of what happens at each stage to ensure the forest reaches Stage 4.

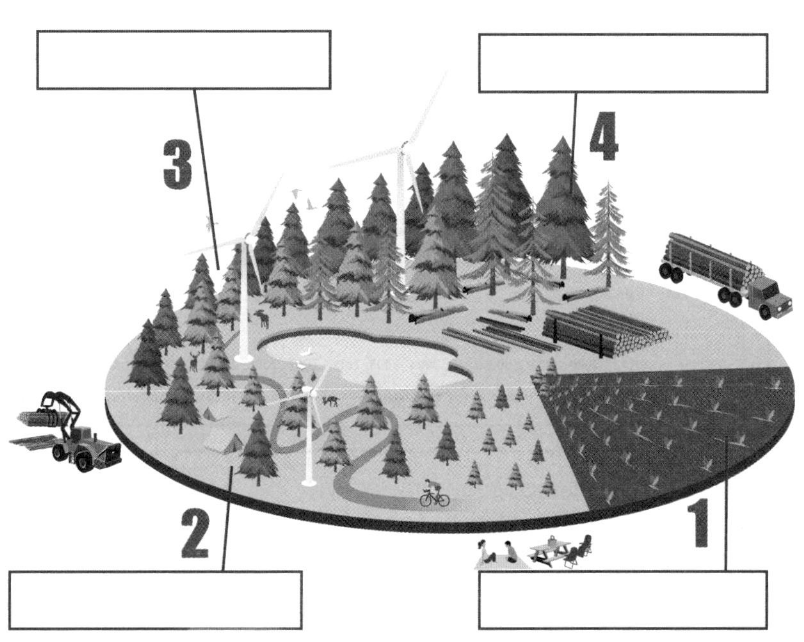

**(ii)** Examine the tweet below and answer the questions.

Coillte
@coilltenews

Status Orange HIGH Forest Fire Risk Warning is in place until Friday 23rd July.

Coillte advises that all outdoor use of fires, barbeques and other open ignition sources be avoided on forest lands and in other high-risk areas.

Learn more: bit.ly/3hITKMc

#BeFireAware"

12:01 PM · Jul 19, 2021 · Hootsuite Inc.

**(a)** List the possible causes of forest fire mentioned in this tweet.

___

___

___

**(b)** Based on your knowledge of weather and climate change, what other causes may also increase the risk of forest fires?

___

___

___

___

**6.** Study the information displayed on the poster below and answer the questions that follow.

**Estimated number of visitors to Irish forests 1999–2015**

| Year | Number of forest visits |
|---|---|
| 1999 | 8,500,000 |
| 2004 | 11,000,000 |
| 2005 | 18,000,000 |
| 2015 | 29,105,759 |

**GeoSkill**

Interpreting information from an article, graph or infographic. Read the title of the graph. What are the x- and y-axes showing?

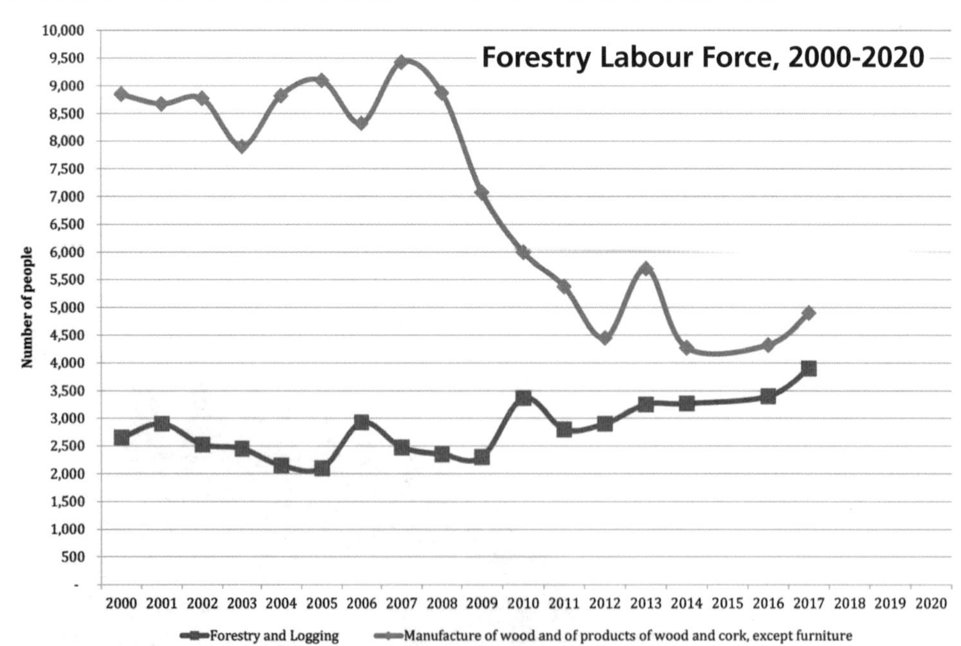


*Source: Teagasc*

The total value of economic activity in wood manufacturing in 2012 was €1,389.1 million.

The total direct value of economic activity in the growing and harvesting forestry in 2012 was €387 million.

**(i)** In 2012, what was growing and harvesting forestry worth to the Irish economy?

______________________________

**(ii)** In which year did Ireland have the highest number of visitors to its forests?

______________________________

**(iii)** Which forestry sector hires more people?

______________________________

**(iv)** What was the total economic worth of forestry (growth and wood manufacturing) to Ireland?

______________________________

## Sustainable Exploitation of Soil

'. The table below shows two ways to manage and exploit soil sustainably.

**(i)** In the spaces provided, add a third solution, and then explain what each solution is, how it works and where it is used. In the last row, suggest and discuss your own solution.

**Exam Hint**

Be mindful of the difference between the questions asked here.
'What It Is' is asking you to describe the type of soil management.
'How It Works' is asking how it benefits the soil.
When choosing the third type of soil management, can you think of any practices not used in Ireland? They may be used in more extreme climates.

| The Solution | What It Is | How It Works and Where It Is Used |
|---|---|---|
| Crop rotation | | |
| Careful spreading of herbicides and pesticides | | |
| ______________ | | |

**(ii)** Below is a list of threats faced by soils around the world. Choose **two**, describe them and explain one practice to help minimise their effects.

Desertification Pesticides Soil erosion Overcropping
Overgrazing Human activities Climate change

| Threat | Description | Practice to Reduce Effects |
|---|---|---|
| | | |
| | | |

**8.** Study the maps below and answer the questions that follow.

- Farm A and Farm B are located on the first map below.
- **Farm A is a dairy farm that also has crops.** The soil is mostly brown soil.
- **Farm B is a sheep-rearing farm.** The soil is a mixture of gley and podzol soil.

**GeoSkill**

Read the legend and text on each map carefully. They are needed to attempt this question.

**Agricultural Regions in Ireland**

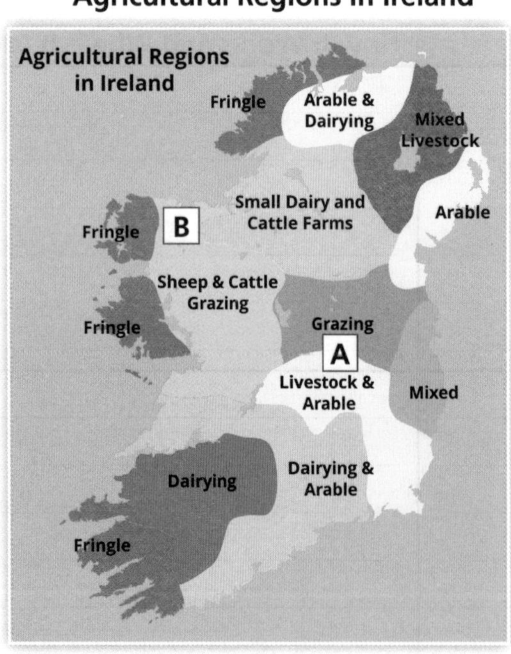


**Soil Map of Ireland**

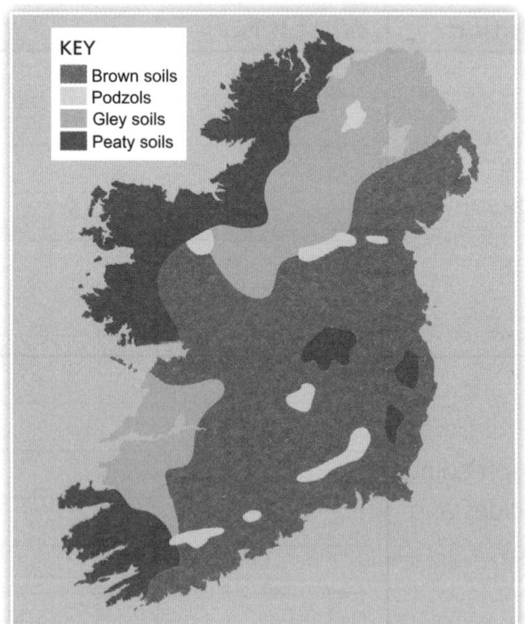


**(i)** Based on your understanding of soil fertility, explain why a farmer would need to practice careful crop rotation on Farm A.

(ii) Choose one type of soil management other than the one mentioned in question (i) and explain how either Farm A or Farm B would need to practise it carefully.

| Soil Management: | Farm A or B: |
| --- | --- |
| | |

Have a look at the infographic below on the importance of soil and attempt the questions.

(i) What percentage of the Earth's surface is covered by grazing?

(ii) Name one threat to soil caused by overgrazing.

SOILS AND PASTURE

Grasses found on pasturelands protect the soil against soil erosion and support soil biological activities.

The livestock sector provides food and income for **1 billion** of the world's poor.

**26%** of the earth's terrestrial surface is occupied by grazing

**Grazing and overgrazing remove the soil cover,** fostering soil erosion and reducing important soil functions such as climate regulation.

**Grass type and pasture rotation** help keep the soil system functional.

**As global demand for meat and dairy products continues to rise,** soil protection and conservation on pasturelands becomes even more critical.

SOILS AND FORESTS

**orests provide livelihoods** r more than a **1 billion** people and are vital r conservation of biodiversity, energy supply, nd soil and water protection.

early **1/3** of the total carbon terrestrial ecosystems is captured forests.

The use of solid biofuels, including wood, is predicted to grow, along with the expansion of agricultural lands **putting at risk the capacity of forest soils to act as carbon sinks in the future.**

As a result of the conversion of forests and native grasslands to croplands,

the soil's capacity to act as a carbon sink can decrease by **20-40%**

(iii) What fraction of the world's carbon emissions are captured by our forests?

(iv) Soil, like trees, absorbs $CO_2$. By what percentage are soils' ability to act as carbon sinks decreased by?

(v) List an economic, social and environmental impact of soil mentioned in this infographic.

**Answer the questions to complete the mind map. This will support your revision.**

## Prompt Questions for Mind Map

**(a)** Can you explain the term 'sustainable exploitation'?

**(b)** What are natural resources? Do you understand the difference between renewable and non-renewable resources?

**(c)** Irrigation is important to exploit water sustainably – why?

**(d)** Can you list three causes and three solutions to overfishing?

**(e)** Why are Ireland's forests an important resource? How can we manage them sustainably?

**(f)** How can we manage soil sustainably?

(a) Sustainable Exploitation

(f) Sustainable Exploitation of Soil

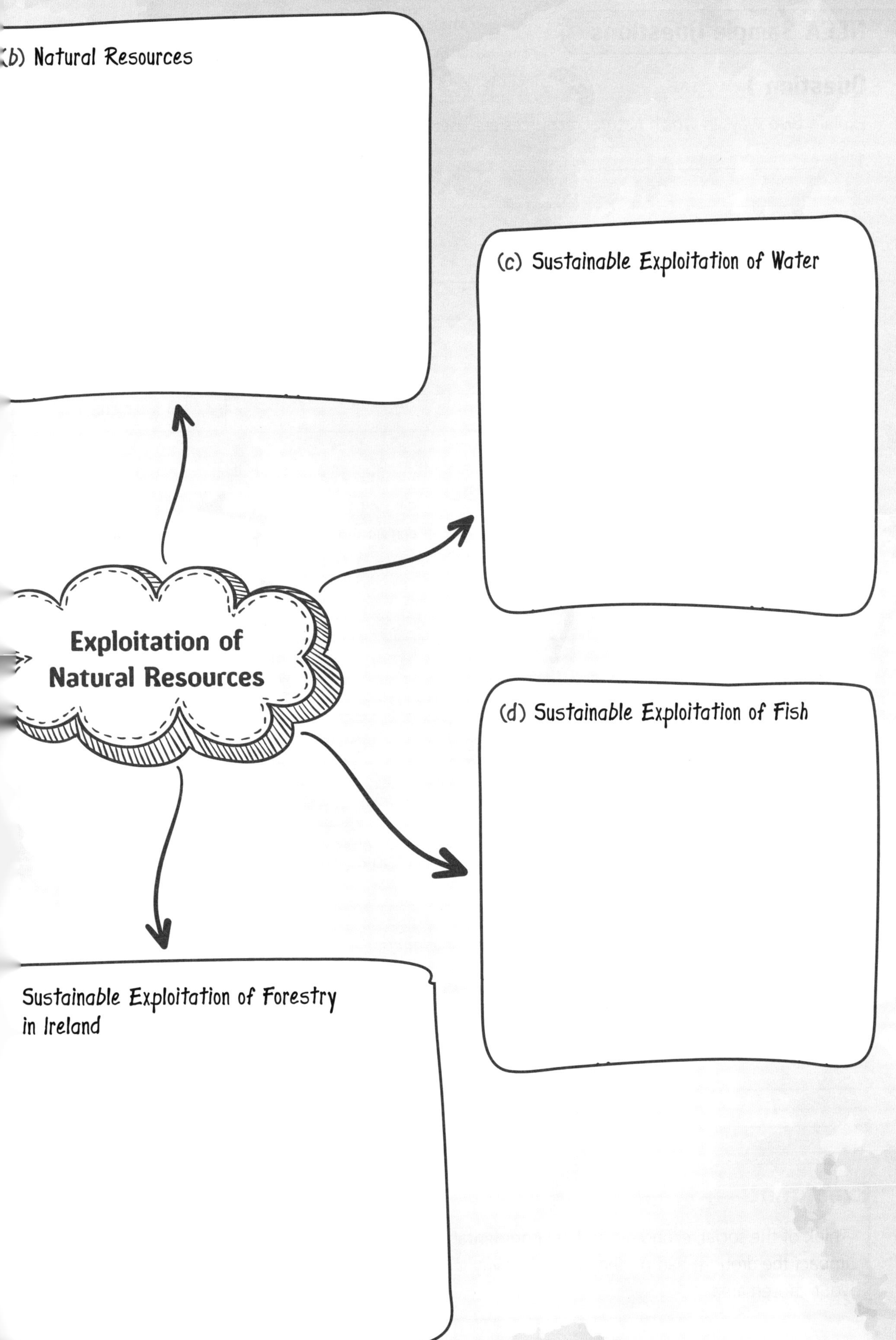
(b) Natural Resources
(c) Sustainable Exploitation of Water
Exploitation of Natural Resources
(d) Sustainable Exploitation of Fish
Sustainable Exploitation of Forestry in Ireland

## NCCA Sample Questions

### Question 1

*This question does not specify if the resource has to be renewable or non-renewable. Whichever resource you choose, include your understanding of sustainable exploitation.*

Explain **two** ways in which natural resources are used in your locality. [10 marks]

1. ______

2. ______

**Marks Awarded**

2 marks for each natural resource named

(2 + 2 = 4 marks)

3 marks for explaining how the resource is used in your locality

(3 + 3 = 6 marks)

### Question 2

*This type of question allows you to use information from any case study you have studied. You can use the irrigation scheme you studied as an example of an impact the drought had on your chosen area.*

(i) **Name** an area that experiences severe drought and explain why drought occurs in this area.

Name of area: ______

(ii) **Describe** and explain the impacts of drought on human activity in this area. [12 marks]

**Exam Hint**

Think of the social, economic and environmental impact the drought had on the human activity in your chosen area.

**Marks Awarded**

- 2 marks for naming your area
- 5 marks for each impact (5 × 2 = 10 marks)
  - 2 marks for naming the impact
  - 3 marks for explaining the impact in detail

Total = 12 marks

# 25 Human Development and Development Assistance

In this section, the Learning Outcomes we will look at are: **3.8** and **3.9**

**Learning Checklist:**

- ☐ I can describe what human development is.
- ☐ I can explain the indicators used to measure human development.
- ☐ I can explain where aid comes from and the different types of aid given.
- ☐ I can explain the role Irish aid plays in helping human development.
- ☐ I can understand the advantages and disadvantages of aid on human development.
- ☐ I can explain how technology aids human development.
- ☐ I can interpret information from infographics.
- ☐ I can take information from articles to support my answer.

## ɫuman Development

. Fill in the blanks below with the words provided.

| Standard of living | Quickly developing | Slowly developing |
|---|---|---|
| Healthcare | Income levels | Freedoms and opportunities |

**Exam Hint**

If you are unsure of the meaning of any of the words here, now is the time to look them up and write down their meaning.

ountries can be ranked on their level of economic development. They can be developed, ________________ ________________ or ________________ ________________. Human ɛvelopment can also be measured. Human development is the process of improving people's ːcess to education and ________________ while also improving their ________________ ___ ________________. The United Nations (UN) gathers and records information on three main indicators. ıese are ________________ ________________, education, and ________________ ___ ________________. Using this information, the UN has developed the Human Development Index to easure the human development of a country.

2. Examine the graphic below. It shows factors measured to determine a country's level of human development.

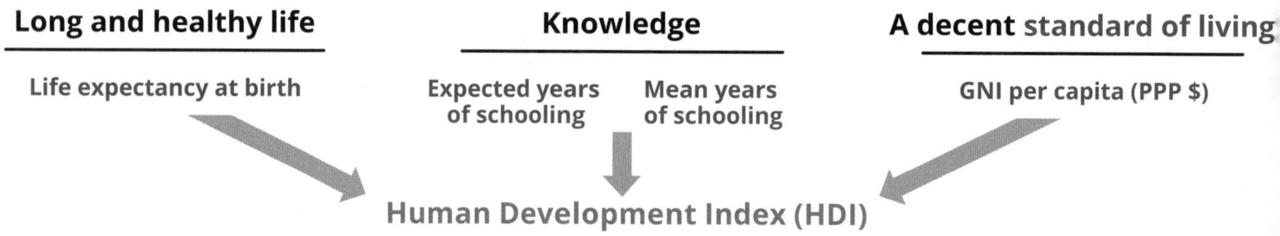

**Long and healthy life** | **Knowledge** | **A decent standard of living**

Life expectancy at birth → Human Development Index (HDI)

Expected years of schooling, Mean years of schooling → Human Development Index (HDI)

GNI per capita (PPP $) → Human Development Index (HDI)

**Human Development Index (HDI)**

(i) Give a brief explanation of your understanding of any **three** of the terms in **red** in the above graphic.

| Term | Explanation |
|---|---|
| | |
| | |
| | |

**(ii)** In your opinion, which of the factors in the graphic on the previous page is the best to use to determine a country's level of human development? Explain the reason(s) behind your choice.

## Exam Hint

When a question asks for your opinion, state it clearly. Give evidence to support your opinion that demonstrates to the examiner you have a clear reason for your choice and a good understanding of the topic being questioned.

______________________________________________

______________________________________________

______________________________________________

______________________________________________

______________________________________________

______________________________________________

______________________________________________

______________________________________________

**3.** Examine Map A and Map B below and answer the accompanying questions.

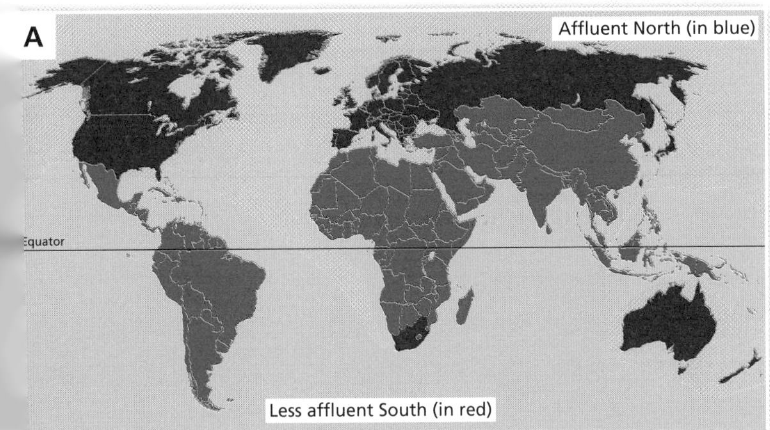


The World's Divided Wealth

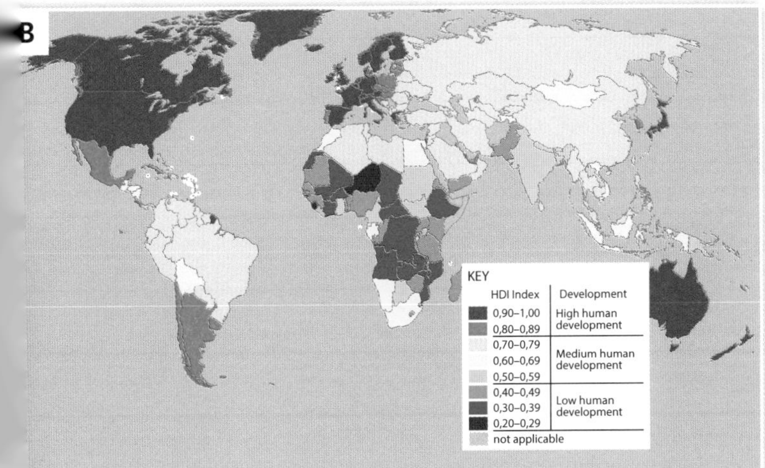


World Map of Human Development

**(i)** Identify one country located in the less affluent South from Map A.

______________________

**(ii)** Identify one country located in the affluent North from Map A.

______________________

**(iii)** What is the HDI score for Ireland in Map B?

______________________

**(iv)** According to Map B, which of these three countries has a HDI score of between 0.3–0.39 – Brazil, Angola or India?

______________________

**(v)** Based on the information provided in both maps, write a short paragraph explaining a possible link between wealth and human development. Use information such as a country's location, affluency or its economic development to help you answer.

## What Is Human Development Aid?

**Exam Hint**

In the short questions here, including examples to complete your definitions is always a good thing.

**2.** Answer the following short questions.

**(i)** Give a definition of the term 'aid'.

**(ii)** Explain the terms 'grant' and 'loan', referring specifically to aid.

Grant:

Loan:

## Sources of Aid

3. (i) Match each logo with the correct term and give a short explanation of each source of aid.

**Remember!**

Clear connecting lines to your answers make it easy for the examiner to read your work.

TRŌCAIRE

Irish Aid
An Roinn Gnóthaí Eachtrachta
Department of Foreign Affairs

Bilateral Aid: ______________________

Multilateral/Development Assistance Aid: ______________________

Non-Governmental Aid: ______________________

(ii) There are four different types of aid. Complete the table by explaining each type of aid and giving an example of it in use.

| 1. Emergency or Short-term Aid | 2. Conditional or Tied Aid | 3. Untied Aid | 4. Long-term Development Aid |
|---|---|---|---|
| Explanation: | Explanation: | Explanation: | Explanation: |
| Example of it in use: | Example of it in use: | Example of it in use: | Example of it in use: |

**(iii)** Examine the two tweets below from Irish Aid. Describe the type of aid described in each one, and give one piece of evidence to support your choice.

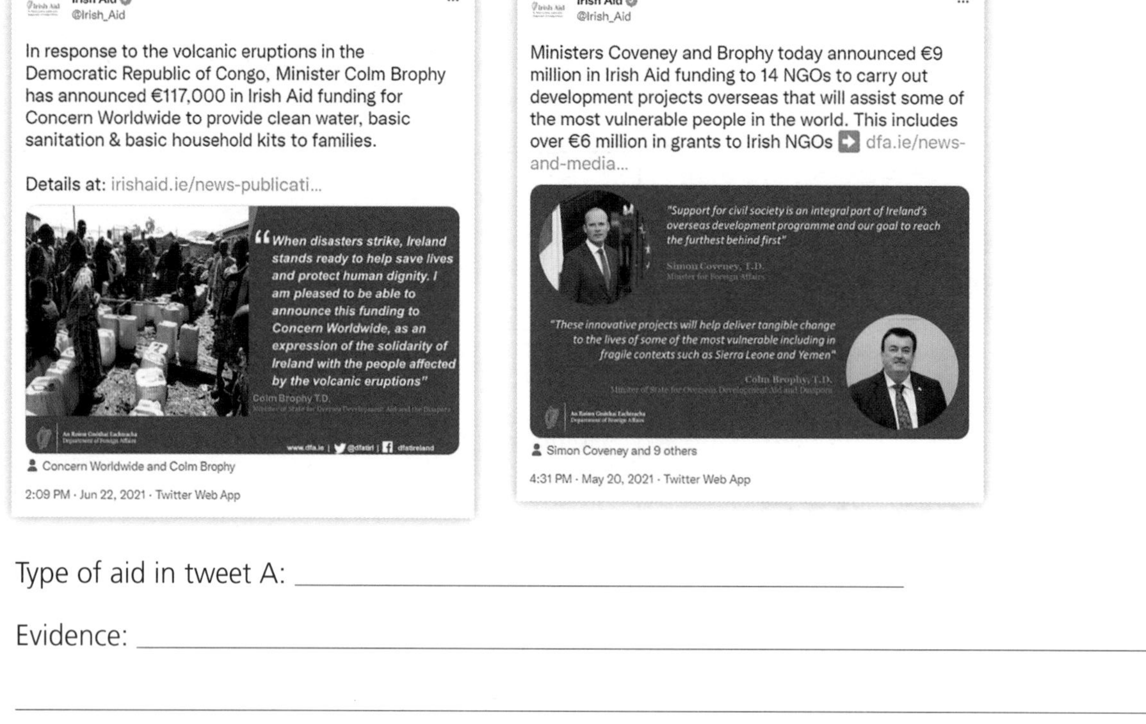

**A**

Irish Aid
@Irish_Aid

In response to the volcanic eruptions in the Democratic Republic of Congo, Minister Colm Brophy has announced €117,000 in Irish Aid funding for Concern Worldwide to provide clean water, basic sanitation & basic household kits to families.

Details at: irishaid.ie/news-publicati...



Concern Worldwide and Colm Brophy

2:09 PM · Jun 22, 2021 · Twitter Web App

**B**

Irish Aid
@Irish_Aid

Ministers Coveney and Brophy today announced €9 million in Irish Aid funding to 14 NGOs to carry out development projects overseas that will assist some of the most vulnerable people in the world. This includes over €6 million in grants to Irish NGOs ➡ dfa.ie/news-and-media...



Simon Coveney and 9 others

4:31 PM · May 20, 2021 · Twitter Web App

Type of aid in tweet A: ______________________

Evidence: ______________________

______________________

Type of aid in tweet B: ______________________

Evidence: ______________________

______________________

## Irish Aid

**4.** Read the following newspaper article and answer the questions that follow.

### Minister Brophy announces further €2 million in humanitarian assistance for the crisis in Venezuela

Minister of State for Overseas Development, Colm Brophy TD, today expressed his concern about the humanitarian situation caused by the Venezuelan migrant crisis and pledged €2 million in humanitarian assistance from Ireland towards the international response to the crisis – a doubling of last year's grant.

Last month, 7,484 Venezuelans were encountered by Border Patrol agents along the US–Mexico border – a record high number.

Irish Aid emergency relief supplies were recently delivered to the Colombian Red Cross for Venezuelan refugees. In 2020 Irish Aid provided €1 million in 2021 in response to the Venezuelan migrant crisis

The majority are escaping long-running economic devastation marked by blackouts and shortages of food and medicine. South America and the Caribbean are one of the worst affected regions of the Covid-19 pandemic. Venezuelan refugees and migrants are particularly vulnerable due to the government's poor response to the Covid crisis.

*Source: Department of Foreign Affairs*

## eoSkill

Taking information from extracts. Link your answer to the extract and use it to strengthen your answer.

## Exam Hint

- Read any article/headline carefully.
- Read the questions carefully.
- Underline any key terms/important facts you feel will help answer questions.
- Answer the questions asked.
- When using facts/information from articles/headlines, quote it directly – do not change it.
- Give as much relevant detail in your answers as you can.

**(i)** Who is the Minister of State for Overseas Development? ____________________

**(ii)** List two emergencies affecting the country of Venezuela.

**1.** ____________________

**2.** ____________________

**(iii)** What type of aid has Irish Aid given Venezuela? ____________________

**(iv)** How much aid in total has Irish Aid given to Venezuela since 2020? ____________________

**(v)** Imagine you are in the role of Minister for State for Overseas Development. The conditions in Venezuela are expected to worsen for the following year.

Write a short speech you will make to both the World Bank and Trócaire, seeking their assistance in dealing with the crisis. Describe the conditions in Venezuela, the type of aid you believe is needed and how it will be used.

**Answer the questions to complete the mind map. This will support your revision.**

(a) Give a brief explanation of the term 'human development'.

This box has been left blank for you to include any additional information you feel needs revising.

(f) Define the four types of aid.

b) List as many indicators as you can that could be used to decide the human development level of a country. Explain two of these.

(c) What scale is used to measure human development? List the levels of development a country may be on this scale.

**Human Development**

(d) What is the difference between sources of aid and types of aid?

List the three sources of aid and explain them.

## NCCA Sample Question

Read the article below and answer each of the following questions.

**Exam Hint**

- Read the article carefully.
- Underline anything you think is important.
- Answer the questions asked.

### Humanitarian Crisis in Somalia Driven by Climate Change

Somalia has a hot desert climate with high temperatures and little rainfall. This makes any rain that falls very important. Climate change is leading to less rainfall in certain parts of the world, including Somalia. Between 2016 and 2018, Somalia experienced below-average rainfall. This led to many problems for farmers, including crop failure, widespread livestock deaths and loss of assets.

As well as farmers, the wider population of Somalia was affected as there was large-scale population displacement, hunger and malnutrition. By 2018 the number of people in need of urgent humanitarian assistance was estimated at 4.2 million.

**(i)** The article stages that 4.2 million people are in need of urgent humanitarian assistance.

Which type of assistance do you think is most appropriate to help the people of Somalia? Tick (✓) the box beside your choice. [3 marks]

Tied aid ☐ Emergency aid ☐ Development aid ☐

**(ii)** Justify your choice in the space below. [10 marks]

*Give valid reasons or evidence to support an answer or conclusion. Use information from the extract and what you have studied in this chapter.*

**(a)** Type of aid: ____________________

**(b)** Explain the type of aid you chose:

____________________

____________________

____________________

____________________

**(c)** Why did you choose this type of aid? Advantages/ Disadvantages:

____________________

____________________

____________________

**(d)** What evidence from the extract supports your choice

____________________

____________________

____________________

____________________

____________________

**Marks Awarded**

**(ii)** Tick the boxes as you include the information listed below in your answer:

**(a)** Choose the type of aid you think best suits this question ☐ 2 marks

**(b)** Explain the type of aid you chose ☐ 4 marks

**(c)** Explain why you think this particular type of aid is the correct choice ☐ 2 marks

**(d)** Support your choice with evidence from the extract ☐ 2 marks

# 26 Life Chances in a Developed and Developing Country

In this section, the Learning Outcome we will look at is: **3.7**

## Learning Checklist:

- ☐ I can describe a country as either developed, developing or slowly developing.
- ☐ I can explain how gender can impact the life chances of young people in developed and developing countries.
- ☐ I can explain how access to healthcare can affect young people in developed and developing countries.
- ☐ I can explain the differences in employment opportunities for young people in developed and developing countries.
- ☐ I can explain how the educational opportunities given to young people in developed and developing countries can affect their chances in life.
- ☐ I can interpret information from infographics. I can take information from articles/infographics to support my answer.

## Developed and Developing Countries

. Examine the demographic transition model below.

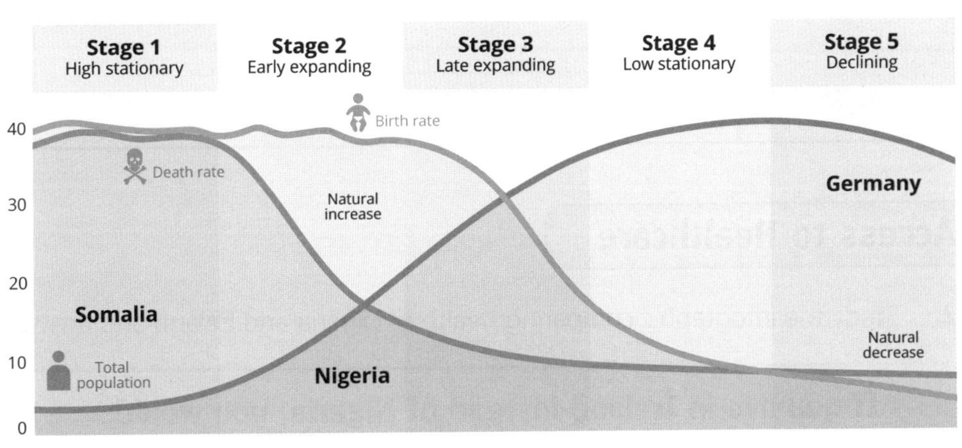


**(i)** Based on your understanding of the demographic transition model and the terms 'developed', 'quickly developing' and 'slowly developing', place Somalia, Nigeria and Germany on the scale below according to the level of development of each country.

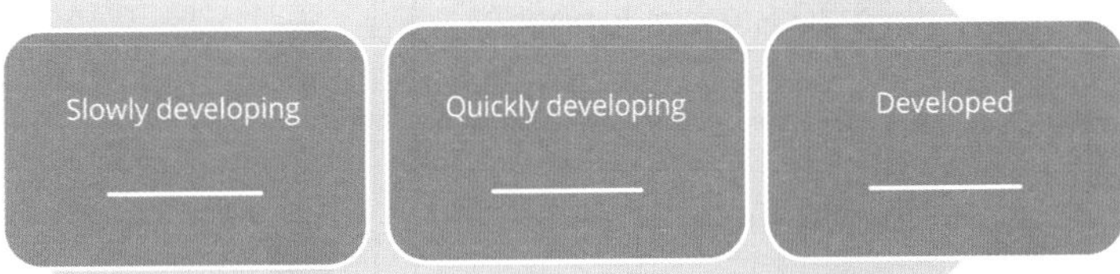


**Remember!**

If you are unsure of the meaning of any of the terms in this question, now is the time to look them up and write out the definitions.

**(ii)** In your own words, expalin what the Human Development Index (HDI) is and what it measures.

**(iii)** Fill out the table below with the information required for each country.

**(a)** State the HDI level as high, medium or low.

**(b)** State which sector most of the population work in: primary, secondary or tertiary.

**(c)** Give an explanation for the link between the HDI level and the type of employment the majority of the population are working in.

| Country | Somalia | Nigeria | Germany |
|---|---|---|---|
| **HDI level** | | | |
| **Employment** | | | |
| **Explanation** | | | |

## Access to Healthcare

**2.** Study the infographic comparing health in Nigeria and Ireland and answer the questions that follow

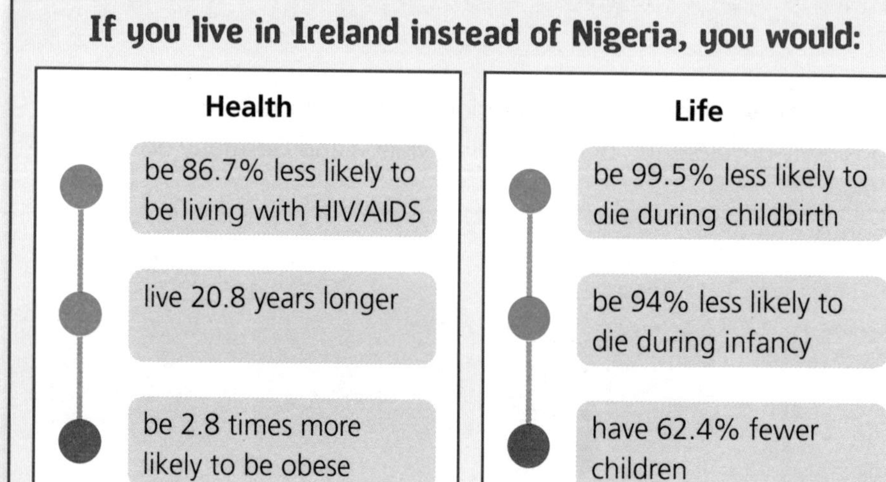

If you live in Ireland instead of Nigeria, you would:
Health
be 86.7% less likely to be living with HIV/AIDS
live 20.8 years longer
be 2.8 times more likely to be obese
Life
be 99.5% less likely to die during childbirth
be 94% less likely to die during infancy
have 62.4% fewer children


**GeoSkill**

Reading and taking information from an infographic. The facts and figures shown are there to be used in your answers.

(i) How much longer is the average life expectancy for a person living in Ireland?

______________________________________________

(ii) Obesity is more of a problem in Ireland. Give a reason why you think this is so.

______________________________________________

______________________________________________

______________________________________________

(iii) Explain the term 'infant mortality'.

______________________________________________

______________________________________________

(iv) What is the difference in infant mortality in Nigeria and Ireland?

______________________________________________

______________________________________________

______________________________________________

. Examine the tables below and answer the questions on the next page.

| Indicators (2017) | Ireland | Nigeria |
|---|---|---|
| Population | 4,995,000 | 206,140,000 |
| Number of public hospitals | 48 | 15 (there are thousands of privately owned hospitals, which are often too expensive for many Nigerian people) |
| Number of doctors per 1,000 people | 2.7 | 0.38 |
| Number of GPs in each country | 2,500 (approx.) | Figure not available though it is estimated that by 2030 there will be a shortage of over 50,000 doctors* |

**Source: www.vanguardngr.com*

| reland | Nigeria |
|---|---|
| ize: 84,421 km² | **Size:** 923,768 km² |
| .9 on HDI scale (high human development) | 0.5 on HDI scale (low human development) |
| tage 4 of Demographic Transition Model | Stage 2 of the Demographic Transition Model |

**(i)** Why might availability/access to public hospitals affect the life chances of a young person in Nigeria who has HIV or AIDS?

**(ii)** Examine the four graphs below which show the number of Covid-19 cases and deaths in Nigeria and Ireland.

Write a brief newspaper article for your school's newspaper which:

- highlights the different effect Covid-19 has had on both countries
- offers possible explanations for these differences (access to healthcare, doctors, etc.)
- offers a type of aid that could possibly help Nigeria better cope with Covid-19.

Use information from the tables on the previous page and the four graphs below to help.

## GeoSkill

There are four graphs in this question. Take your time to examine the heading for the x- and y-axes on each. Take Graphs A and B: these show the steep incline in Covid cases and deaths in Nigeria between February 2020 and October 2021 on the x-axes. The y-axes show these figures in thousands. The same applies to Graphs C and D, which show Covid cases and deaths in Ireland.

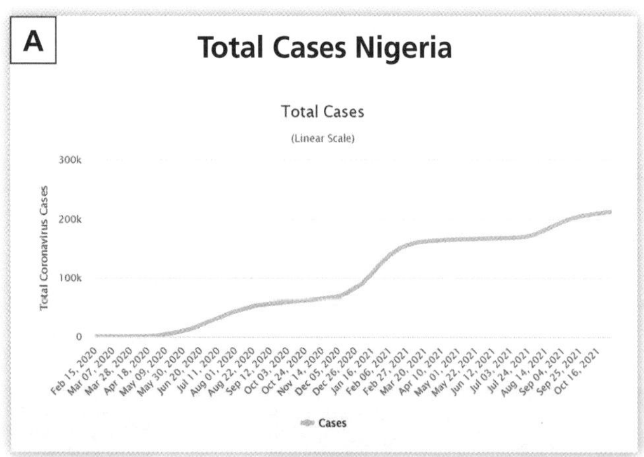


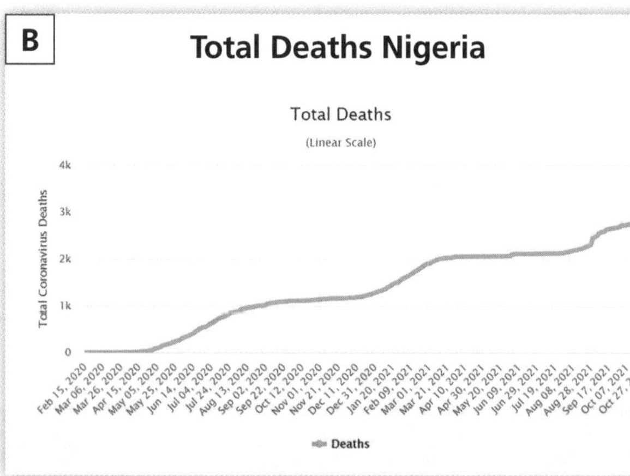


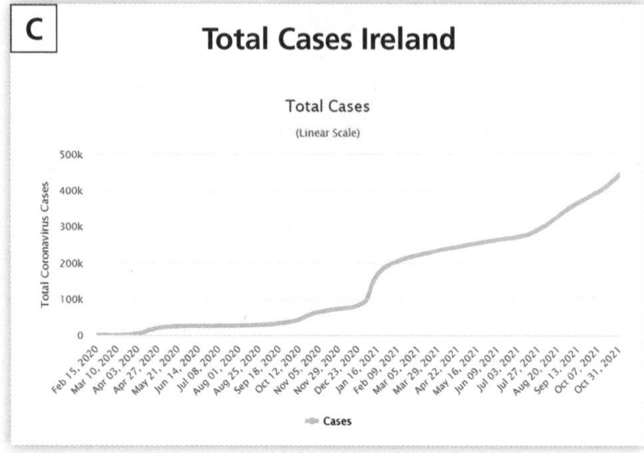


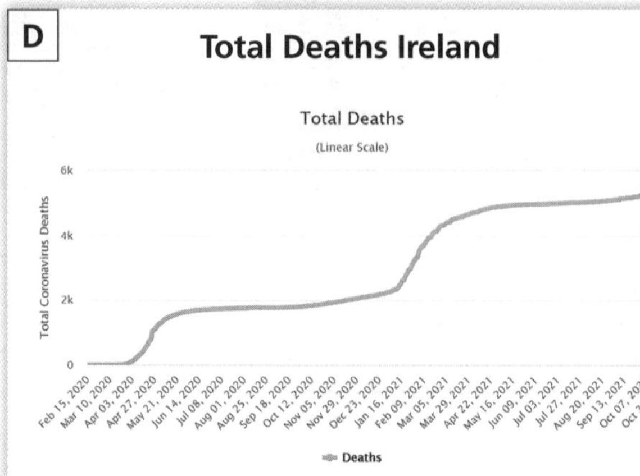

## Exam Hint

When writing newspaper articles, use the facts and figures provided in any graphs or infographics. These will strengthen the points you are trying to make. What trends can you see in the graphs? When did cases/deaths rise? How do the numbers differ?

# The Daily News

**Date:**

1. How has Covid-19 affected each country differently?

______________________________

______________________________

______________________________

2. What possible reasons might be behind this?

______________________________

______________________________

3. What types of aid may help Nigeria?

______________________________

______________________________

## ducational Opportunities: Developed vs Developing

The United Nations have set out a number of goals to try and achieve quality education in the developing world.

**(i)** In the space provided, suggest one way each goal could be achieved in the developing world.

| Jnited Nations Quality Education Goals | Your Suggestions |
|---|---|
| 1. By 2030, ensure that all girls and boys complete free, equal and quality primary and secondary education. | |
| 2. By 2030, increase the number of youths and adults who have relevant skills, including technical and practical skills for better employment, decent jobs and entrepreneurship. | |
| 3. By 2030, increase the supply of qualified teachers in developing countries by sharing teacher-training methods from developed countries. | |

**(ii)** Choose what you believe to be the most important goal (number 1, 2 or 3) and say why you believe it to be the most important of the three goals.

**Exam Hint**

With this question, apply your knowledge from whichever developing country you studied.

Goal: ____________________

Reason:

____________________

____________________

____________________

____________________

____________________

____________________

____________________

____________________

____________________

**(iii)** Based on your studies of education in developed and developing countries, write one more goal the UN could implement to try to achieve quality education in the developing world.

____________________

____________________

____________________

____________________

**4.** In the table below, there are a number of barriers to education listed. In the spaces provided:

- write whether you think the barrier is experienced more so in the developed or developing world
- explain the reason(s) behind your choice.

**Exam Hint**

There are barriers here experienced in both the developing and the developed worlds. But this question is asking where these barriers are experienced **more** and why.

| Barriers | Developed/ Developing | Reason(s) |
|---|---|---|
| **Cost:** Many young people cannot afford college fees so education ends after secondary school | | |
| **Lack of space:** Small schools cannot accommodate all students in a community, meaning young women stay at home instead of going to school | | |
| **Family size:** Large families will often only send young males to school instead of young women | | |

| **Locality:** Students from so-called disadvantaged areas are less likely to progress to college | | |
|---|---|---|
| **Gender:** As few as 20% of young women in the country have attended school | | |

## Gender Equality and Life Chances

5. **(i)** Explain the term 'gender equality'.

______________________________________________

______________________________________________

______________________________________________

______________________________________________

______________________________________________

**(ii)** Study the infographic below and answer the short questions that follow.

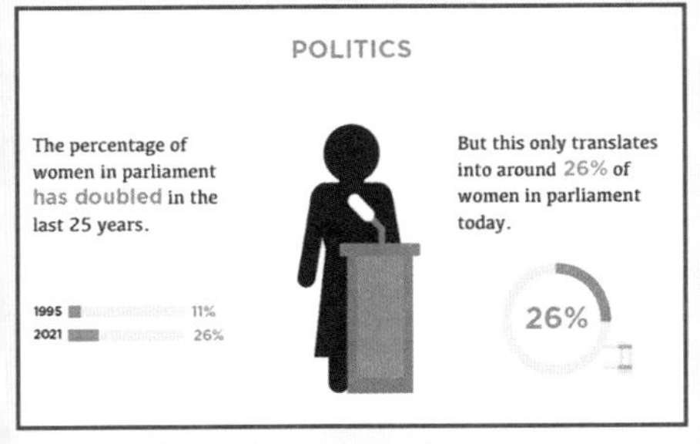

POLITICS
The percentage of women in parliament has doubled in the last 25 years.
But this only translates into around 26% of women in parliament today.
1995 11%
2021 26%
26%


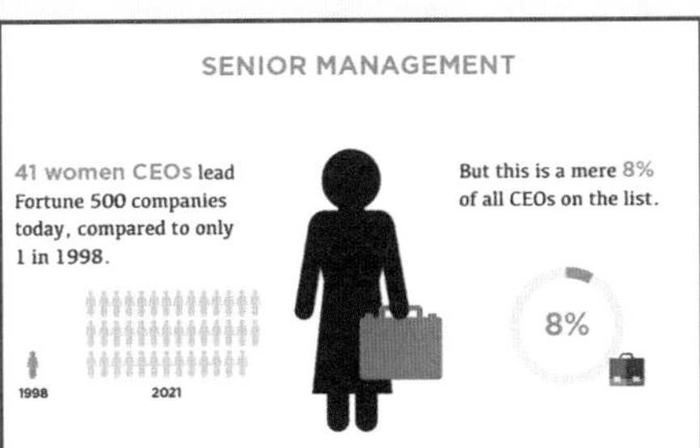

SENIOR MANAGEMENT
41 women CEOs lead Fortune 500 companies today, compared to only 1 in 1998.
But this is a mere 8% of all CEOs on the list.
8%
1998
2021


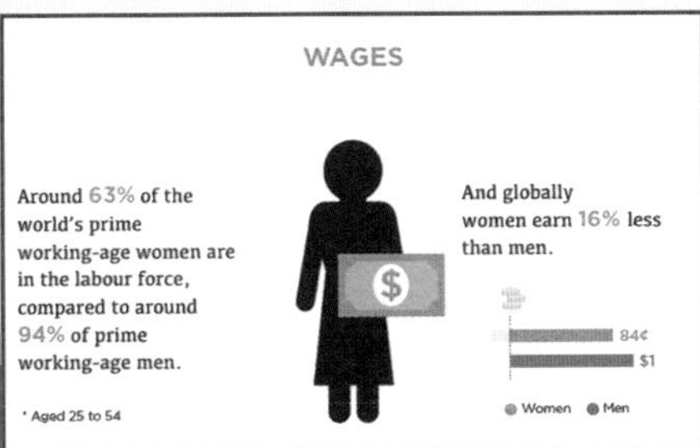

WAGES
Around 63% of the world's prime working-age women are in the labour force, compared to around 94% of prime working-age men.
* Aged 25 to 54
And globally women earn 16% less than men.
84¢
$1
Women
Men


According to the latest data from the Central Statistics Office, the average gender pay gap in Ireland is 14.4%.

Women make up 46% of all those in employment in Ireland and are more likely to work part-time.

*Source: UN Women*

**(a)** What percentage of prime working-age women are working in the world?

______________________

**(b)** What is the difference in wages between men and women in the world today? ________%

**(c)** Give one potential reason why only 8% of the world's CEOs are female.

______________________

______________________

______________________

**(d)** In Ireland, why might women be more likely to work part-time than men?

______________________

______________________

______________________

**(e)** Is the gender pay gap in Ireland higher or lower than the global average?

______________________________________________

**6.** Study the graphs below and answer the short questions.

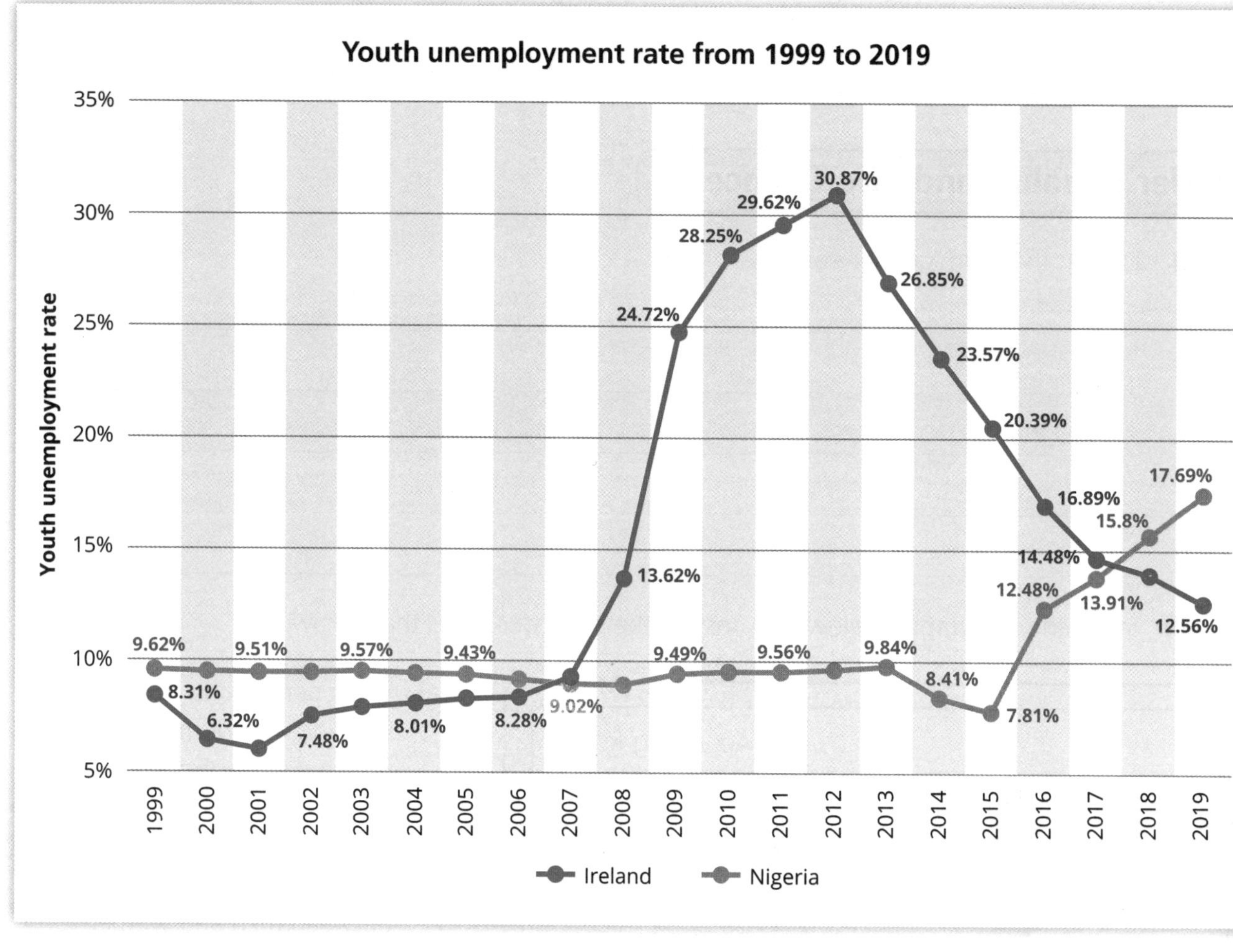


**(i)** In what year was youth unemployment highest in Nigeria? ____________________

**(ii)** In what year was youth unemployment at its lowest in each country?

Nigeria: ____________________ Ireland: ____________________

**(iii)** In what year was youth unemployment highest in Ireland? ____________________

**(iv)** What happened to Ireland's economy in 2008 that may have caused the increase in unemployment seen in the graph?

____________________

**(v)** Describe the trend in youth unemployment in both Ireland and Nigeria over the period shown on the graph. Suggest reasons for the patterns shown.

____________________

____________________

____________________

____________________

____________________

**Answer the questions to complete the mind map. This will support your revision.**

### Prompt Questions for Mind Map

**(a)** List the three categories of development that can be applied to countries. Give an example of a country in each category.

**(b)** Do you know the indicators used to compare life chances in developed and developing countries?

**(c)** Can you compare and contrast healthcare and education in a developed and developing county you have studied?

**(d)** Are you able to explain gender inequality and how it can be measured?

(b) Indicators of Life Chances

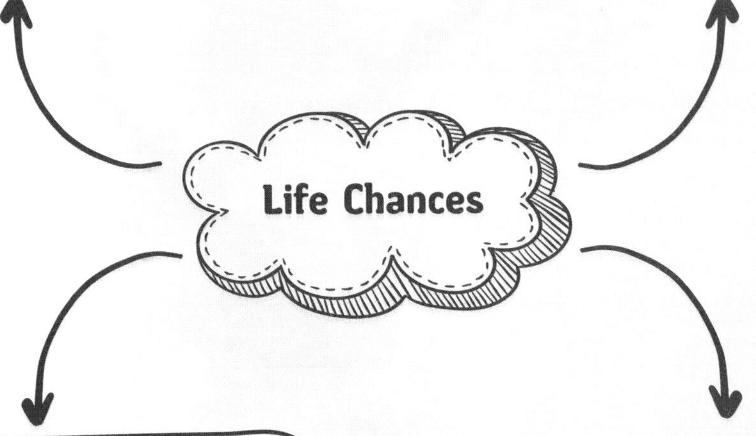


(d) Gender Equality and Life Chances

(c) Access to Healthcare and Education

## Sample NCCA Question

### Question 1

Compare two characteristics of a country categorised as low income/developing and a country categorised as high income/developed. [12 marks]

**(i)** ______________________ is categorised as a developed/high-income country.

______________________ is categorised as a developing/low-income country.

**Exam Hint**

- Name a country which is low income and a country which is high income.
- State clearly the characteristics you will use to compare the two countries.
- Use facts and figures to support each characteristic you choose.

**(ii) 1.** The first characteristic I will use to compare these two countries is:

______________________

______________________

______________________

______________________

______________________

______________________

**2.** The second characteristic I will use to compare these two countries is:

______________________

______________________

______________________

______________________

______________________

______________________

**Marks Awarded**

(i) 1 mark each for naming your two countries (1 + 1 = 2 marks)

(ii) 5 marks for each characteristic

- 2 marks for naming your characteristic (2 + 2 = 4 marks)
- 3 marks for developing each characteristic (3 + 3 = 6 marks)

Total = 12 marks

# 27 Globalisation

In this section, the Learning Outcome we will look at is: **3.9**

## Learning Checklist:

- ☐ I can explain what is meant by the term 'globalisation'.
- ☐ I can explain the impact of globalisation on settlement, population and human development.
- ☐ I can describe the different aspects of globalisation – cultural, economic and political.
- ☐ I can use data to draw charts. I can read key information from tables.
- ☐ I can read grid references from 1:10 000 OS maps and I can draw sketch maps.

## What Is Globalisation?

Answer all questions below.

**(i)** Complete the explanation below by using the words provided.

Goods Economy Connected Globe Political interconnection

lobalisation is the process by which the world ________________ is becoming more connected. Today, eople around the world are much more ________________ to one another. Globalisation allows eople, services, money, ideas and ________________ to move very quickly around the ________________. We can define globalisation as the increasing social, economic and ________________ ________________ of people and countries around the world.

**(ii)** Which of the following is **not** a result of globalisation? Tick (✓) the correct answer.

**(a)** Greater movement of money, goods, services, people ☐

**(b)** Increased global communications ☐

**(c)** A reduction in levels of global inequality ☐

**(d)** Increased levels of international trade ☐

**(iii)** Apple is a transnational corporation that operates in many countries across the globe. The table below shows where Apple stores are located.

| Country | Number of Apple stores |
|---|---|
| United States | 271 |
| China | 50 |
| United Kingdom | 38 |
| Canada | 28 |
| Australia | 22 |
| France | 20 |
| Italy | 16 |
| Germany | 15 |
| Spain | 11 |
| Others | 40 |

*Source: www.statista.com*

**(a)** What is a transnational corporation?

______________________________

______________________________

______________________________

______________________________

**(b)** How many Apple stores are located worldwide?

| Rough work |
|---|
| Answer: |

## Exam Hint

When drawing your graph on the following page, use pencil. Use a ruler to ensure neat, straight lines. Place a title at the top of your bar chart. Double check each figure as you place it.

**(c)** Display the information from the previous page on the bar chart below. The first has been added for you.

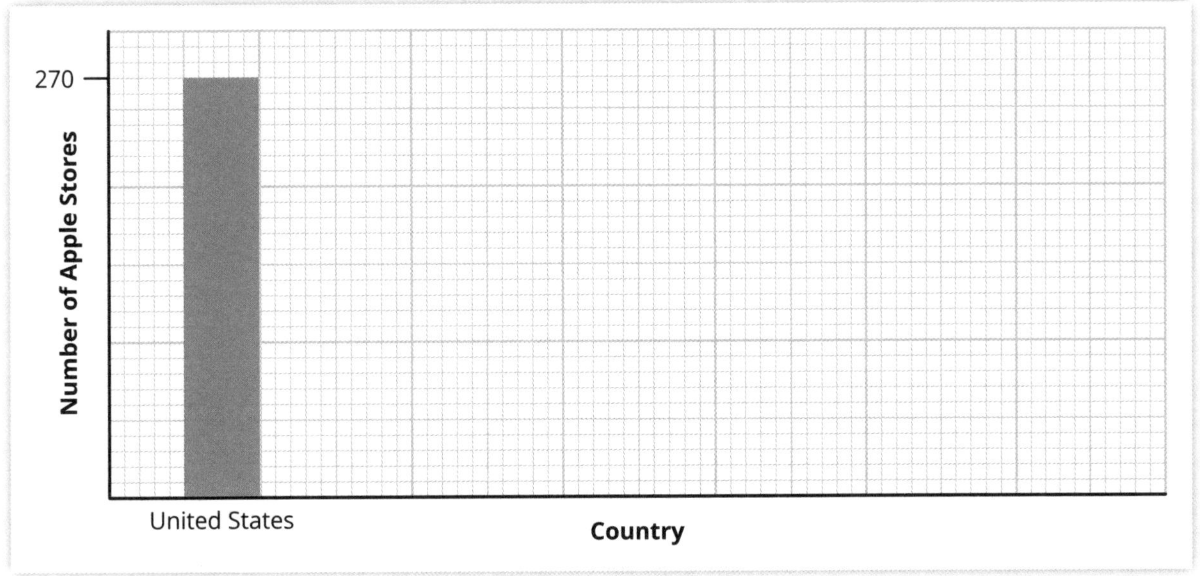


**(iv)** Review the table below showing the number of people (in thousands) who were employed in Ireland's main economic sectors between 1961 and 2004.

**Numbers Employed in Main Economic Sectors (000s)**

| Sector | 1961 | 1981 | 2004 |
|---|---|---|---|
| Agriculture | 379 | 196 | 115 |
| Industry | 259 | 363 | 499 |
| Services | 415 | 587 | 1,206 |
| Total at work | 1,053 | 1,146 | 1,820 |

*Source: CSO, ESRI*

**Remember!**

Primary ➔

Secondary ➔

Tertiary ➔

**(a)** Describe the trend in agricultural employment between 1961 and 2004.

______________________________

______________________________

______________________________

**(b)** Between 1961 and 2004 we see a large increase in the number of people employed in tertiary economic activities. Outline how globalisation may have contributed to this increase.

______________________________

______________________________

______________________________

______________________________

______________________________

______________________________

2. **(i)** Read the article below and answer the questions that follow.

### Ireland's Data Centre Boom is Complicating Climate Efforts

**A surge in the data processing industry will increase Ireland's already too high carbon emissions, making Ireland's response to the climate crisis more difficult.**

Digital Realty's Dublin data centre operates 24 hours a day from a business park in Clonee, Co. Meath. This data hub is how many Irish, UK and Europeans access email, social media, online shopping, Netflix and other internet services.

By 2028, data centres and other large users will consume 29 per cent of Ireland's electricity. The digital 'cloud' can create carbon: it is estimated that when the music video 'Despacito' reached 5 billion streamed YouTube views in 2018, the energy used was equivalent to powering 40,000 US homes a year.

Google and Amazon representatives have said their Irish data centres were energy efficient and entirely supplied – or soon would be – by renewable energy.

*Source: www.irishtimes.ie*

**(a)** Where is Digital Realty's data centre located?

**(b)** What will be the result of the surge in Irish data processing?

**(c)** What evidence is there to show that the digital cloud creates carbon?

**(d)** Explain how technological developments have accelerated globalisation.

**(ii)** Globalisation has both positive and negative impacts for countries across the world. Describe **three** impacts that globalisation has had on a country of your choice.

**Remember!**

Think back to cultural, economic and political globalisation. There are connections here to population, migration, settlement and human development.

## Case Study

Country : ______________________

| Impact 1: |
|---|
| Impact 2: |
| Impact 3: |

**(iii)** 'The developing world has not been as positively impacted by globalisation as other regions.' Briefly explain this statement.

**(iv)** Complete the description below of how globalisation has had an impact on settlement and population in Ireland. Use some of the key terms provided to support you.

| Cheaper transport costs | International migration | Migration to cities |
|---|---|---|
| Growth of towns | Diversity in population | MNCs |
| Skilled workers | Young immigrants | Multicultural |

*lobalisation has made communications across the globe much faster. With the rise of social edia use, increased access to high-speed internet, and online streaming sites broadcasting levision shows across the globe, we are increasingly attracted and drawn to visiting other untries and cultures. Globalisation has attracted many people to come to live in Ireland.*

**GeoSkill**

This is a 1:10 000 map. Your grid reference will be a letter and number, e.g. A1. This scale allows you to see this area in greater detail. Remember to use map evidence in your answers.

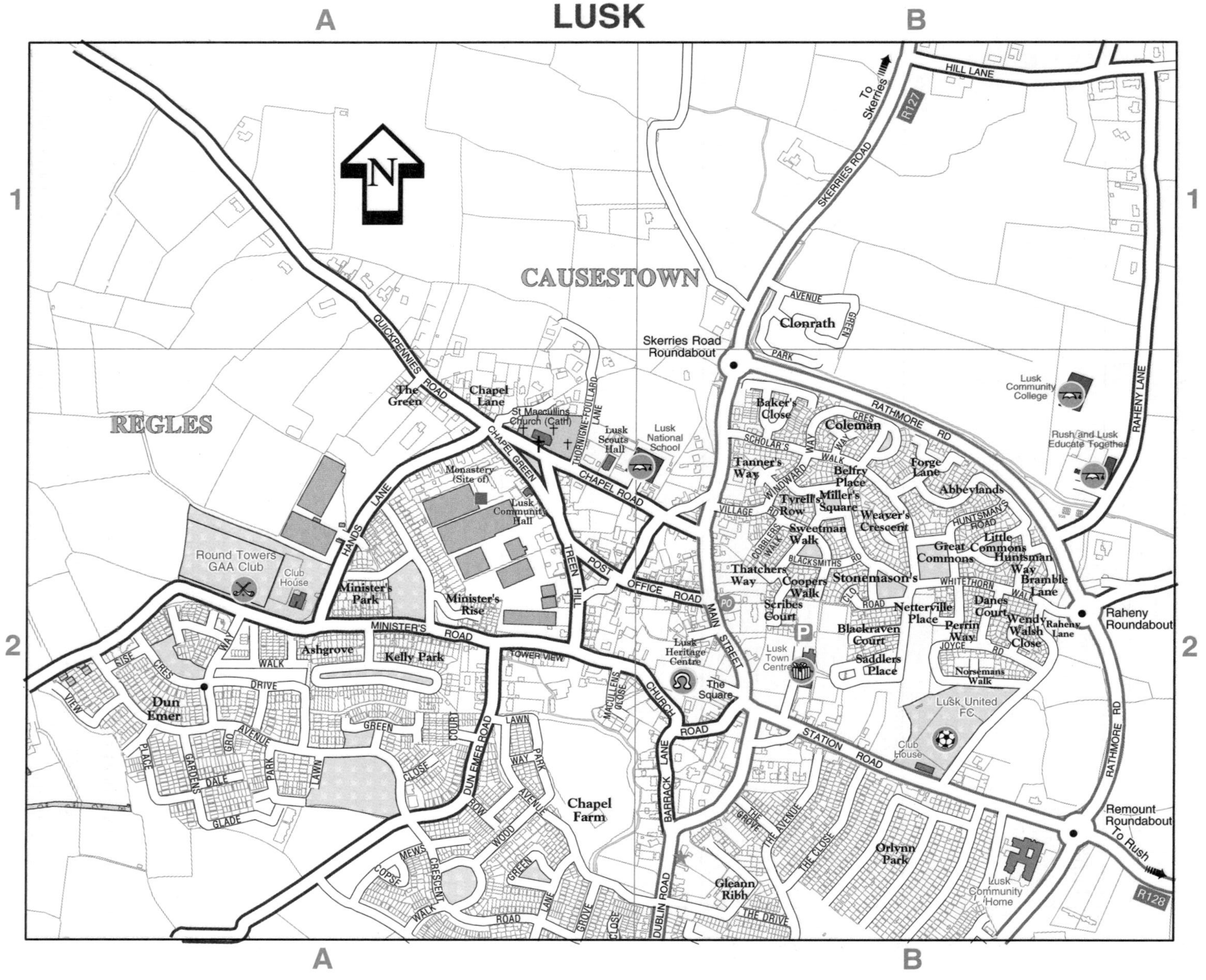

3. A multinational fast food chain has decided to establish an outlet in Lusk. Review the 1:10 000 map extract on the previous page and answer the questions that follow.

**(i)** Name one factor that attracts multinational companies such as this one to Ireland.

______________________________________________

**(ii)** Give the location of the most suitable site for the new fast food outlet to be located.

______________________________________________

**(iii)** Explain two reasons for your choice of location, using evidence from the map extract.

**1.** ______________________________________________

______________________________________________

______________________________________________

**2.** ______________________________________________

______________________________________________

______________________________________________

**(iv)** Outline one positive and one negative impact that this multinational fast food company could have on the local area.

Positive:

______________________________________________

______________________________________________

______________________________________________

Negative:

______________________________________________

______________________________________________

______________________________________________

**(v)** Draw a sketch map of the area shown on the OS map. On your sketch you should include:

- The full length of the R127
- Lusk Community College
- A residential house estate
- A named recreational area

↑

**Answer the questions to complete the mind map. This will support your revision.**

**Prompt Questions for Mind Map**

**(a)** Define 'globalisation'.

**(b)** Outline the three main types of globalisation. Give an example of each one: what happens? Where can it be seen?

**(c)** Explain some of the positives and negatives of globalisation.

**(d)** Describe the impact of globalisation on a region/country that you have studied.

**(e)** How has globalisation had an impact on human development? On climate change? Give examples.

(a) What Is Globalisation?

(d) Impact of Globalisation on Human Development and Climate Change

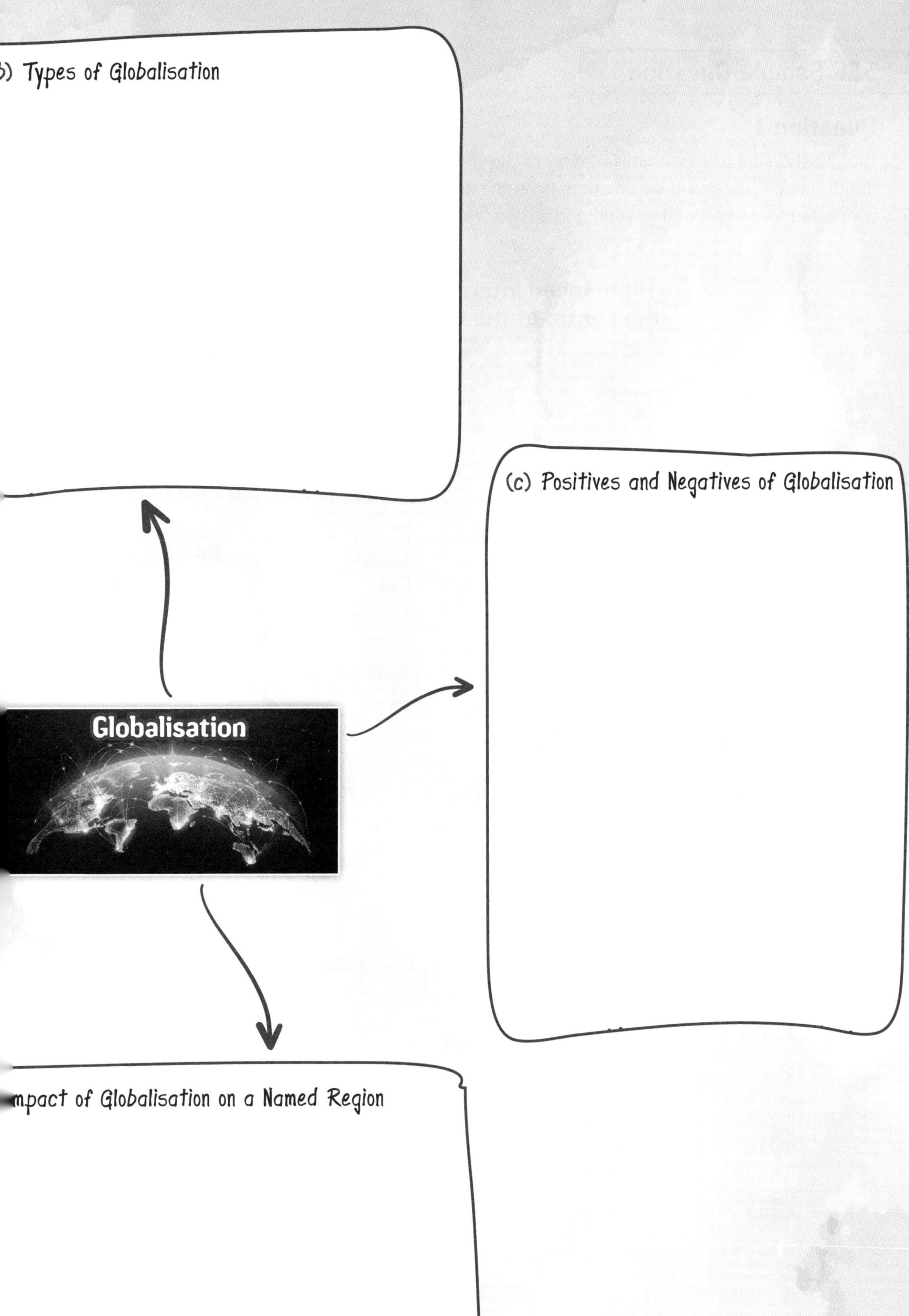
b) Types of Globalisation
(c) Positives and Negatives of Globalisation
Globalisation
mpact of Globalisation on a Named Region

## SEC Sample Question

### Question 1

Globalisation is a process that is leading to the world becoming more connected due to the exchange of goods, people, ideas and information. Read the article below about a rural Irish town becoming more connected to the rest of the world and answer each of the following questions.

**High-Speed Internet Puts Skibbereen at the Centre of the World for Connectivity**

In 2016, Skibbereen became Ireland's first one gigabit town. Before this, Skibbereen was like many rural towns, with very low levels of broadband internet. The access to high-speed broadband has attracted businesses to the town who can now have a global presence.

Fifteen families have moved or relocated to Skibbereen since May 2018, attracted by the high-quality jobs as well as the quality of life. They tell of escaping the daily commuting nightmare, lower housing costs and lower childcare costs.

High-speed broadband is clearly having a positive effect on economic development in the town and is contributing to a sustainable future for Skibbereen.

**(i)** How many families have moved or relocated to Skibbereen since May 2018? [2 marks]

______________________________

**(ii)** Name two pull factors mentioned in the article that attract families to live in the area. [4 marks]

*Pull factors – what is making people want to come to live here?*

**1.** ______________________________

**2.** ______________________________

**(iii)** Imagine you are a setting up a business in Skibbereen. How will having access to high-speed broadband be of benefit to your business? [4 marks]

*Consider how the internet will allow you t[o] send emails, use web browsers or set up [a] website. If the speed was slow, how migh[t] that impact on your new business?*

______________________________

______________________________

______________________________

______________________________

**(iv)** Ships, like those in the photo below, transport goods, people and information all over the world.

B
A
MSC
MSC LEVINA
PANAMA

**(a)** Which ship in the photo is used by tourists to travel around the world? Tick (✓) the correct box. [2 marks]

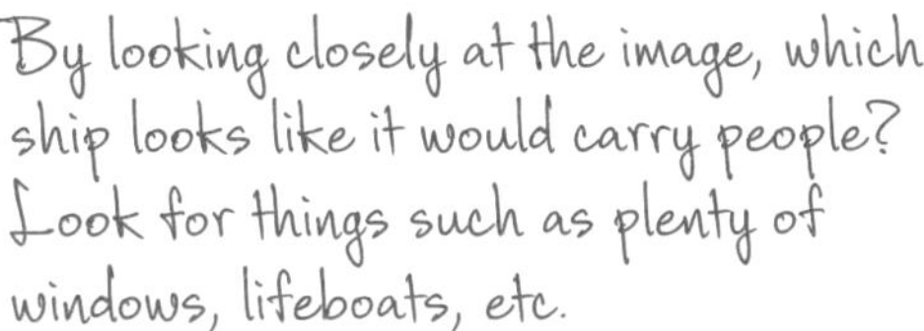
By looking closely at the image, which ship looks like it would carry people? Look for things such as plenty of windows, lifeboats, etc.

A ☐ B ☐

**(b)** The number of ships like the one labelled B entering Irish ports has increased. Explain how globalisation has contributed to this increase. [4 marks]

*Ship B is carrying containers of products that will be brought to shops.*

______________________________________________

______________________________________________

______________________________________________

______________________________________________

**Marks Awarded**

**(i)** Correct figure – 2 marks

**(ii)** Each named pull factor – 2 + 2 = 4 marks

**(iii)** State benefit – 1 mark; development – 3 marks (1 + 3 = 4 marks)

**(iv)** (a) Correct box – 2 marks

(b) Statement – 1 mark; developed explanation – 3 marks (1 + 3 = 4 marks)

Total = 16 marks